REMEMBERING AND FORGETTING NAZISM

REMEMBERING AND FORGETTING NAZISM

Education, National Identity, and the Victim Myth in Postwar Austria

by

Peter Utgaard

Berghahn Books
NEW YORK • OXFORD

Published in 2003 by
Berghahn Books

www.berghahnbooks.com

© 2003 Peter Utgaard

Library of Congress Cataloging-in-Publication Data

Utgaard, Peter.
  Remembering and forgetting Nazism : education, national identity,
and the victim myth in postwar Austria / by Peter Utgaard.
    p. cm.
  Includes bibliographical references and index.
  ISBN 1-57181-187-7 (alk. paper)
    1. National socialism—Austria—Psychological aspects 2. National
characteristics, Austrian. 3. Political culture—Austria. 4. Austria—History—1938–1945. I. Title.

  DB99 .U74 2002
  943.605'3'019—dc21

                                                    2002027711

British Library Cataloguing in Publication Data

A catalogue record for this book is available from
the British Library.

Printed in the United States on acid-free paper

For My Grandparents

Leon Alexander Baker, 1906–1966
Mary Blankenship Baker, 1906–1998

and

Sigurd Bjorn Utgaard, 1895–1997
Florence Heller Utgaard, 1906–1973

CONTENTS

List of Illustrations   viii

Preface   ix

Acknowledgments   xii

Introduction: The "Austria-as-Victim" Myth and
Postwar Austrian Identity   1

Part I: Reversing the Anschluss, 1945–1955

1. From *Blümchenkaffee* to *Wiener Mélange:* Schools, Identity,
   and the Birth of the Austria-as-Victim Myth   25

Part II: Major Themes of the Austria-as-Victim Myth, 1955–1986

2. Remembering and Forgetting the Anschluss   71

3. Remembering and Forgetting World War II, the Holocaust,
   and the Resistance   90

4. Remembering and Forgetting the Allied Occupation,
   Rebuilding, and the State Treaty: The Second Rebirth
   of Austria and New Symbols of National Identity   121

**Part III: The End of the Austria-as-Victim Myth?
Official Memory Since 1986**

5. Fragmentation of the Victim Myth Since 1986:
   From Kurt Waldheim to Jörg Haider   161

Bibliography   198

Index   231

ILLUSTRATIONS

Following page 120

Plate 1 Flak tower near Mariahilferstrasse
Plate 2 Memorial to war dead. Bundesoberstufenrealgymnasium,
          Wiener Neustadt
Plate 3 Monument at Morinzplatz commemorating victims of
          the Gestapo
Plate 4 Memorial to "The Heroes of World War II"
Plate 5 View from the Old Jewish Section of Vienna Central Cemetery,
          looking toward the Christian section
Plate 6 Jewish gravestones in the Old Jewish Section of Vienna
          Central Cemetery
Plate 7 Monument against War and Fascism. The "Gate of Violence"
Plate 8 Monument against War and Fascism. The "Jew Scrubbing
          the Sidewalk"
Plate 9 Monument against War and Fascism. Man looking at two
          of Hrdlicka's pillars

PREFACE

This book is an analysis of how the Austrian education system cultivated postwar Austrian national identity through the vehicle of the
"Austria-as-victim" myth; a myth that came to define the official memory
of the Austrian Second Republic. The victim myth is shorthand for a
number of interconnected themes that turned the Austrian experience
from 1938–1955 (especially the Anschluss, World War II, and the Allied
occupation) into a positive narrative of redemption to mark the (re)birth
of a new democratic, prosperous, neutral, and non-German Austria. The
work examines the history of the victim myth from its birth to its fragmentation in the mid 1980s up to the present.

I conducted research for the project at the archive and library of the
Austrian Education Ministry during the 1995–1996 academic year, but the
roots of the book date to the 1987–1988 academic year that I spent as an
undergraduate student in Baden, Lower Austria, and in Vienna. In retrospect, questions that this book seeks to answer were initially conceived
during that year when the Waldheim controversy raged, and, in the
spring, when Austria marked the fiftieth anniversary of the Anschluss.
When it came to World War II and Nazism, what differentiated Austrians
from Germans? How and why was the Austrian view of the war so different from that of Germans? How did Austria more or less escape the
Cold War? Later I came to realize that these and other questions collectively formed a much bigger question: How did Austrians, who had been
an integral part of the Third Reich, explain their role in the war and the
subsequent rebirth of their nation? For this book, I further refined the
question by focusing upon the role of Austrian education in defining
postwar Austrian national identity.

This volume is organized into three parts. Part I, "Reversing the
Anschluss, 1945–1955," includes chapter 1, "From *Blümchenkaffee* to
Wiener Mélange: Schools, Identity, and the Birth of the Austria-as-Victim
Myth." This chapter covers the origin of the Austria-as-victim myth and
examines the role of Austrian schools in shaping and rebuilding Austrian
identity in the immediate aftermath of World War II. An important topic
of this chapter is how school materials incorporated several themes to
build a unique Austrian identity that was purposefully separated from

German identity. This program to distinguish Austria from Germany was important to building a new Austria, but it also indirectly contributed to victim mythology by implying that participation in the Nazi war of conquest was antithetical to Austrian identity.

Part II, "Major Themes of the Austria-as-Victim Myth, 1955–1986," examines the individual themes of the Austria-as-victim myth. This section covers the period from 1955, when the Allied occupation of Austria ended, to 1986, the year Kurt Waldheim was elected president of Austria. This was the time of the (mostly) unchallenged victim myth, which reached its pinnacle in 1965. Some minor changes in mythology occurred in this period, and they are noted throughout part II; however, there was no fundamental shift away from the victim myth until after 1986. Chapter 2, "Remembering and Forgetting the Anschluss," discusses the importance of the annexation of 1938 and the April plebiscite. Memory of the events of 1938 is key to the overall victim myth, as all other themes of victimization originate with mythology surrounding the Anschluss. In chapter 3, "Remembering and Forgetting World War II, the Holocaust, and the Resistance," three major topics are covered by focusing on specific issues. In particular, this chapter deals with seemingly contradictory mythologies that justify the war and diminish its ideological significance by teaching simplistic truisms and conflating all wars into a single category. Official memory of the Holocaust is also discussed, including an analysis of how the Holocaust and its symbols were appropriated to support the Austria-as-victim myth. The chapter concludes by examining official memory of the resistance. Resistance mythology is key to the overall victim myth and plays an especially important role in legitimizing the Second Republic. Chapter 4, "Remembering and Forgetting the Allied Occupation, Rebuilding, and the State Treaty: The Second Rebirth of Austria and New Symbols of National Identity," expands the parameters of the overall victim myth to include Austria's "unjust" and "unfair" treatment by the occupying powers. Themes covered in this final chapter of part II include the Moscow Declaration of November 1943, the Marshall Plan and rebuilding, negotiations over the State Treaty, and the importance of Austria's neutrality to its victim mythology and national identity.

Part III, "The End of the Austria-as-Victim Myth? Official Memory Since 1986," presents chapter 5, "Fragmentation of the Victim Myth Since 1986: From Kurt Waldheim to Jörg Haider." This chapter explains the shift away from the Austria-as-victim myth that resulted from the combination of the vast media attention surrounding the 1986 election of President Kurt Waldheim and, in 1988, the fiftieth anniversary of the Anschluss. The chapter also notes that the intellectual and political groundwork of the change regarding victim mythology predated the Waldheim controversy. Further, while the years 1986–1988 did mark a significant shift away from the victim myth, evidence presented in this chapter demonstrates that the changing viewpoint was characterized by a fragmentation of the consensus view of Austrian history, which had prevailed up to that time. By the late 1990s, the Austria-as-victim myth had become a superfluous and untenable aspect of Austrian national identity, yet many themes related to the victim myth continued officially to be promulgated.

Unless otherwise noted, translations are my own, and of course, I bear sole responsibility for any shortcomings of this work.

ACKNOWLEDGMENTS

This volume is the culmination of several years of work in German and history, and there are many people who helped me along the way whom I would like to acknowledge. First, my parents, John and Susan Utgaard, deserve special thanks for encouraging my education over the years. Their enthusiastic support of a year of study in Austria during the 1987–1988 school year sent me on a journey where the first seeds for this study were sown. I also want to thank the many great German teachers and professors I have had over the years, including David Mendriski, Eva Landecker, Thomas Keller, Frederick Betz, Andrew Weeks, and Helmut Liedloff. Enormous thanks are owed to the Fulbright Commission for granting me a fellowship that allowed me to spend the 1995–1996 academic year in Vienna. My work at the Austrian Ministry of Education was aided by the friendly staff of the Education Ministry's library and archive. Ingrid Höfler and Josef Flachenecker deserve special mention for their courtesy and unfailing patience in answering my questions and helping me find materials. I also benefited from conversations with Wilhelm Wolf and Walter Denscher of the Austrian Education Ministry. William Wright of the University of Minnesota deserves thanks for his support and for putting me in contact with Lonnie Johnson in Vienna, whose kind advice and contacts helped my work enormously. On his recommendation, I was able to meet and benefit from conversations with Peter Malina of the Institute for Contemporary History, Wolfgang Maderthaner of the Verein für Geschichte der Arbeiterbewegung, Helmut Wohnout of the Karl von Vogelsang-Institut, and Tony Judt, who kindly allowed me access to the library of the independent Institute for Human Sciences. Our friends in Austria Martin Marchart, Markus Nepf, and Solomon and Doris Namala also deserve thanks for their support and camaraderie. I especially want to acknowledge our friend Johanna Pour. Our stay in Vienna was made enjoyable thanks to her friendship and support. Her kindness will always be remembered and appreciated.

I also wish to thank Harry Ritter of Western Washington University and many wonderful people at Washington State University, including Roger Schlesinger, David Stratton, Thomas Kennedy, Fritz Blackwell, Marvin Slind, Richard Law, and Jane Lawrence; my dissertation committee, John

Kicza, Steven Kale, and Rachel Halverson; and especially my mentor Raymond Sun. Since its inception as a dissertation project, this work has benefited enormously from the thoughtful criticism and encouragement of many. I want to thank the anonymous readers from Berghahn Books for making numerous invaluable suggestions for improving the manuscript, as well as the publisher and staff of Berghahn Books, especially Shawn Kendrick, for supporting the project. I also want to thank Anton Pelinka of the University of Innsbruck, who commented on the manuscript, encouraged my work, and answered obscure questions. Heidemarie Uhl of the Austrian Academy of Sciences also commented on the manuscript and generously shared materials. Günter Bischof of the University of New Orleans has been a great well of information, and his generosity, advice, and support have been essential to this work.

In San Diego, I want to thank the students of Cuyamaca College, whose enthusiasm for history is inspirational, the library staff, and many wonderful colleagues, including Therese Botz, Paul Carmona, Pei-Hua Chou, Ezequiel Cardenas, David Detwiler, Susan Haber, Kay Hartig, Marie Ramos, Patricia Santana, Patrick Setzer, Albert Taccone, Michael Wangler, Madelaine Wolfe, and especially Cristina Chiriboga. Also in San Diego, I want to thank the Villalpando family and Benton and Emily Long for their moral support, love, and friendship. Finally, I want to thank my wife Claire. This work would not have been possible without her intellectual advice, companionship, love, and unwavering support.

I dedicate this book to my grandparents. Their love of life and learning influenced me in ways that I have only recently come to appreciate.

INTRODUCTION

The "Austria-as-Victim" Myth and
Postwar Austrian Identity

O n 23 May 1996, a major exhibit opened in Vienna's Schottenstift to commemorate one thousand years of Austrian history. At the same time, in a courtroom in another part of the city, the trial of a teacher accused of teaching National Socialism *(Wiederbetätigung)* was underway. The day before, the presiding judge had badgered the prosecution's student witnesses, openly doubting their testimony that their teacher, "Richard R.," had taught them that "Austria is actually the *Ostmark*" and that the gas chambers were constructed by the Americans during the occupation. A few days later the judge was removed from the case.[1]

These simultaneous events demonstrate two visions of Austria's past. One vision is that of Habsburg glory: beautiful landscapes, splendid palaces, and the art and architecture of *fin-de-siècle* Vienna. This is tourist Austria, and any visitor, especially in Vienna, will immediately be impressed by its trappings. The Hofburg, Opera, Parliament, Burgtheater, Rathaus, museums, and other grand buildings are only minutes from each other as one walks around Vienna's famous Ringstrasse, developed in the nineteenth century.[2] The grandeur of the Ringstrasse and the magnificence of Schönbrunn Palace seem out of proportion to the small Alpine nation, yet the Habsburg past understandably remains important to modern Austrian identity. To many Austrians, the imperial past represents Austrian uniqueness vis-à-vis their German cousins. The empire was home to the "Austrian idea," where the different ethnic groups of Central Europe lived in harmony under the Catholic Habsburg emperor. Austria stood in contrast to Protestant, Prussian-dominated Germany, where the "cult of the nation-state" reigned supreme.[3] The idea of Austria's special mission *(die Österreichische Sendung)* was especially prominent among postwar conservatives.[4] The fact that imperial harmony was a historical myth does not diminish the importance of the multinational idea to Austrian identity.[5] But since 1945, Austria has had a more recent and unsavory legacy to contend with: the collapse of the empire, the bitter politics and civil war of the First Republic, Austro-fascism, union with Nazi Germany, and the complicity of many Austrians in the Nazi war of aggression and racist annihilation. How were these traumatic experiences reconciled and explained as a new Austrian state was built out of the ruins?

In his introduction to the 1997 volume *Austrian Historical Memory and National Identity*, Günter Bischof argues that Austria-as-victim became an essential ingredient of postwar Austrian identity.[6] This work seeks to expand on Bischof's point by arguing that Austria-as-victim became the dominant theme in the official memory of the recent past in postwar Austria, and that the identity and legitimacy of the Second Austrian Republic have largely been based on the Austria-as-victim myth since its founding. Austria-as-victim was the one idea that coherently linked the experiences of the First Republic, Austro-fascism, full participation in the Nazi war of conquest, and the Allied occupation into a positive narrative of absolution and empowerment. This mythological narrative became a fundamental part of Austrian identity in the Second Republic and has enabled Austrian politicians, teachers, school officials, and other nation-builders to turn recent Austrian history into what Charles Maier (with regard to Germany) terms a "usable past."[7] In the postwar Austrian school, the "usable past" offered by the victim myth became an essential ingredient in constructing, to use Benedict Anderson's now famous phrase, the "imagined community" that became the postwar Austrian nation.[8] How Austrian school textbooks reflected and propagated this victim myth as Austria's usable past and key aspect of postwar national identity is the major theme of this work.

A succinct account of Austria's national victim myth includes all of the following themes. Austria was a victim of German aggression, invaded and forcibly annexed in 1938. Austria then suffered through the war years under the yoke of the "Prussians," aided by a handful of misguided Austrians. Through the trials of occupation and forced participation in the Nazi (German) war, Austrian identity awakened and asserted itself. The numerous patriotic resistance groups, operating both abroad and within Austria, manifested the resurgent Austrian identity. Finally, Austria emerged from the ashes, only to face a new trial: an unjustly long occupation by the Allies. Incorporating the lessons of the First Republic and the German occupation, Austrians of all political camps *(Lager)* worked together to build a new Austria, which emerged as a neutral and independent state in a world dominated by calculating superpowers.[9] This mythological narrative enabled Austrians to build a new, positive identity as a prosperous and democratic Austria was constructed out of the ruins.

The post–World War II Austrian nation was a great success compared to the post–World War I First Republic, when there had been no consensus on what it meant to be Austrian or even whether Austria should exist. The successful story of nation-building in post–World War II Austria was largely one of fusing the differing visions of Austria's past into a consensus view. Austria's victim myth was an essential tool used by Austrian nation-builders, especially in the schools, to forge the new consensus.

Regarding the long-term Austrian past, builders of Austrian identity relied on the positive images of imperial times, with an emphasis on heroic deeds, great personalities, and local traditions.[10] Concerning the more recent past, Austria-as-victim provided thematic unity to the years 1918–1945 (and especially 1938–1945). While there were important voices of dissent, the postwar narrative of victimization remained dominant until the Waldheim controversy of the 1980s. Since then, the myth of Austria as a victim and only a victim has been dismantled. Now, Austria's mythology of victimization is usually seen as wholly negative, based on the argument that the victim myth hindered democratic development and contributed to a shameful neglect of the genuine victims of Nazism. There is much to be said for the second part of the argument, but it is more difficult to argue that the victim myth in some way undermined the development of postwar Austrian democracy. Indeed, it can be argued that insofar as the Austria-as-victim myth contributed to postwar reconciliation, it enabled the successful rebirth of Austrian democracy and a renewed sense of national identity.[11] As the prominent Austrian historian Gerald Stourzh notes: "[I]f the Austrians had considered themselves merely the vanquished inhabitants of the German *Ostmark*, of one of the insolvent remains of the Third Reich, the sense of Austrian identity, which was to develop more fully in the decades to follow, could hardly have emerged."[12] Austria's (until recently) trademark politics of cooperative and consensus politics, termed "consociationalism," provided a high level of stability, which replaced the bitter politics of the First Republic.[13] One could go so far as to posit that postwar reconciliation in Austria might have *required* some degree of forgetting. This would follow the idea of the nineteenth-century French scholar Ernest Renan, who remarked: "[T]he essence of a nation is that all individuals have many things in common, and also that they have forgotten many things."[14] By this definition, the postwar Austrian nation had been forged by 1955.

Sources

In *Radetzkymarsch,* Joseph Roth's novel of the twilight of the Austrian Empire, the family patriarch and hero of the Battle of Solferino is outraged when he finds that the school textbooks have altered the exact facts of the battle, in which he had saved the life of Emperor Franz Josef. Upon making inquiries, an official tells *Hauptmann* Trotta that he is overreacting and reminds him that "[a]ll historical deeds are presented differently in schools.... The children need examples that they understand and that make an impression on them. The actual truth they can find out later!" A "shocked" Trotta then resigns from the army he had so dutifully served.[15] The response of the official reminds us that the importance of the school in constructing the nation has been acknowledged throughout the modern period. After the unification of Italy, historian Pasquale Villari stated, with an eye toward Italian education, that proving the continuity of Italian history (a difficult task) was "not merely a scientific need, but a patriotic duty."[16] Indeed, such sentiments were common in the late nineteenth century, as evidenced by the Hungarian sociologist and historian Béla Grünwald, who cynically remarked: "The secondary school is like a big engine which takes in at one end hundreds of Slovak youth who come out at the other end as Magyars."[17] Such a naked statement on the role of schools in building a nation is rarely heard today, but the reasoning behind it has changed very little since the nineteenth century.

Whatever the locale, the school curriculum remains contested ground precisely because the school is recognized as the preeminent site of teaching not only practical knowledge, but also *values*, especially those deemed essential to national (and/or regional) identity. The school is where the impressionable young—the future of the nation—learn the national history, the national literature, and civic values. Few places then are as fruitful as the school for examining how people see themselves, both historically and in the present. The history curriculum is especially important not only because history is where students engage their national past (who we were), but because in so doing, both the present (who we became) and, to some degree, the future (who we as a people will become) are also defined.[18] In short, schools are mirrors of local and national identity because values and priorities are reflected both in the curriculum and in how schools use their resources. For example, occasional debates over teaching evolution remind us about the political power of Evangelical Christians in many American school districts. Sometimes grotesque inequities in funding between academic subjects and athletics reflect a community's priorities, as in the case of Permian High School in Odessa, Texas, where the resources of the football team are far greater than the school's English department.[19] In Austria, the history curriculum is especially important because it is where history and official (or quasi-official) memory meet with most measurable precision. The sources I employ as a window to Austrian historical identity and official memory are school materials, including history textbooks, reading books, yearbooks, commemorative publications, and administrative decrees.

At the same time, there are limits to what can be interpreted from school textbooks, which any textbook study must take into account. For example, typically a textbook author can devote only so much space to a particular theme. Textbook authors also face the challenge of distilling recent historiography for young audiences, as well as the difficulty of accounting for conflicting interpretations and historiographical priorities (i.e., whether to emphasize political history, social history, gender history, etc.). Furthermore, even an author who is well versed in historiography may be hard pressed to match that knowledge to the requirements of the curriculum. Finally, a textbook author (especially in more recent texts) is constrained by the need for a text to be "authoritative," yet also pedagogically challenging to students by incorporating controversial historical questions and critical thinking problems. This is a tall order. One might ask, for example, how a contemporary Austrian textbook should treat the Holocaust in a few pages or even a chapter. How would the Holocaust be defined? Could the author include the background information on anti-Semitism in Europe and Austria? Should legitimate historiographical debates (e.g., the "intentionalists" vs. the "functionalists") be incorporated? Other important questions might include: Who were the perpetrators? Was the Holocaust unique? How many victims were there? Is there a difference between a death camp and a concentration camp?[20] No textbook author (let alone a symposium of scholarly experts) could adequately answer all or even most of these questions in the confines of a textbook chapter.

The aforementioned limitations must be kept in mind when analyzing history textbooks, yet to some degree, the point can also be reversed. The fact that there are considerable limits on what a text can include means that the content reflects conscious choices regarding what to include and what *not* to include. In other words, the content reveals the significance of choices and priorities. The official status of Austrian textbooks makes them an especially valuable tool for exploring official memory. Whereas in the United States textbooks are adapted in a decentralized fashion at the local and state level, in Austria the system for textbook approval is centralized in the Education Ministry. All textbooks must cover required themes in the official lesson plans and must be approved by special committees working with the Education Ministry before they can be used in the schools. As a result, school materials in postwar Austria tended to convey a quasi-official consensus view of history that reflected the dominance of Austria's system of patronage politics (*Proporz*). Aptly named "coalition history," this viewpoint indicated a compromise between the conservative Austrian People's Party (ÖVP) and Socialist (SPÖ) views of history.[21] Coalition history played an important role in the Austria-as-victim myth and is a clear example of politics having an influence on the writing of history. On a more specific level, it is currently impossible to determine to what degree political considerations play a role in the approval or rejection of individual textbooks because the files of the textbook approval committee members are not open to the public. But there is evidence that the personal political positions of approval committee members sometimes play a role in the acceptance or rejection of a work. Christian Sitte, who coauthored a geography textbook for Austrian schools, experienced the approval process and also gathered several files on textbook approval through personal connections. Based on his experience, Sitte has concluded that the personal and political beliefs of committee members *do* play a significant role in whether or not a book will be accepted for use in an Austrian classroom.[22] Another advantage to studying school texts is that in addition to revealing a great deal about national identity, textbooks also disclose how one nation perceives another.[23] These views of other peoples often support a nation's own sense of identity. As we shall see, in the Austrian case, negative views of the Allies buttressed notions of Austria's moral superiority as a neutral country compared to the Cold War powers.

The history textbooks analyzed in this study were published between 1945 and 1996.[24] In some ways, the history-textbook portion of my work follows in the footsteps of a number of highly critical textbook studies.[25] But while there are thematic similarities, this work is more comprehensive in that it examines both history textbooks and reading books and details how textbooks have changed over time in the context of larger events. Most of the history textbooks for this study are from basic secondary education schools (*Hauptschulen*, or HS), general secondary education schools (*Gymnasium* and *Realgymnasium*, or AHS), and the polytechnic schools.[26] The sample of sources from these schools is nearly comprehensive: with few exceptions, every book approved between 1945 and 1996 has been taken into account. This comprehensive coverage of history textbooks was possible for two reasons. First, the period of contemporary history analyzed in this volume (Austrian history from 1938–1955) is taught twice in the curriculum for the HS and AHS schools and once in the polytechnic curriculum.[27] Since these contemporary history topics are taught only in these years, it was practical to survey these texts in a comprehensive manner. Second, with some exceptions, the books examined were limited to those used in HS, AHS, and polytechnic schools.[28] Readers will note that the number of books published increased in the 1970s. This is attributable to the *Schulbuchaktion*, which provided students with free schoolbooks beginning with the 1972–1973 school year.[29]

In addition to history textbooks, my work also incorporates a representative sampling of reading books published since 1945. These works are especially valuable because themes important to identity and history often appear in the prose and poetry selections of reading books. Some of the most revealing information about Austrian victim mythology and identity-building comes from the readers. To my knowledge, this is the first history-centered textbook study to incorporate both history and reading textbooks. Inclusion of the readers also expands the age base of the students, since in addition to HS, AHS, and polytechnic readers, grammar school (*Volksschulen*) books are analyzed. The large number of books in these categories made it necessary to look at these sources in a representative rather than a comprehensive manner. A selection of well over one hundred reading books published between 1945 and 1996 ensures a wide representative sampling.[30]

As stated earlier, the process by which texts are approved, published, and used makes them intrinsically valuable sources as reflectors of official views on history. Nevertheless, a potential weakness with textbooks as a source is that their impact is difficult to gauge since the manner in which historical themes are taught in the classroom cannot easily be assessed. It is therefore important to measure student attitudes in some way. To address this issue, I also examined Austrian school yearbooks (*Jahresberichte*).[31]

These yearbooks are similar to American yearbooks, except that they typically contain more text and fewer photographs. Often included in the yearbooks are reports written by students and teachers concerning class projects on historical themes, as well as reports about field trips to historical sites. These yearbooks go far toward addressing the problem of evaluating students' attitudes toward history, and inclusion of the yearbooks in this work allows Austrian students to speak for themselves, often in very eloquent and revealing ways. Given the vast number of yearbooks, I make use of a representative sampling from both secular and Catholic schools. All nine Austrian provinces are represented in the yearbook selections.

Finally, this study also makes use of important administrative decrees, published in the *Verordnungsblatt für den Dienstbereich des Bundesministeriums für Unterricht*—the governmental organ that disseminates decrees and laws on education that make up official education policy—and the national lesson plans *(Lehrpläne)*, which spell out official guidelines on curriculum and general goals of education. (In some cases, the lesson plans and updates to the lesson plans are published in the *Verordnungsblatt.*) All in all, the combination of primary sources I employ from the Austrian school system covers the spectrum from student to administration.

Historiography of the Victim Myth

The Austria-as-victim myth is now widely recognized, and indeed some scholars believe that Austria's "forgotten" past currently receives too much attention. In a 1997 review, Allan Janik of the University of Innsbruck remarked: "Austrian contemporary historians are ghostbusters. Their aim is to exorcise Austria's political elite and intelligentsia of their self-delusions. They pursue their moral goal with the Manichaean mercilessness of Robespierre and St. Just." Janik further warned that national identity is not merely constructed but also tied to birth and linked to personal identity.[32] The distinguished Austrian historian Ernst Hanisch likewise cautions against moralistic scholarship, pointing out that it is of little value to our historical understanding to replace the victim thesis with an equally simplistic "collective perpetrator" thesis.[33] These concerns should be heeded, for it falls upon the historian to explain rather than condemn. As Tony Judt writes in his study of postwar French intellectuals: "It isn't enough, after all, to 'kill the father'—you have to understand him, too."[34]

Yet for the purposes of this study, Janik's warnings should be qualified in two ways. First, while it is true that national identity is infinitely complex and multifaceted, in the case of Austria there *was* a crisis of national identity in the immediate postwar period (and more so in the interwar period), which is why Austrian politicians and education officials so deliberately addressed the question of Austrian identity. The question at hand is not personal identity, but national identity associated with the nation-state and deliberately cultivated by the state. Here I agree with Robert

Knight, who writes: "National Identity does not exist prior to the forma-tion of the nation-state; it can be advanced—or created—by state institu-tions such as the army or universal education or by the exercise of social and political forces acting within the state's boundaries over a period of time."[35] Second, even if one accepts the argument that scholarship on postwar Austrian memory has swung too far in the direction of condem-nation, that view should be qualified by the fact that for many years the subject of Austrians' complicity in the Nazi regime and its crimes *was* ignored, sometimes quite deliberately.[36] Thomas Angerer argues that Aus-trian historians of contemporary history were themselves part of the prob-lem, as the biographies of many prominent historians embodied coalition history.[37] Indeed, before the Waldheim controversy beginning in 1986, pub-lications critical or revealing of recent Austrian history were rare. The important exception was Austrian literature, in which works such as Hel-mut Qualtinger and Carl Merz's brilliant monologue play *Der Herr Karl* satirized Austrian attitudes toward the Nazi years (see chapter 5 for further discussion).[38] The earliest examples of history works that explored Aus-trian complicity in the war include historian Erika Weinzierl's book *Zu Wenig Gerechte: Österreicher und Judenverfolgung*, published in 1968, which examined the role of Austrians in the Holocaust.[39] Later examples include American scholar Bruce Pauley's 1981 study, *Hitler and the Forgotten Nazis: A History of Austrian National Socialism*, which undermined Austria's victim mythology by focusing on pre-Anschluss Austrian Nazis. Another early example was John Bunzl and Bernd Marin's *Antisemitismus in Österreich* (1983), which systematically analyzed Austrian anti-Semitism—a topic obviously linked with the role of Austrians in the Holocaust.[40]

There were other examples as well (see chapter 5), but it was not until the controversial 1986 election of former Wehrmacht officer and ex-Secretary General of the United Nations Kurt Waldheim that Austria's "unmastered past" received extensive and sustained attention. Since then, historians, lit-erary critics, and others on both sides of the Atlantic have produced a new body of work on Austrian history in the era of World War II. Works on Waldheim and the Waldheim scandal were an important part of this new wave of scholarship, including Richard Mitten's *The Politics of Anti-semitic Prejudice: The Waldheim Phenomenon in Austria* (1992). The Cana-dian historian Robert Keyserlingk's monograph on wartime Allied policy toward the Austrian question, and especially the Moscow Declaration, is essential to understanding the origins of the victim myth.[41] British scholar Robert Knight revealed how the Austrian government deliberately de-layed the claims of Jewish victims in postwar Austria.[42] Works such as *Das Grosse Tabu*, a collection of essays edited by Anton Pelinka and Erika Weinzierl, explicitly addressed the Austria-as-victim myth.[43] The best general history of modern Austria, Ernst Hanisch's *Der Lange Schatten des Staates*, points to the "half-truth" of the victim theory and asserts that the Austrian government supported the victim idea for political gain.[44] Re-cently, the Austrian-born British journalist Hella Pick's book *Guilty Victim:*

Austria From the Holocaust to Haider also addressed the issue of Austrian "guilt" in World War II.[45] Historian Evan Bukey's *Hitler's Austria: Popular Sentiment in the Nazi Era, 1938–1945* can rightly be regarded as the coup de grâce to the Austria-as-victim myth. The culmination of many years of research on popular opinion in Austria, Bukey's work demonstrated not only that there was widespread popular support for the Anschluss, but that a majority of Austrians backed the Nazi regime until the end of the war.[46] Few would now claim that Austria was a victim, and only a victim, of Nazism. Yet the importance of the victim myth to postwar Austrian identity remains underappreciated. Peter Thaler's recent *The Ambivalence of Identity* (2001), for example, makes an impressive contribution to the development of postwar Austrian identity, but pays too little attention to the importance of the victim myth.[47] Nevertheless, the post-Waldheim shift in historiography was significant and was also reflected in Austrian textbooks. As we shall see, in the late 1980s Austrian textbook authors began to abandon the simplistic version of the Austria-as-victim myth, though by no means did all mythological themes disappear.

Austrian Education and Official Memory

The historiography of history and memory is now vast. While a thorough discussion of the epistemological and historiographical issues related to history and memory is beyond the scope of this work, a brief discussion of the historiographical background is helpful.[48] Since the French sociologist Maurice Halbwachs published his pioneering essays on collective memory beginning in the early 1940s, scholars have engaged in a tremendous range of works that explore the links between history and memory.[49] A brief list of only some of the more important ones includes: Paul Fussel's *The Great War and Modern Memory* (1975), David Lowenthal's *The Past is a Foreign Country* (1985), Charles Maier's, *The Unmasterable Past: History, Holocaust, and German National Identity* (1988), Henry Rousso's, *The Vichy Syndrome: History and Memory in France since 1944* (1991 [1987 in France]) and Ian Buruma's *The Wages of Guilt: Memories of War in Germany and Japan* (1995). At the core of these works are key questions as to how the remembered past affects definitions of national identity. The essential epistemological problem raised in many works on history and memory is to what degree the remembered past is distinct from the historical past in the context of postmodern scholarship, which has wrestled the traditionally accepted legitimacy of "truth" and "objectivity" away from history.[50] David Lowenthal eloquently summarizes important distinctions between history and memory: "Unlike memory, history is not given but contingent: it is based on empirical sources which we can decide to reject for other versions of the past."[51]

While differentiating between history and memory, it is also important to acknowledge that writing about memory and historical myths implies by definition that these views or versions of the past exist in opposition to a more "truthful" or "actual" past. Herein rests an enormous epistemological crux, because the idea of a single, accurate, and truthful past has been undermined by the scholarship of the poststructuralist and postmodernist critique, which continues to be vigorously debated.[52] Some scholars (e.g., Ruth Wodak) have come to the conclusion that there is no "*the* past" and that there really is no "Archimedean point" of objectivity that historians can rely upon.[53] With these caveats in mind, this work does not assume that a single, truthful past exists in opposition to the mythological Austrian past, but rather takes the perspective that a historically demonstrable past, which strives for completeness and accuracy, *does* exist, as opposed to a mythological narrative of the Austrian past based on selective memory. Of course, the historical past is constantly changing as scholars continue to examine new evidence, re-evaluate old evidence, and interpret the past in new ways. In sum, while the historical past and the mythological past are both fluid, and while they sometimes intersect, they are nevertheless distinct. My philosophy on the thorny problem of distinguishing history from an emplotted narrative follows that of historian Michael Roth, who argues that historians should approach their work with empirical rigor, pragmatism, and piety, meaning "an attempt at fidelity to (not correspondence with) the past."[54] It is in this spirit then that this work is informed and influenced by current scholarship on memory.[55]

Of particular importance to this study is the recent scholarship focusing specifically on Austrian historical memory and national identity. Heidemarie Uhl has emerged as the leading scholar on Austrian memory with her analysis of Austria's 1988 year of reflection, *Zwischen Versöhnung und Verstörung. Eine Kontroverse um Österreichs historische Identität fünfzig Jahre nach dem "Anschluß"* (1992)—a work which not only incorporates oral history, but takes some 5,000 articles from 330 publications into account.[56] Uhl is also the coauthor of an insightful work on Styrian war monuments, which chronicles how the commemoration of Austria's war dead contributed to and reflected the prevailing idea of Austria-as-victim by casting the fallen soldiers *(Gefallene)* as victims.[57] Another important work is Meinrad Ziegler and Waltraud Kannonier-Finster's *Österreichisches Gedächtnis. Über Erinnern und Vergessen der NS-Vergangenheit* (1993), a sociological analysis based on oral histories of several Austrian survivors of the war. Besides these works, there are also important collections of articles and essays on the subject of Austrian postwar memory, such as the volume edited by Günter Bischof and Anton Pelinka, *Austrian Historical Memory and National Identity* (1997), and the aptly titled *Eiszeit der Erinnerung* (Ice Age of Memory, 1999), edited by Ulf Brunnbauer. The linguistic study *The Discursive Construction of National Identity* (Wodak et al., 1999) should also be mentioned because the authors' analysis of how both elite and everyday Austrians speak about the past bears directly on the question of Austrian historical memory and national identity.[58]

It is my goal to contribute to this rich scholarship by focusing on official memory and national identity in the postwar Austrian school. By "official memory," I mean the way that historical events are portrayed in an official and public manner, that is, sanctioned by the state or a government entity such as a public school. Official memory provides a useful conceptual framework because it underscores the themes and images that comprised the quasi-official narrative, which Austrians considered essential to their national identity. In the case of school materials examined throughout this volume, this official memory reflects a consensus view of history that embraces the Austria-as-victim myth as the unifying theme in Austrian official memory of the recent past. As discussed, school materials are valuable sources precisely because of the consensus view of the past portrayed therein, whereas in other public outlets of memory, such as print and broadcast media, academia, and the rhetoric of political parties, there tends to be more diversity or even competing visions of the past.[59]

The Uniqueness of Austrian Memory?

With more than fifty years of critical distance having elapsed, memory of World War II continues to be contentious ground. The mid-1990s controversy over the atomic bomb exhibit at the National Air and Space Museum is an oft-cited example of the politics of memory in the United States. Some veterans groups were outraged by a planned exhibit, which they believed did not appropriately address the context of the time and therefore threatened to denigrate their own sacrifices. Subsequent political pressure resulted in a much-simplified exhibit.[60] This controversy was emblematic in that it demonstrated an impasse between the memory of veterans' groups and scholars who have complicated the idea of the "good war" (though the supposed naïve acceptance of the "good war"[61] was never as widespread as is often supposed)[62] by highlighting racial hypocrisy in American society and by probing the sensitive topic of how America's enemies were treated.[63] But despite the body of work that has complicated the idea of the "good war" (and enriched our understanding of it), few Americans and few historians call into question the necessity and righteousness of taking up arms against Japanese militarism and Nazism. It is fair to say that most Americans view the era of World War II in positive terms, as far as American national identity is concerned.

In Europe, links to national identity and memory of the war are much more complex because of the varying layers of fascist and Nazi complicity, which changed with time, place, and circumstance. As Tony Judt writes, on the continent, complicity with Nazism was more the rule than the exception:

[I]f one could stop the clock in, let us say, January 1944, most of Europe would have had little of which to complain by contrast with what was about to come.

Another way of putting this is to say that most of occupied Europe either collaborated with the occupying forces (a minority) or accepted with resignation and with equanimity the presence and activities of the German forces (a majority). The Nazis could certainly never have sustained their hegemony over most of the continent for as long as they did, had it been otherwise.[64]

Indeed, it is hard to see where Judt's argument would not apply.[65] This level of complicity set the stage for a willful embrace of postwar amnesia because, as Judt writes, during "the liberation, everyone sought to identify with the winners—in this case the Allies and those who had sided with them before the final victory. Given the nature of the war, which by its end had mutated into a whole series of brutal local civil wars, it was for most Europeans a matter of some urgency."[66] In short, identifying with the winners was how most Europeans came to terms with their immediate past and (re)established national identity and legitimacy. Throughout liberated and conquered Europe, common denominators in coming to terms with the war included highlighting honorable moments (e.g., emphasizing resistance movements), purging a limited and selective number of Nazis and collaborators, and claiming victim status.[67] In France, for example, the idea of the sword and the shield—de Gaulle's sword of Free France in combination with Petain's shield of Vichy, making the best of bad circumstances to preserve the honor of France—became the basis for postwar reconciliation.[68]

In the two Germanys, total defeat and the dominant presence of the Allies meant that the only answer to postwar identity was rejection of the National Socialist past, albeit in different ways.[69] It is generally assumed that because of the strong Allied presence in Germany, Germans "came to terms" with the Nazi past in a more forthright manner than did Austrians.[70] While there is some validity to this argument, it should not be overstated, for there is a large body of scholarship demonstrating that Germans, like all other postwar Europeans, embraced a number of myths that made memories of the Nazi years more palatable. Such myths included the upstanding Wehrmacht, victim narratives based on alleged Allied atrocities (or real ones, as in the case of the Katyn Forest massacre), and Germany's postwar treatment by the Four Powers.[71] Overall, these postwar German myths served to distinguish between the German people and Nazism. The politics of the Cold War bolstered this view in both East and West Germany. In the West German Federal Republic, the nature of the Stalinist regime in the East was seen as proof positive that while Nazism may have been evil, the war against Bolshevism was not entirely without justification. In the East, the Communist leaders of the German Democratic Republic argued that the capitalist West's failure to adequately punish prominent Nazis demonstrated the need for vigilance against fascism and capitalism, which they saw as inseparable. Now, more than ten years after the unexpected reunification of Germany, the shadow of the war remains in the form of slave labor lawsuits and other controversies related to the Nazi past. The problem of violence against foreigners in contemporary Germany suggests that the Germans' progress in coming to terms with the past has not necessarily advanced beyond that of the Austrians.

Given the near universality of European postwar mythmaking and selective amnesia, what then was unique about Austrian postwar memory? Overall, I argue that postwar Austria was unique in at least two ways. First—setting the legal argument aside—Austria, for all meaningful purposes, had become *part of* Nazi Germany. Because most Austrians became full citizens of Nazi Germany, they stood to gain much (and for a time, many did) from the new Nazi order in Europe. The popular annexation of Austria, as well as the linguistic and cultural similarities between Austria and Germany, also makes the Austrian case fundamentally distinct from Vichy France or the occupied Netherlands. Hitler, after all, was not Dutch, but an Austrian by birth and a German by choice.[72] Given these factors, in postwar Austria it was essential not only to eliminate Nazism from Austria, but also to eliminate "Germanness" from Austria. While the Germans distanced themselves from Nazism, the Austrians distanced themselves from all things German, because, in the Austrian view, Nazism and Germany (Prussian traditions in particular) were nearly one and the same. In the Austrian narrative, restoration of the country marked a return to normality, and the feelings and responsibility of those who had cheered the Anschluss in 1938 were forgotten. Besides, losing the war gave even former Anschluss supporters and Nazis ample reason to fall (back) in love with Austria. Thus, despite seven years of shared history (1938–1945), Austrian memories, official and personal, were considerably different from those in Germany.

The second reason why the Austrian case is unique is the longevity and elaborate nature of the victim myth. This stems from the fact that the Austrian victim narrative was linked not only with Austria's postwar image and sense of identity, but also with legal questions of state legitimacy and national economic survival. For postwar Austrian politicians, the victim myth was necessary for the achievement of two key goals: ending the Allied occupation and protecting economic revival by avoiding the payment of reparations. When the occupation ended in 1955, the Austrian government had largely achieved these aims. By then, Austria's victim mythology had evolved into a web of connected themes, which included the Anschluss of 1938, the role of Austrians in the war and the Holocaust, the Austrian resistance movement, the Moscow Declaration of November 1943, and Austria's relationship with the Four Powers from 1945 to 1955— culminating with the State Treaty and Austria's declaration of permanent neutrality. This victim narrative continued to dominate Austrian official memory and was deliberately cultivated as a part of Austrian identity through the mid 1980s.

Because my arguments employ the terms "myth," "victim," and "perpetrator," it is important to clarify how these terms are used throughout this work. By myth, I mean a narrative that explains, justifies, and gives coherence to historical events in a way that legitimizes the outcome. Thus, a mythological narrative is not so much a false account of events as it is a *selective* account of events that serves a specific purpose or teaches a lesson. When I use the term "victim," I mean someone who was acted upon by the Nazi regime and its supporters. The victim category includes those who were the ideological targets of National Socialism (Jews, Communists and political enemies, Gypsies, the mentally ill, etc.), as well as those who suffered directly at the hands of the regime and its supporters (e.g., forced laborers, resistance fighters, prisoners of war, Allied soldiers, etc.). While it is clear that many Wehrmacht soldiers were nonvoluntarily enlisted by the regime, they cannot be considered victims because they were not targets of Nazi ideology. I define perpetrators as all those who committed violent acts upon the previously mentioned victims. The perpetrator category also includes all those who were ideological supporters of Nazi ideology, or who supported significant elements of Nazi ideology, whether or not they were Nazi Party members. This distinction is necessary to better illuminate the Austrian situation, because, as Anton Pelinka points out, both anti-Semitism and antidemocratic ideas existed independently of National Socialism in Austria.[73] Further, the perpetrator category is by no means limited to Germans and Austrians, but also includes Dutch and French SS volunteers, fascist Italians, and many others. Finally, it would be simplistic to assume only a perpetrator/victim dynamic, for there were many who were neither victims nor perpetrators. This group is characterized by those who were neutral vis-à-vis the regime and did not believe in the significant aspects of Nazi ideology, such as *Lebensraum*, anti-Semitism, and German "racial" superiority. Those in the neutral group neither actively supported nor resisted the Nazi regime.[74] I employ these categories in the hope of making sense of and bringing analytical coherence to wartime experiences, though it must be acknowledged that not everyone can be placed squarely into one category.

The aforementioned neutral category is especially important to acknowledge, because the selective memories of those in this group in particular contributed so much to victim mythology. Because the neutrals suffered during and after the war from food shortages, aerial bombardment, lack of heat, loss of family members, and innumerable other hardships, it is understandable that many would consider themselves to be victims. While psychologically comforting, the view that many were simply "victims of the times and circumstances" is of little use in honestly and directly confronting the past. A more accurate picture of the Nazi era and the Allied occupation requires that we differentiate between a victim as someone who was acted upon by the regime and its supporters and a victim as someone who suffered the consequences of the collapse of a regime that he or she had neither actively supported nor actively resisted. This distinction is important because overly broad definitions of victimhood lead to a conflation of victims. In Austria, the failure to distinguish between general suffering and being a victim of the Nazi regime resulted in the creation of a homogenized community of victims that encompassed nearly everyone, from Jews, to Wehrmacht soldiers, to civilians killed in air raids. Based on the victim myth, a new Austrian nation was being forged out of this all-encompassing community of suffering.[75] As Peter Malina and Gustav Spann write, in that suffering there was unity *(die Gemeinsamkeit des Leidens)*.[76] But as Günter Bischof points out, the "hyperinflation" of victims also resulted in a "failure to confront the past" (in the language of *Vergangenheitsbewältigung*), as meaningful categories of causation and responsibility faded from history.[77]

Here, it is important to add two points of qualification. First, this conflation of victims was not unique to Austria, but common to all of what had been Nazi Germany, especially when it came to the themes of aerial bombardment, German refugees, and the Allied occupation. Second, the tendency to cast oneself as a victim is better understood as a human failing rather than a specifically Austrian (or German) trait. Rarely in history have a people collectively gone to the mountain to confess their sins, and postwar Austrians were no exception. What was specifically Austrian, though, and what differentiated Austria from Germany (as noted earlier), was the insistence on victim status and the conviction that Nazism was something largely alien to Austrian culture and civilization. With this definition of victim in mind, my goal is not to "expose" the skeletons in Austria's closet (that has already happened anyway), but to explore the role of schools in propagating the myth of Austrian victimization as a key component of national identity.

Notes

1. Daniel Glattauer, "Lehrer, Richter, Recht und rechts," *Der Standard* (Vienna), 23 May 1996, 8; and Bernhard Odehnal, Martin Staudinger, and Klaus Zellhofer, "Recht, Rechter, Richter," *Falter* (Vienna), no. 22 (May 1996): 8–9.
2. See Carl Schorske's influential essay "The Ringstrasse, Its Critics, and the Birth of Urban Modernism," in idem, *Fin-de-Siècle Vienna: Politics and Culture* (New York: Vintage Books, 1981), 24–115.
3. Edward Timms, "National Memory and the 'Austrian Idea': From Metternich to Waldheim," *The Modern Language Review* 86, part 4 (October 1991): 898–909.
4. Werner Suppanz, *Österreichische Geschichtsbilder. Historische Legitimationen in Ständestaat und Zweite Republik* (Vienna: Böhlau Verlag, 1998), 120–124.
5. See Charles Maier, "Whose Mitteleuropa? Central Europe between Memory and Obsolescence," in *Austria in the New Europe*, ed. Günter Bischof and Anton Pelinka (New Brunswick: Transaction Publishers, 1993), 13.
6. Günter Bischof and Anton Pelinka, eds., *Austrian Historical Memory and National Identity* (New Brunswick: Transaction Publishers, 1997), 4.
7. Charles S. Maier, *The Unmasterable Past: History, Holocaust, and German National Identity* (Cambridge: Harvard University Press, 1988), 121–159.
8. Benedict Anderson, *Imagined Communities* (New York: Verso, 1983). The literature on the construction of nations is extensive. Arnold Publishers is issuing an "Inventing the

Nation" series, which includes Nicholas Doumanis's *Italy* (London: Arnold, 2001). Among the more useful works on nationalism and national identity are Eugene Weber's classic *Peasants into Frenchmen* (Stanford, 1976); Eric Hobsbawm's famous essay "Inventing Traditions," in *The Invention of Tradition*, ed. Eric Hobsbawm and Terence Ranger (Cambridge: Cambridge University Press, 1983); Geoffrey Cubitt, ed., *Imagining Nations* (Manchester: Manchester University Press, 1998); and Nicolas Shumway, *The Invention of Argentina* (Berkeley: University of California Press, 1991). On Austrian identity in particular, see the linguistic study by Ruth Wodak et al., eds., *The Discursive Construction of National Identity*, trans. Angelika Hirsch and Richard Mitten (Edinburgh: Edinburgh University Press, 1999); and Peter Thaler, *The Ambivalence of Identity: The Austrian Experience of Nation-Building in a Modern Society* (West Lafayette: Purdue University Press, 2001).

9. My formulation of the victim myth follows that of several Austrian scholars. See Heidemarie Uhl, *Zwischen Versöhnung und Verstörung. Eine Kontroverse um Österreichs historische Identität fünfzig Jahre nach dem "Anschluss"* (Vienna: Böhlau Verlag, 1992), 82; Meinrad Ziegler and Waltraud Kannonier-Finster, *Österreichisches Gedächtnis. Über Erinnern und Vergessen der NS-Vergangenheit* (Vienna: Böhlau Verlag), 70–71; Siegfried Mattl and Karl Stuhlpfarrer, "Abwehr und Inszenierung im Labyrinth der Zweiten Republik," in *NS-Herrschaft in Österreich, 1938–1945*, ed. Emmerich Tálos, Ernst Hanisch, and Wolfgang Neugebauer (Vienna: Verlag für Gesellschaftskritik, 1988), 601; and lastly, Gerhard Botz, "Geschichte und Kollektives Gedächtnis in der Zweiten Republik," and Brigitte Bailer, "Alle waren Opfer: Der selektive Umgang mit den Folgen des Nationalsozialismus," both in *Inventur 45/55: Österreich im ersten Jahrzehnt der Zweiten Republik*, ed. Wolfgang Kos and Georg Rigele (Vienna: Sonderzahl Verlagsgesellschaft, 1996), 51–85 and 181–200, respectively.

10. Suppanz, *Österreichische Geschichtsbilder*, 133–243, *passim*.

11. Here I am in agreement with Nicolas Shumway, who, in regard to nineteenth-century myths of Argentine national identity, writes of "guiding fictions," which though often fabricated "are necessary to give individuals a sense of nation, peoplehood, collective identity, and national purpose." See Shumway, *The Invention of Argentina*, xi.

12. See Stourzh's remarks in the roundtable discussion about his work *Um Einheit und Freiheit. Staatsvertrag, Neutralität, und das Ende der Ost-West-Besetzung Österreichs 1945–1955*, 4th rev. and exp. ed. (Vienna: Böhlau, 1998) in *Neutrality in Austria*, ed. Günter Bischof, Anton Pelinka, and Ruth Wodak (New Brunswick: Transaction Publishers, 2001), 289.

13. Anton Pelinka, *Austria: Out of the Shadow of the Past* (Boulder: Westview, 1998), 15–18. Also see Anton Pelinka, "Von der Funktionalität von Tabus," in *Inventur 45/55*, ed. Kos and Rigele, 23–32.

14. Ernest Renan made these remarks in a lecture at the Sorbonne on 11 March 1882. See Ernest Renan, "What is a Nation?" trans. Martin Thom, in *Nation and Narration*, ed. Homi Bhabha (New York and London: Routledge, 1990), 8–22. For the original, see *"Qu'est-ce qu'une nation?" Oeuvres complètes*, vol. 1 (Paris: Calmann-Lévy, 1947), 887–907. Also see Lonnie Johnson's discussion of nationalism in Lonnie Johnson, *Central Europe: Enemies, Neighbors, Friends*, 2nd ed. (New York: Oxford University Press, 2002), 134–136.

15. Joseph Roth, *Radetzkymarsch* (Munich: Deutscher Taschenbuch Verlag, 1986), 12.

16. Doumanis, *Italy*, 104.

17. Quoted from Oscar Jászi, *The Dissolution of the Habsburg Monarchy* (Chicago: University of Chicago Press, 1961 [1929]), 329.

18. Laura Hein and Mark Selden make this point eloquently when they write: "Schools and textbooks are important vehicles through which contemporary societies transmit ideas of citizenship and both the idealized past and the promised future of the community.... People fight over textbook content because education is so obviously about the future, reaches so deeply into society, and is directed by the state." See Laura Hein and Mark Selden, "The Lessons of War, Global Power, and Social Change," in *Censoring History: Citizenship and Memory in Japan, Germany, and the United States*, ed. Laura Hein and

Mark Selden (New York: Sharpe, 2000), 3. Also see Hanna Schissler, who writes: "[W]e can extract from school-books what a society believes should be handed on to the young as part of their historical consciousness." Hanna Schissler, "Perceptions of the Other and the Discovery of the Self: What Pupils are Supposed to Learn About Each Other's History," in *Perceptions of History: International Textbook Research on Britain, Germany and the United States*, ed. Volker R. Berghahn and Hanna Schissler (New York: Berg Publishers, 1987), 26.

19. In 1988, Permian High School in Odessa, Texas, budgeted $5,040 for teaching materials for the English Department, while $6,750 was spent on boys' athletic medical supplies, $6,400 was spent for film prints for football games, and approximately $70,000 was spent on chartered jet aircraft for away games (including the Texas high school playoffs). See H. G. Bissinger, *Friday Night Lights: A Town, a Team, and a Dream* (New York: HarperPerennial, 1991), 145–146.

20. I owe thanks to Richard Mitten for pointing to this list of questions related to the Holocaust.

21. It is not entirely clear who first coined this apt phrase now commonly used by Austrian scholars. According to Bernard Schausberger, *Koalitionsgeschichtsschreibung* was coined by Karl Stadler. See Bernard Schausberger, "Die Entstehung des Mythos. Österreich als Opfer des Nationalsozialismus. Eine Dokumentation" (Diplomarbeit, Paris-Lodron-Universität, Salzburg), 1991, 9.

22. Christian Sitte, "Entwicklung des Unterrichtsgegenstandes Geographie, Erdkunde, Geographie und Wirtschaftskunde an den Allgemeinbildenden Schulen (APS u. AHS) in Österreich nach 1945" (Ph.D. diss., University of Vienna, 1989), 413–429, *passim*.

23. See Deborah S. Hutton and Howard D. Mehlinger, "International Textbook Revision: Examples from the United States," in *Perceptions of History*, ed. Berghahn and Schissler, 142.

24. Some textbooks from the *Ständestaat* and the Nazi period are also included in chapter 1.

25. For a study based on fifteen texts published between 1973 and 1985, see Peter Malina and Gustav Spann, "Der Nationalsozialismus im Österreichischen Geschichtslehrbuch" in *NS-Herrschaft in Österreich*, ed. Tálos et al., 577–599; for a study based on twenty-three texts published between 1972 and 1983, see Eduard Fuchs, *Schule und Zeitgeschichte. Oder Wie kommen Jugendliche zu Politischen Klischeevorstellungen* (Vienna and Salzburg: Geyer Edition, 1986); for a brief study based on seven texts published between 1980 and 1987, see Josef Thonhauser and Ingrid Gassner, "Was können Schüler aus Geschichte-Lehrbüchern für die Vergangenheitsbewältigung lernen?" in *Kontroversen um Österreichs Zeitgeschichte. Verdrängte Vergangenheit, Österreich-Identität, Waldheim und die Historiker*, ed. Gerhard Botz and Gerald Sprengnagel (Frankfurt and New York: Campus Verlag, 1994), 428–450; for a textbook study based on eighteen texts (dates not given), which emphasizes issues of Austrian identity, see Josef Thonhauser, "Österreichbewusstsein und Vergangenheitsbewältigung im Spiegel der Lehrbücher," *Zeitgeschichte* 15, no. 1 (1987): 37–53.

26. For a general overview of Austrian education, see *The Austrian Educational System* (Vienna: Federal Press Service, 1990).

27. In HS and AHS schools, the history of the years 1938–1955 is taught in the fourth and eighth classes. Recently, the Nazi era and the postwar era have been split between the seventh and eighth classes. Overall, then, Austrian history from 1938 to 1955 is part of the curriculum in the years roughly corresponding with American junior high and the final two years of high school.

28. Currently, there are separate textbook lists for at least twelve types of schools, including schools for agriculture and forestry (*Land- und Forstwirtschaftliche Berufsschulen*). It should be noted that it is common for the same textbook authors to submit a slightly altered version of their books to be approved for different types of schools. This means that there are not significant differences in the content of the textbooks for the various types of schools.

29. The *Schulbuchaktion* is a government program that supplies Austrian students with free textbooks. Students receive coupons from their schools, which they use to purchase texts at local bookstores. The textbook program also vastly increased the number of

reading books. See Bundesministerium für Finanzen und Bundesministerium für Unterricht und Kunst, *10 Jahre Schulbuchaktion* (Graz: Leykam Universitätsbuchdruckerei, 1982), 17–18, 32. Another result of the *Schulbuchaktion* was the creation of a lucrative market in textbooks for Austrian publishers. Some 111 publishers print books for the *Schulbuchaktion*, and approximately 3,000 jobs stem directly from the free book program. See Sitte, "Entwicklung des Unterrichtsgegenstandes Geographie," 400–401.

30. Note also that readers for the fourth class (seventh-grade age) focus on local themes. This is done either in individual volumes dedicated to one province, or in supplemental volumes for individual provinces read in combination with a "base" volume. My sampling of fourth class readers includes examples from all nine Austrian provinces.

31. "*Jahresbericht*" translates directly as "annual report." I translate "*Jahresbericht*" as "yearbook," since these documents resemble American-style high school yearbooks.

32. See Allan Janik's review of Bischof and Pelinka, *Austrian Historical Memory and National Identity*, in *Central European History* 30, no. 4 (1997): 625.

33. Ernst Hanisch, "Die Präsenz des Dritten Reiches in der Zweiten Republik," in *Inventur 45/55*, ed. Kos and Rigele, 33–47.

34. See Tony Judt, *Past Imperfect: French Intellectuals, 1944–1956* (Berkeley: University of California Press, 1992), 4.

35. Robert Knight, "Education and National Identity in Austria after the Second World War," in *The Habsburg Legacy: National Identity in Historical Perspective*, ed. Ritchie Robertson and Edward Timms (Edinburgh: Edinburgh University Press, 1994), 180.

36. Robert Herzstein reported that when he began his research into Kurt Waldheim's past in the 1980s, he was aided by Austrian scholars who specifically asked that their assistance not be acknowledged, because—in Herzstein's words—"[p]resumably, their careers might suffer." See Robert Herzstein, "The Present State of the Waldheim Affair: Second Thoughts and New Directions," in *Austrian Historical Memory and National Identity*, ed. Bischof and Pelinka, 116–134.

37. See Thomas Angerer, "An Incomplete Discipline: Austrian Zeitgeschichte and Recent History," in *Austria in the Nineteen Fifties*, ed. Günter Bischof, Anton Pelinka, and Rolf Steininger (New Brunswick: Transaction Publishers, 1995): 207–251.

38. Der Herr Karl is the Viennese "average Joe," made famous in *Der Herr Karl* by Carl Merz and Helmut Qualtinger, first performed in 1961. See Carl Merz and Helmut Qualtinger, *Der Herr Karl* (Vienna: Akadamietheater, 1987).

39. Erika Weinzierl, *Zu wenig Gerechte. Österreicher und Judenverfolgung 1938–1945* (Graz: Verlag Styria, 1985).

40. Bruce Pauley, *Hitler and the Forgotten Nazis: A History of Austrian National Socialism* (Chapel Hill: The University of North Carolina Press, 1981); and John Bunzl and Bernd Marin, *Antisemitismus in Österreich. Sozialhistorische und soziologische Studien* (Innsbruck: Inn-Verlag, 1983).

41. Robert Keyserlingk, *Austria in World War II: An Anglo-American Dilemma* (Montreal: McGill-Queen's University Press, 1988).

42. Robert Knight, ed., *"Ich bin dafür, die Sache in die Länge zu ziehen." Wortprotokolle der österreichischen Bundesregierung von 1945–52 über die Entschädigung der Juden* (Frankfurt am Main: Athenäum, 1988).

43. See Anton Pelinka and Erika Weinzierl, eds., *Das große Tabu. Österreichs Umgang mit seiner Vergangenheit* (Vienna: Edition S., 1987).

44. Ernst Hanisch, *Der Lange Schatten des Staates. Österreichische Gesellschaftsgeschichte im 20. Jahrhundert* (Vienna: Ueberreuter, 1994), 399. Also see Walter Manoschek, "Verschmähte Erbschaft. Österreichs Umgang mit dem Nationalsozialismus 1945 bis 1955," in *Österreich 1945–1995. Gesellschaft, Politik, Kultur*, ed. Reinhard Sieder et al. (Vienna: Verlag für Gesellschaftskritik, 1995), 94–106; and Siegfried Mattl and Karl Stuhlpfarrer, "Abwehr und Inszenierung im Labyrinth der Zweiten Republik," in *NS-Herrschaft in Österreich*, ed. Tálos et al., 601–624. Also see Jacqueline Vansant, "Challenging Austria's Victim Status: National Socialism and Austrian Personal Narratives," *The German Quarterly* 67, no. 1 (winter 1994): 38–57.

45. By design, the journalist Pick's work is a personal reflection on postwar Austria with a strong emphasis on the political career of Bruno Kreisky. Despite the title, it cannot be considered a comprehensive work on postwar Austria or postwar Austrian memory. See Hella Pick, *Guilty Victim: Austria from the Holocaust to Haider* (New York: I.B. Tauris, 2000).
46. For Bukey's earlier work on the subject. see Evan Bukey, "Popular Opinion in Vienna After the Anschluss," in *Conquering the Past: Austrian Nazism Yesterday and Today*, ed. Frank Parkinson (Detroit: Wayne State University Press, 1989), 151–164.
47. See Thaler, *The Ambivalence of Identity*.
48. For a useful analysis of the historiographical issues related to history and memory, see Patrick Hutton, *History as an Art of Memory* (Hanover: University Press of New England, 1993).
49. Maurice Halbwachs, *On Collective Memory*, ed. and trans. Lewis A. Coser (Chicago: University of Chicago Press, 1992). The English volume *On Collective Memory* is translated from two works, *Les cadres sociaux de la mémoire* (1952) and *La topographie légendaire des évangiles en terre sainte: Etude de mémoire collective* (1941).
50. For example, French scholar Pierre Nora implies that historical knowledge as it was formerly conceived is no longer possible. According to Nora, memory is the only avenue historians have left for examining the past. Of particular interest is Nora's concept of *lieux de mémoire*, or "sites of memory"—meaning sites where historical memory is deliberately evoked—which includes monuments, artifacts, rituals, and objects such as school textbooks. See Nora's general introduction "Between Memory and History" in *Rethinking the French Past: Realms of Memory. Volume I: Conflicts and Divisions*, ed. Lawrence D. Kritzman, under the direction of Pierre Nora, trans. Arthur Goldhammer (New York: Columbia University Press, 1996).
51. David Lowenthal, *The Past is a Foreign Country* (London: Cambridge University Press, 1985), 212–213.
52. Poststructuralism and postmodernism are sometimes used interchangeably. For a lucid discussion of postmodernism and related theories, see Steven C. Hause, "The Evolution of Social History," *French Historical Studies* 19, no. 4 (1996): 1191–1214.
53. See Ruth Wodak et al., *Die Sprachen der Vergangenheiten. Öffentliches Gedenken in österreichischen und deutschen Medien* (Frankfurt am Main: Suhrkamp, 1994), 12–14.
54. Michael S. Roth, *The Ironist's Cage: Memory, Trauma, and the Construction of History* (New York: Columbia University Press, 1995), 16. For a brilliant critique of the excesses of literary critics' assaults on history, see John H. Zammito, "Are We Being Theoretical Yet? The New Historicism, the New Philosophy of History, and 'Practicing Historians,'" in *The Journal of Modern History* 65 (December 1993): 783–814.
55. As far as my position on memory relates to the larger debate on the postmodern critique, I would agree with Saul Friedlander, who in regard to postmodernism and the Holocaust writes: "[N]otwithstanding the importance one may attach to postmodern attempts at confronting what escapes, at least in part, established historical and artistic categories of representation, the equivocation of postmodernism concerning "reality" and "truth"—that is, ultimately, its fundamental relativism—confronts any discourse about Nazism and the Shoah with considerable difficulties." See Friedlander's introduction in Saul Friedlander, ed., *Probing the Limits of Representation: Nazism and the "Final Solution"* (Cambridge: Harvard University Press, 1992), 20. For further works on the limitations of the postmodern critique, see Georg Iggers, *Historiography in the Twentieth Century: From Scientific Objectivity to the Postmodern Challenge* (Hanover: Wesleyan University Press, 1997), especially 118–147; and Richard Evans, *In Defense of History* (New York: Norton, 1999). It is interesting to note that Richard Evans served as an important witness against the British Holocaust denier David Irving in his recent failed libel lawsuit against historian Deborah Lipstadt in Great Britain. See Ian Buruma, "Blood Libel: Hitler and History in the Dock," *The New Yorker*, 16 April 2001, 82–86.
56. See Uhl, *Zwischen Versöhnung und Verstörung*.

57. See Stefan Riesenfellner and Heidemarie Uhl, eds., *Todeszeichen. Zeitgeschichtliche Denkmalkultur in der Steiermark vom Ende des 19. Jahrhunderts bis zur Gegenwart* (Vienna: Böhlau, 1994).

58. See Wodak et al., *The Discursive Construction of National Identity*.

59. For an analysis of how Austrian and German media have covered historically controversial issues, see the aforementioned Wodak et al., *Die Sprachen der Vergangenheiten*, and Heinz Wassermann, *"Zuviel Vergangenheit tut nicht gut!": Nationalsozialismus im Spiegel der Tagespresse der Zweiten Republik* (Innsbruck: Studienverlag, 2000).

60. See the articles and discussions in the special section "History and the Public: What Can We Handle? A Round Table about History after the Enola Gay Controversy," in *The Journal of American History* 82, no. 3 (December 1995): 1029–1144.

61. Studs Terkel, *The "Good War"* (New York: Ballantine, 1984).

62. See Chad Berry, "Public, Private, and Popular: The United States Remembers World War II," in *Austrian Historical Memory and National Identity*, ed. Bischof and Pelinka, 163–182.

63. See John Hope Franklin, "Their War and Mine," *Journal of American History* 77, no. 2 (September 1990): 576–579; and John Dower, *War Without Mercy: Race and Power in the Pacific War* (New York: Pantheon, 1996). Also see Paul Fussell, *Wartime: Understanding and Behavior in the Second World War* (New York: Oxford University Press, 1989).

64. Tony Judt, "The Past Is Another Country: Myth and Memory in Postwar Europe," *Daedalus* 121, no. 4 (fall 1992): 85.

65. The Hitler-Stalin pact of 1939 does not seem to have contributed to any sense that the Great Patriotic War was in any way unjust or unnecessary.

66. Judt, "The Past Is Another Country," 86.

67. See István Deák, Jan T. Gross, and Tony Judt, eds., *The Politics of Retribution in Europe: World War II and Its Aftermath* (Princeton: Princeton University Press, 2000).

68. See Henry Rousso, *The Vichy Syndrome: History and Memory in France since 1944*, trans. Arthur Goldhammer (Cambridge: Harvard University Press, 1991). Also see Judt, *Past Imperfect*, 46–47.

69. See Mary Fulbrook, *German National Identity After the Holocaust* (Oxford: Polity Press, 1999); Jeffrey Herf, *Divided Memory: The Nazi Past in the Two Germanys* (Cambridge: Harvard University Press, 1997); Frank Trommler, "The Creation of History and the Refusal of the Past in the German Democratic Republic," in *Coping with the Past: Germany and Austria after 1945*, ed. Kathy Harms, Lutz Reuter, and Volker Dürr (Madison: University of Wisconsin Press, 1990), 79–93; and Bill Niven, *Facing the Nazi Past: United Germany and the Legacy of the Third Reich* (Routledge: New York, 2002), especially 41–61.

70. While he did not specifically address Austrian memory of the war, Daniel Goldhagen has high praise for postwar West Germans and their willingness to confront their past. See his comments on the German public's reception to his controversial (and simplistic) book in the afterword to the Vintage Edition of the work. Daniel Goldhagen, *Hitler's Willing Executioners: Ordinary Germans and the Holocaust* (New York: Vintage Books, 1997): 465–466.

71. See Omer Bartov, "Defining Enemies, Making Victims: Germans, Jews, and the Holocaust," *American Historical Review* 103, no. 3. (June 1998): 771–816; Robert Moeller, *War Stories: The Search for a Usable Past in the Federal Republic of Germany* (Berkeley: University of California Press, 2001); Elizabeth Heineman, "The Hour of the Woman: Memories of Germany's 'Crisis Years' and West German National Identity," *The American Historical Review* 101, no. 2 (April 1996): 354–395; and Jane Kramer, "Letter from Germany: The Politics of Memory," *The New Yorker*, 14 August 1995, 48–65.

72. There is some question about the degree to which Hitler's ideological anti-Semitism dated to his Austrian, and especially Viennese, experiences. Ian Kershaw argues that while Hitler's ideological and racist anti-Semitism cannot be traced to his Austrian years, Hitler must have been anti-Semitic in his personal relations, as well as influenced by Austrian political anti-Semitism. See Ian Kershaw, *Hitler 1889–1936: Hubris* (New York: W.W. Norton, 1998), 63–69. Brigitte Hamann also points to Austrian political anti-Semitism and its likely influence on Hitler, but argues that Hitler was on friendly terms

with numerous Jews. Hamann believes that anti-Semitism as the "core of his *weltanschauung* cannot be answered by looking at his years in Linz and Vienna," and that the "great turning point" in Hitler's ideological development must have developed during the Great War and the chaos of its immediate aftermath. See Brigitte Hamann, *Hitler's Vienna: A Dictator's Apprenticeship* (New York: Oxford University Press, 1999), 351–352.

73. Pelinka, *Austria: Out of the Shadow of the Past*, 184.

74. For a detailed delineation between perpetrators, victims, and bystanders as they relate to the Holocaust, see Raul Hilberg, *Perpetrators, Victims, Bystanders: The Jewish Catastrophe, 1933–1945* (New York: HarperCollins, 1992).

75. I use the phrase "community of suffering" throughout this work. This phraseology is inspired by the terminology of other historians. Günter Bischof writes of an "Austrian victims collective." See Günter Bischof, *Austria in the First Cold War, 1945–55: The Leverage of the Weak* (New York: St. Martin's Press, 1999), 63. Likewise, Heidemarie Uhl writes of a "time of collective suffering among the entire population." See Heidemarie Uhl, "Erinnern und Vergessen. Denkmäler zur Erinnerung an die Opfer der nationalsozialistischen Gewaltherrschaft und an die Gefallenen des Zweiten Weltkrieges in Graz und in der Steiermark," in *Todeszeichen*, ed. Riesenfellner and Uhl, 147.

76. See Peter Malina and Gustav Spann, "Der Nationalsozialismus im Österreichischen Geschichtslehrbuch," in *NS-Herrschaft in Österreich*, ed. Tálos et al., 594.

77. Bischof and Pelinka, *Austrian Historical Memory and National Identity*, 3–4.

Part I

REVERSING THE ANSCHLUSS, 1945–1955

FROM *BLÜMCHENKAFFEE* TO *WIENER MÉLANGE*

Schools, Identity, and the Birth of the
Austria-as-Victim Myth

When the last Allied soldier left Austria in the fall of 1955, Austrians could look back on ten years of profound change.[1] Austria had been reborn in the spring of 1945 with the provisional government's declaration of independence, but from the beginning, Austria was faced with a material crisis and a crisis of identity. In those lean years following the war Austrians drank *Blümchenkaffee*, coffee so weak one could see through it to the floral designs on the bottom of coffee cups. By 1955, the physical rebuilding of Austria, greatly assisted by Marshall Plan aid, was largely complete, and the shortages of food and fuel were mostly a memory. Simultaneously, Austrian political leaders and educators had laid the groundwork for a new Austrian identity based on a mixture of tradition, Austrian uniqueness vis-à-vis Germany, democratic values, and the myth of Austria-as-victim. The time of *Blümchenkaffee* was coming to an end. Austrian coffee was now richly brewed, and more and more Austrians could afford to drink *Wiener Mélange*—strong coffee mixed with steamed milk and often served with sugar and a small glass of water on the side.

The end of the war brought the rebirth of Austria, but the new Austria faced a crisis that went beyond the acute shortages of the immediate post-war period. More than just food and other necessities were in short supply; Austria needed a political, social, and cultural identity that was completely distinct from Germany. It was essential to Austria's long-term viability and key to attaining political leverage with the Four Powers that Austria rapidly distance itself from its recent association with Nazi Germany. A new Austria had to be invented, and a sense of identity had to be built out of whatever remains of the past were still useful in combination with new ideas. Foremost among these ideas was the Austria-as-victim myth, which had already been propagated by the provisional government in April 1945. The very legitimacy of the Second Republic rested on this idea, which not only coherently explained Austria's recent ordeals, but also lent a positive, even honorable cast to the travails of annexation, war, and military collapse.

In Austrian textbooks, the victim myth became the unifying theme in the narrative of postwar Austrian history and was cultivated as an important part of Austrian identity. This promotion of victim status is related to, but distinct from, questions as to what actually constitutes Austrian national identity, or what exemplifies the Austrian character. While defining a people or a nation is philosophically and historically difficult, the Austrian case is rendered especially complex because of Austria's varied history and its historical, cultural, and linguistic connection with Germany.[2] There is a rich historiography—but by no means a consensus—on the theme of Austrian identity and what it means to be an Austrian.[3] The emphasis here is to explore how Austrian schools employed the Austria-as-victim theme to build a new and officially sanctioned identity of Austrian fortitude, political courage, perseverance, and cultural sophistication out of which a new nation would be built.

The task of imparting a sense of national identity to Austria's youth was an onerous one for Austrian educators: political division in the 1920s and early 1930s, Austro-fascism, union with Nazi Germany, and full participation in the war constituted a recent past from which it was difficult to borrow. The Austria-as-victim myth gave school officials the thematic unity that was needed to make sense of those turbulent years. Indirectly supporting this mythology was the separate issue of distinguishing Austria from Germany and inculcating a unique Austrian identity among the students. As Werner Suppanz demonstrates in his fine study *Österreichische Geschichtsbilder*, Austrian patriots explicitly argued that Austria's unique, non-German culture and history dated at least to the Middle Ages (and for some, even to Roman times) and continued through the age of Enlightenment into the nineteenth century.[4] Austria's uniqueness was further reinforced in school materials, which highlighted the themes of *Heimat* (homeland), *Landschaft* (landscape), culture, Catholicism, and work. This image of an eternal and unique Austria was distinct from the Austria-as-victim myth, yet it validated and supported the victim mythology by casting Austrian culture and life as completely alien to that of Germany. By implication, Austria became the very antithesis of Nazi Germany. By 1955, the mythology of victimization and the cultivation of Austrian uniqueness had combined to form an official memory of the recent Austrian past that supported the legitimacy of the Second Republic by bolstering Austria's claim to victim status.

Ständestaat and Nazi Education

The education officials of post–World War II Austria were painfully aware of the failure of the post–World War I First Republic and the *Ständestaat* (the Dollfuss-Schuschnigg period, termed by many as the Austro-fascist dictatorship) to build a strong and unified sense of Austrian identity. After the collapse of the Habsburg Empire, there was no consensus on what it meant to be Austrian.[5] With the end of the First Republic in 1934, schoolbooks of the *Ständestaat* sought to emphasize Austrian uniqueness by focusing on themes, such as *Heimat* and *Landschaft*, that would appear again in the Second Republic. But ultimately the *Ständestaat*'s attempt to build a sense of national identity failed. One reason for the failure was the mixed message sent by *Ständestaat* nationalism. For example, a 1935 book for grade school children, *Mein Vaterland, mein Österreich*, imparted the message: "We Austrians are Germans. We belong to the German people. Whoever is a good Austrian is at the same time a good German. The federal chancellor Dr. Dollfuss, who died for our fatherland, said: 'We happily recognize our Germanness [*Deutschtum*].'"[6] Students also read about the *Ständestaat*'s public works program, the *österreichische Arbeitsdienst*, which clearly emulated similar programs in Nazi Germany.[7] The flaws in the *Ständestaat* program of building national identity were numerous. First, the *Ständestaat* excluded Socialists (and Nazis) from Austrian political life, thereby creating groups of outcasts from the beginning. Second, the Austrian identity propagated by the *Ständestaat* was insufficiently distinct from German identity. Austria did not come across as unique and dissimilar to Nazi Germany, but rather as the poorer cousin of the Germans. Austrians had a clear sense of local identity, but the idea of an Austrian nation separate from the German nation remained underdeveloped.[8] This failure of nation-building contributed to the relatively smooth nature of the 1938 Anschluss (annexation) and aided the Nazis' efforts to remove the trappings of the Austrian nation as the formation of new *Gaue* (Nazi administrative districts) and the implementation of Nazi administration and law proceeded. The *Ständestaat* had already paved the way by eliminating Socialists and Communists from political life and preaching German patriotism. As a result, the Austrian populace correctly saw many of the changes brought by the Anschluss as lateral changes, rather than revolutionary changes.

After the Anschluss, the Nazis quickly and systematically sought to eliminate symbols of Austrian identity, and Austrian schools rapidly experienced the effects of the Nazi *Gleichschaltung*—the coordination and nazification of all aspects of life. In June 1940, the Austrian Education Ministry closed its doors as a result of the *Ostmarkgesetz* (*Ostmark* law), which eliminated the last legal remnants of Austria.[9] By that time, many Nazi features had become part of life in Austrian schools, including the Nuremberg race laws, portraits of Hitler in classrooms, the German greeting "Heil Hitler!" and German handwriting, and posters in classrooms to remind students of the success of the April 1938 plebiscite. After the war began, students were asked to collect bones and scrap metal for the war effort.[10] The Nazi curriculum was also introduced as subjects such as history and biology being taught from the Nazi point of view.[11] Students were introduced to "science" books already used in Germany, such as Jakob Graf's, *Familienkunde und Rassenbiologie für Schüler*, and reading books with messages to the youth of the Reich from Adolf Hitler and poems by Baldur von Schirach, the leader of the Hitler Youth.[12]

The Anschluss was also a boon to Austrian Nazis, who lost no time in making their mark on Austrian schools. Previously dismissed Nazi teachers were reinstated, and many schools organized Anschluss celebrations.[13] In the 1938 yearbook for Laa an der Thaya, the teacher Othmar Rieger recounted the Anschluss and wrote of coming out from the shadow of a "sad time."[14] In Baden, students witnessed Field Marshall Hermann Göring drive through the city. A thrill for one girl, *Fräulein* Berghammer, came when Göring stopped his vehicle to receive a bouquet of flowers from her.[15] In another school in Klagenfurt, a teacher organized a book burning.[16] Yearbooks from 1938 often also included articles by teachers on the goals and challenges of National Socialist education.[17] Collectively, these measures taken by the Nazi government in Austria demonstrate not only the impact of National Socialism on Austrian schools, but also the concrete nature of the Anschluss.[18]

Casting Austria as a Victim

After the war, the effects of the Nazi *Gleichschaltung* had to be reversed. The new Austrian government began a campaign to build Austrian identity based on Austrian uniqueness vis-à-vis Germany, local traditions, and a selective view of long- and short-term Austrian history. The glory of the Babenbergs and the Habsburgs, the Turkish wars, the grandeur of Austrian architecture, and the Austrian landscape were areas ripe for harvesting images of national identity.[19] However, the long-term view of Austrian history was inadequate to the task of explaining the immediate antecedents of the Second Republic. The First Republic, Austro-fascist government, union with Nazi Germany, and World War II—watershed events in and of themselves—also amounted to a collective massive rupture from the Habsburg past.[20] In post–World War II Austria, these topics had to be addressed to make sense of the Second Republic. In building the new nation, it was imperative, though extremely difficult, to claim a positive legacy from these turbulent years. The one unifying theme capable of explaining the years 1918–1945 in a way meaningful to Austrian identity was the idea of a victimized Austria, an idea which the Austrian government embraced immediately as a pillar of legitimacy and which became key to Austrian identity in the Second Republic.

In the public sphere, Austrian political leaders embraced the idea of Austria-as-victim in the Proclamation of 27 April 1945, a time when many Austrians in the Nazi armed forces were still fighting Allied soldiers. The proclamation claimed to nullify the Anschluss, declared Austria independent, and named a variety of ways in which Austria was a victim of

Germany, including forcible occupation of a helpless people, degrading Vienna to the status of a provincial city, economic and cultural plunder, robbing the Austrian people of natural resources, selling off priceless artistic and cultural objects (which even the "hard peace of St. Germain" had protected), and forcing Austria into a war or conquest that "no Austrian ever wanted."[21] Thus, as Anton Pelinka, points out, the legitimacy of the Second Republic was dependent from the beginning on not facing up to the past: "The neglect of Austria's past began exactly on 27 April 1945, when the provisional government declared Austria a victim and only a victim."[22]

The victim myth was further elaborated as a political doctrine by both Austria's provisional government and its first postwar elected government in an annotated collection of documents, *Justice for Austria! Red-White-Red-Book*, published in 1946.[23] The Foreign Office had taken the lead in the summer of 1945, arguing against the "annexation" theory of the Anschluss. Instead, it put forth the view that Austria had been "occupied and liberated." As Günter Bischof writes, this "'Rip Van Winkle myth' of dormant Austrian statehood" became official state doctrine, and the occupation theory soon radiated throughout government policy.[24] The *Red-White-Red-Book* was unequivocal in viewing Austria as a victim of both German aggression and the world's neglect: "Her fall—inevitable under the conditions which then reigned—was the bursting of the dike through which the elements of the brown deluge were to pour over the whole of Europe. *Their first victim, left in the lurch, by the whole world, was Austria*" (emphasis in original).[25] The *Red-White-Red-Book* also covered many other important aspects of the Austria-as-victim myth, including Austria's role in the war, the alleged damage to Austria's economy caused by the annexation, and the role of the Austrian resistance in liberating Austria. Fifty years later, it is easy to see the *Red-White-Red-Book* as a distortion of history that took events out of context and relied on an abstract view of the Austrian state as a victim—a view which stripped Austrians of any agency in the Anschluss and ignored the fact that Austrian democracy was destroyed in 1934 by Austrians, four years before the Anschluss.

The *Red-White-Red-Book* was indeed the manifesto of the Austria-as-victim myth, but it was not simply a cynical falsification of history. It was a direct answer to the Allies' November 1943 Moscow Declaration, which named Austria a victim of German aggression, but at the same time warned "that she has a responsibility for participation in the war on the side of Hitlerite Germany, and that in the final settlement account will inevitably be taken of her contribution to her liberation."[26] That the Moscow Declaration was more a tactical device designed to undermine support for the Nazi regime than a statement of Allied political policy did not matter, because the Allies never publicly disavowed the Moscow Declaration as a meaningful statement of political intent. Thus, the Allies, too, played a key role in legitimizing the Austria-as-victim myth from the beginning. Indeed, this was acknowledged at the time by American diplomats such as Martin Herz, who early in 1947 remarked that because

American policy was to "encourage a separate Austrian nationalism, we cannot be surprised, and should in fact find comfort in the fact that most Austrians deny ever having had anything to do with Germany.... It stands to reason that the emphasis on Austria's separateness from Germany results in a corresponding feeling of guiltlessness."[27]

The larger significance of the *Red-White-Red-Book* was that it was unequivocal in arguing Austria's victim status and that therefore Austria deserved to be treated differently from Germany. Once officially declared a victim, Austria became a liberated rather than a conquered nation. With their country so designated, Austrian statesmen could argue against paying reparations or losing territory to Germany's wartime foes, while in domestic politics, Austrian politicians avoided alienating those who had been in, or sympathetic to, the Nazi camp.[28] Church leaders, too, contributed to the myth by openly declaring the Church and Austrian citizens to be victims of a catastrophe. Austria's victim status was stated unequivocally in a joint pastoral letter of Austrian bishops in October 1945: "No group has sacrificed more ... than Christ's church.... But we also know that the entire German people, and the entire Austrian people even less so, cannot be made responsible.... Fortunately, [the Nazi plan] to choke off and destroy Austrians' love for their *Heimat* and fatherland did not succeed. No, we love our beautiful *Landschaft*, we love Austrian ways and temperament, and we love Austrian style and culture and carry in us the belief in a new ... Austria."[29] The targets of Nazi ideology—Jews, communists, and others—remained conspicuously absent from the bishops' exoneration of the Austrian people. While it would be easy to dismiss these remarks as hubris, in the immediate postwar context they provided comfort to a hungry and defeated flock.[30] Personal suffering, political rhetoric, and the position of the Church all reinforced each other to forge a new Austrian community—an all-encompassing community of suffering.

The *Red-White-Red-Book* was important not only as an official statement of Austria's victim status, but also as an early example of coalition history. Born of the consociational politics of the Second Republic, coalition history was characterized by compromise between the Social Democrats and the conservative Austrian People's Party. This unique brand of Austrian politics provided the Second Republic stability over the years, but it also hindered meaningful confrontation with darker aspects of Austria's past.[31] Throughout the *Red-White-Red-Book*, all groups within Austrian society are seen as victims of Nazism. Credit for resistance to Nazism is likewise parceled out equally to every social group: Catholic conservatives, Socialists, and Austrian soldiers forced to fight with the Wehrmacht all become resisters. In the early years of the Second Republic, the country's restoration and the goal of distancing Austria from Germany depended on cooperation and consensus-building among the major political parties—parties that had fought a civil war only eleven years earlier. Coalition history contributed to political peace, but gave legitimacy to two specific myths. The first was that Socialists and conservatives were equally to blame for the violent political division of the First Republic. The second was the idea that both the Socialists and conservatives suffered equally at the hands of the Nazis. The legend emerged that leaders who had once hated each other had learned the lessons of putting Austria first and of getting along while imprisoned in German concentration camps.[32] Forty years after the war, this idea remained alive and well. In 1985, Austrian President Rudolf Kirchschläger evoked this idea in the introduction to a book commemorating the rebirth of Austria in 1945. It was a time that demanded "reflection on the courage which blessed those men who remained loyal to our country in hard times and laid the foundation of the Second Republic, but also reflection on the spirit of cooperation, which alone was responsible for leading the enterprise [the rebirth of Austria] to success."[33]

While the coming together of Socialists and conservatives in concentration camps was partly a legend, the postwar spirit of compromise embodied by the legend was real and in many ways defined the political stability of the Second Republic.[34] But as Anton Pelinka has noted, coalition history also created taboo areas. While intense rivalries continued behind the scenes, public inquiries into the bitter divisions of the First Republic were shelved because any discussion of the First Republic would automatically lead to a discussion of how Austria collapsed as a state and was smoothly incorporated into the Third Reich.[35] It was politically easier to blame the Anschluss on the Germans and a token handful of Austrians rather than to look closer to home for explanations of Austria's demise. At the grassroots level, though, there is evidence that by no means were all Austrians comfortable with the Austria-as-victim explanation of the recent past. Heidemarie Uhl's pioneering study of Styrian memorials demonstrates that the victim consensus did not dominate war memorials until after 1950. Indeed, in the immediate aftermath of the war, numerous locally sponsored memorials in Styria were dedicated to racial and political victims of Nazism, Allied soldiers, and members of the Austrian resistance. But such local initiatives gave way to the victim consensus being constructed at the national level.[36] Contributing to the change in commemoration patterns was the looming question of the disenfranchised Nazis, who, sooner or later, would become voters again. As the Allies disengaged from denazification (see chapter 4), political parties competed with each other for the votes of former Nazis, and denazification denigrated into a rapid succession of amnesties. A significant side effect of the series of amnesties was the formation of the Party of Independents (VdU), the forerunner of the Freedom Party of Austria (FPÖ). In any event, the competition for the votes of the newly enfranchised ex-Nazis made soul-searching over the immediate past even more unlikely.[37] Despite the negative effects of letting bygones be bygones, it must be pointed out that Austrian politicians in the late 1940s had little choice. A renewal of the fierce partisan politics of the First Republic would have led to disaster for Austria. Coalition history served a valuable purpose by creating political harmony, a truly precious commodity in Austria. This consensus view of history was especially evident in school materials and other areas where cooperation was necessary. However, it should be added that outside the sphere of consensus politics, Austrian political parties had, and continue to have, their own views of Austria's past, which are in sharp contrast with one another.[38]

Reversing the *Gleichschaltung* of Austrian Education

The driving reason behind the postwar spirit of cooperation between the conservatives and Socialists was the Allied occupation and the fear that Austria would be permanently divided and forced to pay crippling reparations. Political cooperation was needed to overcome the Austrian government's limited freedom of action due to the occupation. Austrian education officials, too, were subject to the occupation authorities, though the degree of Allied involvement in education decisions varied from zone to zone and from issue to issue. The first task was to get the schools up and running in an atmosphere of privation. The organization of the school system itself had long been a contentious political issue in Austria and promised to be so again. In the immediate postwar context, it was agreed to return to the structure of the school system as it was during the First Republic, with the understanding that the question of reform would be revisited.[39] Significant reform, however, was not enacted until 1962, after years of negotiation and disagreement. The first two years of Allied occupation saw by far the highest level of Allied involvement. The stated goal of the Allies was: "To ensure the institution of a progressive long-term educational program designed to eradicate all traces of Nazi ideology and to instill into Austrian youth democratic principles."[40] A top priority of the Allies was to eliminate Nazi teachers from schools. Lack of Allied unity on denazification procedures weakened the process, but the greater problem was the huge number of implicated teachers. Some 60 percent of *Volksschule* teachers, roughly 50 percent of *Mittelschule* teachers, and approximately 25 percent of *Fach-* and *Berufsschule* teachers had some direct connection to the Nazi Party.[41] School materials also had to be purged of Nazism. Officials eliminated Nazi texts, and, after approval by the Education Ministry and the Allied Quadripartite Committee on Education, Austrian education officials introduced new books as quickly as possible. By the end of 1948, 7.3 million copies of some 286 different titles had been printed. All new books were required to contribute to Austrian national consciousness, promote democracy, and emphasize Austrian culture.[42]

In the early occupation years especially, there was considerable Allied interest in the Austrian education system. In the American zone, for example, aside from the issue of denazification, there were criticisms of how schools were organized and how students were forced to choose between a vocational and an academic track at a young age.[43] But for the ten-year occupation period as a whole, the Allied presence was felt more through the potential for intervention rather than actual practice. Foreign language study remained important to the Allies throughout the occupation, but direct intervention waned dramatically after the initial occupation period. By the end of 1948, the Allies lifted schoolbook censorship, except in the subjects of geography and history. Some Allied imports such as the American-inspired youth book clubs and parents' clubs had long-lasting effects, but in general, education was a largely Austrian affair during most of the Allied occupation.[44] In any case, the defeat of Nazi Germany, the occupation by the Allies, and the emergence of anti-Nazi Austrian political leaders created circumstances in which there was a general consensus on education policy.

One area of consensus among the Allies and Austrian education officials and politicians was the need to build a, new, positive, and democratic Austrian identity. How this was to be done was another question. Central to the identity-building plans of Austrian education officials was eliminating "Germanness" from the curriculum and replacing it with "Austrianness." This was not an easy task, given the level to which Austrian schools had been subjected to the Nazi *Gleichschaltung*. Postwar Austrian school officials were faced with the doubly difficult task of educating children and young adults in difficult material circumstances, as well as re-educating students who had been educated in the Nazi curriculum for as many as five and one-half school years. In short, Austrian school officials had to reverse the Nazi *Gleichschaltung*, and Austrian political leaders lost no time in taking on this task. The Communist Ernst Fischer was appointed the first education minister by the provisional government formed in April 1945.[45] Fischer immediately began a textbook reform and eliminated the use of Nazi lesson plans.[46] Fischer also addressed the issue of Austrian identity by pragmatically, and ironically, adopting a conservative view of Austrian uniqueness. In an April 1945 editorial in the newspaper *Neues Österreich*, Fischer wrote:

> We are a people with a unique history and culture. We know that not everything in our past or in our present character is laudable, but we can still point to a contribution to world culture that is worthy of notice. We do not deny it. We are proud of Haydn and Mozart, Schubert and Bruckner, Grillparzer, Raimund, and Nestroy. We are proud of our great architects who created Saint Stephen's Cathedral, the Church of St. Charles, the Belvedere Palace.... We are proud of our peasant leaders.... We are proud of our Viennese ... we are proud of the battles and achievements of the Austrian working class.[47]

With the exception of Fischer's remarks about the Austrian working class, all of these topics became (or in many cases returned as) themes of identity in Austrian schoolbooks. The Communists, however, did not have the same resonance among Austrians as did Fischer's themes of identity, and he lost his post when the Austrian Communist Party was devastated in the November 1945 elections.

Fischer was replaced by Felix Hurdes from the conservative Austrian People's Party. Hurdes, who had been imprisoned by the Nazis, was a leading proponent of "Austrianism" and implemented several concrete measures to build Austrian identity. Hurdes's Austrianism, unlike the Austrianism of the *Ständestaat*, which viewed Austrians as the "better" Germans, was strongly anti-German. Indeed, Hurdes later remarked that "Austria had to be made a counter concept to Nazi Germany."[48] Overall, Hurdes and other conservatives traced Austrian uniqueness back to the medieval and baroque past. It was, as Peter Thaler argues, an "emerging Austrian national ideology centered on demarcation from Germany."[49] Many in the Socialist Party were against Hurdes conservative vision of creating "unconditional Austrians," and were especially wary of the ÖVP's ties to the Catholic Church.[50] The prominent Socialist Friedrich Adler, in particular, rejected the idea of an Austrian nation separate from the German cultural community.[51] An examination of the textbooks and the relevant decrees makes it clear that, despite Socialist reservations, much of Hurdes's vision was implemented. The official organ for disseminating education policy was (and still is) the monthly *Verordnungsblatt für den Dienstbereich des Bundesministeriums für Unterricht*, which appeared in February of 1946. The inaugural issue of the *Verordnungsblatt* called for the "dismantling of all that was un-Austrian" (*Abbau alles Unösterreichischen*) and building Austrian consciousness.[52] The policy of emphasizing democracy and a healthy, nonchauvinistic Austrian patriotism was clearly manifested in the lesson plans (*Lehrpläne*) for Austrian teachers. In German classes, teachers were to "awaken the love of *Heimat*" by emphasizing fairy and folk tales for younger children, while older students were to read and discuss works by Austrian authors and learn to appreciate work and the beauty of the *Heimat*. History teachers were to fight "historical lies" and teach students about Austria's mission as a conveyor of Western culture to "the many small countries of Central and Eastern Europe."[53] In 1949, these themes were further emphasized in specific classes on citizenship (*Staatsbürgerliche Erziehung*), which linked the Austrian political nation with the cultural nation through an emphasis on past and present Austrian achievements.[54] Distasteful reminders of the Nazi years were also removed from the Austrian schools as German writing (*Deutsche Normalschrift*) was discontinued and the crucifix was returned to the Austrian classroom.[55]

The most notorious example of Austrianism was the introduction of *Unterrichtssprache* (language of instruction) to replace German in Austrian schools. Going hand in hand with *Unterrichtssprache* was the commission of the *Österreichisches Wörterbuch* (Austrian dictionary) in 1951. Some ridiculed *Unterrichtssprache* as the new language of "Hurdestani."[56] In 1952, *Unterrichtssprache* was changed to account for minority Croatian, Slovenian, and Hungarian schools, so in German-speaking schools, the new designation for German class became *deutsche Unterrichtssprache*.[57] The designation *deutsche Unterrichtssprache* was finally eliminated in favor of *Deutsch* for the 1955–1956 school year—the year in which the Allied occupation of Austria ended.[58] In Hurdes's defense, Robert Knight points out that the term *Unterrichtssprache* dated to the Austrian Empire. Knight adds that the revival of the term began when Ernst Fischer was education minister and that Hurdes had hoped that the term could quietly be put to rest.[59] Whatever Hurdes's role and intentions in the affair, it is clear that many perceived the term as a deliberate flight from *Deutsch*.

Besides the goals and actions of Austrian education officials, of great importance was of course the end result of texts being read by students in and out of the classroom. It was while reading and interacting with officially approved reading books that students were exposed to several themes important to building Austrian identity. The themes of patriotism, culture, *Heimat*, *Landschaft*, Catholicism, and work were all commonly found in Austrian reading books between 1945 and 1955. Many of these themes were mainstays of prewar texts as well, but in the context of postwar Austria, these themes took on a new importance in identity-building. Collectively, these themes underscored the uniqueness of Austria and thereby distanced Austria from Nazi Germany. In this sense, I argue that the insistence on Austrian uniqueness contributed to the myth of Austrian victimization, albeit indirectly.[60]

A New Austria Emerges in the Textbooks: Heroic Figures and Austria's "Mission"

Austrian history was rich in heroic deeds, and there was an abundance of symbols to draw from, but patriotism was a delicate theme in postwar Austria because recent Austrian history included many aspects that were antithetical to a positive sense of Austrian identity, such as the ethnic division of the empire, World War I, the disdained First Republic, the *Ständestaat*, and, above all, union with Nazi Germany. To overcome these obstacles, the authors and editors of reading books borrowed selectively from Austrian history to link Austria's present to a positive past. Two of the most basic symbols of nationalism were the flag and the national anthem, which was commonly printed in Austrian reading books. The flag was a particularly valuable symbol, since it had a Catholic connotation and deep historical roots. Students read about the origins of the flag in the story "Rot-weiß-rot," which told of Duke Leopold's adventures on a medieval Crusade to the Holy Land. Leopold was a great warrior, and "as the story is told, when the battle was over, his snow-white battle dress was so red from blood, that only the stripe covered by his belt remained white." After the battle, Leopold changed his coat of arms from a red eagle in a white field to a red shield divided by a white band. "Today, these are again the colors of our fatherland: red-white-red."[61] Thus, the origins of the Austrian national flag were traced to a time long before the nation-states of the nineteenth century. Unlike Germany, Austria had a pedigree going back to the Crusades and a historical role as a protector of Christianity. The Austrian flag also linked the recent past with the heritage from the Crusades through the coat of arms. The black eagle on the coat of arms bore the red-white-red shield and on each foot, there was a shackle with a broken chain to symbolize Austria's breaking free from fascist bondage.

The story behind the national anthem—which was commonly featured in reading books—is especially interesting. The old Austrian national anthem had been the Haydn Hymn, a tune also used for the German national anthem. In the aftermath of the war, the Haydn Hymn was linked with Nazi Germany, so it was decided to adopt a new melody and commission new lyrics. Mozart's "Bundeslied" was decided upon for the tune, and after a contest was held, Paula Preradovic's poem "Land der Berge, Land am Strome" (Land of Mountains, Land on Rivers) was chosen to supply the lyrics for the new Austrian national anthem. But this decision did not go unchallenged. Many thought that the Haydn Hymn was Austrian "cultural property" and saw no reason to give up the tune. It was even argued that retaining the Haydn Hymn would be a kind of reparation *(Wiedergutmachung)* of Austrian cultural property. Some raised the question of authenticity, suggesting that Mozart may not have written the melody, since it was composed so close to his death. Mozart's background as a Freemason also came into question, but ultimately these arguments were refuted. In any case, the association of the Haydn Hymn with Nazi Germany could not be overcome.[62] The result was a new, symbolically significant national anthem that students commonly encountered in their reading books. The melody linked the Second Republic to the cultural heritage of Mozart, while the lyrics of Preradovic's poem evoked the beauty of the Austrian landscape ("Land der Berge, Land am Strome, Land der Äcker, Hämmer, Dome") and Austria's difficult, but ultimately successful, march through history ("Heiß umfehdet, wild umstritten. Liegst dem Erdteil du inmitten.... Deiner Sendung Last getragen: Vielgeprüftes Österreich!"). [63]

Local heroes, such as the Tyrolean Andreas Hofer, untainted by any link to Germany or Germanness, also served as useful symbols of national identity. As explained in a 1952 reading book, Hofer, born in 1767, was highly respected in his valley as an honorable farmer, and eventually became famous for leading the regional fight against Napoleon: "Andreas Hofer's name spread out from his home mountains, yes, he is known throughout the world, wherever one values simplicity, selflessness, and loyalty." Hofer successfully led the Tyroleans against a French army of fifty thousand, but when the emperor sued for peace, "Hofer allowed himself to be misled by hotheads without a conscience and reached ... once more for the weapons," which resulted in his death.[64] In the context of postwar Austria, a figure like Hofer took on renewed significance, since he was an example of a patriotic Austrian who gave his life to defend Austria from foreign invaders and represented the Austrian *Volk*.[65] The most well-known tribute to Andreas Hofer is Julius Mosen's "Andreas Hofer Lied," which appeared in several reading books:

Dort soll er niederknien;
der sprach: "Das tu' ich nit.
Will sterben, wie ich steh',
will sterben, wie ich stritt,
so wie ich steh' auf dieser Schanz';
es leb' mein guter Kaiser Franz,
mit ihm das Land Tirol!"[66]

Another hero from Austrian history who appeared regularly in history and reading books was Prince Eugene of Savoy. Poems such as "Prinz Eugen, der edle Ritter"[67] chronicled the exploits of the man, who led Austria's expansion at the expense of the Ottoman Turks.[68] In addition to patriotic ideals based on Austria's past, students also read more direct appeals to patriotism and loyalty to the new Austria. One text included a passage from President Karl Renner on the basic values of democracy.[69] Another example of a direct appeal to patriotic values was Hermann Bahr's "Habt den Mut zu Österreich!" which exhorted students to "Believe in Austria! Hope for Austria! Because, youth, Austria is in you!"[70]

When it came to *Kultur*, or culture, there was no shortage of confidence in Austria. Textbook authors tapped this well with aplomb to make culture an important theme in the national identity of the new Austria. Austrian students learned that their country had not only a rich cultural history, but also a cultural mission of world significance. The passage "Österreich grüßt dich" by Edwin Grabherr evoked many themes of national identity, but put special emphasis on Austria's unique geographical and cultural position in Europe, with the Rhine, "the holy river of the German people," on the western frontier and the "blue band of the Danube … which still unites the peoples of the once so powerful house of Austria" flowing through the country. Further, Austria brought music, art, science, and protection to its neighbors: "With the cross in one hand, and the sword in the other, it protected the peoples of its own empire and the Christian Occident from the onslaught of foreign powers.... But also greeting you is the new Austria … not in doubt over the loss of what it once was and what it had, but rather with Christian courage. It still is what it was and—God willing—always will be: protector and propagator of the German spirit, [and] conveyor and teacher to other peoples. Austria is the German lighthouse in the East."[71]

The author's emphasis on Austria as part of a greater German cultural community is unusual for this time period, but all of the other themes, such as the Austrian landscape, are typical. What is most significant about this passage is the absolute self-confidence concerning Austria's cultural position in Europe. Another passage concerning Austria's cultural mission took a patronizing tone. In "Kulturelle Völkerverständigung—eine österreichische Aufgabe," by Dr. J. Plohovich, students read about the suffering Austrians experienced in two bitter world wars because of their failure to realize their true mission—"international cultural understanding." Plohovich wrote that despite its poor economic position, Austrians still had a lot to offer because "the Austrian was a European before other peoples had a clear concept of 'Europe' ... when the Austrian defended his home against Huns, Avars and Turks, he defended Europe."[72] (This "bulwark of Christendom" theme had a long tradition in Austria, though, as Lonnie Johnson notes, it had also been claimed by many Central European peoples.)[73] Plohovich went on to assert that even though Austria was materially poor, "we are rich in cultural values," and that with the war over, Austrians "look forward to seeing American, English, French, and Russian dramas and films." But despite this expressed desire to learn from others, when it came to culture, the author made it clear that Austria had more to teach than to learn, writing that we Austrians "cannot permit ourselves to neglect cultural exchange with our immediate neighbors. Here, to a certain extent, we will have to do the work of pioneers and, in so doing, we will be able to make the virgin territory accessible to the West."[74] This assumption of cultural superiority was not diminished by the occupation. If anything, the idea of an Austrian cultural "mission" was strengthened by the presence of "uncultured" occupation forces of the Western powers and especially the troops of the Red Army. The immediate background of Nazi rule likewise strengthened the Austrian concept of cultural achievement, because in the postwar context, Austrians severed their cultural ties to Germany. Playing second fiddle to the Germans in the cultural realm had been a particular source of outrage in the official Austrian view, as reflected in the Proclamation of 27 April 1945 discussed above.

Austria: Land of Music

No part of the cultural realm was emphasized more than music, and Austrians were not shy about stressing their musical heritage as part of Austrian national identity, often proclaiming Austria as *Land der Musik*, a tradition that continues today. Austria's emphasis on musical tradition had already begun in the First Republic, most notably with the establishment of the Salzburg Festival, whose organizers were very conscious about stressing Austria's baroque past as an important part of Austrian identity.[75] On the national level, the government made it a priority to reopen the State Opera and also sponsored a "world tour" of Austrian cultural achievement.[76] Beginning in 1948, the Education Ministry sponsored a music competition with the goal "to encourage the love of singing among our youth, to stimulate their understanding of music, and to promote the singing of native songs."[77] Music was also emphasized in Austrian reading books. For example, in a passage titled "Land der Musik," Ernst Hartmann writes: "If any description is fitting for Austria, it is the description 'Land of Music.'" Hartmann then lists the achievements of several Austrian musicians, including Ludwig van Beethoven, who, "despite his Rhenish origins, can be claimed by Austrian music, and so with complete justice, because from his twenty-first year until his death, he lived in

Vienna; his life and work belong to Austrian cultural history."[78] In other reading books, students often found passages dealing with other heroes of Austrian music, such as Franz Grillparzer's "Erinnerungen an Beethoven," or stories about Franz Schubert.[79] Of course, Mozart is the most obvious example of Austrian musical excellence, and continues to serve as the symbol of Austrian musical genius. Franz Frangruber's "Der kleine Mozart und die große Kaiserin" tells the story of the boy Mozart playing before Empress Maria Theresa. Frangruber concluded the narrative by telling students that Mozart's "name is famous and celebrated throughout the world, and his fatherland, Austria, is very proud of him."[80]

Sometimes the emphasis on music approached the obsessive, if not the bizarre. During the 1953–1954 school year in Burgenland, Haydn Festival Weeks marked the cultural high point of the year. The climax of the festival was the return of Franz Joseph Haydn's skull to Eisenstadt.[81] After his death and initial burial in Vienna in 1809, his skull had been removed for the purpose of phrenological study. In the 1820s, Haydn's body was moved to Eisenstadt, but his skull remained at the Gesellschaft der Musikfreunde in Vienna until 1954, when it was reunited with his body in the crypt of the Eisenstadt Bergkirche.[82]

Austria indeed had an illustrious musical tradition, and it made sense to emphasize this tradition to students in the new republic. Music seemingly provided an ideologically pure source of national pride, and it was a theme that had resonance. After all, Beethoven and Mozart were internationally renowned and celebrated, and Vienna and Salzburg were centers of music. But upon closer examination, this emphasis on music was problematic in some ways. Like many institutions throughout the country, Nazism had also tainted Austria's illustrious music traditions. For example, shortly after the Anschluss, Jews were dismissed from the Vienna Philharmonic and the Vienna Symphony. Many top Austrian musicians, including Wilhelm Kienzl, Josef Reiter, and Leopold Reichwein, had openly supported Hitler and Nazism since 1933.[83] Furthermore, the emphasis on achievement in culture and music also carried occasional chauvinistic undertones. Music and culture were defined in exclusive and specific ways—music meant a certain *kind* of music. The image of Austria as a highly cultured nation sometimes merged directly with the Austria-as-victim myth. One teacher, Franz Joachim, wrote about the importance of teaching Austrian cultural achievements in history classes to build a positive sense of Austrian identity, noting that "Little Austria is a great power in the area of culture and spirit." That the Nazis had demoted the cultural importance of Austria was especially outrageous to Joachim. Particularly galling was the "historian" Johannes Haller, who had traced German cultural achievement to Prussia and Saxony in his textbook *Epochen der deutschen Geschichte*. "Instead [of Austrian achievements] the Greater German Reich had to be praised, which … only brought Austria … a sea of blood and tears … [and with final defeat, ultimately] pulling our innocent *Heimat* along with it into the rottenness."[84]

It is significant that culture was seen as such an integral part of national identity and as something un-German and uniquely Austrian. Joachim's comments hint at an instructive aspect of the victim myth: anger and resentment toward Germany often had more to do with high-handed German behavior or slighting of Austria than it did with anti-Nazi ideology. But more problematic than specific Austrian cultural chauvinism were references to Austria's cultural mission and Austria's historical role in protecting "the Occident" from the East. In the context of immediate postwar Austria, references to the ominous East may have alluded to Austria's occupation by the "Asiatic" Red Army. A student learning of Austria's cultural mission could very easily make the connection that the recently lost war was justifiable, insofar as it was a war to protect the Occident (*Abendland*).

Heimat Austria

Patriotic stories from Austria's past and the emphasis on Austrian culture and Austria's cultural mission were the themes of national identity that displayed the most confidence. There were many other themes emphasized in Austrian reading books that were more subtle in their contribution to Austrian national identity. Among these was the idea of *Heimat*, which emphasized the importance of local roots. An almost untranslatable word, *Heimat* means more than just "home" or "homeland." Concerning *Heimat* in Germany, scholar Christopher Wickham emphasizes the emotions and geographical implications of the term, arguing: "Central to both traditional and revisited conceptions of *Heimat* are the components of longing and belonging. The desire for a place of identity traditionally looked backward to a real, imagined, or even mythical place of security with clear regional characteristics." [85] The Tyrolean Heimatschutzverein (Tyrolean Club for the Protection of *Heimat*) defined *Heimat* to students as

> a word full of wonder, which denotes something which people especially love. The feeling for the *Heimat* accompanies a person throughout his entire life und does not let go of him, even if he emigrates. Indeed, it holds onto him tighter, the farther away he goes, and often awakens painful desires. *Heimat* encompasses not only the surroundings, cities, villages or lonely farmyards, not only mountain[s] and valley[s], lakes and waterfalls, springs and wild creeks, the animals at home and in the forest, the flowers in the fields, meadows and Alpine pastures [*Almen*], but also the people living among them, their lives, their morals and customs. [86]

In short, *Heimat* is an inescapable and wonderful attachment to local roots. Indeed, the idea that there is no place like *Heimat* is conveyed in a vignette by Anton Wildgans, a staunch supporter of Austrian patriotism during the First Republic. [87] The narrator has seen beautiful sights all throughout the world, including Ceylon, Nepal, and the Riviera, but concludes: "*Heimat*, with one word, remains *Heimat*; and although on the oceans I breathed the purest, cleanest, dust-free air for months on end, here I feel as if I have lungs again."[88] Wildgans's sentiment that there may be beautiful places elsewhere in the world but still no place like *Heimat* is common in other texts as well. For example, the poem "Das Lied von der Heimat," by Viktor Buchgraber, conveys this idea, while emphasizing the eternal attachment to *Heimat*:

> Wohl, es gibt fettere Weiden,
> Länder voll Honig und Milch.
> Anderswo geht man in Seiden,
> hier trägt man Loden und Zwilch.
> Aber mit nichts zu erkaufen,
> Glanz meiner Heimat bist du!
> Wollt' ich—weiß Gott—wohin laufen,
> fände doch Glück nicht und Ruh'.
> …
> Und je älter ich werde,
> umso verwurzelter nur
> bin ich in dieser Erde,
> folgend der Väter Spur.
> Bin wohl ein Zweig von jenen,
> Blut auch von ihrem Blut:
> Weil all mein Sorgen und Sehnen
> fest in der Heimat ruht.[89]

Idyllic life in small villages was also a staple of *Heimat* stories and poems. For example, Robert Reinik's poem "Das Dorf" describes the simple joy of riding in a hay wagon through a village:

> Steht ein Kirchlein im Dorf, geht der Weg dran vorbei
> und die Hühner, die machen am Weg ein Geschrei
> …
> Und der Wagen voll Heu, der kommt von der Wiese,
> und obendrauf sitzen Hans und die Liese.
> Die jodeln und jauchzen und lachen alle beid',
> und das klingt durch den Abend, es ist eine Freud'!
> Und dem König dem Thron, der ist prächtig und weich,
> doch im Heu zu sitzen, dem kommt doch nichts gleich!
> Und wär' ich der König, gleich wär' ich dabei
> und nähme zum Thron mir einen Wagen voll Heu.[90]

Idyllic country life is also portrayed in the story "Mein Heimatland," by Heinrich Kotz. Four children embark on a five-hour hike to a mountain peak. When the well-equipped children (*Nagelschuhe* and *Rucksäcken*) reach the overlook, they are greeted by a beautiful sight: "The sky is blue and the mountain wind whistles…. Sunshine is everywhere." Two of the girls are so inspired that they begin to sing:

Wohl ist die Welt so groß und weit
und voller Sonnenschein,
das allerschönste Stück davon
ist doch die Heimat mein![91]

Again, the idea is expressed that though there may be other nice places in the world, nowhere else is as pure and wonderful as the *Heimat*.

The practice of publishing different or modified books for individual provinces allowed for stories and poems on *Heimat* with specific local themes.[92] Editors often included poems written in local dialect, which linked language with *Heimat* as well. Dialect poems offered students a chance to read in a language that was unmistakably their own. If anything was purely Austrian and *not* German, it was a dialect *Heimat* poem such as "Tirol isch lei oans":

Tirol isch lei oans,
isch a Landl a kloans,
aber a liabs und a feins,
und dös Landl isch meins[93]

Otto Pflanzl's "Mein Hoamat, Mein Sålzburg" likewise strongly connects dialect with the *Heimat*:

Mein Homat, mein Sålzburg, di hålt i in Ehr'n,
koan Fleck auf der Welt kunnt ma liaber nu wer'n!
Då bin i hålt glückli, då gfreit mi mein Leb'n,
für mi kann's auf Erd'n nix Schener's mehr geb'n![94]

Poems and sayings also enabled children to link the *Heimat* with distinctly local cultural and geographical features. For example, in a reader for students from Upper Austria, the saying "Aus da Hoamat" named the symbols of Upper Austria's four distinct regions:

Innviertel
    Roß und Troad,
Mühlviertel
    Flachs und Gjoad,
Hausruckviertel,
    Obst und Schmalz,
Traunviertel
    Salz[95]

Some students read texts that were unequivocal in expressing the uniqueness, beauty, and even superiority of their own region. In a section titled "Heimat Vorarlberg," one author discusses the beautiful landscape of Vorarlberg and explains the unique character of the Swabian, Swiss, and Allemanic peoples who settled near the Bodensee (Lake Constance). The people are characterized by "healthy enterprise, creativity, a down-to-earth nature, thriftiness, and a love of *Heimat*." Furthermore, "Vorarlberg is a land of mountains, whose beauty is second to no other Alpine region, either domestic or foreign."[96] Reading books for Tyrolean children also strongly emphasized the mountains and the symbols of Alpine life. Two poems by Karl Schönherr demonstrate the strong connection between *Heimat* and the mountains of Tyrol. "A rechter Tiroler" (A True Tyrolean) reinforces the idea of permanent attachment to the *Heimat*:

> A Tiroler, dear hängt an sein Hoamat,
> dear hängt an sein Berg und sein Wald,
> ischt er noch so weit wöck in der Fremdn—
> zrugg ziachts 'n ins Landl mit Gewalt.[97]

Another Schönherr poem, "Bin a Tiroler Bua" (I'm a Tyrolean Fellow), emphasizes ties to the mountain landscape and the impossibility of feeling at home in a city with its narrow houses:

> Laßt's miar mein grob'n Lod'nrock
> und meini Nöglschuah,
> i will a frischi Almluft, bin a Tirolerbua!
> ...
> Und enkri Häuser brauch i nit,
> miar war's drein z'eng und z'schmol,
> do hätt' mei Jodler gor nit Platz,
> dear braucht a ganzes Tol.[98]

The distinctive clothing of Alpine life—a Loden coat and spiked shoes— also links the narrator to Tyrolean *Heimat*. It is interesting to compare "Der Steirer Land," by Jakob Dirnböck, to the Tyrolean examples. Departing from the style of the Tyrolean poems, Dirnböck emphasizes the proud industrial tradition of Styria and connects the strength of Styrian iron with the strength of Styrian oaks, thus combining the industrial with the bucolic:

> Wo durch Kohlenglut und des Hammers Kraft
> starker Hände Fleiß das Eisen zeugt;
> wo noch Eichen stehn, voll und grün von Saft,
> die kein Sturmwind je noch hat gebeugt:
> Dieses schöne Land ist der Steirer Land,
> ist mein liebes, teures Heimatland![99]

While Dirnböck's "Der Steirer Land" successfully combines industrial imagery with rural imagery, it is an atypical poem. The overwhelming emphasis of *Heimat* was on the purity of rustic life. This theme worked especially well in associating national identity with the lifestyle of Austria's rural and Alpine provinces, but as a nation-building tool, *Heimat* had the drawback of excluding urban Vienna. Distrust between Vienna and the provinces had long been a feature of Austrian life, but the large population and status of Vienna made the metropolis an unavoidable topic. Students faced the issue of Vienna and *Heimat* directly when they read a poem by Anton Wildgans titled "Ich bin ein Kind der Stadt":

Ich bin ein Kind der Stadt. Die Leute meinen,
und spotten leichthin über unsereinen,
daß solch ein Stadtkind keine Heimat hat.
In meine Spiele rauschten freilich keine
Wälder. Da schütterten die Pflastersteine.
Und bist mir doch ein Lied, du liebe Stadt![100]

In this poem, the child narrator is apologetic about not having a "real" *Heimat*. The boy loves the city, but it is still unclear if Vienna can really count as *Heimat*. A story for Tyrolean children addressed Vienna in a different way. Two Tyrolean children, Christl and Gerda, visit Vienna and see many important sites, including St. Stephen's Cathedral, affectionately known as *der Steffl*. When the children return to Tyrol and reminisce about their trip, they become teary-eyed and actually miss Vienna.[101] The story was an obvious attempt to explain the importance of Vienna to children in the provinces, yet despite the emotional scene, the attachment to Vienna does not come close to the eternal ties of *Heimat*.

The idea of *Heimat* was a useful theme in building national identity in that the emphasis on idealized images of local life enabled children to link their sense of identity with familiar places and concrete objects. The local emphasis of *Heimat* also served to distance Austrian identity from German identity. But the emphasis on eternal ties to the land and local traditions also presented difficulties. Vienna, as we have seen, was difficult to fit into the concept of *Heimat*. Another problem with *Heimat* was that while it was useful as an identity-builder, it was of limited use in fostering a sense of nationality based on citizenship and democratic values. After all, *Heimat* was an inherently *exclusive* concept, as noted by Hans-Georg Pott, who wrote: "No notion of *Heimat* is thinkable without that of the distant or foreign."[102] If one was eternally tied to one's *Heimat*, then by definition, an outsider could not join the society.

Closely linked to *Heimat* as a recurring theme in Austrian reading books was the theme of *Landschaft*, or scenic landscape. Reading book authors understandably focused on the theme of the beautiful Austrian scenery to help build national identity, though sometimes to an exaggerated degree. For example, in an informative passage titled "Die Landschaft Österreichs," Felix Braun describes a Viennese vista: "From Belvedere looking to St. Stephen's tower with the melodic hillsides of Kahlenberg in the background.... The landscape of Austria: it is so rich and so varied ... that nothing could be more difficult than its comprehensive praise."[103] Mountains and Alpine themes were especially common in reading book passages on *Landschaft*. Peter Rosegger's descriptive passage "Der Dachstein" recounts some mountain climbers' ascent of the Dachstein, which is praised not only as one of Austria's finest mountain peaks, but as one of the world's greatest peaks. After a strenuous trek, "the bold mountain climbers finally reach the magnificent pinnacle of the Dachstein, where there is room for only a few, because so few are chosen to look face to face at this great glory of God." Rosegger then explains that the Dachstein intersects three provinces (Salzburg, Styria, and Upper Austria), all of which claim the peak, whose beauty is so great that "its praise spreads into the songs of the farthest countries."[104] Another book for the province of Salzburg follows the exploits of the *Valtlbauern Kinder*, Micherl and Eva Edlinger. Among their adventures is accompanying a Viennese doctor on a hike. Young Micherl is impressed by the hiking abilities of the doctor, remarking "sie sind gar nicht so ungeschikt, die Stadtleut" (these city folks aren't so bungling after all). The highlight of the excursion is when the three reach a scenic overlook where the sun shines down on the magnificent Alpine peaks. After viewing the farms below, "they turn around again with their back to the village—there it shines like a giant precious stone. 'The Übergossene Alm,' exults Everl. 'Yes, the Übergossene Alm!' says the doctor, "Salzburg's largest glacier.""[105] A related recurring theme of the Austrian Alpine *Landschaft* was the Alpine meadow, or *Alm*, and life surrounding summer work on the *Alm*.[106] For example, Paul Tschurtschenthaler's story "Heimfahrt von der Alm" describes the return of cattle from the high country: "The cattle are coming! From down the road the whips crack, and the bright cheering crowd stands up. Now the *Kranzkuh* appears. She sways her *Stirnschmuch* of tinsel and glass threads. Then a boy comes as driver in holiday garb with a flower wisp on his hat. Behind him the bells of a dozen cows ring and sound out."[107]

Such traditional scenes in combination with the beautiful landscape of Austria suggest a mainstay of the Austrian economy—the tourist industry. Tourism was and still is a major part of the Austrian economy, and even though times were lean throughout Europe, the recovery of the Austrian economy during the reconstruction period depended on reviving the tourism industry.[108] Günter Bischof argues that two of the most important reasons for the revival of Austrian tourism were, first, Marshall Plan funds that were devoted to tourism and related infrastructure and, second, the return of large numbers of German tourists beginning in the early 1950s.[109] Austrian education officials did their part by disseminating to teachers guidelines on tourism that had been compiled by the Ministry of Trade and Rebuilding (Bundesministerium für Handel und Wiederaufbau). The cooperating ministries sponsored an essay contest on tourism and offered specific advice regarding student behavior toward tourists. Four points in particular were promoted as ways students could help the tourist industry: (1) greeting guests in a polite manner, (2) providing information in a friendly way, (3) doing good deeds, and (4) caring about personal grooming and wearing proper clothing. The pamphlet also offered photographs of beautiful scenery and of positive and negative examples of how children could contribute to tourism. One set of pictures presents a "before and after" sequence of a country house. The "before" picture shows a drab building with shuttered windows and cracks in the plaster. In the "after" picture, the windows of the house are decorated with flower boxes, while a smiling pretty girl in traditional dress sits on a rustic bench in front of the house.[110] These "before and after" photographs have interesting implications for the theme of *Heimat*, because they suggest that the beauty of *Heimat* is not automatic, but rather something that has to be cultivated. Students were instructed to embrace a stereotype by converting drab scenes of country life into charming and idyllic pictures.

While tourism was essential to the Austrian economy, it also brought up a paradox in nation-building imagery. The Austrian *Landschaft* and idyllic life in mountain villages were key to attracting tourists, but their association raised uncomfortable questions: Weren't tourism and *Heimat* in direct contradiction to each other? Could a piece of *Heimat* be bought? These questions were not ignored. In an informative passage from 1953, Heinrich Kotz warns Tyrolean students that even though tourism brings profits, "it also brings danger for the *Heimat* along with it. Many farm boys leave the plow and seek easier and better paid employment in a tourist enterprise, [and] some country girls would rather work in a hotel than on their parents' farm…. All too easily, one forgets native morals and begins to copy foreign ways and foreign habits."[111] Kotz's remarks remind us of the fundamental conflict of *Heimat* (and its adjunct *Landschaft*) versus tourism, which was sometimes seen as a dangerous aspect of modernization. Indeed, modernization itself and all that it represented (e.g., the city, cosmopolitanism) were what *Heimat* stood against.[112] Kotz's concerns about the danger to *Heimat* were not new; they had been raised when Austria was first faced with modernity, as evidenced by the nineteenth-century Tyrolean innkeeper who was spit upon for promoting tourism in the Ötztal.[113] The postwar warning not to forget "native morals" and to avoid "foreign ways and foreign habits" clearly demonstrates that *Heimat* is by definition a closed concept. One cannot adopt strange ways and maintain loyalty to one's *Heimat* at the same time.

Catholic Austria

Roman Catholicism was another recurrent theme in Austrian reading books. Austria was the home of the Catholic Reformation and remains a country with a largely Catholic population.[114] The old village churches, mountain chapels, huge urban cathedrals, and rural monasteries make the physical symbols of Catholicism a permanent part of Austrian life. Catholicism was and still is intimately linked with the school system. A crucifix commonly hangs on the wall of Austrian classrooms, and teachers at private Catholic schools are paid by the state. Religious instruction is a part of the curriculum, though it is by no means exclusively Catholic; minority religious groups are also entitled to in-school religious instruction. Such characteristics are common to many Catholic countries, but in

Austria, Catholicism took on new significance to Austrian identity in the postwar years as it served to underline the differences between Austrians and Protestant Prussians (though not the mostly Catholic Bavarians in the south of Germany, who are generally viewed more sympathetically than Germans from the north). Notwithstanding the large number of German Catholics, the idea of the Catholic virtue of Austria versus the cold Protestantism of Prussia dated at least to the Thirty Years War. As Werner Suppanz points out, Austrian patriots drew the contrast especially sharply when comparing Frederick the Great (violator of the Pragmatic Sanction and conqueror of Silesia) with Empress Maria Theresa, the mother of sixteen children.[115] Because Austrian politicians and school officials strongly associated Nazism with Prussian traditions (a view supported by some of the historiography of the time),[116] the age-old conflict between Prussia and Austria took on new significance in the postwar era. Since Austria had rivaled Prussia for years, it stood to reason that this traditional stance had not changed during the Nazi years. In this context, one function of emphasizing Catholic traditions in Austrian reading books was to stress Austrian distinctness from Germany. Furthermore, many poems and descriptive passages with Catholic themes were linked with other themes of Austrian uniqueness, such as regional dialects, *Heimat*, and *Landschaft*. For example, in the poem "Gott grüße dich!" Julius Sturm explains the significance of the Austrian greeting, noting that it is more than just a how-do-you-do:

Gott grüße dich! Kein andrer Gruß
   gleicht dem an Innigkeit.
Gott grüße dich! Kein andrer Gruß
   paßt so zu aller Zeit.
Gott grüße dich! Wenn dieser Gruß
   so recht von Herzen geht,
gilt bei dem lieben Gott der Gruß
   soviel wie ein Gebet.[117]

While this greeting is also used in Catholic areas of Germany, such as Bavaria, in the postwar context, "Gott grüße dich" and "Grüß Gott" had a pro-Austrian connotation. Nothing would give away the origins of a German national more quickly than to use the greeting "Guten Tag," instead of "Gott Grüße dich!" or "Grüß Gott!" Since National Socialism and Protestantism were intimately associated with Germany, this focus on Catholicism had the benefit of distancing Austria from Germany, though it cannot be said that this was why Catholicism was emphasized in Austrian textbooks. What *can* be said, as Werner Suppanz argues, is that the emphasis on Catholicism reflected the values and influence of Austrian conservatives (and again, oddly enough, the first postwar education minister, the Communist Ernst Fischer). Austrian Socialists tended to be wary of linking postwar Austrian identity so explicitly with the Church.[118]

Several books also arranged themes chronologically so that students could read stories and poems that coincided with the seasons or holidays. Austria's numerous Catholic holidays fit well into this pattern, with students reading stories and poems such as "Allerseelen,"[119] "Heilige Nacht,"[120] and "Ostern in den steirischen Bergen."[121] Another example is Joseph Georg Oberkofler's story "Advent," which linked Advent to *Heimat*, with its "sweet anxiousness of expectation and the peaceful rest after coming home!" In the story, Advent signals the end of the year and a time of rest, as evidenced by nature itself: "[T]he fields have given grain ... [and] the herds have returned home. Everything is home." Advent becomes a force that draws people to their *Heimat*: "[I]n the weeks before Christmas the word *daheim* [at home] takes on a wonderful luminous power. An all-powerful desire to be home grabs our hearts."[122] A more direct link between the land and Catholicism appears in the story of Saint Florian. The author tells the story of how the Roman emperor Diocletian hated Christians. Florian and forty other Christians encamped in Lauriacum (now Lorch on the Enns) refused to abandon their religion. Florian was sentenced to death and drowned in the Enns River. When his corpse washed up on shore, "it was surrounded by a gleam of light.... And so the pious widow Valeria found him. She had the body taken away by a team of oxen. After some time, the animals would move no farther. Valeria recognized this as a sign from God that Florian was to be buried here. Today, the St. Florian abbey soars above this spot."[123] This story signaled the deep roots of Austrian Catholicism by linking the abbey with an event from Roman times.

Of course, the theme of Catholicism made sense to students because it *was* typical to be Catholic in Austria. Yet there were some problematic aspects to the theme of Catholicism as not everyone was Catholic. While Protestants were not truly included, Protestant students could relate to many stories and poems in Austrian reading books. Jews, on the other hand, were not at all represented in the postwar reading books. Overall, the theme of Catholicism provided an additional brick to the foundation of the emerging postwar national identity, but it also excluded some from Austrian life because it was a theme of identity based not on pluralistic democratic values, but rather on a cultural attribute. Given the Catholic imagery in the postwar textbooks, it is worth noting that Austrian Jews are sometimes referred to as *Mitbürger* (fellow citizens) instead of simply as *Bürger* (citizens). As defined in Austrian schools, "Austrian" generally meant Catholic, as indeed was and still is most often, but not always, the case.

Work

The theme of work (*Arbeit*) was also common in the reading books of the reconstruction period (see chapter 4 for official memory of the reconstruction). There was plenty of work to be done in rebuilding Austria, and instilling Austrian youth with an appreciation of work was an important part of building Austrian identity. The need to rebuild Austria meant that all types of professions were important and worthy of honor. A poem by Ernst Weber, "Arbeiter," emphasizes the importance of work for the future of the country:

> Arbeiter sein—wir alle müssen's.
> Arbeiter sein—wir alle wissen's,
> daß nur die Arbeit aus Not und Nacht
> das deutsche Volk ans Licht gebracht,
> daß nur ein rastloses Schaffen und Sinnen
> uns eine Zukunft kann gewinnen.[124]

Students encountered a more succinct explanation of the importance of work in an East Tyrolean saying:

> Wer nit arbeitet, soo a nit essen,
> Faulder, mörk dies, tues nit vergößn![125]

Ostensibly, all types of work were equal in importance. This is the message conveyed in Johannes Trojan's poem "Der beste Beruf":

> Ein jeder Stand der Welt ist gut,
> wenn treu ein Mann das Seine tut,
> Magst Kaufmann oder Tischler sein,
> Horn blasen oder Saaten streu'n;
> …
> ob auf der See fährst, sturmumweht;
> acht hab auf eins, vergiß es nicht:
> Was du auch bist, tu deine Pflicht![126]

The idea that regardless of profession, one's work was important was not as mundane as it might initially appear. Austria was a country where one's profession was intimately linked with one's class and party. Industrial workers tended to be closely affiliated with the Socialist Party, while farmers typically supported the conservative Austrian People's Party. It was imperative that these groups find common ground if the Second Republic was to survive. Both rural work and urban industrial labor were honored in the reading books of the reconstruction period, yet the former, such as farming and handicrafts, was portrayed more often and in a more positive manner than the latter. One reason for this imbalance was the link that rural work had to the themes of *Heimat* and *Landschaft*, which, as we have already seen, were important elements of Austrian identity.

Among rural workers, farmers were at the top of the honor roll. To be a farmer was nothing short of being part of the *Heimat* itself. For example, in "Nie stirbt das Land," Joseph Georg Oberkofler writes of the farmer's eternal attachment to the land:

Dies ist das Land, das uns ernährt,
...

Wir wollen nichts auf dieser Welt,
nur Sonn und Tau für unser Feld.
Wir wollen nichts.
...

Nie stirbt das Land, dem Land geweiht,
der Bauer lebt in Ewigkeit.
Nie stirbt das Land.[127]

In another story about farm life, the attachment of farmers to the land is also eternal. In this case, the author expresses dismay that any farmer would let anyone else harvest his crop, because a "real farmer cannot do that; for him, it is as if the seeds lay in his own heart."[128] For author Friedrich Rückert, to be a farmer is quite simply "Das beste Werk auf Erden" (The Best Work on Earth):

Das beste Werk auf Erden ist,
Korn in die Scholle zu säen,
und aller Freuden reichste ist,
die vollen Schwaden mähen!
Rund geht der Wurf des Säemans
und rund des Schnitters Eisen.
Das ganze leben auf und ab
liegt zwischen diesen Kreisen.[129]

The prevalence of poems and stories extolling the idyllic nature of rural life is noteworthy in that it was contrary to the larger reality. While much of Austria was rural, postwar Austria was an industrialized country and was increasingly becoming more so. Indeed, the large-scale plants and projects such as the Linz steel works and the Kaprun hydroelectric complex (see chapter 4) were more important to the rebuilding than the small-scale workshops. Perhaps in recognition of this fading way of life, some poems and stories took a defiant and defensive posture. For example, Richard Billinger's "Wir Bauern" vehemently defends the religion of farmers, perhaps in reaction to more secular urban areas of Austria, such as Vienna:

Wir Bauern dulden keinen Spott
an unserm Herrn und Helfer Gott!
Was wären wir wohl ohne ihn?
Eine Ehschaft ohne Gatten,
ein Bienstock ohne Königin,
ein Baum ohne Frucht und Schatten.[130]

The poem about a content and happy farmer, "Der glückliche Bauer," by Alfred Huggenberger is another example that lauds the virtue of bucolic life:

Ich habe ein Hause auf dem sonnigen Rain;
da schaut mir der Morgen zum Fenster herein.
Und ringsum die Felder, die Matten sind mein;
da reifen die Saaten, da blüht mir der Wein.
Ich herrsche, ein König, auf sicherem Thron;
mein Schwert ist die Pflugschar, ein Kremphut die Kron'.[131]

What is particularly notable about this poem is the level of autonomy enjoyed by the farmer.

Also enjoying autonomy were rural craftsmen, whose work was portrayed as equally as honorable as that of the farmer.[132] Industrialized society was a threat to craftsmen, and it was important to distinguish between craftsmanship and industrial production. In "Handwerker," by Paul Bosson, a young boy views craftsmen in action and enjoys the various noises of the workshop that make it an important part of village life. The story concludes by stating that as "beautiful and exact as a machine works, it cannot create what the hand ... can make from raw material."[133] Another positive portrayal of craftsmen is found in Ferdinand von Saar's poem "Die Handwerker":

Hantierend bei Tag,
hantierend bei Nacht,
erwerben wir mühsam
das tägliche Brot
für Weib und Kind
und unser Gesind.
Wir sind die Kleinen,
doch will es uns scheinen,
man soll uns halten in Ehren,
niemand auf Erden kann uns entbehren.[134]

These favorable representations of craftsmen stand in contrast to the images of industrial workers. While there were some positive portrayals of laborers in reading books of the reconstruction period, the overall image of industrial work was neutral at best. Sometimes workers were shown in an overtly negative or pathetic way. For example, in "Ein alter Arbeiter spricht," Hans Haidenbauer tells the story of a man who wastes his life in a factory:

An dreißig Jahren hab' ich
beim Ofen hier geschafft,
warf in die weißen Gluten
Metall—und meine Kraft!
Ich warf die schönsten Jahre
hinein in seinen Bauch;
nun ist er überflüssig
geworden—und ich auch![135]

While Alfred Huggenberger's farmer rules his farm as a king, the old worker in Haidenbauer's poem leads a dreary life chained to a furnace. In the world of postwar Austrian reading books, it was clearly better to be a farmer than an industrial worker. The significance of this difference in portrayals of work went beyond students receiving an inaccurate picture of labor in Austria. The greater significance was the image of a work force that matched other themes of Austrian identity, such as *Heimat* and *Landschaft*. It is also important to note that these images were overwhelmingly conservative in their depiction of Austria and Austrians. One might have expected Socialists to press for less traditional imagery, especially concerning the theme of work. William T. Bluhm argues that the Socialists went along with a conservative education and identity program because it was also linked to democratic values, which the Social Democrats shared, and because the Socialists were more concerned with exercising influence in other areas of the government.[136] However, while much of the imagery and many of the themes in the schoolbooks of the time were conservative, the Socialists did vigorously attempt to put their mark on the curriculum. In particular, Socialist officials involved with Austrian education sought to link ideas of international understanding and cooperation with the uniqueness of Austrian identity.[137]

The school system helped to create this national identity during the occupation period by focusing on themes of *Heimat, Landschaft*, Austria's heroic past, and Austrian cultural achievements. While such motifs are common to all modern nations, they took on a special importance in postwar Austria. In many ways, the Second Republic was a new country, distinct from Germany, whose identity was being shaped by a number of images that collectively defined Austrian identity. Later, many of these images came to be resented as stereotypes and clichés, but it is important to remember that idyllic representations of the Austrian landscape, *Heimat*, Catholicism, Austrian culture, and life in the country, were themes emphasized by Austrians themselves. Long before Hollywood defined Austria in *The Sound of Music*, Austrians defined themselves using the same images that later came to be seen as kitschy stereotypes.[138]

Austria's long history and local traditions were fertile ground for fashioning images of national identity. The fact that Austria could in some ways be traced back nearly one thousand years made it seem as if Austria had been a given, or a *Selbstverständlichkeit*, for an eternity. The year 1946 was the 950th anniversary of the birth of Austria, or at least the 950th anniversary of the first occasion when the word "Ostarrîchi" was written down. At a celebration to commemorate the Ostarrîchi anniversary, President Renner called attention to Austria's long-standing existence, saying: "Now it lives again! A new beginning has been made, as by the settlers of Ostarrîchi a thousand years ago!"[139] But ironically, it was Austria's most recent history that made it clear that Austria was *not* eternal.[140] Austria ceased to exist as a state in 1938, and it was reborn only through the victory of the Allies. Austrian schools had to address this episode of Austrian history in a meaningful way. The answer to the dilemma was a myth already embraced by Austrian politicians: the Austria-as-victim myth.

The Shadow of the War in the Textbooks

In the late 1940s and the early 1950s, building Austrian identity, overcoming material shortages, and achieving normalcy were the priorities of the Austrian school system. In the early years of the Second Republic, the themes of the Austria-as-victim myth were still expanding and were not fully incorporated as part of the curriculum. Nevertheless, certain concepts were already common in textbooks of the occupation period. By 1955, the victim myth had joined other motifs and had become a fundamental part of Austrian identity.

Only one history book covering the World War II years was approved for use during the occupation period. *Allgemeine Geschichte der Neuzeit von der Mitte des 19. Jahrhunderts bis zur Gegenwart*, by Franz Heilsberg and Friedrich Korger, was published in 1953, and subsequent versions with minor revisions were used in Austrian classrooms until the early 1970s. The authors treated the Anschluss as the "occupation of Austria" and emphasized the forced takeover of Austrian economic assets. Austrian involvement in the war was minimized and characterized as forced participation. According to the authors: "Austrians had to fight in the *German* army for Hitler's boundless goals of conquest. But ever more common posters in the streets of Vienna, naming those hung for 'high treason' and the transports, which went to the *German* concentration camps, demonstrated the growing resistance" (emphasis added).[141]

This passage demonstrates what became a classic formula of the Austria-as-victim myth: Austrian participation in the war was downplayed and immediately countered with accounts of Austrian resistance. Another facet of the victim myth shown in this passage is the emphasis on the war being a German—and only a German—war. This use of language was no coincidence, for the 1946 provisional lesson plan for *Mittelschulen* reminded teachers to instruct students that the war was to be understood in the context of "reactionary Prussian militarism."[142] Indeed, as Werner Suppanz points out, after the war, Austrian patriots seized upon anti-Prussian feeling and the link between Prussian militarism and Nazism as key elements of pro-Austria propaganda.[143]

The war was also briefly covered in books for other subjects such as civics (*Staatsbürgerkunde*). In the 1950 text *Österreichische Staatsbürgerkunde*, Robert Endres provides students with a succinct version of recent Austrian history:

> On 12 February 1934 the democracy collapsed. Four years later, Austria became the booty of National Socialism. Under the pretense of a "liberation," German troops occupied the country. Austria lost its name—the country was re-baptized as the *Ostmark*.... Austria's economic assets and its people were put into the

service of German war policy. The small country had to make unspeakable sacrifices for foreign interests. But the will to resist was not broken, as proven by the many who fell in battle for Austria's freedom. In 1945 our republic again stood as a democratic state, thanks to the victory of the Allied armies over Hitler's Germany.[144]

Again Austria appeared solely as a victim, and again the Austrian resistance movement was immediately cited to counter any hint of support for the war. Another *Staatsbürgerkunde* textbook from 1954 briefly covered the Anschluss as a violation of international law and mentioned nothing else about the war.[145] Later history books would be more extensive and would also include other themes, such as the Allied occupation, but already in the occupation period, it was clear that the authors of history and social studies texts had embraced the victim myth.

In addition to history books, reading books also touched on important historical themes. For example, one text included the Proclamation of 27 April 1945 (discussed above).[146] A text used in the province of Vorarlberg, *Von heut' und ehedem*, stands out for including several passages about the war. In Julian Thurnher's story "An der Front" (On the Front), students read about an Austrian farmer-turned-soldier named Gottfried Stark. While at his post, Stark muses about the senselessness and suffering of war. But when his thoughts turn to home, he resolves to keep fighting: "[W]hat if the enemy were to stand in our own country? Then the well-kept villages and small towns of the *Heimat* ... would certainly become a horrible pile of rubble; wife and child would have to manage as homeless beggars under a foreign people. Never and never can that be!" Stark then survives an attack at dawn, which is repelled after heavy casualties, before the story concludes: "Honor is due to the heroes who ... love the people and the *Heimat* more than their own life."[147] This remarkable story reflects victim mythology in at least two ways. First, the war is void of any ideological context. Second, the war is justified as a war of defense through the figure of the rural Austrian farmer, shuddering at the thought of foreign armies threatening the villages of his *Heimat*.

Von heut' und ehedem also included four excerpts from soldiers' letters. A 1941 letter from Friederich Dünser to his family amounts to a tourist's description of the weather and landscape of arctic Norway. Josef Giesinger, who was stationed at the Murmansk front in November 1943, likewise writes about the plants and landscape, and describes the wonder of the northern lights. Then there is Seppl, from "somewhere in Ehrenaika," writing to his friend Karl: "Last week we were together in France, today I'm writing from Africa. That's how it goes with us; that is what they call 'the life of a soldier.'" The tone of these letters is strikingly similar. All of the authors seem to find it quite normal that they are in foreign lands—being far from home is, after all, part of a soldier's life. Another letter from Friedrich Natter, who wrote from Bjatiogorsk in the Caucasus, is even more significant:

Here we felt content as sons of the mountains. The people are friendly to us here, too, although we came to the country as "conquerors." They are people too, after all, with the same worries and joys as we. We did not feel like enemies. How nice it must be to see and experience such foreign lands in peace! Being together with the people of this country we feel clearly how inhuman the war is and how it only brings unhappiness to people and countries, all of whom are innocent of unleashing the war's fury. May a time soon come when people and countries are united in peace![148]

Unlike the others, Natter's letter hints at the ideological nature of the war. The idea that many in the Caucasus welcomed the soldiers may well have been true, but it is nonetheless a one-sided view that justifies the Nazi presence deep inside the Soviet Union. On the other hand, both the soldiers and local civilians are victims of a larger force, "the war," which itself has become a historical actor, dragging people into misery with its "fury." But more unusual than the tone of the correspondence is that such letters would be included in a postwar textbook at all, considering that the stated goal of Austrian education officials was to sever any link between Austria and Germany. As a reading book, this work was not subject to censure by the Allied authorities. It is therefore especially revealing for its extensive coverage of the war and for its portrayal of Austrians as both participants in the war and victims of the war.

Another story from *Von heut' und ehedem*, Leopold Arthofer's "Jubelfeier im Kazet," tells the touching story of a priest imprisoned in the Dachau concentration camp outside of Munich. When the priest mentions that the twentieth anniversary of his ordination is approaching, civilian workers at the camp invite him to not one but two secret dinners to celebrate the anniversary. At the second dinner, the wife of the host, Mrs. Filippitsch, remarks that she cannot believe what she has seen and questions the humanity of the SS men at the camp. She also explains that her "husband was tricked when he accepted the job here as garbage man" and that they "knew nothing of the proximity of the concentration camp and even less [about the fact] that prisoners were employed in the operation. If we could, we would have left from here on the first day, but my husband has his orders. How will this all someday end? This Dachau is a pit of murder and we cannot help at all."[149] It is significant that the perpetrators of crimes in the camp are clearly defined as members of the SS, thus distancing everyone else in the story from Nazi ideology. Furthermore, since the protagonist of the story is a priest, the victim category is occupied by a Catholic Austrian. (No story in the book mentions Jews as victims.) Finally, the story also emphasizes the theme of helplessness: "We did not know," and "We would help, but we cannot."

"War is hell" truisms abounded in stories dealing with the war, resulting in a view that cast the war as a natural disaster, which Austrians had to survive as best they could. In a reading book for Carinthian schools, students read about the province's ordeals in several wars in a section called "Einst und jetzt," under the heading "Kriege sind ein großes Unglück [Wars Are a Great Calamity]!":

> Had people in later times always remembered that times of war bring no blessing to the *Heimat*, then perhaps our people and province would not have had to experience so many terrible wars. Barely had the [recently] migrated Germans from Bavaria and Franconia brought order back [to Carinthia], when Hungarians and Turks marched into the province.
>
> Much later, the French, too, tore all of Carinthia into two pieces, and at the end of the First World War, the Yugoslavians wanted to sever an entire piece of Carinthian land.... In such times of emergency, the Carinthians have always held together and thereby prevented much misfortune.... The hand of peace that the Carinthian people were always ready to offer is why foreign peoples like to come to our peaceful mountain country as guests during the winter and summer. The French, the Italians, the Yugoslavians, the Germans, and all of the others, who even come from across the ocean to visit us, are welcome if they do not come as enemies and do not disturb the peace of the *Heimat*.[150]

It is fascinating how this passage never explicitly mentions World War II, but rather speaks of war in general, thus placing World War II into a continuum of wars and invasions through which Carinthians have suffered and survived by sticking together. From the point of view of this text, a student might even have concluded that Allied occupation troops belonged in the category of earlier invaders of Carinthia.

Heimkehr

One aspect of the war that continued to be a part of many Austrians' lives in the reconstruction period involved loved ones who were missing *(vermisst)*. Many held out hope that their friends and family members would be among the survivors of prisoner of war camps and would soon come home. This intense anxiety and grief over personal losses was a formative aspect of the victim myth, as the pain of families easily melded into the official rhetoric of a victimized Austria. Poems and stories in reading books that dealt with the issue of the missing undoubtedly had a direct personal relevance to many Austrian students whose fathers were missing in action. For example, Ernst Thrasolt's poem "Vermißt" (Missing) reflects the agony over not knowing the fate of a loved one:

> Vermißt! Vermißt!
> Lebst du noch oder bist du tot?
> Sage, melde uns, wo du bist!
> fielst du in des schlimmen Feindes Hand,
> lebendig, gesund, von Wunden rot?
> Liegst du frierend, fiebernd am Waldesrand?
> haben die Unsern dich unerkannt
> in einem Massengrab begraben?
> ...

Lebst du oder bist du tot?
Gib uns doch ein Zeichen von dir?
 Laß still die alte Hausuhr steh'n,
klopf' nachts dreimal an die Kammertür!
Der du deiner Mutter erschienen bist,
kannst du uns hilflos leiden sehn?
Und wie unsre Mutter krank, grau geworden ist?
Höre uns, Herr Jesus Christ![151]

In another reading book, students read a more hopeful account of a family at Christmas whose father is still away, but alive. When the son, Rudi, asks his mother if he should put his father's picture with the Christmas tree, the mother replies that he "wrote us today that soon he will be back home forever from the far foreign land. His letter is my most wonderful Christmas present this year." The mother then reminds her son how lucky they are compared to so many others. True, they have had to wait a long time for the father's return, but "there are still many families who know nothing of their far-away loved ones, if they are still alive or if they have long been at rest." Mother and son then participate in a nationwide gesture of remembrance: "[T]onight everyone in our country is placing two burning candles in the window. They are a sign that we remain united in our hearts and that we wish strength and comfort to the lonely and those who are far away on Christmas eve."[152] In another example, students read the story of a welcome home celebration for POWs returning to Salzburg. It is the moment that so many had hoped for, that is, *Heimkehr*, or homecoming, and people from throughout the province of Salzburg have come to the city to greet the returning prisoners who had "fought for the *Heimat* in the far-off foreign land" before their ordeal as POWs began. As the author explains, being a prisoner "may have been harder than the time of war itself. In enemy country they often had to do heavy work with unimaginable hunger, in deep mine shafts, in stone quarries, and in factories.... Who can measure the privation, suffering, and the great homesickness which these sons of our province have suffered!" After being welcomed by the mayor, a spokesman for the veterans thanks the mayor for the reception and pledges their readiness to "participate in the work of building a bright future for our province of Salzburg."[153]

In all of these examples, the missing and prisoners of war are victims of the war, but the tone of the third narrative is especially significant. The first two examples emphasize the pain of loss, hope, and solidarity with other families who have also suffered loss and experienced the anxiety of not knowing the fate of their loved ones. But Leopold Wally's story "Heimkehr" goes beyond the emotions of loss to express extreme victimization rhetoric. In Wally's story, the POWs fought a war of defense for the *Heimat* and then were forced into a life of slave labor in Soviet POW camps. The types of labor that the hungry soldiers had to perform is also significant. Students could have easily concluded that there was no real difference between forced labor in Nazi concentration camps and that in Soviet POW camps. It is also interesting to note that Russia is not specifically mentioned in the story, though there is little doubt that any student reading this story would know where the soldiers had been imprisoned. Finally, it is significant that the POWs have survived and returned eager to help rebuild Austria. They had been victims of Russian brutality, but they are ready to get on with life. The lesson of the POWs is perseverance, and there is no need to discuss why the soldiers were imprisoned in the first place.

The victim status of returning soldiers was reaffirmed by the archbishop of Salzburg in a pastoral letter for All Saints Day in November 1945. Archbishop Andreas Rohracher wrote: "When I, on this day, direct a heart-felt welcome to all returnees, I mean above all our brave soldiers, who have come home from the war, whether they have returned directly from the front, from prisoner of war camps or from the military hospitals … [and] yes, I also direct a welcome to those returnees who were ostracized or persecuted in jails or concentration camps, held prisoner, forced to flee the country, or confined, and now have regained their freedom and *Heimat*."[154] In his welcome, the archbishop not only lumps soldiers and persecuted victims of the regime into a single category, but those persecuted by the regime are named second, almost as an afterthought. But in the context of the times, it is unlikely that a great deal of soul-searching would have occurred. In the fall of 1945, hungry and displaced Austrians were not apt to put themselves in the shoes of the Nazi regime's victims. By declaring everyone a victim, the archbishop was also calling for reconciliation, knowing that bitter infighting would hamper rebuilding efforts in Austria. In making his welcome to all *Heimkehrer*, the cleric demonstrated political leadership in unifying Austrians and boosting morale. However, in his position as a moral leader, Archbishop Rohracher neglected to raise the issue of responsibility.

When the occupation ended in 1955, the myth of Austrian victimization at the hands of Germany was already well established in Austrian political life and was rapidly becoming a staple theme of Austrian identity in schools. Furthermore, the victim myth was linked to other motifs of Austrian identity in two ways. First, the themes that reinforced the uniqueness of Austria supported the idea that Austrians, as a people separate from the Germans, never went along with the annexation of 1938 in the first place and therefore were exonerated for participating in subsequent Nazi crimes. Second, the image of Austrians as a people who were Catholic, rural, and cultured, with an imperial, but not imperialist, past, meant that Austrian identity was incompatible with the crimes of the Nazi regime. In short, the fundamental characteristics of the newly reconstructed Austrian identity were antithetical to Nazism, which was intimately linked with Prussian-dominated Germany.

In many ways, these images of Austrian identity reflected reality (e.g., most Austrians *were* Catholic and Mozart *did* live and compose in Vienna) and had the benefit of providing a sense of unity. Given the bitter divisions of the First Republic, the importance of this sense of unity in postwar

Austria, though strained at times, cannot be overstated. But the chosen themes of identity also exacted costs. Overt racist nationalism had been discredited by the Nazi defeat, but cultural chauvinism remained alive as Austrian school texts imparted a sense of identity based not just on the ideals of democracy and pluralism, but also on a religious and cultural basis that excluded as well as defined. The definition of culture in Austria played a major role in exclusionary national identity, as did the emphasis on local identity. Overall, these factors helped to create an Austrian identity filled with contradictions—contradictions that are evident throughout the history of the Austria-as-victim myth. When compared to Germans, Austrians portrayed themselves as a unique people; yet when Austrians faced the east, they cast themselves as a beacon of German and European culture and the protector of the Occident.

In spite of these contradictions, the Austria-as-victim myth, with its emphasis on Austrian uniqueness, played an essential role in building the Second Republic. It was integral to the process of creating the political and social legitimacy of a new Austria. By 1955, a nation once doubted by its own citizens was emerging.[155] The crisis of identity was coming to an end. The voice of a young boy in the story "Woran ich oft denke ..." (What I often think of ...) demonstrates the sentiment of the mid 1950s: "The last evidence of the hard-lost war gradually disappeared, and peaceful times returned to the village. We children felt it on the dinner table, because the good mother could put more fat on the noodles and could salt up a freshly slaughtered pig at least once a year. We could again slip into real shoes with real leather soles, and teachers as well as parents were greatly relieved no longer to have to hear the clatter of wooden shoes."[156] The war was over, and it was time to forget about it and get on with life. The era of *Blümchenkaffee* had come to an end.

Notes

1. An earlier abbreviated draft of this chapter was published in the *Austrian History Yearbook*, vol. 30 (1999).
2. The most controversial question of all could be summarized as "How German is Austria?" This question was vigorously debated when the German historian Karl Dietrich Erdmann put forth the idea of three successor German states to Nazi Germany and generally sought to place Austrian history in a broad German context. Separating this approach from nationalist ideology proved elusive, and for many, Erdmann belonged in the camp of antidemocratic, right-wing German nationalism. Erdmann's ideas were so explosive that even discussing them proved to be difficult. Historian Harry Ritter's analysis of Erdmann's ideas and the controversy surrounding them in the *German Studies Review* provoked a caustic reply from some Austrian historians who believed Ritter himself was in sympathy with *völkisch* and racist concepts of the nation. See Harry Ritter, "Austria and the Struggle for German Identity," *German Studies Review. Special Issue: German Identity* (winter 1992): 111–129; Margarete Grandner, Genot Heiss, and Oliver Rathkolb, "Österreich und seine deutsche Identität. Bemerkungen zu Harry Ritters

Aufsatz 'Austria and the Struggle for German Identity,'" *German Studies Review* 16 (October 1993): 515–520; and Harry Ritter, "On Austria's German Identity: A Reply to Margarete Grandner, Gernot Heiss, and Oliver Rathkolb," in the same issue (521–523). For the ideas in question, see Karl Dietrich Erdmann, *Die Spur Österreichs in der deutschen Geschichte: Drei Staaten, zwei Nationen, ein Volk?* (Zurich: Manesse-Verlag, 1989).

3. For a synthesis of works and major arguments on Austrian identity, see the chapter "On Austrian Identity: The Scholarly Literature" in Wodak et al., *The Discursive Construction of National Identity*, 49–69.

4. Suppanz, *Österreichische Geschichtsbilder*, 140, 148.

5. For a discussion on Austrian identity during the First Republic, see Hans Haas, "Staats- und Landesbewusstsein in der Ersten Republik," in *Handbuch des politischen Systems Österreichs. Erste Republik, 1918–1933*, ed. Tálos et al. (Vienna: Manzsche Verlags- und Universitätsbuchhandlung, 1995), 472–487.

6. *Mein Vaterland, mein Österreich* (Vienna: Österreichischer Bundesverlag, 1935), 5.

7. *Ich bin ein Österreicher* (Vienna: Österreichischer Bundesverlag, 1935), 62–64. For other patriotic school texts from the *Ständestaat* period, see *Der Österreicher hat ein Vaterland* (Vienna: Österreichischer Bundesverlag, 1935); *Hoch Österreich* (Vienna and Leipzig: Österreichischer Bundesverlag, 1935); and Otto Ender, ed., *Das Neue Österreich. Staatsbürgerkunde mit Bildern* (Vienna and Innsbruck: Tyrolia Verlag, 1935).

8. See Stanley Suval, "The Search for a Fatherland," *Austrian History Yearbook*, vols. 4–5 (1968–1969): 275–299; Carla Esden-Tempska, "Civic Education in Authoritarian Austria, 1934–38," *History of Education Quarterly* 30, no. 2 (summer 1990): 187–211; Hanns Haas, "Staats- und Landesbewußtsein in der Ersten Republik," in *Handbuch des politischen Systems Österreichs. Erste Republik, 1918–1933*, ed. Tálos et al., 472–487; and Herbert Dachs, "'Austrofaschismus' und Schule—Ein Instrumentalisierungsversuch," in *"Austrofaschismus." Beiträge über Politik, Ökonomie und Kultur, 1934–1938*, ed. Emmerich Tálos and Wolfgang Neugebauer, 2nd ed. (Vienna: Verlag für Gesellschaftskritik, 1984), 179–197.

9. *Verordnungsblatt für innere und kulturelle Angelegenheiten*, June 1940, 11. Stück, 61.

10. Ibid., June 1938, 6. Stück, no. 25, 23–26; ibid., April 1938, 1. Stück, no. 4, 2; ibid., April 1938, 1. Stück, 1, no. 7, 2; ibid., October 1938, 13. Stück, no. 60, 140; ibid., March 1939, 5. Stück, no. 41, 50; and ibid., January 1940, 1. Stück, no. 17, 15–16. (Where applicable, "no." refers to the decree number.)

11. Ibid., June 1940, 11. Stück, 70–72.

12. See Jakob Graf, *Familienkunde und Rassenbiologie für Schüler* (Munich: J.F. Lehmanns Verlag, 1934); and Friedrich Hackenberg et al., *Deutsches Lesebuch für Jungen, Zweiter Teil* (Frankfurt am Main: Verlag Moritz Diesterweg, 1942).

13. *Verordnungsblatt für innere und kulturelle Angelegenheiten*, June 1938, 5. Stück, no. 21, 17–19.

14. Staats-Realgymnasium in Laa a. d. Thaya (1911/12—1937/38). XI. *Jahresbericht über die Schuljahre 1936/37 und 1937/38* (Laa a. d. Thaya, 1938), 9. The events of the Anschluss were also recounted in *Unser Heim. Blätter der Staatserziehungsanstalt Traiskirchen*, 13. Jahr. 6. Folge (Traiskirchen, 1938), 51–58, and many other yearbooks.

15. *Jahres-Bericht des Oberlyzeums und Realgymnasiums für Mädchen der Gesellschaft für erweiterte Frauenbildung in Baden bei Wien* (Baden, 1938), 1.

16. *Jahresbericht der Handelsakademie und der kaufmännische Wirtschaftschule in Klagenfurt, 1937–1938* (Klagenfurt, 1938), 15–16.

17. *Jahresbericht des Staatsgymnasiums in Krems an der Donau, 1937/38* (Krems, 1938), 20–24.

18. For more on Austrian schools under the Nazi regime, see Helmut Engelbrecht, *Geschichte des österreichischen Bildungswesens. Erziehung und Unterricht auf dem Boden Österreichs. Band 5. Von 1918 bis zur Gegenwart* (Vienna: Österreichischer Bundesverlag, 1988), 304–350; and Herbert Dachs, "Schule und Jugenderziehung in der 'Ostmark,'" in *NS-Herrschaft in Österreich*, ed. Tálos et al., 217–242.

19. On the medieval past, the Turkish wars, and the symbolic importance of the baroque, see Suppanz, *Österreichische Geschicthsbilder*, 109–113, 148, 162–165, 170–177, 183–188.

20. Anton Pelinka summarizes these changes under the heading "Changing Identities" in *Austria: Out of the Shadow of the Past*, 9–12.

21. Bundesministerium für Unterricht, *Freiheit für Österreich. Dokumente* (Vienna: Österreichischer Bundesverlag, 1955), 11–14.

22. Quoted from Schausberger, "Die Entstehung des Mythos," 6–7.

23. *Gerechtigkeit für Österreich! Rot-Weiss-Rot-Buch. Darstellungen, Dokumente und Nachweise zur Vorgeschichte und Geschichte der Okkupation Österreichs* (Nach amtlichen Quellen). Part I was published in the summer of 1946 by the Austrian State Printing House. I quote from the English translation of this work, which was published in 1947. Note that red-white-red is the color scheme of the Austrian flag.

24. Bischof, *Austria in the First Cold War*, 52, 60–62.

25. *Red-White-Red-Book*, 5.

26. Quoted in Keyserlingk, *Austria in World War II*, 152. See chapter 4 for further discussion on the importance of the Moscow Declaration.

27. Quoted from Reinhold Wagnleitner, "The Sound of Forgetting Meets the United States of Amnesia: An Introduction to the Relations between Strange Bedfellows," in *From World War to Waldheim: Culture and Politics in Austria and the United States*, ed. David Good and Ruth Wodak (New York: Berghahn Books, 1999), 7.

28. Schausberger, "Die Entstehung des Mythos," 31.

29. Ibid., 78–79.

30. See, for example, Marianne Baumgartner, *"Jo, des waren halt schlechte Zeiten..." Das Kriegsende und die unmittelbare Nachkriegszeit in den lebensgeschichtlichen Erzählungen von Frauen aus dem Mostviertel* (Frankfurt am Main: Peter Land, 1994).

31. Pelinka, *Austria: Out of the Shadow of the Past*, 15–17.

32. Manfried Rauchensteiner argues that while imprisoned Austrian politicians from different camps did learn the importance of working together, no set plan for future cooperation was made in the Nazi concentration camps. See Manfried Rauchensteiner, *Die Zwei. Die Große Koalition in Österreich, 1945–1966* (Vienna: Österreichischer Bundesverlag, 1987), 19.

33. Franz Danimann and Hugo Pepper, eds., *Österreich im April '45* (Vienna: Europaverlag, 1985), 9.

34. Given the divisive nature of Austrian politics in the First Republic, the stability achieved by the postwar coalition was a remarkable achievement. See William E. Wright, "Austria and the Dear School of Dame Experience," in *Coping with the Past*, ed. Harms, Reuter, and Dürr, 66–78.

35. See Anton Pelinka, "Der verdrängte Bürgerkrieg," in *Das große Tabu. Österreichs Umgang mit seiner Vergangenheit*, ed. Anton Pelinka and Erika Weinzierl (Vienna: Edition S, 1987), 143–153; Anton Pelinka, "The Great Austrian Taboo: The Repression of the Civil War," in *Coping with the Past*, ed. Harms, Reuter, and Dürr, 56–65; Matthew Paul Berg, "Between Kulturkampf and Vergangenheitsbewältigung: The SPÖ, the Roman Catholic Church, and the Problem of Reconciliation, *Zeitgeschichte* 24, nos. 5–6 (1997): 147–169; and Elizabeth Klamper, "Ein einig Volk von Brüdern. Vergessen und Erinnern im Zeichen des Burgfriedens," *Zeitgeschichte* 24, nos. 5–6 (1997): 170–185.

36. Uhl, "Erinnern und Vergessen," 114–146. Also see Heidemarie Uhl, "Transformationen des österreichischen Gedächtnisses. Geschichtspolitik und Denkmalkultur in der Zweiten Republik," in *Eiszeit der Erinnerung. Vom Vergessen der eigenen Schuld*, ed. Ulf Brunnbauer (Vienna: Promedia, 1999): 49–64.

37. For works on the history and significance of the VdU and FPÖ, see Anton Pelinka, "SPÖ, ÖVP, and the 'Ehemaligen': Isolation or Integration?" and Max Riedlsperger, "FPÖ: Liberal or Nazi?" both in *Conquering the Past*, ed. Parkinson, 245–256 and 257–278, respectively; and Max Riedlsperger, *The Lingering Shadow of Nazism: The Austrian Independent Party Movement Since 1945* (Boulder: East European Quarterly, 1978). For controversial Austrian People's Party and Socialist campaign posters seeking the votes of returning veterans, see Norbert Hölzl, *Propaganda-Schlachten. Die österreichischen Wahlkämpfe 1945 bis 1971* (Munich: R. Oldenbourg Verlag, 1974), 41.

38. The Verein für die Geschichte der Arbeiterbewegung serves as guardian of Socialist history while the Karl von Vogelsang-Institut represents the historical views of the ÖVP.

39. The organization of the school system was based on laws not only from the First Republic (notably the reforms of 1927) but also dating to the monarchy. See Josef Schermaier, *Geschichte und Gegenwart des allgemeinbildenden Schulwesens in Österreich* (Vienna: Verband der wissenschaftlichen Gesellschaften Österreichs, 1990), 1–2. The role that the Church would play in public education was a particularly divisive issue in the negotiations over school reform. See Erika Weinzierl, "Kirche und Schule in Österreich, 1945–1948," *Kirchliche Zeitgeschichte* 1 (1989): 165–170.

40. Engelbrecht, *Geschichte des österreichischen Bildungswesens. Band 5.*, 399.

41. Ibid., 400–401.

42. Ibid., 404–405.

43. Alfred Hiller, "US-amerikanische Schulpolitik in Österreich, 1945–1950," *Österreich in Geschichte und Literatur* 2 (1980): 65–79.

44. Engelbrecht, *Geschichte des österreichischen Bildungswesens. Band 5.*, 405, 409–410. It is interesting to note that enrollment in and offerings of French and Russian courses decreased dramatically when the occupation ended in 1955. See ibid., 409.

45. I use the terms "Education Ministry" and "education minister" throughout this work. The exact title of the ministry and the duties of the minister have changed a number of times since 1945, but education and teaching *(Unterricht)* have remained core functions of the ministry, which at times has simultaneously been the Ministry for Sports, Art, and Cultural Affairs.

46. Engelbrecht, *Geschichte des österreichischen Bildungswesens. Band 5.*, 397.

47. William T. Bluhm, *Building an Austrian Nation: The Political Integration of a Western State* (New Haven and London: Yale University Press, 1973), 131–132. Disappointed over the policies and actions of the Soviet Union, Fischer later left the Communist Party. See Ernst Fischer, *Das Ende einer Illusion. Erinnerungen 1945–1955* (Vienna: Verlag Fritz Molden, 1973).

48. Hurdes made this remark in a 1966 interview. See Bluhm, *Building an Austrian Nation*, 133.

49. Thaler, *The Ambivalence of Identity*, 59.

50. Knight, "Education and National Identity in Austria after the Second World War," 187–188.

51. Thaler, *The Ambivalence of Identity*, 115–116.

52. *Verordnungsblatt für den Dienstbereich des Bundesministeriums für Unterricht*, 1946, 1./2. Stück, 1.

53. *Lehrpläne für die Hauptschulen, mit einem Vorwort von Viktor Fadrus* (Vienna: Verlag für Jugend und Volk, 1947), xiv–xx. Also see *Provorische Lehrpläne für die Mittelschulen* (Vienna: Österreichischer Bundesverlag für Unterricht, Wissenschaft und Kunst, 1946); and Fritz Fellner's remarks on the Austrian obsession with the "special mission." See Fritz Fellner, "The Problem of the Austrian Nation after 1945," *Journal of Modern History* 60 (June 1988): 281.

54. Bluhm, *Building an Austrian Nation*, 134–135. Also see Matthew Paul Berg, "Political Culture and State Identity: The Reconstruction of Austrian Social Democracy, 1945–1958" (Ph.D. diss., University of Chicago, 1993).

55. *Verordnungsblatt für den Dienstbereich des Bundesministeriums für Unterricht*, 1946, 3. Stück, no. 42, 69; and ibid., 1946, no. 66, 97.

56. Bluhm, *Building an Austrian Nation*, 133.

57. *Verordnungsblatt für den Dienstbereich des Bundesministeriums für Unterricht*, 1952, Stück 10, no. 110, 215.

58. Ibid., 1955, Stück 10, no. 84, 218.

59. Knight, "Education and National Identity in Austria after the Second World War," 189.

60. Johann Schoiswohl overstates the case somewhat when he argues that the emphasis on all things Austrian was part of a deliberate "strategy of guilt alleviation." See Johann Schoiswohl, "Schule Nach Auschwitz. Fünf Thesen zur Struktur der Österreichischen Pflichtschule in der Unmittelbaren Nachkriegszeit," *Zeitgeschichte* 15, no. 6 (1988): 245–261.

61. Heinrich Kotz et al., *Junge Saat. Lesebuch für Tiroler Volksschulen. Band II* (Innsbruck and Vienna: Tyrolia Verlag, 1952), 365–366. Heinrich Kotz was a teacher and school inspector

from Tyrol. During the First Republic, he also served in the Tyrolean Landtag as a member of the Christian-Social Party. Kotz was a prolific author of textbooks, and his career spanned from the Austrian Empire to the Austrian Second Republic.

62. *Verordnungsblatt für das Schulwesen in Steiermark*. Jahrgang 1947. 15 March 1947, Stück 1–3; and "Eine neue Bundeshymne für Österreich?" *Die Furche*, 17 April 1946. Both are quoted from Dirk Lyon et al., *Österreich-'bewußt'sein-bewußt Österreicher sein? Materialien zur Entwicklung des Österreichbewußtseins seit 1945* (Vienna: Österreichischer Bundesverlag, 1985), 58–62.

63. Ibid., 60. There is no official translation of the Austrian national anthem. The following translation is provided by the Austrian Press and Information Service: "Land of mountains, land on the river,/Land of fields, land of cathedrals,/Land of hammers, rich in outlook./You are the native home of great sons,/A people uniquely gifted for the beautiful,/Much applauded Austria./Fiercely embattled, ferociously contested,/You lie at the center of the globe,/Like a strong heart./Since the days of your early ancestors/You have borne the burden of a sublime calling,/Much-tried Austria./Courageously we stride/Into the new times, free and devout,/Industrious and of firm heart./In unison choruses of brotherhood/We pledge our allegiance to thee,/Fatherland,/Much-loved Austria."

64. Kotz et al., *Junge Saat. Lesebuch für Tiroler Volksschulen. Band II*, 395–397.

65. Andreas Hofer as a symbol of Tyrol had been firmly established by the 1890s. See Laurence Cole, "Patriotic Celebrations in Late-Nineteenth- and Early-Twentieth-Century Tirol," in *Staging the Past: The Politics of Commemoration in Habsburg Central Europe, 1848 to the Present*, ed. Maria Bucur and Nancy M. Wingfield (West Lafayette: Purdue University Press, 2001), 75–111.

66. "There he was supposed to kneel down;/he said: 'That I won't do./I want to die, as I stand,/I want to die, as I fought,/as I stand on this entrenchment;/long live my good Emperor Francis,/and with him Tyrol!" Heinrich Kotz et al., *Junge Saat. Lesebuch für Tiroler Volksschulen. Band III* (Innsbruck and Vienna: 1953), 619–620.

67. Friedrich Korger and Josef Lehrl, eds., *Lesebuch für Mittelschulen. III. Band* (Vienna: Österreichischer Bundesverlag, 1954), 155–156.

68. Werner Suppanz points out that while Prince Eugene remained important as a symbol after the war, he was not emphasized nearly as much as he had been by the *Ständestaat*. Suppanz asserts that a possible reason for less on emphasis on Prince Eugene in the postwar period is that the Nazis had appropriated the seventeenth-century warrior. See Suppanz, *Österreichische Geschichtsbilder*, 176–177. Indeed, the Seventh SS Volunteer Mountain Division had been named after Prince Eugene. See I. C. B. Dear and M. R. D. Foot, eds., *The Oxford Companion to World War II* (New York: Oxford University Press, 2001), 816.

69. Friedrich Korger and Josef Lehrl, eds., *Lesebuch für Mittelschulen. IV. Band* (Vienna: Österreichischer Bundesverlag, 1952), 298–303.

70. Josef Bitsche, Albert Eberle, and Rudolf Hansen, *Von heut' und ehedem. Lesebuch für die Oberstufe der Vorarlberger Volksschulen, 6. bis 8. Schulstufe* (Bregenz: Verlag J. R. Teutsch, 1953), 494.

71. Ibid., 494–495.

72. Friedrich Demel and Wilfrieda Lindner, *Lesebuch für Handelsakademien. I. Band* (Vienna: Hölder-Pichler-Tempsky, 1948), 17–20.

73. See Johnson, *Central Europe*, 64–84.

74. Demel and Lindner, *Lesebuch für Handelsakademien. I. Band*, 17–20.

75. See Michael P. Steinberg, *The Meaning of the Salzburg Festival: Austria as Theater and Ideology, 1890–1938* (Ithaca: Cornell University Press, 1990), esp. chap. 4, "German Culture and Austrian Kulturpolitik." Also see Stephen Gallup, *A History of the Salzburg Festival* (London: Weidenfeld and Nicolson, 1987).

76. Karl Gutkas, *Die Zweite Republik. Österreich, 1945–1985* (Munich: R. Oldenbourg Verlag, 1985), 55.

77. *Verordnungsblatt für den Dienstbereich des Bundesministeriums für Unterricht*, 1948, 3. Stück, no. 14, 25–26.

78. *Heimat und weite Welt. Lesestoffe für die 7. und 8. Schulstufe der österreichischen Volksschulen*, 3rd rev. ed. (Vienna: Österreichischer Bundesverlag, 1954), 215–216.
79. R. Bamberger and J. Stöger, eds., *Aus der Heimat. Lesebogen für Schule und Heim* (Vienna: Verlag Leinmüller, 1949), 20–21 and 21–23.
80. Kotz et al., *Junge Saat. Lesebuch für Tiroler Volksschulen. Band II*, 391.
81. Hauptschule für Knaben und Mädchen in Eisenstadt. *73. Jahresbericht, Schuljahr 1953/54* (Eisenstadt, 1954), 2.
82. See Neil Butterworth, *Haydn: His Life and Times* (Tunbridge Wells: Midas Books, 1977), 138–139. In his own 1946 work, Karl Geiringer writes that before the war he had shown the "reverently preserved" skull to "countless admirers of Haydn." See Karl Geiringer, *Haydn: A Creative Life in Music* (New York: W.W. Norton, 1946), 174–175.
83. Erik Levi, *Music in the Third Reich* (London: Macmillan, 1994), 210. Also see Michael Kater, *The Twisted Muse: Musicians and Their Music in the Third Reich* (New York: Oxford University Press, 1997), 11, 29–30.
84. *Bundesrealgymnasium in Laa an der Thaya, XV. Jahresbericht. Städtische Wirtschaftsschule in Laa an der Thaya, V. Jahresbericht. Schuljahr, 1945–46* (Laa an der Thaya, 1946), 6–10.
85. Christopher J. Wickham, *Constructing Heimat in Postwar Germany: Longing and Belonging* (Lewiston, N.Y.: Mellen Press, 1999), 8.
86. Kotz et al., *Junge Saat. Lesebuch für Tiroler Volksschulen. Band III*, 395–396.
87. Steinberg, *The Meaning of the Salzburg Festival*, 56.
88. Kotz et al., *Junge Saat. Lesebuch für Tiroler Volksschulen. Band III*, 487–488.
89. "True, there are lusher pastures,/Lands full of honey and milk./Elsewhere one wears silks,/here one wears Loden and ticking./But with no regrets,/You are the splendor of my *Heimat*!/God knows, were I to go away,/I would find neither happiness nor peace./…/And the older I get,/the more rooted/I am in this ground,/following my fathers' path./After all, I stem from them,/Blood of their Blood:/Because all my cares and desires/rest firmly in my *Heimat*." *Heimat und weite Welt. Lesestoffe für die 7. und 8. Schulstufe der österreichischen Volksschulen*, 11.
90. "A small church sits in the village, a path runs by/and the chickens, they make a racket on the path/…/And the wagon full of hay, comes from the pasture,/and up on top sit Hans and Liese./They both yodel and cheer and laugh,/and it rings through the evening, it is a joy!/And to the king on his throne, it is splendid and soft/yet to sit in the hay, there is nothing else like it!/And were I the king, I would get right at it/and would take a wagon full of hay as my throne." Heinrich Kotz et al., *Junge Saat. Lesebuch für Tiroler Volksschulen. Band I* (Innsbruck: Tyrolia Verlag, 1952), 203.
91. "True the world is so big and far/and full of sunshine,/but the most beautiful piece of all/is my *Heimat*!" Ibid., 210–211.
92. The fourth class was designated as the year when students would put particular emphasis on their province and *Heimat*.
93. "There is only one Tyrol,/it's a small land,/but beloved and fine/and that land is mine." Heinrich Kotz et al., *Tirolerland. Anhang zum Lesebuch "Mein Heimatland" für die vierte Schulstufe der Tiroler Volksschulen* (Vienna: Hölder-Pichler-Tempsky, 1949), 3. The phrase "Tirol isch lei oans" also makes reference to the partition of Tyrol after World War I. The word "lei" is actually Carinthian dialect meaning "only." During the 1919–1920 border disputes in Carinthia, a similar phrase was used as a slogan for preserving the unity of Carinthia: "Kärnten isch lei oans." I owe thanks to Anton Pelinka for this information.
94. "My *Heimat* my Salzburg, I hold you in honor,/no place in the world could be more beloved by me!/There I am just happy, there I enjoy my life,/for me nothing in the world could be more beautiful." *Unser Lesebuch. 4. Schulstufe. Heimat Salzburg* (Salzburg: Otto Müller Verlag, 1954), 186.
95. "Innviertel/horse and *Troad*/Mühlviertel/flax and *Gjoad*,/Hausruckviertel,/fruit and lard,/Traunviertel/Salt" *Aus da Hoamat. Anhang zum Lesebuch "Mein Heimatland" für die vierte Schulstufe der oberösterreichischen Volksschulen*, 3rd rev. ed. (Vienna: Hölder-Pichler-Tempsky, 1953), 3.
96. Bitsche et al., *Von heut' und ehedem*, 392–393.

97. "A Tyrolean, he is devoted to his *Heimat*,/he is devoted to his mountains and forests,/if he is far away in the unknown—/he is pulled back to the province with force." Kotz et al., *Tirolerland*, 141.

98. "Give me my rough Loden coat/and my spiked shoes,/I want some fresh mountain pasture air, I'm a Tyrolean fellow!/.../And I don't need narrow houses,/in there it's too crowded and cramped for me,/there my yodeler wouldn't have enough room/he needs an entire valley." Richard Bamberger and J. Stöger, eds., *Aus der Heimat. Lesebogen für Schule und Heim* (Vienna: 1949), 6.

99. "Where through hot coals and the hammer's power/strong hands forge the iron;/ where oaks still stand, full and green from sap,/which no strong wind has yet bent;/ This beautiful land is the Styrian land,/it is my beloved, precious *Heimatland!*" *Viertes Lesebuch. Ausgabe für das Bundesland Steiermark,* 3rd rev. ed. (Vienna: Hölder-Pichler-Tempsky, 1954), 101.

100. "I am a child of the city./People think,/and make fun of our kind,/[saying] that such a city child has no *Heimat.*/True, in my games there is no rustling of/forests. Instead, the pavement clatters./Yet to me you are a song, you dear city!" Bamberger and Stöger, *Aus der Heimat,* 13–14.

101. Kotz et al., *Junge Saat. Lesebuch für Tiroler Volksschulen. Band I,* 223–224.

102. Quoted in Wickham, *Constructing Heimat in Postwar Germany,* 54.

103. Korger and Lehrl, *Lesebuch für Mittelschulen. III. Band,* 5–13.

104. *Steirische Heimat. Anhang zum Lesebuch "Mein Heimatland" für die vierte Schulstufe der steirischen Volksschulen,* 2nd ed. (Vienna: Hölder-Pichler-Tempsky, 1951), 64.

105. Note that Übergossene Alm is the name of the glacier; it evokes the image of a glacier pouring out over the meadow. See Helene Tramer-Soeser, *Die Valtbauernkinder. Anhang zum Lesebuch "Mein Heimatland" für die vierte Schulstufe der Salzburger Volksschulen* (Vienna: Hölder-Pichler-Tempsky, 1947), 3–5.

106. *Alm* imagery remains common in Austria. Many Austrian television commercials make use of the *Alm* in either a pious or comic way. There is also a popular Austrian soft drink, called "Almdudler," which is similar to ginger ale.

107. Kotz et al., *Junge Saat. Lesebuch für Tiroler Volksschulen. Band II,* 113.

108. For a postwar book promoting Austria and Austrian tourism, see Ernst Marboe, *The Book of Austria.* trans. G. E. R. Gedye (Vienna: Austrian State Printing and Publication House, 1948).

109. Günter Bischof, "'Conquering the Foreigner': The Marshall Plan and the Revival of Postwar Austrian Tourism," in *The Marshall Plan in Austria,* ed. Günter Bischof, Anton Pelinka, and Dieter Stiefel (New Brunswick: Transaction Publishers, 2000), 357–401.

110. Karl Melchard, "Fremdenverkehrsaufklärung der Österreichischen Schuljugend verbunden mit einem Preisausschreiben," *Beilage zum Verordnungsblatt für den Dienstberiech des Bundesministeriums für Unterricht,* 1950, 5. Stück, 4, 7–8. The photographs are on unnumbered pages between pages 4 and 5.

111. Kotz et al., *Junge Saat. Lesebuch für Tiroler Volksschulen. Band III,* 397.

112. See the discussion in Elizabeth Boa and Rachel Palfreyman, *Heimat: A German Dream* (New York: Oxford University Press, 2000), 2.

113. The story was recounted in 1948 by Austrian Minister of Trade Ernst Kolb as he warned colleagues about the dangers of xenophobia for the tourist industry. See Bischof, "'Conquering the Foreigner,'" 370.

114. In 1993, 78 percent of Austrians were Roman Catholic. *Austria: Facts and Figures* (Vienna: Federal Press Service, 1993), 10.

115. Suppanz, *Österreichische Geschichtsbilder,* 194–199. Wolfgang Kos also writes of the Austrian tendency to use Prussia as a foil in his foreword to *Inventur 45/55,* ed. Kos and Rigele, 10–11.

116. See, for example, William Montgomery McGovern, *From Luther to Hitler: The History of Fascist-Nazi Political Philosophy* (New York: Houghton Mifflin, 1941).

117. "God greet you! No other greeting/compares to it in sincerity./God greet you!/No other greeting/is fitting for all occasions./God greet you! When this greeting/truly comes

from the heart,/dear God counts this greeting/as much as a prayer." Josef Bitsche, Albert Eberle, and Rudolf Hansen, *Heimat und Vaterland. Lesebuch für die Mittelstufe der Vorarlberger Volksschulen* (Dornbirn: Verlag der Vorarlberger Verlagsanstalt, 1953), 1.

118. Suppanz, *Österreichische Geschichtsbilder*, 72–76.

119. Kotz et al., *Junge Saat. Lesebuch für Tiroler Volksschulen. Band II*, 114–115.

120. Friedrich Korger and Josef Lehrl, eds., *Lesebuch für Mittelschulen. II. Band* (Vienna: Österreichischer Bundesverlag, 1951), 354–355.

121. Friedrich Korger and Josef Lehrl, eds., *Lesebuch für Mittelschulen. I. Band* (Vienna: Österreichischer Bundesverlag, 1947), 87.

122. Heinrich Kotz and Sylvia Del-Pero, *Der Weggenoss. Vierter Band Eines Tiroler Lesewerkes* (Innsbruck and Vienna: Tyrolia Verlag, 1954), 10–11.

123. *Aus da Hoamat. Anhang zum Lesebuch "Mein Heimatland" für die vierte Schulstufe der oberösterreichischen Volksschulen*, 12.

124. "To be workers—we all must./To be workers—we all know,/that from privation and the night, only work/brought the German people into the light,/that only restless production and planning/can win us a future!" Bitsche et al., *Von heut' und ehedem*, 35.

125. "Who does not work, should not eat,/lazy ones take note, do not forget!" Kotz et al., *Tirolerland*, 136.

126. "Every station of the world is good,/if a man loyally does his own,/Be he salesman or carpenter,/blowing horns or sowing seed;/…/whether sailing the seas, tossed by storm,/remember one thing, do not forget it:/Whatever you are, do your duty!" *Mein Heimatland. Lesestoffe für die vierte Schulstufe der österreichischen Volksschulen* (Vienna: Hölder-Pichler-Tempsky, 1947), 47–48.

127. "This is the land that nourishes us,/…/We want nothing in the world,/only sun and dew for our field./We want nothing./…/The land never dies, the consecrated land,/the farmer lives in eternity./The land never dies." Kotz and Del-Pero, *Der Weggenoss*, 106–107.

128. Felix Timmermann, "Bauernleben," excerpted from his "Bauernpsalm," in Anna Harmer et al., *Lesebuch für die Lehranstalten für Frauenberufe 1. Teil* (St. Pölten: Preßverein St. Pölten, 1949), 49.

129. "The best work on earth is,/to sow seeds in the fields,/and the richest joy is,/to cut the full swaths!/Around goes the toss of the sower/and around the reaper's iron./All of life up and down/lies between these circles." Bitsche et al., *Von heut' und ehedem*, 53.

130. "We farmers will not tolerate ridicule/of our Lord and helper God!/What would we be without him?/A marriage without a spouse,/a beehive without a queen,/a tree without fruit and shade." Ibid., 55.

131. "I have a house on the sunny ridge;/there the morning shines through my window./And all around the fields, the pastures are mine;/there the seeds ripen, there blooms for me the wine./I rule, a king, on a secure throne;/my sword is the plow share, a Kremphut the crown." Bitsche et al., *Heimat und Vaterland*, 71.

132. "For example, see two stories by Heinrich Kotz, "Der Zimmermann" and "Der alte Schmiede," in Kotz et al., *Junge Saat. Lesebuch für Tiroler Volksschulen. Band I*, 190–193.

133. Kotz and Del-Pero, *Der Weggenoss*, 107–110.

134. "Bustling by day,/bustling by night,/laboriously we earn/the daily bread/for wife and child/and our *Gesind*. We are the small,/yet it seems to us,/one should hold us in honor,/no one on earth can spare us." *Mein Heimatland* (Vienna: Hölder-Pichler-Tempsky, 1947), 48.

135. "For thirty years I have/worked by this furnace,/I threw metal into the white coals/—and my strength!/I threw the most beautiful years/into its belly;/now it has become useless/—as have I!" Harmer et al., *Lesebuch für die Lehranstalten für Frauenberufe*, 87.

136. Bluhm, *Building an Austrian Nation*, 136.

137. Berg, "Political Culture and State Identity," 161–185.

138. A point overlooked in Jacqueline Vansant's critical analysis "Robert Wise's *The Sound of Music* and the 'Denazification' of Austria in American Cinema," in *From World War to Waldheim*, ed. Good and Wodak, 165–186.

139. See Walter Pohl, "Ostarrîchi Revisited: The 1946 Anniversary, the Millennium, and the Medieval Roots of Austrian Identity," in *Austrian History Yearbook*, vol. 27 (1996): 24.

140. Franz Mathis argues that "recurrent allusions to Austria's long history, regularly made at the various anniversaries and intended to foster Austrian identity, actually hinder it." See Franz Mathis, "1,000 Years of Austria and Austrian Identity: Founding Myths," in *Austrian Historical Memory and National Identity*, ed. Bischof and Pelinka, 23.

141. Franz Heilsberg and Friedrich Korger, *Allgemeine Geschichte der Neuzeit von der Mitte des 19. Jahrhunderts bis zur Gegenwart* (Vienna: Verlag Hölder-Pichler-Tempsky, 1953), 149, 157.

142. *Provisorishce Lehrpläne für die Mittelschulen* (Vienna: Österreichischer Bundesverlag für Unterricht, Wissenschaft und Kunst, 1946), 85–86.

143. Suppanz, *Österreichische Geschichtsbilder*, 33–35.

144. Robert Endres, *Österreichische Staatsbürgerkunde*, 6th rev. ed. (Vienna: Verlag für Jugend und Volk, 1950), 41–42.

145. Walter Jähnl and Franz Stidl, *Das österreichische Gewerbebuch. Band I, Teil 7. Staatsbürgerkunde*, 3rd exp. and rev. ed. (Vienna: Österreichischer Gewerbeverlag, 1954), 32.

146. Friedrich Korger and Josef Lehrl, eds., *Lesebuch für Mittelschulen. IV. Band* (Vienna: 1952), 305–309.

147. Bitsche et al., *Von heut' und ehedem*, 354–357.

148. Ibid., 359–362.

149. Ibid., 357–358.

150. *Viertes Lesebuch. Ausgabe für das Bundesland Kärnten* (Vienna: Hölder-Pichler-Tempsky, 1954), 177–178.

151. "Missing! Missing!/Are you still alive or are you dead?/Tell us, report to us, where you are!/did you die at the hand of a bad enemy,/[are you] living, healthy, red from wounds?/Are you laying on the edge of a forest, freezing with fever?/did our own [soldiers], not recognizing you,/bury you in a mass grave?/.../Are you alive or are you dead?/Won't you give us a sign of yourself?/Let the old clock be still,/knock three times on the door!/You who appeared to your mother,/can you see us suffering helpless?/And how our mother has become sick and gray?/Hear us Lord Jesus Christ!" Kotz et al., *Junge Saat. Lesebuch für Tiroler Volksschulen. Band III*, 620–621.

152. *Viertes Lesebuch. Ausgabe für das Bundesland Steiermark*, 143–144.

153. *Unser Lesebuch. 4. Schulstufe. Heimat Salzburg*, 331–333.

154. Quoted from the appendix in Schausberger, "Die Entstehung des Mythos," 84.

155. According to one survey from 1956, when asked the question "Are you personally of the opinion that we are a sub-group of the German people or a separate Austrian people?" 49 percent of Austrians answered "The Austrians are a people of their own," compared to 46 percent who answered "The Austrians are part of the German people." See Thaler, *The Ambivalence of Identity*, 167. One obvious flaw in such a survey is that many Austrians may have chosen to answer "yes" to both questions if given the opportunity.

156. *Viertes Lesebuch. Ausgabe für das Bundesland Kärnten*, 147–148.

Part II

Major Themes of the Austria-as-Victim Myth, 1955–1986

Chapter Two

REMEMBERING AND FORGETTING THE ANSCHLUSS

Und dann is eh der Hitler kommen…Naja – des war eine Begeis-
terung…ein Jubel, wie man sie sich überhaupt nicht vorstellen kann –
nach diesen furchtbaren Jahren…die traurigen Jahre…Endlich amal hat
der Wiener A Freid g'habt…a Hetz…ma hat was g'segn, net? Des ken-
nen S'Ihna gar net vurstelln…Naja, also, mir san alle…i waaß no…am
Ring und am Heldenplatz g'standen…es war wia bein Heirigern…es
war wia a riesiger Heiriger…! Aber feierlich.

— Der Herr Karl on the Anschluss[1]

Few events have contributed more directly to the Austria-as-victim myth
than the Anschluss, the keystone and first major theme of the victim
myth. The two main reasons for this are the aggressive nature of the
Anschluss and the statement in the Allies' Moscow Declaration of November 1943 that Austria was "the first free country to fall victim to Hitlerite
aggression."[2] However, like any historical event, interpretation of the
Anschluss can be distorted by focusing on select details at the expense of
the larger picture. Such was the case in Austrian schoolbooks from 1955
through the mid 1980s. During this period, texts generally presented the
Anschluss to students in terms only of victimization: the Austrian state was
victimized by German aggression, and Austrian citizens either did not support the Anschluss or supported it only under extenuating circumstances.

The events of February and March 1938 are well known, but have been
interpreted in a variety of ways.[3] The Austrian chancellor, Kurt von Schuschnigg, was summoned to meet Hitler at his Bavarian hideaway in
Berchtesgaden, where he was threatened and forced to accept the Nazi
Arthur Seyss-Inquart into his cabinet. After returning to Austria, Schuschnigg attempted to forestall Hitler's design for domination of Austria
by planning a plebiscite on the future of the Austrian state. Before such a
plebiscite could be carried out, Hitler ordered German troops into Austria
on the evening of 11 March 1938. Under orders from Schuschnigg, the

Austrian army offered no resistance. The first major Austrian city reached by the Germans was Linz, the capital of Upper Austria. Five German divisions reached Linz by noon of 12 March 1938. As the Luftwaffe flew overhead, the Wehrmacht troops were applauded by crowds bearing flowers. The enthusiasm grew when the imminent arrival of Hitler was announced. By the time Hitler arrived to give an address from the Rathaus balcony, a crowd of between sixty and eighty thousand was roaring its approval.[4] Hitler told the assembled Linzers that Providence had given him a mission "to restore my dear homeland to the German Reich. I have believed in this mission, I have lived and fought for it, and I believe I have now fulfilled it."[5] Hitler spent the night of 12 March in Linz, and it was there—likely influenced by his positive reception—that he decided to incorporate Austria directly into the Reich, rather than erect a Nazi puppet government under Seyss-Inquart.[6] By the next evening, Seyss-Inquart presented Hitler with the first article of a newly promulgated law stating: "Austria is a province of the German Reich." The Führer was moved to tears and remarked that "a good political action saves blood." Meanwhile, the Nazis were busy arresting their enemies in Vienna.[7]

Hitler arrived in Vienna on 14 March, where he was met by huge and euphoric crowds; an estimated 250,000 people crowded into the Hero's Square (Heldenplatz) to see and hear the Führer.[8] Vienna's Cardinal Innitzer called on Hitler during his first day in the city and honored him with the Nazi salute.[9] On 10 April a Nazi-sponsored plebiscite was overwhelmingly approved, making official what was already clear: Austria had ceased to exist and was now annexed into the Reich as the *Ostmark*.

There is no question that threatening Austria's chancellor and moving troops into Austria were acts of aggression. However, a more complete story of the Anschluss must address the questions of how Austrians reacted to the Anschluss and how they greeted the German invaders. When these issues are examined, Austria's victim status becomes dubious. Historian Evan Bukey pinpoints many of the key questions surrounding the Anschluss, writing that "there can be no doubt that the initial enthusiasm was both genuine and spontaneous" and that there was insufficient time for the Nazis to "stage manage" events. Bukey also argues that "it is clear that the populace was profoundly relieved" at the avoidance of violence and that there were high hopes "for a dramatic improvement in the material conditions of everyday life...." The most controversial aspect of Bukey's analysis is the idea "that millions of people welcomed the Anschluss as a chance to put an end to the so-called Jewish Question," as evidenced by the fact that the Anschluss pogrom "was perpetrated by the Austrian Nazis and their accomplices, not by the German invaders." Despite the popularity of the Anschluss, Bukey further points out that "no more than a third of the populace could be considered dyed-in-the-wool believers [in Nazism]." Rather, most Austrians were saying a cheerful goodbye to the failed system and greeted "the Anschluss as both a powerful 'agent of change' and the fulfillment of an ancient dream."[10]

Bukey's nuanced analysis raises critical historiographical questions: What is ideological support? How great is the distinction between support for the Anschluss and support for National Socialism? First, it may be useful to measure ideological support in terms of function, or in terms of support for major aspects of National Socialist ideology, such as anti-Semitism. The limitation of such a view is that it casts too wide a net for Nazi support not only in Germany and Austria, but throughout much of Europe. At the same time, anti-Semitism and other fundamental ideological tenets of Nazism, such as hatred of communism and a strong belief in German cultural superiority, were not introduced to Austria by Germans, but had long histories of their own.[11] Second, to what degree can support for Anschluss be defined as support for National Socialism? During the First Republic, the idea of Anschluss had supporters in many different ideological camps. Austrian historian Gerhard Botz has identified six distinct groups of Anschluss supporters: (1) "proletarian-Socialists," who were especially active in 1918 and 1919; (2) "small-scale farmers in the provinces" (bäuerlich-kleinbürgerlich); (3) "bureaucrats and academics" (growing in number after 1925); (4) "the upper middle class," which was oriented toward a tariff union; (5) "lower-middle-class Nazis on a revolutionary path" (e.g., participants in the 1934 failed coup); and (6) "middle-class Nazis on an evolutionary course" toward Anschluss.[12] A number of plebiscites from the early years of the First Republic attest to the lack of belief in Austria as a viable state and the support of Anschluss as the answer to Austria's problems. In April 1921, a plebiscite in Tyrol resulted in a 90 percent vote in favor of Anschluss. A similar vote in Salzburg resulted in a 78 percent pro-Anschluss result, while a plebiscite planned for Styria in 1922 was canceled due to pressure from the Entente powers, which had banned any Anschluss in the peace treaty with Austria.[13]

While Botz's categories are useful in identifying different strands of Anschluss thought, it should be noted that some of the groups held similar beliefs. Further, it should be added that these different Anschluss visions took on a new context after the 1933 Nazi takeover of power in Germany. There could no longer be any doubt that Anschluss did not just mean union with Germany—it meant union with Nazi Germany. In this context, it can be argued that there was at least some affinity between support for the 1938 Anschluss and support for Nazi ideology, though many Austrians may well have naïvely held on to alternative visions of Anschluss. Conversely, to be anti-Anschluss meant to be anti-Nazi, but not necessarily democratic.[14] The already complicated picture becomes even murkier when we consider those who soured on the Anschluss after the fact. There were some who had a change of heart based on a rejection of Nazi ideology, but, as Evan Bukey demonstrates, most Austrians continued to consider themselves Germans, remained loyal to Hitler, and rejected the Austrian patriotism of the Catholic conservatives and Communists.[15] Indeed, the famed revival of pro-Austrian sentiment did not date to the Anschluss, but to the 1943 Nazi defeat in Stalingrad, when fears rose that the Third Reich would lose the war. Many rediscovered Austria, but this renewed sense of Austrianness had more to do with the prospect of defeat and the perception of second-class treatment by Germans than with a rejection of National Socialist ideology.[16]

However, the postwar restoration of Austria demanded a different and much simpler interpretation of the Anschluss. In the official memory of the Nazi era, the absence of Austrian support for the Anschluss was essential to the victim narrative and the legitimacy of the state. When enthusiasm for the Anschluss was discussed, it was explained only in terms of economic misery and Nazi propaganda. Once the question of heartfelt support was dismissed, an individual's support for the Anschluss became superficial and fleeting, merely the product of being temporarily duped by Nazi propaganda and the hope for a full belly. The tendency to ignore or downplay ideological support for the Anschluss became a key ingredient in perpetuating the Austria-as-victim myth in Austrian textbooks' treatment of the Anschluss.[17]

The Anschluss in Textbooks: Austria Forsaken and Invaded

Treatment of the Anschluss in textbooks from 1955 to 1986 is best understood if examined in three parts: the political background to the Anschluss, the reception that German troops and Hitler received in Austria, and the April 1938 plebiscite, which finalized the Anschluss. The first of these elements concerns the coercive meeting between Hitler and Schuschnigg and international reaction, or lack of reaction, to Hitler's designs on Austria. Textbooks typically emphasized the lack of foreign support given to Austria, a view that distorted the record because it ignored the fact that many Austrians were agitating for the Anschluss. While it is true that the Western powers did nothing to stop the takeover, it would have been difficult for them to protest violently against an action so enthusiastically received by so many Austrians. While the Austrian state was a victim of German aggression, it is difficult to view Austria in the same category as Czechoslovakia, which was egregiously sacrificed by the appeasement of the parliamentary powers. But Austrian officials argued vigorously that Austria was indeed in that category as they, quite understandably, sought to avoid reparations payments and hoped for an early end to the occupation. In a visit to the United States late in 1946, Foreign Minister Karl Gruber argued publicly that "Austria was not only the first victim of Hitler, but she was also the first victim of the policy of appeasement."[18]

Austrian schoolbooks represented the official view. Austria was depicted as a country doubly victimized by the Germans and the indifference of the Western powers. A 1962 history text demonstrates the notion of an Austria abandoned by the rest of the world. Anton Ebner and Matthias Partick chronicle Hitler's meeting with Schuschnigg before blaming other countries for failing to come to Austria's rescue: "In this desperate hour, Austria tried in vain to find help from Great Britain, France, or Italy, but none of these powers wanted to guarantee Austria's independence." The authors then quote Schuschnigg's resignation speech, which was broadcast on Austrian radio, but they ignore Schuschnigg's statement that Austria is not ready to spill "German blood," editing his remarks to read "... we yield to violence." Finally, when covering the Anschluss itself, the authors once again note the silence of the world: "On the morning of the twelfth of March German troops marched into Austria. And the world was silent; merely Mexico protested against the occupation of Austria."[19] The emphasis on the lack of foreign support shifts the focus away from any discussion of Austrian support for the Anschluss. It is also significant that the authors avoid Schuschnigg's statement about not spilling "German blood." On the one hand, the radio address was valuable to the victim myth as Schuschnigg concluded his speech by saying "Gott schütze Österreich" (God Protect Austria), but on the other hand, Schuschnigg's statement about "German blood" was antithetical to the postwar vision of Austrian identity.[20] A similar interpretation is presented in a book from 1973: "Because Schuschnigg could find help neither with the Western powers nor with [Austria's] neighbors, he resigned on the evening of 11 March 1938 to avoid bloody confrontations."[21] Another text combines these specific elements into an account in which Austria avoided a war with Germany due to the failure of Western aid: "In a radio address, he [Schuschnigg] called on the army and [all] Austrians to avoid bloodshed.... [After the invasion] Austria ceased to exist. The Western powers accepted the fact with an empty and completely useless protest." At the bottom of the page, students are given a question for discussion: "Why didn't the Western powers help to preserve the independence of Austria?"[22]

It is clear that the authors view the demise of Austria in terms of Allied appeasement to German aggression, and as a result, they portray Austria as a victim and only a victim. Also noteworthy is the portrayal of Schuschnigg, who is cast as defiant, heroic, and left in the lurch by appeasement. Yet Schuschnigg never did ask the Western powers for direct aid, as he explains in his 1969 memoir *Im Kampf gegen Hitler*, published in English in 1971 as *The Brutal Takeover*: "It is true that we asked for assistance or advice *neither from London nor from Paris* [emphasis added].... Could we have done anything else if we did not wish to make it easy for Hitler to accuse Austria of breach of the agreement [made at Berchtesgaden] from the outset?" Schuschnigg then asserts that Austria's precarious position in 1938 would be best understood in the context of larger European security issues, writing that "[t]he European order of 1938 stood or fell by the concept of collective security."[23] Despite the publication of Schuschnigg's version of events, textbook authors clung to a view that emphasized Austria's abandonment and victim status. A text from 1972 puts the Anschluss in the context of appeasement and implies that Austria's fate was in the category of Czechoslovakia's: "[After the Anschluss t]he little state in the heart of Europe had ceased to exist. The first aggression of Hitler went by unpunished. That this victim would not be the last was predictable."[24] The authors' choice of diminutive vocabulary ("little" Austria) further emphasizes Austria's victim status. The idea that a helpless Austria had been abandoned by the Western powers and the world had long-lasting resonance. For example, a text from 1981 reads: "In this critical situation, Schuschnigg turned to all Austrians. He called for a plebiscite. Hitler used this intention as a pretext to attack. A call for help from the Austrian government remained without echo."[25] As late as 1988, students read: "Finally on 11 March 1938 Schuschnigg resigned ... after it was shown that no support from the Western powers was expected. On the following night, German troops marched into Austria. Austria ceased to exist as a sovereign state."[26]

Another important element of the mythology of the Anschluss is the German military invasion. The Wehrmacht's arrival onto Austrian soil presents a strong case for Austria's victim status, but also contains the seeds to negate this view. Foreign troops marching into Austria obviously constitutes an act of aggression, but the bellicose nature of the military operation comes into question when one considers the positive reception given to German troops. Enormous, cheering masses greeted the Germans as they arrived, and Hitler was met by wildly enthusiastic crowds. Meanwhile, the Nazis rounded up political enemies, and Austrian Jews were immediately subject to persecution. Indeed, much of the violence associated with the Anschluss was carried out against Jews by Austrian Nazis and other ordinary anti-Semites. Vienna, especially, saw a violent pogrom against Jews.[27] But these well-known events—which would have undermined Austria's victim status—were mostly ignored in Austrian schoolbooks until the mid 1980s.

A 1955 government publication for grade school children to commemorate ten years of the Second Republic simply skips the Anschluss and puts it and World War II in the context of a long-term view of Austrian history: "Foreign warriors came into the country often and ravaged it. Many people died of a horrible disease, the plague. Yet the Austrians never gave in. Master builders built churches and palaces. Poets, painters and musicians accomplished great works of art. Inventors and scholars made life more pleasant and beautiful. In the year 1939 another war began. It lasted six years. Back then, many Austrians had to die in foreign countries, many even in the homeland."[28] While grade school children could hardly be expected to confront the enormous problems of Austria's immediate past, this passage instilled a view that placed Austria in the position of victim, not only during World War II, but also throughout its history. "Foreign warriors" often "ravaged" Austria, but Austria always persevered. Another 1955 commemorative publication addresses the Anschluss specifically, but does not even mention the Germans, let alone Austrian support for the annexation and National Socialism: "In March 1938 Austria was occupied. Her name disappeared from the map and was not allowed to be spoken. Many Austrians were persecuted, thrown in jail, even murdered, because of their religion, because of their belief in Austria, [and] because of their love of freedom."[29]

This passage demonstrates a pattern evident throughout the late 1950s and the early 1960s in which Anschluss coverage was brief and simple. Heavy use of the passive voice, too, served to disperse responsibility for supporting the Anschluss. Austria "was occupied" and Austrians "were persecuted," but the perpetrators, many of whom were Austrians, have disappeared into the ether provided by the passive construction. In many cases, there was no need to explain Austrian support for the Anschluss because it was not mentioned in the first place. In a 1957 text, for example, students read that "heavily armed German soldiers, accompanied by tanks and aircraft, crossed Austria's borders. Therewith our Fatherland lost its freedom and independence."[30] In a 1961 text, students read: "Hitler occupied Austria with violence and progressively subjugated one country after another ... by exploiting people's desire for peace."[31] A reading book from 1956 portrays Austria as a victim of not only the Germans, but also the Allies. In the passage "Zwischen den großen Kriegen," Alois Schmied-bauer suggests that the Anschluss and the Allied occupation were both unjust ordeals experienced by Austria: "[With the Anschluss] Austria ceased to exist as its own state," and "chained to the history of Germany," Austrians were "ensnared" into the war. From the ruins of war, Austria "rose again, impoverished and destroyed, occupied for ten years by four Great Powers."[32]

The Anschluss and Austria's Redemption

As the Second Republic went into its second decade of existence, the Anschluss was an issue that could not go unexplained. By the mid 1960s, schoolbooks no longer ignored the Anschluss, but sought instead to draw a lesson of redemption from it. One important theme was the idea that Austrian consciousness was born out of the Anschluss; only after Austria disappeared as a state did Austrians appreciate what they had lost. This is the message of a 1965 publication in memory of Adolf Schärf, one of the founders of the Second Republic: "On 12 March, German troops are already in Vienna, [and] Dr. Schärf is brought from his apartment to jail.... And yet in these days a miracle happens. Austria, which disappeared from the map, begins to live in the heart. There, where it was dead so long."[33]

The idea of the Austrian change of heart has validity, but the timing of this shift as described in this passage is misleading. There is some truth to the idea that Austrians appreciated their independence only when faced with their unequal partnership with Germany, but this sentiment first gained momentum after Germany began to lose the war, not a few days after the Anschluss.[34] Another commemorative publication from 1966 is particularly revealing of coalition history. The lesson of the Anschluss is put in vague terms of the need for Austrians to cooperate with one another, while explanations about the causes and consequences of the Anschluss are conspicuously absent. Indeed, students are specifically told *not* to confront the past:

> Because the good Austrians among the workers, the farmers, and the middle class did not talk to each other and did not stick together, it just happened. One day it was over with Austria, and there was no more "Grüß Gott" and "Guten Tag," but only "Heil Hitler." ... Your parents and grandparents do not like to talk about these years, you know why. Back then, many Austrians forgot that the state is worth more than the party, and that, in hard times especially, one must love his fatherland from the heart. You may not condemn them for this, though. While they lost the fatherland, they also won it back for you.[35]

In other words, students should put the past behind them and not condemn their parents.

Another method of teaching about the Anschluss was to learn the positive lesson of resistance to the Anschluss. A reading book from 1965, *Wir Schweigen Nicht* (We Will Not Be Silent), is remarkable in that the entire book is devoted to themes such as the Anschluss, the war, and resistance. In a story by Friedrich Funder, "Als Österreich den Sturm Bestand" (When Austria Withstood the Storm), students read an account of the Anschluss that includes a strong dose of coalition history: "[Despite the Anschluss] I felt comfort from many voices, which gave witness to the loyalty ... that people of the most varied backgrounds ... [had to] Austria.... [Later, many in the group were captured and sent to Dachau.] In Dachau, an Austrian community of a special kind soon formed. [There, they rejected their *Lager* for the belief that:] Austria is our political affiliation [In unserem Lager ist Österreich]!"[36]

The legend that Austrian political leaders learned the lesson of cooperation in the concentration camps was also propagated in a 1973 reading book in a story by Rudolf Kalmar titled "Als Österreich seine Freiheit verlor." After describing the difficult transport to Dachau, the narrator recounts:

> Now we stood in the square, tired, hungry, and mocked in striped uniforms, and felt for the first time the entire staggering ridiculousness of our outward appearance. Ministers and state secretaries next to Austrian workers, high military [officers] and bureaucrats of the administration next to young Communists, men of all world views, all professions and classes.... In the following years of indescribable suffering, we put everything divisive aside and sought out the true source of unity: humanity—whether we were poor or rich, great names or unknown people, had this or that profession, were Catholics or atheists, middle class or Socialists, revolutionaries or conservatives, Austrians or Germans, Dutch or French, Italians or Belgians, Luxemburgers or Greeks. We stuck together, although we knew that doing so could cost each one his head.[37]

Again, the coalition lesson was hammered home through the symbol of the concentration camp, but the absence of Jews in this and other concentration camp stories is significant. In this and other schoolbooks, the concentration camp is not a symbol of Jewish persecution; rather, it is a symbol of Austrian defiance and patriotism. The concentration camp was where Austrians finally put aside their class differences. This point was made clear in a speech delivered by H. Heidinger, a member of the Styrian Landtag, at a 1968 school celebration to commemorate fifty years of the Austrian republic. Heidinger chronicles the bitter feuds of the First Republic and then remarks that the differences were finally overcome through the "common suffering in concentration camps" and the need to free Austria from the Allied occupation.[38] It is a powerful idea, but in the creation of this legend, Austrian Jews were often left out.[39] The most important lesson taught through the symbol of the concentration camp was the political lesson of cooperation—in other words, the coalition lesson.[40]

Even more common than the coalition lesson represented in the passages above was the emphasis on resistance to the Anschluss that negated or minimized Austrian support for the Anschluss, which was usually never discussed in the first place. Textbooks typically cited Gestapo arrests of Austrian patriots and the immediate formation of resistance groups. For example, in 1967 students read: "Tens of thousands of upstanding Austrians were taken to prison or concentration camps. Despite the danger, groups formed again and again, which fought against the principles of National Socialism and carried out resistance against the oppression of the population."[41] A work edited by Franz Heilsberg and Friedrich Korger was the only contemporary history textbook approved in the period between 1945 and 1955 (as mentioned above). It is not surprising that this work continued to emphasize the elements of the victim myth, but it is worth noting that it remained in use, largely in its original form, through a fifth edition in 1969. The customary mention of the world's indifference to the Anschluss is accompanied by the usual silence on Austrian support for the Anschluss.[42] After describing the German occupation, the text immediately identifies Austria and Austrians as victims. Hitler is also decried as a hypocrite for giving Mussolini a free hand to Italianize the South Tyrol (Alto Adige) with its large population of German speakers. After covering the woes of the South Tyroleans, the authors provide a one-sided account of Austria immediately after the Anschluss: "Many people well known for their pro-Austrian convictions were sent to concentration camps [and the Nazis plundered Austrian economic resources]..... The forced transfer of assets (seizure of foreign property, or 'aryanization') created the [postwar] 'German property' problem in Austria. For years, this was an almost impossible to solve problem with the State Treaty negotiations."[43] Besides neglecting to link aryanization which Jewish persecution, this passage also encapsulates another aspect of the victim myth by alluding to Soviet seizures of property after the war.[44]

In textbooks of the 1970s and later, Austrian support for the Anschluss was no longer ignored, though it continued to be discounted in both overt and subtle ways. Anschluss supporters were identified as minority Nazis or desperate and unemployed people. In particular, the authors underplayed Austrian support for the Anschluss by immediately discussing resistance groups, whose actual numbers were minuscule compared to Anschluss supporters. For example, in a 1972 text, students read: "The end of Austria's independence filled the National Socialists as well as the many unemployed with joy.... A flood of propaganda leaflets and reports strengthened these expectations even more and distracted the population from the goals of National Socialism.... Already on 12 March 1938 the arrests of leading former politicians of all political camps began. Meanwhile, resistance groups of all political affiliations formed."[45] This passage especially reflects the coalition lesson that resistance to Nazism was carried out equally by all ideological groups. A text from 1973 also mentions support for the Anschluss, but casts it in purely economic terms:

> In the year 1938 a part of the population cheered the Germans who were marching in, because they hoped for a rapid improvement of the economic circumstances. But many upstanding Austrians stood quietly aside in deep sadness over the downfall of the republic. The leaders of the "Fatherland Front" and their organizations, but also many Social Democrats and Communists, were sent to concentration camps, the horror of which was deliberately kept secret from the general population.... A bitter disappointment was Hitler's "solution" of the South Tyrol question. In a treaty with Mussolini, the resettlement of German-speaking South Tyroleans to German territory was agreed upon.[46]

This version of events represents a conservative mythology in several ways. First, ideological support for National Socialism is absent, as support for the Anschluss is explained only in terms of hope for economic improvement. Second, the *Ständestaat*'s Fatherland Front is placed in a prominent resistance role (a problematic categorization), along with Socialists and Communists. Third, the general population is exonerated from knowing about any activities in concentration camps. Finally, the South Tyroleans are portrayed as a people betrayed by Hitler.

Another text from 1975 again emphasizes economic misery as the main cause for support for the Anschluss. After reading an account of the economic problems of the First Republic, students read: "One may not wonder then why so many looked to the neighboring industrial state for rescue." Later, when the Anschluss is discussed, the economic reason is again mentioned along with an immediate reference to resistance groups: "Many Austrians cheered the troops marching in on those days—be it because they hoped for betterment of economic circumstances, [or] be it that they believed in a secure future in the domain of a great, militarily powerful empire. Yet many other Austrians stood quietly aside in deep sadness about the downfall of the republic.... [In] March, 90,000 Austrians, or 4 percent of the adult male population [from all political backgrounds] were arrested."[47] In this case, the authors presented the coalition lesson with a detailed list of those victimized by the Anschluss, a list from which Jews are conspicuously absent. Most textbooks did cover the Holocaust and

Nazi policy toward Jews, but it is significant that the violence against Jews that accompanied the Anschluss is rarely mentioned in textbooks. The victim category was reserved for Austrians who were persecuted for political reasons. Many of those arrested at the time of the Anschluss were also Jewish, but this fact is never emphasized. For example in a 1976 text, students read: "[O]n 12 March 1938, German troops marched into Austria. Austria had found a violent end as an independent state and republic [*sic*].... Soon the Gestapo squads were underway, and in Vienna alone they arrested thousands of ... political opponents with Schuschnigg at the top. They all disappeared behind the walls of jails or in concentration camps.... A quiet fight against the National Socialist intruders began."[48] Again, the victims of the Gestapo round-up are Austrian political leaders, while Jewish persecution in connection with the Anschluss is not mentioned. It is also noteworthy that the large number of arrests made at the time did not have the long-term impact that the high numbers cited by the textbooks would suggest. The majority of those Austrians initially arrested were released within a few weeks or months.[49] Finally, the passage above introduces a fiction. The authors assert that the Anschluss brought an end to the Austrian First Republic, which is inaccurate, since the First Republic ended in 1934, when the *Ständestaat* was created.

As late as the early 1980s, little had changed in the textbooks' presentation of popular support for the Anschluss. Jews were still ignored, Austrians were still the primary victims of the Anschluss, and authors cited hope for economic improvement as the primary reason for Anschluss support. A text from 1982 emphasizes all of these themes, stating that many cheered the Anschluss, including "Austrian National Socialists, but also ... people who simply hoped for improvement of the bad economic situation and an end to unemployment. After all, Hitler's propaganda did not skimp on promises!" In the meantime, the Gestapo arrested many "leading personalities and functionaries of the Christian Social Party, of the Social Democrats, and of the Communists."[50] The issue of agency also played a subtle role in textbook portrayals of the Anschluss. Typically, supporters of the Anschluss were presented as being interested only in economic improvement and as people who were not in charge of their own destiny. For example, in a 1985 text, students read: "Thousands of *curious* Austrians lined the streets. Many greeted the marching [troops] happily with calls of '*Hoch*' and '*Heil*.' Thousands of Austrians, who were suspected by the Nazi regime, were arrested in the same hour" (emphasis added).[51]

In summary, between 1955 and 1986, students were presented with a view of the Anschluss in which popular support for union with Germany was either qualified or not mentioned at all. This made sense in that the myth of Austrian victimization would have been severely undermined by a view of the Anschluss wherein a majority of Austrians had been in favor of union with Nazi Germany. The contention that Austrians were either against the Anschluss or merely curious onlookers preserved the victim status that had become key to legitimizing the Second Republic.

The April 1938 Plebiscite

The plebiscite held on 10 April 1938 resulted in overwhelming approval for the Anschluss, with over 99 percent voting in favor of union with Nazi Germany. While the Nazi-sponsored plebiscite was hardly democratic, the results cannot be dismissed. As Evan Bukey writes: "The available evidence suggests that a substantial majority of the populace welcomed the opportunity to participate in the electoral process to resolve the question of national identity and to exercise the right to vote denied for over half a decade."[52] Furthermore, the Nazis also received public endorsements on the plebiscite from the Socialist leader Karl Renner and Vienna's Cardinal Innitzer. As Anton Pelinka points out, Renner's approval of the plebiscite and his subsequent support for the annexation of the Czech Sudetenland into the Reich in the fall of 1938 were embarrassing incidents in the life of this giant Austrian political figure. These episodes were ignored both in Austrian textbooks and by Renner's biographers.[53] Textbooks likewise ignored or minimized popular support for the plebiscite.

By far, the most common interpretation embraced by textbook authors was to emphasize Nazi propaganda as the sole reason for the plebiscite's success. For example, a 1962 supplementary text (*Lehrbehelf*) in contemporary history explains the overwhelming vote in favor of the plebiscite as the result of "a flood of propaganda slogans" and hope for economic improvement.[54] A text from 1968 also emphasizes these themes: "With the help of controlled propaganda and political pressure, a majority of over 99 percent in the Anschluss plebiscite of 10 April 1938 was achieved. Yet soon after, a deep disappointment took hold, even among Austrian National Socialists, as all of the leading positions were occupied by Reich Germans."[55] This passage strips all agency from the voters, while revealing disappointment with the Nazi regime based not on ideological opposition, but on anger over favoritism toward Germans. A 1968 publication to celebrate fifty years of the Austrian republic embodied many themes of the Anschluss myth, including a failure to mention Austrian support for the union an emphasis on the indifference of the Western powers to the Anschluss. The authors also attributed the 99 percent "yes" vote for the April plebiscite to Nazi propaganda, but in quoting a report from the Tyrolean Gestapo, the authors inadvertently undermined their case: "[Of those who supported the plebiscite] only 15 percent were 'true fighters and absolutely reliable National Socialists,' 30 percent were 'National Socialist in name,' while another 10 to 20 percent were 'casual supporters,' who felt an affinity to certain parts of the party program. These figures are compared to the 30 to 40 percent who opposed the movement because of Marxist or clerical beliefs."[56] While the authors clearly meant to demonstrate minimal support for the Nazis, the numbers they cite suggest that at least 55 percent of Tyroleans supported part of the Nazi program. The authors succeed in undermining the validity of the plebiscite, but they also affirm Austrian support for Nazism. But what is most interesting about this publication is its title, *50 Jahre Republik Österreich*. By declaring the Austrian republic to be fifty years old in 1968, the authors glossed over the *Ständestaat* and the Nazi years, suggesting a continuity from the First Republic to the Second Republic. This dubious fiftieth anniversary of the Austrian Republic was touted by the Austrian government in several publications, and numerous schools had special celebrations of the fiftieth anniversary. In Linz, for example, one school organized an exhibition titled "'50 Jahre Republik' in Bild, Dokument und Plakat" ("50 Years Republic" in Pictures, Documents and Posters).[57]

Textbooks for the newly introduced polytechnic schools (a result of the 1962 school reform) were particularly woeful due to their lack of basic information. In a 1974 text, the authors cover the events of the Anschluss with a list of events that concludes with a nearly complete dismissal of the importance of the plebiscite. Under the heading "The downfall of Austria," students read: "10 April 1938: plebiscite on the Anschluss with Germany, not secret, therefore 99 percent yes-vote."[58] A 1982 text for polytechnic schools also covers the Anschluss with a list of key events and concludes with a question for discussion: "10 April 1938: 'plebiscite' on the incorporation of Austria into the German Reich—99.9 percent yes. Compare this result with similar decisions in other totalitarian regimes—draw parallels."[59] Here, students were introduced to totalitarian theory in its most simplistic form. A 1985 text for polytechnic schools eschews the list form of expression, but also dismisses any significance of the plebiscite: "[T]here was no real secrecy [of the voting, and] therefore also a result of 99 percent yes-votes for the already completed Anschluss with the Greater German Reich."[60]

The coalition lesson was also linked to accounts of the plebiscite. In a 1978 reading book, students read a story by Karl Bruckner, "Heute, am 10. April 1938," about a Socialist family's experience with the plebiscite. While the Germans are "stormily greeted by fanatical worshipers of their god-like leader," the family remains defiant: "But to that majority of Austrians—who despite long years of economic privation did not allow themselves to be deceived by the political oppression, the propaganda of the Nazis, and their lofty promises—we three also belong: father, mother and I, who, after years of unemployment, emigrated to Brazil, and then, drawn by homesickness, returned home only a few weeks ago." After being terrified at the polling place, the family members have no choice but to vote "yes" in the plebiscite. Later, in their apartment, a neighbor knocks on the door: "[It was] Mr. Friedl from the second floor. A retired state bureaucrat. He and his wife are devout Christian Socials, tolerant people, who reject violence and party hatred and seek understanding with those who think differently on political matters. Mr. Friedl explains, whispering: 'Have you heard yet—in the polling place a man who voted "no" has been beaten. You all be careful!'"[61] This story introduced students to several familiar themes. First, in claiming that the family being portrayed was part of a majority of Austrians who rejected Nazism outright, the author introduces what is at best a half-truth. Based on outright political support for the NSDAP in Austria, the author is accurate in his claim that a majority of Austrians did not support Nazism. But this view comes into question when measured in terms of support for the Anschluss. Even more significant in this passage is the coalition lesson reflected in the relationship between families in the apartment building. The idea of the Socialist family getting along so well with the tolerant Christian Socials could have been an anecdotal reality, though it certainly was not typical of Austrian political attitudes. Cordial to one another and full of mutual respect, the common ordeal of facing the Nazis and their undemocratic plebiscite brings the families closer together. By introducing the two families from different political camps, the story creates a retroactive consensus on Austria. The roots of the postwar coalition and the rejection of Nazism are portrayed as inherent to Austria at precisely that time when Austria was disappearing.

The most damaging rebuttal to the idea that there was no real support for the plebiscite are the public endorsements of Cardinal Innitzer and the Socialist leader Karl Renner. In the texts of the 1950s and 1960s, authors ignored their endorsement of the Anschluss. By the late 1970s, textbook authors began to address the issue. But in a familiar fashion, the support of these prominent men was again attributed to the influence of Nazi propaganda: "The National Socialist propaganda worked so cleverly that it even succeeded in convincing the Austrian bishops' conference, with Cardinal Innitzer at the head, of the advantages of the Anschluss and prompted them to make a corresponding election appeal. Even Dr. Renner, who the National Socialists did not arrest in order to win over the Social Democrats, declared on 3 April that he would approve the Anschluss."[62] While mentioning the approval of the bishops and Karl Renner was, in one sense, a departure from mythological accounts of the plebiscite, the approval of these representatives of socialism and conservatism is attributed solely to the cleverness of Nazi propaganda. A 1979 text also mentions the approval of the bishops and Karl Renner, but only in an exceptionally vague manner: "Differing reasons caused the Church leadership as well as the Social Democrat Dr. Renner to publicly declare that would vote yes [on the plebiscite]."[63]

The pattern of dismissing support for the plebiscite as the result of propaganda continued into the early 1980s. A text from 1983 provided students with a more detailed account of the Nazi propaganda machine than earlier texts, explaining that before the plebiscite, "food was given out to families, and over 20,000 children had the opportunity to travel to Germany for vacation, where Austrian workers were also shown the economic advances made by the National Socialist government." When it came to the Church and Renner, students read that each acted pragmatically, as the bishops wished "to secure the position of the Church" and Renner "hoped to save jailed Social Democrats...." In the end, the plebiscite passed with "a nearly unanimous result" because of "clever propaganda" and "fear, which had grasped a part of the Austrian population after tens of thousands of arrests and arbitrary firings, above all, in public service."[64] This text begins to move away from mythology by offering some concrete reasons why Austrians supported the plebiscite. The influence of Nazi propaganda and the fear generated by the Gestapo are certainly important factors, but the authors continue to neglect the other side of the coin. One reason why Nazi propaganda was so successful in the first place is because it was often heard by willing ears.[65]

There was real and genuine support for the Anschluss in March 1938, and there was real support for the plebiscite of April 1938. These facts were antithetical to the Austria-as-victim myth and were not included in Austrian history or reading textbooks between 1955 and 1986. Because the Anschluss was the keystone to the overall myth, it was particularly important to portray Austrians as victims of the Anschluss rather than willing and active participants in Austria's demise. The Anschluss myth also served to differentiate Austrians from Germans and contributed to a unique sense of Austrian identity and purpose. The Anschluss became the symbol of the time when the *Lager* of right and left came together and staked out a common vision for Austria. But while the myths surrounding the Anschluss legitimized the Second Republic and laid the groundwork for the postwar coalition, many legitimate victims were forgotten.

Notes

1. "[In Viennese dialect] Now that was a surprise…a celebration that you can't even imagine—after these terrible years…the sad years…finally a Viennese had some happiness …a hot time…we really saw something, you understand? You can't even imagine it… yeah, all of us…I still remember…standing on the Ring and the Heldenplatz…It was like going to the Heuriger [wine taverns]…it was a huge Heuriger…! Really festive." See Merz and Qualtinger, *Der Herr Karl*, 18–19.
2. However, in a part of the declaration that the Austrian government often ignored, Allied statesmen also wrote: "Austria is reminded, however, that she has a responsibility for participation in the war on the side of Hitlerite Germany, and that in the final settlement account will inevitably be taken of her contribution to her liberation." Keyserlingk, *Austria in World War II*, 152. See chapter 4 for further discussion of the Moscow Declaration.
3. The definitive military history on the Anschluss is Erwin A. Schmidl, *Der "Anschluß" Österreichs. Der Deutsche Einmarsch im März 1938* (Bonn: Bernard & Graefe, 1994). Also see Alfred D. Low, *The Anschluss Movement, 1931–1938, and the Great Powers* (New York: Columbia University Press, 1985); Gerhard Botz, *Wien, vom "Anschluß" zum Krieg. Nationalsozialistische Machtübernahme und politisch-soziale Umgestaltung am Beispiel der Stadt Wien, 1938/39* (Vienna: Jugend und Volk, 1978); and Radomir Luza, *Austro-German Relations in the Anschluss Era* (Princeton: Princeton University Press, 1975). For good short accounts of the Anschluss in English, see the Hitler biographies by Ian Kershaw, *Hitler, 1936–1945: Nemesis* (New York: W.W. Norton, 2000), 63–86; Alan Bullock, *Hitler: A Study in Tyranny* (New York: HarperTorchbooks, 1964), 411–439; and also Joachim Fest, *Hitler*, trans. Richard and Clara Winston (New York: Penguin, 1974), 807–820. Also

see Kurt Schuschnigg, *My Austria* (New York: Alfred A. Knopf, 1938), and his later memoirs, idem, *Austrian Requiem* (New York: G.P. Putnam's Sons, 1946), and idem, *The Brutal Takeover: The Austrian Ex-Chancellor's Account of the Anschluss of Austria by Hitler* (New York: Athenaeum, 1971).

4. Evan Bukey, *Hitler's Hometown: Linz, Austria 1908–1945* (Bloomington: Indiana University Press, 1986), 163.

5. Quoted in Bullock, *Hitler*, 433.

6. Ibid., 433. Also see Keyserlingk, *Austria in World War II*, 48.

7. Bullock, *Hitler*, 433–434.

8. Judith Miller, *One, by One, by One: Facing the Holocaust* (New York: Touchstone Books, 1990), 61.

9. Paul Hoffman, *The Viennese: Splendor, Twilight, and Exile* (New York: Anchor Books, 1988), 237. Innitzer also publicly endorsed the April plebiscite for union with Germany.

10. Evan Bukey, *Hitler's Austria: Popular Sentiment in the Nazi Era, 1938–1945* (Chapel Hill: University of North Carolina Press, 2000), 33–34.

11. Anti-Semitism, for example, was an important part of Austrian political life during the First Republic. In March 1921, some sixty-two Austrian organizations and clubs encompassing approximately four hundred thousand members participated in an international anti-Semitism conference in Vienna. See Albert Lichtblau, "Antisemitismus— Rahmenbedingungen und Wirkungen auf das Zusammenleben von Juden und Nichtjuden," in *Handbuch des politischen Systems Österreichs. Erste Republik, 1918–1933*, ed. Tálos et al., 454–471. Also see Andrew Gladding Whiteside, *Austrian National Socialism Before 1918* (The Hague: Martinus Nijhoff, 1962); Bruce Pauley, *From Prejudice to Persecution: A History of Austrian Anti-Semitism* (Chapel Hill: University of North Carolina Press, 1992); and Pauley, *Hitler and the Forgotten Nazis*.

12. Gerhard Botz, *Der 13. März 38 und die Anschluss-Bewegung. Selbstaufgabe, Okkupation und Selbstfindung Österreichs 1918–1945* (Vienna: Dr. Karl Renner Institute, 1978), 9.

13. Ibid., 10. Also see Alfred D. Low, *The Anschluss Movement, 1918–1919, and the Paris Peace Conference* (Philadelphia: American Philosophical Society, 1974).

14. The crux of the postwar debate about the collapse of the First Republic directly relates to this issue. Conservatives have traditionally viewed the *Ständestaat* as a defensive anti-Nazi dictatorship, while Socialists have viewed the *Ständestaat* as a fascist government, which ultimately aided the Nazi seizure of power by eliminating the Socialists from political life and snuffing out democracy in Austria. This partisan view of history is now being re-examined. See the contributions in Günter Bischof, Anton Pelinka, and Alexander Lassner, eds., *The Dollfuss/Schuschnigg Era in Austria: A Reassessment* (New Brunswick: Transaction Publishers, 2003).

15. Bukey, *Hitler's Austria*, 43–152, *passim*.

16. Ibid., 192–193.

17. In the late 1980s, Evan Bukey criticized Austrian historians for neglecting to examine popular support for the *Anschluss* and Nazism, arguing that "[w]ithin the Alpine republic, historians have long acknowledged the mass enthusiasm that welcomed the Anschluss, but by emphasizing the domination of Austrian society by Reich German officials and by publishing evidence of widespread suffering, discontent, and even resistance to the Hitler regime, they have generally evaded the problem of political consent, unwittingly contributing their own share to the collective amnesia." Evan Bukey, "Popular Opinion in Vienna after the Anschluss," in *Conquering the Past*, ed. Parkinson, 151.

18. Bischof, *Austria in the First Cold War*, 66–67.

19. Anton Ebner and Matthias Partick, *Lehrbuch der Geschichte für die 4. Klasse der Hauptschulen und Mittelschulen* (Salzburg: Salzburger Jugend-Verlag, 1962), 125. The same wording also appeared in Anton Ebner and Matthias Partick, *Lehrbuch der Geschichte und Sozialkunde. Band IV für die 4. Klasse der Hauptschulen* (Salzburg: Salzburger Jugend-Verlag, 1967), 132; as well as Anton Ebner, Matthias Partick, and Georg Stadler, *Lehrbuch der Geschichte und Sozialkunde. Vom Wiener Kongreß bis zur Gegenwart*.

Band III für die 4. Klasse der allgemeinbildenden höheren Schulen (Salzburg: Otto Müller Verlag, 1968), 139–140.

20. Hanns Haas points out that Hitler ordered troops to move into Austria only after Schuschnigg announced that Austria would not fight. See Hanns Haas, "Der Anschluss," in *NS-Herrschaft in Österreich*, ed. Tálos et al., 15–16.

21. Franz Göbhart and Erwin Chvojka, *Geschichte und Sozialkunde. Vom Ersten Weltkrieg bis zur Gegenwart. Lern- und Arbeitsbuch* (Vienna: Verlag Carl Ueberreuter, 1973), 125. The same wording appears in the 1981 edition of the same book.

22. Roderich Gey, *Durch die Vergangenheit zur Gegenwart. Ein Lehr- und Arbeitsbuch für Geschichte und Sozialkunde für die 8. Klasse der allgemeinbildenden höheren Schulen* (Vienna: Österreichischer Agrarverlag, 1974), 73–74. The same passages appear in the 1987 second revised edition of this work. See pages 66–67.

23. Schuschnigg, *The Brutal Takeover*, 245–247.

24. Franz Berger and Norbert Schausberger, *Zeiten, Völker und Kulturen. Lehrbuch der Geschichte und Sozialkunde für die Oberstufe der allgemeinbildenden höheren Schulen. Band für die 8. Klasse. Geschichte des 20. Jahrhunderts* (Vienna: Österreichischer Bundesverlag, 1972), 97–98. This text remained unchanged through the second edition in 1977.

25. Josef Scheipl et al., *Geschichte und Sozialkunde 4. Arbeitsbuch für die 4. Klasse der Hauptschulen* (Vienna: Ferdinand Hirt and Carl Ueberreuter, 1981), 95.

26. Walter Aspering et al., *Gestaltete Welt 3. Von der Neuzeit zur Gegenwart. Ein Lehr- und Arbeitsbuch für Geschichte und Sozialkunde* (Vienna: Ed. Hölzel, 1988), 139.

27. See Hans Witek and Hans Safrian, *Und keiner war dabei. Dokumente des alltäglichen Antisemitismus in Wien 1938* (Vienna: Picus Verlag, 1988) and Bukey, *Hitler's Austria*, 131–152.

28. Arbeitsgemeinschaft, eds., *Unser Österreich, 1945–1955* (Vienna: Österreichischer Bundesverlag, 1955), 3.

29. Othmar Franz Lang and R. Ritter, *Unser Österreich, 1945–1955* (Vienna: Österreichischer Bundesverlag, 1955), 10.

30. Franz Berger et al., *Zeiten, Völker und Kulturen. Ein Lehr- und Arbeitsbuch für den Geschichtsunterricht an Haupt- und Untermittelschulen. 4. Band. Das Zeitalter der Weltpolitik und der Technik* (Vienna: Hölder-Pichler-Tempsky, 1957), 172.

31. A. Klein and Heinz Weber, *Einst und Jetzt. Bilder aus der Geschichte. 1. Teil* (Graz: Stiasny Verlag, 1961), 19.

32. Lehrerarbeitsgemeinschaft beim Landesschulrat Salzburg, eds., *Unser Lesebuch, 6.–8. Schulstufe. Heimat und Welt* (Salzburg: Otto Müller Verlag, 1956), 431–432.

33. Othmar Franz Lang, *Das war Bundespräsident Dr. Adolf Schärf* (Vienna: Österreichischer Bundesverlag, 1965), 40.

34. Bukey, *Hitler's Austria*, 192–193.

35. Klemens Zens, *Schaut Ringsumher. Zum Österreichischen Nationalfeiertag* (Vienna: Österreichischer Bundesverlag, 1966), 21–22.

36. Wilhelm Gross and Hermann Lein, eds., *Wir Schweigen Nicht. Dokumentarische und literarische Aussagen zur Zeitgeschichte* (Vienna: Österreichischer Bundesverlag, 1965), 181–186.

37. Hans Hörler and Hans Müller, eds., *Die Weltenuhr. Ein Lesebuch für Schule und Haus* (Vienna: Österreichischer Bundesverlag für Unterricht, Wissenschaft und Kunst, 1973), 97–100.

38. *Jahresbericht Bundesgymnasium und Bundesrealgymnasium Leibnitz/Expositur Radkersburg Musisch-pädagogisches Realgymnasium* (Leibnitz, 1969)

39. There were at least sixty-three Jews among the prisoners of the early transports to Dachau from Austria, known as the "transport of prominents." See Jonny Moser, "Österreichs Juden unter der NS-Herrschaft," in *NS-Herrschaft in Österreich*, ed. Tálos et al., 187–188.

40. Ruth Beckermann remarked accurately: "The Second Republic was not founded as the antithesis of National Socialism and fascism, but as the antithesis of the experiences of the civil war [of 1934]." See Ruth Beckermann, *Unzugehörig. Österreicher und Juden nach 1945* (Vienna: Löcker Verlag, 1989), 41.

41. Franz Berger et al., *Zeiten Völker und Kulturen. Ein Lehr- und Arbeitsbuch für den Unterricht in Geschichte und Sozialkunde. 3. Band für die 4. Klasse der Hauptschulen und der allgemeinbildenden höheren Schulen. Das Zeitalter der Weltpolitik und der Technik* (Vienna: Hölder-Pichler-Tempsky, 1967), 172.

42. Franz Heilsberg and Friedrich Korger, *Lehrbuch der Geschichte für die Oberstufe der allgemeinbildenden höheren Schulen. 4. Band Allgemeine Geschichte der Neuzeit von der Mitte des 19. Jahrhunderts bis zur Gegenwart* (Vienna: Österreichischer Bundesverlag für Unterricht, Wissenschaft und Kunst, 1969), 149.

43. Ibid., 149–150.

44. Note that this reference to the Soviet seizure of "German property" did *not* appear in the 1953 edition of this work. It is a safe assumption that the Russian authorities would have objected to this passage. See Heilsberg and Korger, *Lehrbuch der Geschichte für die Oberstufe der Mittelschulen,* 149.

45. Walter Göhring and Herbert Hasenmayer, *Zeitgeschichte. Ein approbiertes Lehr- und Arbeitsbuch für Geschichte und Sozialkunde* (Vienna: Verlag Ferdinand Hirt, 1972), 103. The same text appeared on page 103 of the 1986 third revised edition published by Ed. Hölzel, Vienna.

46. Wilhelm Breitfuss and Herbert Glaser, *Sozialkunde und Wirtschaftskunde (mit Einschluß der Zeitgeschichte für den Polytechnischen Lehrgang),* 2nd rev. ed. (Salzburg: Otto Müller Verlag, 1973), 156. Note that the sections on contemporary history were written by Anton Ebner, a familiar name in Austrian history textbooks.

47. Anton Ebner and Harald Majdan, *Geschichte 4 für die Oberstufe der allgemeinbildenden höheren Schulen* (Vienna: Österreichischer Bundesverlag für Unterricht, Wissenschaft und Kunst, 1975), 111, 152–153.

48. Alexander Novotny, ed., *Österreichisches Lehrbuch für Geschichte und Sozialkunde. Menschen und Völker im Wandel der Zeiten. Ausgabe für die 4. Klasse. Vom Wiener Kongreß bis zur Gegenwart,* 3rd rev. ed. (Eisenstadt: E. Rötzer Verlag, 1976), 156, 204. The identical passages appeared in the 1972 edition of this work.

49. See Gordon Brook-Shepherd, *The Austrians: A Thousand-Year Odyssey* (New York: Carroll & Graf Publishers, 1997), 329.

50. Leopold Rettinger and Leopold Hohenecker, *Zeitbilder. Geschichte und Sozialkunde 4. Vom Wienerkongreß bis zur Gegenwart* (Vienna: Verlag Carl Ueberreuter, 1982), 93–94, 104. The same passages appear in a different book by the same authors. See idem, *Geschichte und Sozialkunde. Vom Wienerkongreß bis zur Gegenwart. für die 4. Klasse* (Vienna: Verlag Carl Ueberreuter, 1982 [reprint]), 97, 106.

51. Herbert Hasenmayer, Erich Scheithauer, and Werner Tscherne, *Aus Vergangenheit und Gegenwart. Ein approbiertes Arbeits- und Lehrbuch für Geschichte und Sozialkunde,* 2nd ed. (Vienna: Verlag Ferdinand Hirt, 1985), 88.

52. Bukey, *Hitler's Austria,* 34.

53. Anton Pelinka, "Karl Renner: A Man for All Seasons," *Austrian History Yearbook,* vol. 23 (1992): 111–119. For a psychological explanation of Renner's actions, see Peter Loewenberg, "Karl Renner and the Politics of Accommodation: Moderation versus Revenge," *Austrian History Yearbook,* vol. 22 (1991): 35–56.

54. Anton Ebner et al., *Unser Republik im Wandel der Zeit* (Vienna: Österreichischer Bundesverlag, 1962), 41–42.

55. Walter Knarr, Gustav Otruba, and Hans Mairinger, *Der Mensch im Wandel der Zeiten. III. Teil. Lehrbuch der Geschichte und Sozialkunde. Vom Ausbruch des Ersten Weltkriegs bis zur Gegenwart* (Vienna: Österreichischer Gewerbeverlag, 1968), 107.

56. Franz Berger, Anton Kolbabek, and Hermann Schnell, *50 Jahre Republik Österreich* (Vienna: Österreichischer Bundesverlag, 1968), 65–66.

57. *Jahresbericht Zweites Bundesgymnasium Linz, 1969–1970* (Linz, 1970), 58–60.

58. Anna Schödl and Renate Forstner, *Sozialkunde, Wirtschaftskunde, Zeitgeschichte* (Vienna: Jugend und Volk, 1974), Z22.

59. Gerhard Atschko, Peter Dusek, and Helmut Rauch, *Sozial- und Wirtschaftskunde (inkl. Zeitgeschichte) für den Polytechnischen Lehrgang* (Vienna: Bohmann-Verlag, 1982), 61. Also see the 1989 edition for the same passages.

60. Anna Schödl and Renate Forstner, *SWZ. Sozialkunde, Wirtschaftskunde, Zeitgeschichte* (Vienna: Jugend und Volk Verlag, 1985), 104. The same passages appear in the 1993 edition on pages 110–111.

61. Lucia Binder et al., eds., *Aus dem Reich der Dichtung 4. Literatur für dich* (Vienna: Jugend und Volk, 1978), 16–20.

62. Ebner and Majdan, *Geschichte 4*, 152–153.

63. Irmgard Bohunovsky, Helmut Rumpler, and Gerd Schindler, *Weltgeschichte im 20. Jahrhundert* (Vienna: Verlag für Geschichte und Politik, 1979), 79.

64. Herbert Hasenmayer, Johann Payr, and Kurt Tschegg, *Epochen der Weltgeschichte 3. Vom Ersten Weltkrieg bis zur Gegenwart. Ein approbiertes Arbeits- und Lehrbuch für Geschichte und Sozialkunde* (Wirtschaftsgeschichte) (Vienna: Verlag Ferdinand Hirt, 1983), 31–32.

65. Gerhard Botz, "Schuschniggs geplante 'Volksbefragung' und Hitlers 'Volksabstimmung' in Österreich," in *Anschluß 1938. Protokoll des Symposiums in Wien am 14. und 15. März 1978*, ed. Rudolf Neck and Adam Wandruszka (Vienna: Verlag für Geschichte und Politik, 1981), 220–243.

Chapter Three

REMEMBERING AND FORGETTING WORLD WAR II, THE HOLOCAUST, AND THE RESISTANCE

> [D]a war a Jud im Gemeindebau, a gewisser Tennenbaum… sonst a netter Mensch…da ham's so Sachen gegen die Nazi g'schrieben g'habt auf de Trottoir…auf die Gehsteige…und der Tennenbaum hat des aufwischen müassn…net er allan… de andern Juden eh aa… hab i ihm hing'führt, daß ers aufwischt…und der Hausmasta hat zuag'schaut und hat g'lacht…er war immer bei aner Hetz dabei …Nachn Kriag is er z'ruckkumma, der Tennenbaum. Is eahm eh nix passiert.
>
> — Der Herr Karl[1]

> [A]ll opposition in the Third Reich must be rated as an act of resistance even where it was merely a case on the part of individuals to "remain decent."
>
> — Karl Stadler, Austrian historian[2]

A ustrians were full participants in World War II. One million two hundred eighty-six thousand Austrians served in the Wehrmacht, Luftwaffe, and Kriegsmarine, fighting on every front.[3] After the annexation, the Austrian economy merged with the German economy, supplied the war effort, and joined in the economic exploitation of occupied Europe. The Austrian vehicle manufacturer Steyr A.G., for example, established subsidiaries throughout occupied Eastern Europe.[4] Austria also became the site for key wartime industrial facilities, including aircraft factories and plants building the deadly "wonder weapons," such as the V-1 and V-2 rockets. Most significantly, Austrians also fully participated in crimes of National Socialism, not only in Eastern Europe and the Balkans, but also on *Ostmark* soil, especially at the Mauthausen concentration camp and its subcamps (*Nebenlager*). The war record challenges the Austria-as-victim myth, but until the mid 1980s, the participation of Austrians in the Nazi war was not only overshadowed by the victim myth, it actually was fully incorporated as *part of* the victim myth. The Anschluss was only the first pillar in the overall victim myth. Once it was established that Austrians did not believe in the annexation and that Austrians were victims, and only victims, of the Anschluss, it stood to reason that Austrians had not supported the war either.

There were several distinct mythological themes related to the war. First, the war was portrayed as purely a German war—a theme that was reinforced through the cultivation of Austrian uniqueness. Second, the war was stripped of its ideological character and explained through platitudes; students were taught that war was "bad," but learned little of the ideology of World War II. Third, the Holocaust was often minimized and/or merged with wartime suffering in general. A fourth theme was the resistance, which was initially acknowledged for symbolic importance, and was later broadly defined, overemphasized, and ultimately used as a counterweight to the crimes of National Socialism. Taken together, these themes resulted in a view that presented World War II as either a catastrophe beyond human control, such as an avalanche, or the work of one diabolical man alone—Adolf Hitler.

Unlike the Anschluss, World War II was discussed in some detail in the official lesson plans for Austrian schools. Typically, a lesson plan would simply list themes to be covered, but sometimes it offered specific comments under the heading *Bemerkungen* (remarks). The 1955 lesson plan for *Mittelschulen* is particularly revealing of official attitudes toward the war: "With the discussion of the theme 'War and Peace,' the example of World War II—a foolhardy and criminal war of aggression and conquest, caused by the fascist states—should be shown."[5] This list of themes is in line with the historiographical thinking of the time, which identified the war as criminal, but did not give special weight to the racist dimension of Nazi ideology. The "remarks" for teaching World War II to the eighth class (equivalent to seniors in high school) are more detailed:

> [F]ascist systems are to be clearly earmarked ... as subversive movements that undermined world peace. The collapse of democracy and the victory of fascism ... should be presented as the main causes for the outbreak of the war. In this connection, the systematic preparation for war by the National Socialist state (early rearmament, withdrawal from the League of Nations) ... should be pointed to.... *The spiritual connection of the preparations for war with the world view of reactionary Prussian militarism is to be made clear to the students* [emphasis added].[6]

When blame for the war was clearly mentioned, the accusing finger was pointed directly at Prussia—the cultural antithesis of Austria.

By 1967, this anti-German language no longer appeared in the lesson plans.[7] Lesson plans after the late 1960s typically consisted only of a list of themes to cover along with vague and wordy pedagogical advice. For example, the 1975 lesson plan for *Hauptschulen* lists the following themes to cover without comment: "National Socialism and the unleashing of the

Second World War. The Second World War and its political, social, and economic consequences."[8] The 1984 lesson plan for AHS schools lists: "Communism, fascism, National Socialism. Austria between the wars. The Great Powers. The Second World War. Freedom and resistance movements."[9] Such broad topics gave teachers and textbook writers plenty of room to interpret history, as long as the main themes were covered. One change worth noting in the later lesson plans is the increased emphasis on the resistance—a sign of the increased attention being given to resistance movements and their symbolic importance. History classes in polytechnic schools, which opened their doors in the mid 1960s, focused only on contemporary history. In 1967, the first lesson plan for polytechnic schools was printed. It offered vague guidelines for reviewing the major events up to World War I and informed teachers that special emphasis was to be put on the development of democratic life and its endangerment.[10] The same wording appeared in the 1976 and the 1981 *Lehrplan des Polytechnischen Lehrganges*.[11] Overall, lesson plans after the late 1960s offered few signs of victim mythology in the Austrian schools. History and reading textbooks, however, were a different matter.

World War II in the Textbooks

When Austria regained full sovereignty in 1955, official Austrian identity depended on a view that emphasized Austrian uniqueness and distanced Austria from Germany. At the same time, it was no secret that Austrians had served in the Nazi armies. The participation of so many Austrians in the war presented a contradiction: How could the memory of the war dead and the service of the living be honored when that service was for a regime that had eliminated Austrian independence and sought to eradicate Austrian identity? The answer was the Austria-as-victim myth, which merged the experiences of soldiers, civilians, and Jews into one wartime experience and united all into a community of suffering. While an extensive historiography on the ideological and racist nature of the war was not yet fully developed, many fundamental aspects of the war's nature were clearly understood. For example, the violent anti-Semitism and extreme anticommunism of the Nazis, as well as the aggressive and premeditated nature of the war, were all well known. In any case, textbooks of the time rarely explored the ideological motivations behind the conflict; rather, textbook authors explained the war through the platitude that "war is bad." For example, a 1955 commemorative text for younger children, presents the war as something that Austrians had absolutely no control over—an event that simply "happened": "In the year 1939 another war began. It lasted six years. Many Austrians had to die in foreign places, many even in the *Heimat*…. In these years it seemed as if Austria would be lost forever. But this war too came to an end…. Your fathers and mothers could again make decisions about their own lives in our *Heimat*."[12] Another commemorative text goes even further, comparing the war to a disease and a beast, totally beyond human control:

> A new war came, creeping like a malignant disease. It struck everyone like a terrible fever. It ripped fathers from wife and child, sons from parents and siblings. It forced the men of our country into uniforms that they did not want to wear. It forced weapons into their hands, which they did not want to use, and sent them to a death that they did not want to die—to the Arctic and to Africa, to Russia and to the ocean. The world sank into destruction, blood, and suffering. *The war was an evil animal* [emphasis added].[13]

According to this view, Austrian soldiers were victims of the war, forced against their will to participate and die in the great conflict. The war itself becomes a historical actor, an "evil animal" that causes destruction. A 1967 history text demonstrates the idea that the war was equally hard on everyone. Heavy use of the passive construction also suggests that the war was not a man-made event, but rather a disaster that just "happened": "Homes were destroyed, streams of refugees jammed the streets, many people died or became cripples. Children lost their parents, mothers their sons.... Hundreds of thousands of men now had to carry the heavy burden of [being] prisoners of war for years."[14]

Reading books, too, avoided the ideological significance of World War II and did not venture beyond the "war is bad" theme. For example, in a reader from 1983, the story "Krieg" (War), by Ursula Wölfel, tells the tale of a young girl who inquires about relatives who have passed away. The girl's father explains to her that some of her relatives were killed in the war and that people in a nearby house were killed in an air raid. The girl is relieved to find out that there is no more war in her own country, but sad to find out that war still occurs in other parts of the world. When watching the television news, the girl is horrified by scenes of warfare and cries out: "WHY DO PEOPLE ALWAYS MAKE WAR?" The father replies: "Because they are too dumb and too selfish.... Because they have still not noticed that war only brings unhappiness to everyone." The story goes on to explain about white against black racism in an unnamed country; tells the reader that governments, not people, begin wars; and explicitly mentions the destructive power of atomic weapons and napalm, before finally concluding with the father saying: "Nothing other than unhappiness has ever come through war! If everyone in every country said that, then there could be no more war."[15] This story again exemplifies the "war is bad" truism. By explicitly being linked with wars in general, World War II becomes like all other wars, and the suffering of everyone is put into a single category. At the same time, this story is not as neutral as it might first appear. It is clear that the relatives whose memory has sparked the young girl's questions were killed in an Allied air raid. Furthermore, the author steers the story away from World War II to racial strife, atomic weapons, and napalm—all of which point to the United States. Finally, the mention of napalm and the girl's horror at televised reports of war clearly hint at the Vietnam War, which again evokes the United States. This story reflects the broad change in attitude toward the United States that resulted from the Vietnam War (see the analysis below).

The tendency to portray World War II simply as a horrific experience devoid of any ideological context was not limited to works by minor authors. The numerous stories and poems by the German war veteran Wolfgang Borchert also contributed to an understanding of the war in terms of platitudes and generalizations. Borchert wrote chilling poems, stories, and radio plays about the effects of the war, in which he was wounded and imprisoned by the Nazis for having a defeatist attitude. Borchert's expressionist career was cut short by his death in 1947. At issue here is not aesthetic quality, but the contribution that the tone of Borchert's works—which appeared frequently in postwar Austrian reading books[16]—made to the understanding of the war. Borchert's poem "Lesebuchgeschichte" (Storybook Story), which appeared in several Austrian books, typifies the author's emphasis on the dehumanizing effects of war. In the poem, a soldier returns home from the war and kills another man for his bread. When confronted by a judge who tells him: "Du darfst doch keinen totschlagen [You may not kill anyone]," the soldier answers with a simple "Warum nicht [Why not]?"[17] The emphasis on dehumanization and on the destructive effects of war is clear in this poem. In and of themselves, these themes are completely valid, and Borchert's examination of the impact of war on the human condition is certainly important. Yet such themes contributed to an overall view that saw the war as a historical force in and of itself. Such a view resonated with Austrians in part because it was valid to a limited degree. The dehumanizing effects of warfare are well known, and in many ways, war can be a historical actor, as it affects so many aspects of human life. But the dehumanizing effects of war coexist with ideological as well as situational factors.[18]

One of the most graphic and dramatic examples of how Austrian civilians came face to face with the horrors of war was to experience Allied bombing raids. Reading books especially adopted the theme of air attacks, as already noted in the story "Krieg." These stories contributed to the "war is bad" message by emphasizing the horrors of air raids, but without mentioning why Allied planes were bombing Austrian cities in the first place. Among the authors of stories and poems about Allied air raids is Paula von Preradovic (who also wrote the text to the Austrian national anthem). Her poem "Fliegeralarm" (Air Raid Warning) appeared in a book with Gertrud Fussenegger's "Luftangriff auf Innsbruck" (Air Raid on Innsbruck), which included a picture of American B-17 bombers dropping their payload on an unspecified target.[19] A story in a 1961 reading book combined an air raid story with an important symbol of Austrian culture, the State Opera House in Vienna. In "Unsere Staatsoper" (Our State Opera), Alfred Jerger recounts an ascent out of the Staatsoper's air raid shelter. The opera company had convinced itself that the Allies were purposefully not bombing Vienna's historic city center, but on 12 March 1945 they were shocked when they emerged from the shelter and "hurried over to the opposite side of the Operngasse, where many people were standing. Then we looked back and stared in horror: Our beloved opera house stood in towering flames!"[20] A 1973 story by Hans Erich Nossak, titled "Nach einem Luftangriff" (After an Air Raid), describes the horrors of Hamburg after the massive 1943 Royal Air Force fire bomb raid. The narrator recounts how rats and flies rule the city and thrive on the innumerable dead. He makes his way to his burnt-out home, hoping to find some belongings: "I could not help but to look closely, [to see] if perhaps the little Madonna had remained hanging by chance. But we had nothing left, not even a tiny little something from the things that were dear to us and that belonged to us."[21] The victim imagery in this passage is especially strong as the suffering of the population is linked with the desecration of the holiest symbol of Catholicism; not even the little Madonna on the wall survives the wrath of Allied bombers.

These stories emphasized an aspect of the war to which civilians could most directly relate. Parents and grandparents could have told students of personal experiences, and many students had family members who had been killed in such air raids. But these air bombardment stories also contributed to the victim myth by emphasizing the horrors brought upon the Austrian and German civilian population, without explaining the reasons why such air raids were launched in the first place. This theme was also evoked outside of Austrian schools. In Vienna, plaques abound noting buildings that were bombed and rebuilt after the war. But the greatest physical reminder of Allied air raids are the giant concrete flak towers that still stand in Vienna.[22] The most prominent of the towers, located one block from the busy shopping street Mariahilferstrasse, has been converted into the city aquarium. As children play in the surrounding park, the victim myth is reflected in giant lettering painted across the top of the tower, which reads: "Smashed to pieces in the still of the night" (see plate 1). The message recalls the destruction of air raids in Vienna, but the question "Why?" remains unanswered. In the context of the Austria-as-victim myth, the answer is that Austria was unjustly and brutally bombed by Allied warplanes.

While the previous examples demonstrate a tendency to ignore the ideological nature of the war, some Austrian schoolbooks made an effort to address the issues. But more often than not, these attempts at an ideological explanation either dismiss or subtly justify the war. In a commemorative publication in remembrance of President Adolf Schärf, the author glosses over the political climate of the 1930s and 1940s, and explains that a person living through those times "could have been … a convinced monarchist, a republican democrat, an authoritarian patriot, an ardent National Socialist, or a democratic Austrian. We would hope that there are not too many who, like Herr Karl, were all [of these]." The author then offers exoneration, writing: "Nothing is being accused of [he] who erred in good faith. The times were confusing enough. And not everyone has the ability to unravel confusion, to see through darkness, and to separate the false from the real."[23] This "let bygones be bygones" attitude was typical of the postwar period, when the emphasis was on moving beyond the divisions of the past toward a stable and unified future. Other texts went beyond the postwar coalition lesson, going so far as to justify World War II as a defensive war against the Soviet Union. A history text from 1962 includes the passage: "[Hitler] saw clearly that peaceful coexistence between communism and National Socialism was not possible in the long run."[24] Another text from 1976 implies that the war in the East was justifiable as a defensive thrust against Soviet power: "Above all, Soviet intentions to conquer the Baltic states and Romania … were troubling to Germany. Under the pretext that the Soviet Union was secretly massing troops against Germany, Hitler opened the war against Russia on 22 June."[25] The message seems to be that Hitler used a pretext to start the war, but the authors imply that his move was in response to Soviet imperialism, which made Germany "uncomfortable."

It is well known that the war against the Soviet Union was an ideological war in which Nazi racism played a key role. Furthermore, the myths that the regular German army was not ideologically motivated and did not participate in war crimes have long been exposed.[26] In Austria (as in Germany), the long-standing pretense of the innocence of the regular army contributed to the Austria-as-victim myth by ennobling the experiences of Austrian veterans. Key to upholding this view was to portray the war against Russia as a normal or even chivalrous war. For example, the story "Als Arzt im Rußlandfeldzug" (As a Doctor in the Russian Campaign), by Peter Bamm, paints the war in the East as an upstanding campaign. The narrator is a field surgeon who has been operating for many hours. Two Russian prisoners who had been previously treated are caught, after having set fire to four hundred liters of gasoline. The narrator interrogates the wounded prisoners: "Did you [two] ignite the gasoline?"—"Yes!"—"Why?"—They shrug their shoulders—"Have you been treated fairly?"—"Yes!"—"Did you get something to eat?"— "Yes!"—"Were you mistreated when taken prisoner?"—"No." The narrator is then completely beside himself over what to do next, saying: "In no book of military justice in the world does it say anything other than the death penalty for sabotage in a combat area. What should I do?" In the end, the surgeon decides to let the two off. Two years after the incident, the doctor is put before a court martial.[27] It is understandable that textbooks would seek to ennoble the experiences of the soldiers, many of whom were Austrian. But the function of such stories was also to divorce the troops from the crimes of the Nazi regime. The war was bad, the Nazi leadership was bad, but the soldiers were noble, and in some cases, so was their cause—the fight against Bolshevism. While the cause of the war was ultimately discredited, the Wehrmacht remained, for many, a symbol of wartime pride and decency.

Stalingrad

The ultimate symbol of Wehrmacht sacrifice and honor was the monumental battle of Stalingrad. In a few cases, textbook authors did not glorify the battle. A reading book from 1964 includes a story about Stalingrad from the Russian point of view,[28] and in a 1973 history book, the author reminds students that the "Soviet victory at Stalingrad proved how falsely Hitler had estimated the resistance capacity of Slavic peoples."[29] But these examples are exceptions, for it was far more common for history and reading books to treat the battle of Stalingrad as a monument to Wehrmacht honor. From a patriotic Austrian point of view, there was a great irony in raising the battle of Stalingrad to heroic status. As the turning point in the war, the Wehrmacht's defeat at Stalingrad marked the beginning of the process whereby Austria could be reborn. The fact that Austrian schoolbooks did monumentalize Stalingrad is strong evidence that the reputation and experiences of the Wehrmacht were as important to Austrians as they were to Germans. German B movies about the heroic soldiers at Stalingrad, such as 1959's *Hunde, wollt ihr ewig leben?* (Dogs, do you want to live forever?),[30] surely resonated in Austria as well.

One thread that ran through many Stalingrad stories was the (largely accurate) idea that the army was put into an impossible position and betrayed by Hitler. This view preserved the honor of the army by divorcing it from the Führer. For example, in a 1957 history text, the authors call Stalingrad "a great human tragedy," and explain that Hitler ignored his generals and forbade a withdrawal, resulting in the German army's encirclement by the Red Army. Ultimately, "160,000 soldiers fell victim to the fighting, the cold, and the hunger, [and] many tens of thousands became prisoners of war. This horrible battle meant the turning point in the European theater."[31] The idea that Hitler had betrayed the army took a more graphic form in a 1965 student poster project in Vienna: the horrors of war were emphasized, and Hitler was named a traitor to his own people.[32] A history text from 1963 is unusual in that it specifically mentions Austrians in its coverage of Stalingrad, pointing out that "many Austrians belonged to this army [the doomed German Sixth Army]. Even though they stood at lost posts, history cannot overlook their heroism or the great amount of suffering that they were forced to endure."[33] Leopold Wally's story "Die Mutter von Stalingrad" (The Mother from Stalingrad) from a 1960 reading book depicts Stalingrad with great melodrama. It tells the story of a German woman, Gertrud Kadereit, who had escaped from Stalingrad and made her way back to Königsberg in East Prussia, only to be returned to a prisoner camp near Stalingrad. After the war, she is finally reunited with her husband, who had been in an American POW camp. Wally's account of the actual battle is especially worthy of note:

> Stalingrad! Back then, in the January days of the year 1943, millions of people sat feverishly by their radios and followed the reports about the terrible winter

battle for the major Russian city on the Volga, *not far from the border between Europe and Asia*.

Over three hundred thousand men, among them tens of thousands of Austrians, had been surrounded by Russian armies during the Christmas days of the year 1942, and since then defended themselves, frustrated on the frozen fields before the city and in the rows of buildings shot to pieces.

In vain! Help from the outside was no longer possible, the ammunition supplies ran out, terrible cold, hunger, and frustration broke the resistance of the defenders [emphasis added].[34]

In this version of Stalingrad, the battle is nothing less than a struggle for Western civilization, as is made clear by the reference to the supposed border between Europe and Asia. In Wally's view, the Wehrmacht was holding the line against the Asiatic Russians, and he further justifies the war in the East by repeatedly using the word "defenders" to describe the Wehrmacht in Stalingrad—more than one thousand miles from Germany.

From the German point of view, it was important to make some sense out of the loss of so many who had died in the wrong place for the wrong cause. This was even truer for Austrians, who sought to ennoble the suffering of those who had died for a cause that was ultimately anti-Austrian. One way to honor the dead was to justify the war in the East as a war to protect Europe from Asiatic Russia. With Stalingrad, it was also common to elevate the suffering of the German Sixth Army to a Biblical level. This was evident in a poem by Peter Huchel titled "Dezember 1942," which was by published in a 1978 reading book:

> Wie Wintergewitter ein rollender Hall.
> Zerschossen die Lehmwand von Bethlehems Stall.
> Es liegt Maria erschlagen vorm Tor,
> ihr blutig Haar an die Steine fror.
> [Three soldiers offer gold and myrrh, as a crow and a dog roam around a bare farmstead]
> …
> Vor Stalingrad verweht die Chaussee.
> Sie führt in die Totenkammer aus Schnee.[35]

By locating the nativity scene at Stalingrad with a horrifying image of a frozen and bloody Mary, Huchel links the very fate of Christendom with Stalingrad. The conclusion is that the German loss at Stalingrad—a death chamber of snow—dealt Western civilization a nearly fatal blow.

War Memorials

While poems and stories served to memorialize the troops, monuments to honor the fallen were built by Austrian towns, villages, and schools. In this, there was nothing unique about Austria's treatment of its war dead.

However, what *was* unique was the connection with the Austria-as-victim myth. The Second Republic was in part built on the fiction that Austrians were exclusively victims of Nazism, but at the same time, those who had died in the Nazi war could hardly be forgotten. Labeling Austrians who had served in the German forces as traitors would have been absurd, as well as political suicide. (Indeed, public castigation of Nazis, let alone nonparty veterans, was politically unwise. The SPÖ undoubtedly lost several voters to the ÖVP with a 1945 campaign poster that proclaimed "All Nazis to Siberia.")[36] As a result, when it came to Wehrmacht veterans, the victim myth created an uncomfortable contradiction. Only the defeat of the Nazi armies allowed Austria to be reborn, yet Austrians had to honor the memory of those who had died for National Socialism. But given that the postwar mythology had created an all-encompassing community of victims, this contradiction was easily addressed. Heidemarie Uhl demonstrates that from 1950 through the early 1980s, Styrian war memorials, often sponsored by veterans organizations, emphasized honor, duty, and sacrifice for the *Heimat*.[37] By generalizing sacrifice and suffering, and referring to the *Heimat* instead of Germany, the service of the veterans and the fallen could be honored.

In this context, war monuments had an impact on schools in several ways. Many schools erected war monuments on their grounds or within school buildings (see plate 2). Monuments were also the subject of stories in textbooks. For example, in the story "Der Kriegerdenkmal" (The War Memorial) in a 1973 reading book, students read: "In almost every town of our *Heimat*, a marble plaque reminds us ... of soldiers who sacrificed their lives for the fatherland during the two world wars.... Read the names on the war memorials in your town! ... That these soldiers sacrificed their lives for the *Heimat*—about that we should always think."[38] Remembering and honoring the war dead were also themes in yearbooks. For example, a commemorative program from 1958 lists the school's war dead under the caption "those who lost their lives for the *Heimat*."[39] Another commemorative program from 1962 includes a list of war dead under the heading "the victims of the world war 1939–1945." Among them are five teachers and 124 former students who were killed on all fronts of the war.[40] But while the Austria-as-victim myth created this contradiction, it also answered it by uniting everyone—soldiers, Jews, political prisoners, and civilians—into a single community of suffering. Because the victim myth encompassed everyone, those who were persecuted by the regime lost any claim to the uniqueness of their suffering.

The Holocaust in the Textbooks

In *Hitler's Austria*, Evan Bukey notes that "while historians have written that the 'twisted road to Auschwitz' was 'built on hate and paved with indifference,' they have paid little attention to the route running through the *Ostmark*. Should they take a closer look, they would find a branch surveyed, engineered, and graded to meet the demands of a critical mass of the Austrian people."[41] Bukey's powerful statement is a reminder that the active complicity of many Austrians in the Holocaust and the anti-Semitic violence that preceded it run counter to the Austria-as-victim idea. The Anschluss of 1938 was accompanied by a brutal pogrom in Vienna in which both Nazi and non-Nazi Austrians persecuted Jews. In the aftermath of the annexation, thousands of Jewish apartments and other properties were confiscated. Gerhard Botz refers to these seizures, which benefited many Austrians materially, as a Nazi substitute for social policy.[42] Some sources suggest that Austrians were highly overrepresented as guards and executioners in concentration camps. The well-known Nazi hunter Simon Wiesenthal estimates that 75 percent of concentration camp guards were Austrians—an astounding figure, if accurate, when we consider that Austria's pre-Anschluss population was seven million compared to sixty-five million Germans.[43] More clear is that many Austrian civilians knew about Nazi atrocities, given that the notorious Mauthausen concentration camp and numerous smaller camps were located on Austrian soil. Finally, over sixty-five thousand Austrian Jews were murdered in the Holocaust.[44] These grim statistics would seem to undermine the idea of Austrian victimization, but in the context of the Austria-as-victim myth, the Holocaust actually became *part of* the myth rather than its negation.

One of the most problematic factors of the Austria-as-victim mythology was the need to present the Holocaust not as a unique aspect of the war, but as part of the larger pattern of suffering experienced by *everyone*. This is demonstrated in a history text from 1962, in which the authors state: "Above all, National Socialism turned itself against the Christian churches and against Jewry, on whom one put all of the guilt of Germany's precarious situation."[45] Here, the authors acknowledge Nazi persecution against Jews, but it is equated with—or made secondary to—persecution against the Catholic and Protestant churches. The message that there was nothing unique about the persecution of the Jews often came across when authors summarized the impact of the war. In a commemorative text from 1966, the authors imply that *everyone*—from Jews to soldiers killed fighting the Russians—is a victim of the war: "Seventy thousand Austrians died in a murderous war that they never had wanted. Twenty-five thousand were killed by bombs, further tens of thousands were locked up, and many were tortured to death or executed in the torture chambers of the concentration camps."[46] Another history textbook from 1973 covers the Holocaust in some detail, but when summing up the war, the authors homogenize all victims, resulting in problematic comparisons:

> Yet the brutalization of morals was not limited to the Third Reich. In the woods of Katyn near Smolensk, thousands of hurriedly buried bodies were found, [of] Polish officers obviously shot to death in the Soviet Union. The treatment

of prisoners of war, especially the Germans in the Soviet Union and the Soviet Russians in Germany, was hard and callous. Air raids and atomic bombings of purely residential areas took the lives of many completely innocent people, above all women and children.[47]

These examples serve as a counterweight to the Holocaust, and demonstrate an ethical relativism that undermines the uniqueness and scope of Nazi crimes. The authors' equivocation of the treatment of German and Russian POWs reflects the view that brutality was to be found in equal measure on all sides. This view has since been empirically proven to be false. According to Christian Streit's research, 37 percent of German POWs in Russian hands died, while 58 percent of Russian POWs in German hands perished.[48] The message of this passage—that is, everyone suffered and every side perpetuated war crimes—related to the Austria-as-victim myth by implicitly arguing that there was nothing unique about crimes against the Jews. The Holocaust was seen as one of many atrocities committed by all sides. The community of victims idea also served coalition history and fostered political unity in the postwar period. Armed with this idea, textbook authors passed on the notion that Austrians from all political walks of life and all religious groups suffered under the Nazis. Furthermore, many authors avoided the issue of large-scale participation in Nazi crimes by blaming them on Hitler alone, as in the following text from 1967: "[After becoming chancellor in 1933]… *he* [Hitler] persecuted *his* political opponents, sent Jews, Catholics, Socialists, and Communists to the notorious concentration camps, and had over six million people murdered" (emphasis added).[49]

It can also be argued that the placement of material in texts served to undermine the uniqueness of the Holocaust. For example, a reading book from 1977 contains three pages of excerpts from Anne Frank's diary. On the following page, a story and a poem appear that serve as a counterpoint to the diary. "Das Wohnzimmer im Kastanienbaum" (The Living Room in the Chestnut Tree) is a dialogue between two children playing in a park. The park is on a site where a house was bombed during the war, killing a little girl named Sonja. One of the children suggests that they pretend that Sonja is still alive. The other child disagrees, saying:

"That does no good. We cannot reverse what happened."
"No?"
"No. But we can do something else."
"What?"
"*Be careful*, so that something like that does not happen again."
"Yesterday I saw on television how they dropped bombs. In Vietnam."

On the same page there is also a poem by Marie Luise Kaschnitz titled "Hiroshima." Thus, the editors of the book followed the excerpt from Anne Frank's diary with stories and poems that indirectly connect the death of young Sonja in World War II to the (obviously American) war in

Vietnam and the bombing of Hiroshima. Overall, the editors of this reading book embraced a moral relativism that thematically linked Anne Frank, Sonja, the Vietnamese, and the Japanese in Hiroshima into a single chain of victimization.[50]

As we saw earlier, an important postwar legend held that Austrians of different political camps, who had fought a bitter civil war in 1934, forged a sense of unity through the common ordeal of persecution at the hands of the Nazis. This interpretation has some basis in fact, but in teaching the coalition legend, the concentration camp became primarily a token of Austrian political unity, rather than a symbol of Jewish persecution. In many history and reading books, the result was concentration camps without Jews. For example in the story "Zeit Ohne Gnade" (Time without Mercy), from a 1965 reading book, the author Rudolf Kalmar recounts the horrors of medical experiments conducted at Dachau by German Luftwaffe doctors. At one point in the story, the narrator is interrogated by an SS guard looking for a candidate for medical experimentation:

> "You?" he asked me. His terse style was supposed to seem military, although it was nothing other than the expression of his lower-Bavarian primitiveness, brutal and simple-minded at the same time.
> "Yes, sir!" I answered.
> "How old?"
> "Forty-two."
> "How long in the camp?"
> "Since 1938."
> "Nationality?"
> "Austrian."
> (The Dachau concentration camp was probably the only place in all of greater Germany where the Austrians so long and doggedly called themselves Austrians, so that even the SS had become used to it.)
> Hofmann had an aversion to Austrians.
> On average, they were too intellectual for him, a thought he was accustomed to expressing with other words in his lower-Bavarian manner.[51]

This story is a prime example of how the concentration camp became first and foremost a symbol of Austrian victimization and defiance, rather than a symbol of Jewish persecution. It is also noteworthy that the cultured Austrian, through the defiance and courage of the intellectual narrator, comes across as the exact opposite of the lower-Bavarian brute. Another example is from a 1955 text published to celebrate ten years of the Second Republic. In this case, the concentration camp is again seen as a site of persecution for many Austrian groups. But the Jews are alluded to in only the vaguest of terms: "Religious groups and priests were persecuted. Monks and nuns could no longer work in the places where they had served our country through hundreds of years. The temples were destroyed. The symbols of faith were destroyed."[52]

By the early 1980s, there were some notable exceptions to the mythological accounts of the Holocaust common to Austrian textbooks. In a 1982 history text for polytechnic schools, the authors covered the Holocaust and also addressed contemporary Austrian anti-Semitism. The authors wrote of "anti-Semitism without Jews" (i.e., how anti-Semitism persists in a country with so few Jews) and challenged students to look beyond Jewish stereotypes.[53] A 1983 history book for business high schools also provided extensive coverage of the Holocaust and mentioned the Austrian roots of Hitler's anti-Semitism.[54] These books are early examples of a break with the victim myth, but these improvements were by no means universal and did not represent a fundamental shift away from the Austria-as-victim myth. In the larger context, the above examples remained the exception to the rule.

For example, a 1985 text barely mentions the Holocaust. In a chapter on National Socialism, students read about the fundamentals of Nazism in which Nazi racial ideology is covered in a few brief sentences and one photograph.[55] While the authors briefly mention anti-Semitism, they never link anti-Semitism with the Holocaust. Further in the text, a photograph of the concentration camp Mauthausen appears, but in the context of discussing the resistance. In the accompanying text dealing with concentration camps, students read: "The National Socialist leaders ... did not care at all about the life of the individual. Hundreds of thousands of opponents were annihilated in the concentration camps." This text is followed by two points for students to discuss: "Attempt through books, reports, or films about concentration camps, or through a visit to one [a camp] to understand what prisoners had to suffer there!" and "In class, discuss what every person can do, what every person must do, so that such horror can never happen again!" While the text challenges students to investigate concentration camps further, the emphasis is clearly put upon political prisoners. Furthermore, the authors' statement that "hundreds of thousands of opponents were exterminated in concentration camps" would be accurate only if they had taken pains to distinguish between Nazi political enemies and "racial" enemies. Since the authors do not make this distinction, students were left with a gross underestimation of the extent of the Holocaust. Further de-emphasizing the Holocaust, the authors conclude their coverage of the war with two separate lists of casualties—soldiers and civilians. Jews and other victims of the Holocaust are not included in either list.[56] Ultimately, the Holocaust portrayed in this book, *Aus Vergangenheit und Gegenwart*, is a Holocaust without Jews.

Yet in the same text where the Holocaust is treated in so cursory a manner, the authors found time and space to provide detailed coverage of the atomic bombings of Hiroshima and Nagasaki: "The effect was horrible. Of the approximately 400,000 residents of Hiroshima, some 80,000 were killed.... Every fourth inhabitant of Hiroshima did not survive the catastrophe. Most of the survivors died later on from illnesses resulting from the radiation and wasted away."[57] The atom bomb and nuclear energy had already been the subject of discussion in textbooks for some time. In the early 1960s, there were even some positive portrayals of the potential for atomic energy, but by the late 1960s, Austrian history books, and especially Austrian reading books, emphasized the horrors of atomic weapons.[58] A 1966 reader for polytechnic students, *Schaffensfreude, Lebensfreude*, includes three stories about the atomic bomb. The first is an eyewitness account of the New Mexico test in July 1945. The second story "... als die Sonne auf die Erde fiel" (When the Sun Fell to the Earth), by Walther Pluhar, gives an account of the bombings of Hiroshima and Nagasaki. The third atomic bomb story included in the text is an excerpt from Karl Bruckner's novel *Sadako will leben* (Sadako Wants to Live). Bruckner's work, which was commonly featured in Austrian textbooks, is based on the life story of the young Japanese girl Sadako Sasaki, who died from leukemia as a result of exposure to radiation from the bombing of Hiroshima. Sadako struggled to fold one thousand paper cranes, hoping to evoke the legendary power of the cranes to cure the sick. Though she died before she could fold them all,[59] Sadako lived on in the memory of her classmates and became an important symbol of the horrors of nuclear weapons and a symbol for peace in the atomic age.[60] In the short excerpt from this story, Bruckner describes the Hiroshima explosion from the pilots' point of view: "[T]hey saw that the head of this horrible mushroom was made of a fireball that exceeded every human conception of hell's fire. This fire of the primeval world was so horribly unearthly that the witnesses stuck to their seats as if they were paralyzed."[61] Another book includes an excerpt from *Sadako will leben*, in which Sadako's mother, Yasuko Sasaki, witnesses the atomic explosion from the Mitsubishi shipyard where she works: "Yasuko sank to her knees upon viewing this horrible fire cloud. She stared full of terror at this work of demons. Because only they [demons] could have ignited this otherworldly giant torch to punish humans. But why? What had they done? And her children?"[62]

The first use of atomic weapons was relevant to Austria in the sense that it was relevant to all of humanity. In the context of a world faced with the omnipresent threat of nuclear annihilation, it is not surprising that Austrian reading books would include references to Hiroshima and Nagasaki. But aside from these reasons, the bombings of Hiroshima and Nagasaki had no direct relevance to Austria, while the Holocaust did. Over sixty-five thousand Austrian Jews were murdered in concentration camps, and some Austrians benefited materially from the persecution of Austrian Jews. In this context, then, Austrian textbook authors and school officials can be criticized for distorting history through emphasis. While Cold War-related atomic angst can account for some of the emphasis on Hiroshima, the increase in Hiroshima stories also coincided with revulsion at the Vietnam War.

The American war in Vietnam, especially the air campaign, had a profound impact on both the self-image and the international image of the United States. As the level of violence escalated in a war that lacked clear objectives and had a dubious beginning, more and more voices began to question and challenge the moral standing of the United States. Among the voices was Telford Taylor, who had been a prosecutor at the Nuremberg trials. Taylor linked the United States with Nazi war crimes in his 1970 book *Nuremberg and Vietnam: An American Tragedy*.[63] Such comparisons had already taken hold with the American New Left, many of whom were quick to compare American involvement in Vietnam with Nazi crimes. The severity of these accusations is less surprising when seen as a reaction to a Cold War culture that had witnessed the abuses of McCarthyism, the reckless labeling of any form of dissent—including advocating for civil rights—as "communist," the threat of nuclear war, and now an undeclared war in Southeast Asia. But even though there were a multitude of good reasons to denounce the Vietnam War, including the My Lai massacre, carpet-bombing, and the widespread use of Agent Orange, comparisons between the United States' military campaign in Vietnam and Nazi Germany's war of annihilation were overdrawn, historically misleading, and ultimately tenable only through the lenses of ethical relativism.

While the war in Vietnam created deep divisions among many Americans that have not yet been fully addressed,[64] the impact of the Vietnam War on America's image in Europe was almost universally negative. As Richard Pells writes: "Europeans no longer saw the Americans as benevolent liberators. Now television newscasts showed American soldiers napalming Vietnamese children, burning peasant huts, bringing the Cold War to the Mekong Delta."[65] In countries such as Austria, Germany, and Japan, the "CARE packet" image of America faded and was replaced by an image of B-52 bombers destroying villages.[66] Significantly, for many Austrians (as well as Germans and Japanese) this was not necessarily a new image, but the revival of an older one, for it was an older generation of American airmen who had laid waste to Austrian cities during World War II. The ultimate American air raids were on Hiroshima and Nagasaki, and it was during the Vietnam War that the theme of atomic bombings was increasingly emphasized in history books and especially in reading books. While it is understandable that Austrian students should learn about the horrors of nuclear war through the vehicle of the only atomic attacks that have actually occurred, when examining the context in which Austrian schoolbooks covered these events, it is safe to say that atomic horror stories, and especially the Sadako story, became a staple of Austrian books to an extreme degree. It is no exaggeration to say that Austrian children were more likely to encounter the ordeal of Sadako in their schoolbooks than they were to learn about Anne Frank. As a symbol, Hiroshima was weighted more heavily than the Holocaust in reading books, though not always in history books. This emphasis on Hiroshima reinforced the Austria-as-victim myth by increasing the pool of atrocity victims to include the American-inflicted Japanese atomic casualties. By implication, Hiroshima became the American Auschwitz.[67]

In addition to the subtle role Hiroshima played in Austrian mythology of the Holocaust, direct links were also made between Hiroshima and the Holocaust. A 1981 history text includes an eyewitness description of the bombing of Hiroshima, followed by a summary of the war that links casualties of the atom bomb, concentration camp victims, and even some former Nazis into a single chain of victimization:

> With this dropping of the atomic bomb, more than 100,000 people found their death in seconds or were so [severely] injured that they wasted away from the results of the radiation and died an agonizing death. In present-day Hiroshima and Nagasaki, many deformed children are born as a result of this event. The total losses of the Second World War amount to approximately 40 million dead.
>
> Next to the horror and insanity of the war, it came to *unimaginable atrocities in the Third Reich*. In concentration camps, for example Auschwitz [and] Mauthausen, some 10 million people were murdered—mostly gassed. Above all, Jews (6 million) were among these people.
>
> But also many out-of-favor Germans, yes even former members of the Nazi Party were arrested through so-called People's Courts—usually without any real chance at defense—[and] often sentenced to death [emphasis in original].[68]

By making everyone a victim, this summation diminishes the crimes of the Nazis and analyzes the war only through the "war is bad" platitude. Again, any unique quality of the Holocaust melts away into a view in which the Holocaust was one of many horrible things that happened during World War II.

At the same time, there is evidence that many Austrian students learned about the war in ways that went beyond the banal statements presented in their books. For the twentieth anniversary of the Austrian Second Republic in 1965, the director of the high school for girls in Graz, Robert Rieder, delivered a speech in which he directly addressed the dangers of anti-Semitism, though he was careful to point the finger at Germany:

> Do you know what anti-Semitism means? The word means race hatred, race hatred against the Jews.
>
> And do you know who tirelessly and passionately preached this race hatred? Adolf Hitler and his Nazis were the fanatical theoreticians and atrocious practitioners of this anti-Semitism.
>
> And do you know what anti-Semitism led to during the war?
>
> The Germans built huge factories to exterminate the Jews. The Jews were suffocated in gas chambers, and their corpses were burned in the adjoining cremation ovens.[69]

In 1978 in the East Tyrolean town of Lienz, the head of the parents' association arranged to show the exhibition "Judentum im Dritten Reich" (Jews in the Third Reich) at the high school. In addition, the chair of Jewish studies at the University of Vienna traveled to Lienz to deliver a talk, which, despite being widely publicized, attracted only thirty-two people.[70] This incident demonstrates both interest in and apathy toward Austria's role in the Holocaust. On another occasion on the eve of the Austrian national holiday, in a speech titled "Mit dem Terror leben" (Living with

Terror), Father Bartholomäus Rubatscher covered the Holocaust extensively and took Austrians to task for their role in it: "It is a shameful chapter in Austrian history that the extermination of so many Jews was largely accepted with resignation by the Austrian population."[71]

The most direct way Austrian students commonly came into contact with the Holocaust was to embark on a field trip to the Mauthausen concentration camp in Upper Austria. In their yearbook reports, many Austrian students recall being moved by a visit to Mauthausen. In a 1985/1986 yearbook, the student Astrid Heubrandtner wrote: "We must not ever forget Mauthausen!... It is up to us to make sure that something like that never happens again!"[72] Claudia Zinnagl, a student from Salzburg was moved to write a poem about Mauthausen:

> Mauthausen
> Groß und grau liegt es auf einem Hügel
> Beherrschend.
> Schülerschwärme ergießen sich im Hof. Unwissendes Sprachgewirr belebt die kalten Mauern,
> die schon so viel Grausames gesehen haben.
> [the tour is described, then]
> Man steigt in sein Auto, fährt, um nie wiederzukommen.
> Fährt in das nächste Gasthaus, um den Schrecken herunterzuspülen.[73]

One teacher from Bad Ischl, Ingrid Moser, brought her class to a memorial ceremony at the Ebensee concentration camp, a smaller subcamp overshadowed by the larger Mauthausen. Despite its small size, at one point there were over eighteen thousand prisoners at Ebensee, and several companies used slave labor there to produce ammunition and rocket parts. The Nazi architect and director of the German economy Albert Speer and the German rocket scientist Werner von Braun had both visited Ebensee on different occasions. At the memorial service, students were able to talk directly to surviving inmates of Ebensee, most of whom now live outside of Austria.[74] Other teachers developed elaborate lesson plans incorporating interviews with concentration camp survivors and other primary sources.[75] Such examples demonstrate that many Austrian teachers and students were interested in directly confronting Austria's past to a degree that went far beyond their textbooks. But a trip to Mauthausen could cover only so much ground. In one report, the students' view of the Holocaust was changed by their trip to the camp, but one is left wondering what they thought before their visit: "Several of us thought that this documentation [the film and exhibits at the visitors' center] had been exaggerated. But those who had felt that way were soon reformed. Upon seeing the fresh flowers on the litter of the cremation oven, every cheerful discussion went silent."[76] While the students learned a valuable lesson from their visit to Mauthausen, the skepticism of several students before their visit is significant. The Holocaust did not resonate with some students until they were directly confronted with one piece of its horrific machinery—the cremation oven.

The Resistance in Textbooks

In November 1943, the Allies' Moscow Declaration reminded Austria that "she has a responsibility for participation in the war on the side of Hitlerite Germany, and that in the final settlement account will inevitably be taken of her contribution to her liberation."[77] This passage was an important counter to the opening statement of the declaration, which declared Austria a victim of German aggression. The Allies were thus sending a clear message that resistance to the Nazi regime would be rewarded. In the postwar context, Austrian legitimacy rested on demonstrating the role Austrians played in their own liberation; it was important for the Austrian government to demonstrate that there had been an effective resistance to the Nazi regime. The *Red-White-Red-Book* is the earliest example of the Austrian government seeking to document the importance of Austrian resistance. In the 1950s and 1960s, Austrian school texts reflected the symbolic value of resisters. The texts made the link between resistance and the Moscow Declaration, but resistance to Nazism did not otherwise receive much attention. For example, a 1957 text mentions resistance at the end of the war almost as an afterthought: "Austrian resistance groups wanted to spare the *Heimat* further senseless destruction and bring about a rapid end to the war. But they were frequently too weak to follow through."[78] Another text put the importance of the resistance in the context of the Allied warning that Austria must participate in its own liberation. After discussing the Moscow Declaration, the authors state: "From then on, the activity of the resistance movement increased substantially. The decisive defeat of the German army at Stalingrad and air raids … led to passive resistance.… Soon the active fight of individual resistance groups began, above all in Tyrol, the Salzkammergut, and the Carinthian border area."[79] In a 1968 text, the authors emphasize the Austrian resistance in terms of its contribution to the legitimacy of the Second Republic. In this case, the authors put Austria in the context of countries overrun by Nazi Germany: "[R]esistance movement[s], supported by the Allies, formed in almost every country, above all in Poland and Russia, Yugoslavia, Norway, and France ('maquis' or 'résistance'), but also in Austria."[80]

It is one of the many contradictions of the Austria-as-victim myth that authors placed Austria in the camp of occupied countries even though it was more typical for Austrians to be the occupiers of those same nations. It is also interesting to note that the authors covered resistance in Germany under a separate heading, with emphasis on the Kreisau Circle and the White Rose. Those involved in the conspiracy to assassinate Hitler are singled out for high praise: "It is owing to the men of 20 July 1944, for having saved the honor of the German people, in obeying the call of their conscience."[81] The "men of July 1944" were an important symbol for postwar Germany and Austria. Not only did the conspirators represent an example of resistance from the right, but as army officers, they helped preserve the image of the regular army as upstanding. However, what is often forgotten about the "men of July 1944" is that, for many of them, their resistance was inspired not so much by a rejection of Nazi ideology, but by Hitler's conduct of the war, which they rightfully believed would lead to defeat. The "men of July 1944" were heroic but not uncomplicated figures. As Omer Bartov points out, the generals who rebelled had earlier helped make "possible the regime and the organization of the army that facilitated the disasters and crimes against which they ultimately rebelled."[82]

While the Austrian government emphasized resistance for political purposes, the resisters themselves remained largely forgotten. They were wanted only for their symbolic value. Not until 1988 did the government offer resistance fighters an indemnity in the pitiful amount of between 2,500 and 5,000 schillings (roughly between $250 and $500). Meanwhile, former soldiers and prisoners of war received pension credit for their time of service.[83] It was largely due to this neglect that a group of resisters and victims of persecution, led by Herbert Steiner, founded the Dokumentationsarchiv des Österreichischen Widerstandes (Archive of the Austrian Resistance), or DÖW, in 1963. The stated mission of the archive was to "serve the education of youth in contemporary history through documentary evidence. They [Austrian youth] should be made aware of the results of the loss of independence and freedom of Austria, as well as the heroic fight of the resistance fighters."[84] Heidemarie Uhl points out that in the early 1960s, the founding of the DÖW was essential in order to counter a memory of the war that was strongly influenced by veterans' organizations hostile to the resistance. Indeed, in the April 1963 issue of the veterans' publication *Der Kamerad*, an article boldly declared: "We front soldiers have absolutely nothing in common with our countrymen, who, with weapons in their hands, killed or betrayed our own comrades."[85] Since its founding, the DÖW has published countless works on resistance and persecution, and has become a controversial and politically active organization. Founded as a corrective to honor the forgotten, the DÖW became a complicated institution. By acting as a constant reminder of Austrian resistance and in raising the memory of the persecuted, the DÖW developed into a leading iconoclast of the Austria-as-victim myth. Yet at the same time, the DÖW contributed to mythmaking in its own right.

In the 1970s, the DÖW began a project called "Resistance and Persecution in Austrian Provinces, 1934–1945." By beginning the discussion of resistance in 1934, the DÖW demonstrated its leftist orientation by including the Austro-fascist years along with the Nazi years. Historically, this was a legitimate position to take, but in the Austrian context it was also a political stand. To correct the perceived bias, the DÖW also sponsored the publication of a "supplementary" work on the *Ständestaat*'s Fatherland Front, calling it a "not unimportant aspect of the Austrian battle against National Socialism and Hitler's Germany." The publication of this work was cited "as evidence of the political-scientific plurality of the DÖW."[86] Thus, while the DÖW clearly leaned to the left, coalition history still made its mark on the archive and its work. In addition to being a research center, the DÖW is also a politically active organization that fights tirelessly against right-wing extremism, actively educates Austrian youth, and advocates for immigrants' rights. An example of the DÖW's success in the political arena is its role in banning the British historian and Holocaust denier David Irving from making a 1989 lecture tour in Austria.[87] (This is the same David Irving who, in 2000, lost a lawsuit in Great Britain where he had accused American Holocaust historian Deborah Lipstadt of defamation.)[88] As a watchdog of right-wing extremism, the DÖW has impeccable credentials, but as a research institute, the DÖW can be criticized on a number of levels.

The broad definition of resistance embraced by the DÖW and its coupling of "resistance and persecution" are both problematic. For example, in its project "Resistance and Persecution in Austrian Provinces, 1934–1945," the DÖW purposely adopted a broad definition of resistance, stating that "the entire spectrum of resistance, opposition, and discontentment—that is, every nonconformist reaction to the dictatorship—should be documented."[89] This definition is the result of inappropriately combining different historiographical schools. In the 1970s, historian Martin Broszat's idea of *Resistenz*, which is distinct from *Widerstand* (resistance), introduced a new category that encompassed nonconformity and other behavior that indirectly challenged the Nazi state's claim to total control.[90] While studies of various forms of nonconformity added new nuances to historians' understanding of Nazi Germany, the *Resistenz* concept was also potentially misleading. Many historians began to focus on nonconformity *at the expense of* the larger picture of conformity and support for the regime.[91] For example, in *Inside Nazi Germany*, Detlev Peukert writes on several themes of daily life, including contradictions in the mood of the "little man," Edelweiss pirates, and the swing movement.[92] This excellent book is not the work of an apologist historian, but taken out of the context of cooperation with and support for the Nazi regime, some of Peukert's themes could be misinterpreted. Furthermore, the important subtle distinctions between resistance and *Resistenz* were sometimes glossed over, resulting in too broad a definition of resistance. This was sometimes the case with the DÖW, which contributed to the victim mythology by overemphasizing resistance to Nazism.[93]

In the 1970s, the DÖW expanded its mandate to document Nazi persecution on racial, religious, and national grounds, later enlarging its realm of research to include victims of forced sterilization and euthanasia. The DÖW also claims not to spare in any way the Austrian participation in "Nazi terror measures."[94] But in practice, grouping resistance with persecution distorts history and contributes to the Austria-as-victim myth. An ambitious oral history project sponsored by the DÖW demonstrates how the concept of resistance can be obfuscated. The multivolume collection of interviews, *Erzählte Geschichte*, seeks to demonstrate a broad spectrum of resistance in Austrian society dating to the prewar years.[95] By lumping resisters and victims of persecution together, the books blur the fundamental difference between resistance and persecution: a resister takes action and assumes risk, while a victim of persecution is acted upon. For example, a Jew forced to scrub the sidewalk with a toothbrush has no option other than to continue scrubbing or be beaten or killed. What resisters and the persecuted *do* have in common is opposition to the regime, but there is a difference between opposition by choice and opposition by definition. Furthermore, giving persecuted individuals the same status as resisters dramatically increases the pool of those opposed to the regime, as the number of Austrians who "resisted" the regime jumps into the hundreds of thousands. The experiences of resisters and the persecuted are both used to support a notion of Austrian identity whereby the Second Republic was born out of their suffering. It is a bitter irony that the groups added to the resistance pool, especially Jews, have largely disappeared from the Second Republic, which is in part legitimized by their "resistance." Furthermore, it should be pointed out that the Austrian government did little to welcome Austrian Jews back after the war and has been painstakingly slow in offering any compensation.[96] It was not until the late 1990s that compensation was agreed to.[97]

Another criticism that can be leveled at the DÖW is its contribution to a historiographical imbalance. The broad definition of resistance feeds coalition history and allows for a nearly endless number of categories wherein resistance to Nazism can be studied. This, in turn, has led to a mountain of works on the Austrian resistance.[98] This tendency has been even stronger outside the realm of works sponsored by the DÖW. Indeed, the definition of resistance has become so broad that Chancellor Dollfuss—who was murdered by Nazis in 1934, almost four years before the Anschluss—is named as a resister. In 1972, the prominent Austrian historian Erika Weinzierl wrote: "Already in 1938 there was a not undangerous resistance against National Socialism, whose early opponents, as with after 1938, came from all political parties, even if they no longer officially existed after 1934. Its most prominent victim was federal chancellor Engelbert Dollfuss, killed in the course of the 25 July 1934 National Socialist putsch."[99] While Dollfuss was obviously a victim of Nazi violence, it requires a bending of terminology to name him a resister. The term "resistance" connotes challenging a higher authority from a disadvantaged position. One might argue that it is a stretch to use the same terminology for post-1938 resistance groups and for Dollfuss, who was the head of state at a time when the Nazi Party was outlawed. But in the context of the Austria-as-victim myth and coalition history, it made perfect sense to call Dollfuss a "resister." In so doing, the Austro-fascist government could be seen as a necessary defensive measure against Nazi Germany, and conservatives could salvage the memory of the 1934 civil war. Dollfuss's status as a resister to Nazism was argued explicitly with the 1984 publication of Gottfried-Karl Kindermann's *Hitler's Niederlage in Österreich. Bewaffneter NS-Putsch, Kanzlermord und Österreichs Abwehrsieg 1934.* In 1988, the English translation was published with the title *Hitler's Defeat in Austria, 1933–1934: Europe's First Containment of Nazi Expansionism.* Facing the title page is a leaf featuring a photo of Dollfuss's death mask. In his acknowledgments, Kindermann praises publishers Hoffmann und Campe (Hamburg), C. Hurst & Co. (London), and Westview Press (Boulder) for undertaking unsubsidized publication despite the book's "uncomfortable premises and its re-examination of historical events which many find convenient to pass over in silence." He also thanks the Lower Austrian government and its governor, Siegfried Ludwig, for underwriting the English translation (a form of support that apparently did not count as a subsidy). Governor Ludwig also wrote the second of two prefaces (the first written by the ÖVP's Alois Mock) in which he took the opportunity to convey familiar themes:

> In looking back on the First Republic, one should not forget that mistakes were made on all sides, often fraught with serious consequences. It ought not to be a matter today of seeking mutual recrimination for errors and misunderstandings of the past. To my mind, the principle of shared responsibility is indisputable.... The lesson to be drawn for the present and for all future times is surely that, regardless of ideological considerations, a political opponent must never be looked upon as an enemy. And that partnership and cooperation in the interests of the people and the state ought to be paramount. This, in my view, is an incontestable precept.

Ludwig's remarks, and Kindermann's book in general, sent a message to the Austrian left: the mantle of resistance was part of the coalition lesson, and that lesson belonged to *all* Austrians.[100]

How extensive and how effective was the Austrian resistance? The historiographical imbalance makes it difficult to answer these questions. Wolfgang Neugebauer, the director of the DÖW, acknowledges that the Austrian resistance never threatened the Nazi regime and even warns that the resistance must be seen in light of the large-scale support for the Nazi state.[101] But despite this caveat, the sheer volume of works on the resistance, combined with the "resistance and persecution" coupling, detracts from the larger reality of the war. Ultimately, placing so much emphasis on the resistance does overshadow the one-half million Austrians who joined the Nazi Party and the 1.28 million Austrians who served in the Nazi armed forces.[102] Serving in the Wehrmacht was much more typical of the Austrian experience than belonging to a resistance group. Austrians killed Russians, not Nazis.

Despite its overall ineffectiveness, the Austrian resistance was important in providing legitimacy to the Second Republic and was a powerful part of the overall Austria-as-victim myth. While the DÖW was not directly involved in the textbook-writing process, the tone set by the DÖW was reflected in Austrian school texts from the 1970s on. The DÖW's tendency to group resistance with persecution also became ubiquitous in government publications about the war.[103] While the textbooks of the 1950s and 1960s covered resistance minimally with an eye toward the Moscow Declaration, the new, broader definition of resistance and the emphasis on nonconformity, which originated among academic historians, fit perfectly into the Austria-as-victim myth. The pool of resisters grew to a size un-dreamed of by the authors of the *Red-White-Red-Book* as many textbook authors overemphasized the Austrian resistance. One text from 1972 sug-gests that even the army was a potentially strong source of resistance: "Austrians called to military service were consciously not put into closed Austrian units, but were divided among soldiers from all parts of the Reich. That way, they could not easily find contact [with each other]."[104] This text implies that it was only because Austrian soldiers were spread out among German units that a more active resistance did not occur, but there is no evidence to support such a claim. The issue of emphasis is most noticeable when comparing coverage of the resistance to coverage of the Holocaust. A 1976 text includes a table, under the heading "The Aus-trian Resistance in Numbers," that lists deported and murdered Jews along with resisters.[105] This table ignores any distinction between resist-ance and persecution. By listing people from both groups under the "resist-ance" heading, the number of resisters is greatly inflated. The overall picture has been obfuscated through emphasis. A text from 1980 includes one and a half pages on the White Rose, the Stauffenberg plot, the Aus-trian 05 movement (in which a group of army officers sought to stop the battle for Vienna by passing on information to the Red Army), and parti-sans, followed by one-half page on the Holocaust. A "Sources and Litera-ture" section immediately follows the brief discussion of the Holocaust, where students could read in detail about Inge Scholl and the White Rose and about the conspiracy to assassinate Hitler on 20 July 1944.[106] A 1981 text follows the same pattern. A brief account of the Holocaust is followed by nearly three pages on the resistance, including coverage (again) of the Scholl siblings and the Austrian martyr Franz Jägerstätter, who was exe-cuted for refusing to serve in the Wehrmacht.[107]

By far the most common theme concerning the resistance was the coali-tion history idea of "resistance for everyone." It was important for Aus-trian identity and unity that all political camps be represented in the official memory of the resistance. A reading book from 1965 unabashedly blends resistance and persecution and stresses the importance of the suf-fering of these groups to Austrian legitimacy: "They [the resisters and the persecuted], through their blood and suffering, forged the Austrian peo-ple together, in their thousand-year path through history, into a new form. The creative will of these people to the rebirth of their country created a new Austrian national feeling."[108] This same theme is emphasized in a memorial at the former site of Gestapo headquarters in Vienna (see plate 3). An odd historical twist of this site is that the Gestapo was housed in the old Hotel Metropole, where Mark Twain spent several weeks during his sojourn to turn-of-the-century Vienna. While there, Twain wrote a short unpublished manuscript titled "Conversations with Satan."[109]

Of course, the major problem with explicitly linking the legitimacy of the Second Republic with the achievement and suffering of resisters was the unfortunate reality that the Austrian resistance movement had little practical success and never seriously threatened the Nazi regime. In a world where students were much more likely to have family members with experience in the army rather than the resistance, the overemphasis on the resistance could easily ring hollow. But in the context of the victim myth, this danger was minimal because the all-encompassing community of suffering made resisters merely one of many groups. The only thing that separated the suffering of resisters from others was the resisters' symbolic importance. This is acknowledged in a history textbook from 1975 in which the authors devote five pages to the Austrian resistance movement before concluding: "For the future of Austria, the military successes of the resistance movement were not decisive ... rather [what was important was] the coming into being of a new fatherland consciousness, across all party lines."[110] Key to the symbolic power of the resistance myth was the idea that all political groups had a stake in the resistance. It was this familiar coalition lesson that made "resistance for everyone" passages so common in Austrian textbooks. In 1985, for example, students read: "There were opponents of the Hitler dictatorship in all circles, regardless of world-view or party membership."[111] The same text is accompanied by a list of casualties from the Austrian resistance movement that includes 51,500 Austrian Jews.[112] With persecuted Jews being added to the mix of resisters, the legitimacy function of the resistance was strengthened.

Although memory of the resistance was exploited and appropriated, it should be emphasized that there *was* resistance to National Socialism in Austria. This resistance was intrinsically important and of real symbolic value to the Second Republic.[113] When considering Austrian memory of the resistance, the point should not be to deny the Austrian resistance its rightful claim, but to give it its due by being forthright. This point is made eloquently by Evan Bukey, who writes that it is "worth inquiring whether the conflation of resistance and persecution has not dishonored the memory of those who took a conscious stand against Hitler's despotism."[114] An attempt to honor the resistance in a 1983 textbook points out how the victim myth has made it nearly impossible to strike a balance between honoring and appropriating the memory of the resistance. The text includes an excerpt from a diary recounting the execution of Dr. Heinrich Maier by the Gestapo just before eastern Austria fell to the Red Army: "With the last execution of 22 March 1945, Dr. Maier, too, *had to give his life for his fatherland*. With his last words 'Long live Christ, the King, and a free Austria!' the executioners seized him, and in the next seconds his head fell" (emphasis added).[115] By itself, there is nothing remarkable about this passage honoring a martyr of the resistance. However, if we compare the language of the passage with reading book passages honoring soldiers "who died for the *Heimat*," we are left with a question: Could Nazi soldiers and resisters to the Nazis both die for the same fatherland?[116] In the context of the Austria-as-victim myth, the answer is yes. Soldiers, civilians, Jews, and resisters all belonged to a single community of suffering (see plate 4).

Notes

1. "[T]here was a Jew in the apartment complex, a certain Tennenbaum…in spite of that a nice fellow…he wrote some things against the Nazis on the pavement…on the sidewalks…and Tennenbaum had to wash it off…not him alone…the other Jews too…I led him there so he would clean it up…and the building manager was watching and laughing…he was always around for mischief…After the war he came back, this Tennenbaum. Nothing happened to him anyway." Merz and Qualtinger, *Der Herr Karl*, 19–21.

2. Quoted from Evan B. Bukey, "Popular Opinion in Vienna After the Anschluss," in *Conquering the Past*, ed. Parkinson, 162 fn.

3. Rüdiger Overmans, "German and Austrian Losses in World War II," in *Austrian Historical Memory and National Identity*, ed. Bischof and Pelinka, 295. This figure does not include Austrians who served in the SS or Waffen SS. See ibid., note 6.

4. See Florian Freund, "Kriegswirtschaft, Zwangsarbeit und Konzentrationslager in Österreich," in *Österreicher und der Zweite Weltkrieg*, ed. Wolfgang Neugebauer and Elisabeth Morawek (Vienna: Österreichischer Bundesverlag, 1989), 100–119.

5. See the "Neuverlautbarung der Provisorischen Lehrpläne für die Mittelschulen" in *Verordnungsblatt fur den Dienstbereich des Bundesministeriums für Unterricht*, Stück 10a (Vienna, 15 October 1955), 81.

6. Ibid., 84.

7. *III. Sondernummer zum Verordnungsblatt für den Dienstberiech des Bundesministeriums für Unterricht*, Stück 10a (Vienna, 1 October 1967), 109.

8. *Lehrplan der Hauptschule*, 5th ed. (Vienna: Österreichischer Bundesverlag für Unterricht, Wissenschaft und Kunst, 1974), 125. The same wording is in the 1979 eighth edition. See *Lehrplan der Hauptschule*, 8th ed. (Vienna: Österreichischer Bundesverlag, 1979), 92.

9. *Lehrpläne der allgemeinbildenden höheren Schulen. I. Band* (Vienna: Österreichischer Bundesverlag, 1984), 87–88.

10. *Lehrplan des Polytechnischen Lehrganges* (Vienna: Österreichischer Bundesverlag, 1967), 44.

11. *Lehrplan des Polytechnischen Lehrganges* (Vienna: Österreichischer Bundesverlag für Unterricht, 1976), 46; and *Lehrplan des Polytechnischen Lehrganges* (Vienna: Österreichischer Bundesverlag, 1981), 54–55.

12. Arbeitsgemeinschaft, *Unser Österreich, 1945–1955*, 2–3 (unnumbered pages).

13. Lang and Ritter, *Unser Österreich, 1945–1955*, 10.

14. Ebner and Partick, *Lehrbuch der Geschichte und Sozialkunde*, 138.

15. Karl A. Dostal, ed., *Umgang mit Texten 3. Lesestücke für die dritte Klasse der Hauptschule und der AHS* (Vienna: Verlag Leitner, 1983), 163–167.

16. For example, see Borchert's "Nachts schlafen die Ratten doch" in *Die Weltenuhr*, ed. Hörler and Müller, 107–110.

17. Binder et al., *Aus dem Reich der Dichtung 4. Literatur für dich*, 7.

18. See, for example, the work of Christopher Browning, especially *Ordinary Men: Reserve Police Battalion 101 and the Final Solution in Poland* (New York: HarperPerennial, 1992).

19. Arbeitsgemeinschaft, eds., *Österreich Lesebuch. Band 4* (Vienna: Verlag Carl Ueberreuter, 1983), 117, 179–180.

20. Hans Bernt et al., eds., *Arbeit—Freiheit—Menschenwürde. Vom Biedermeier zur Gegenwart. Österreich—erlebt und erschaut* (Vienna: Hölder-Pichler-Tempsky, 1961), 139–141.

21. Hörler and Müller, *Die Weltenuhr*, 103–105.

22. A popular story claims that removal of the towers remains an elusive problem to solve as the amount of explosives necessary to bring them down would damage the surrounding areas.

23. Othmar Franz Lang, *Das war Bundespräsident Dr. Adolf Schärf* (Vienna: Österreichischer Bundesverlag, 1965), 5.

24. Ebner and Partick, *Lehrbuch der Geschichte und Sozialkunde*, 133.

25. Novotny, *Österreichisches Lehrbuch für Geschichte und Sozialkunde*, 167–169. This 1976 edition is virtually the same as the 1972 edition.

26. See Omer Bartov, *The Eastern Front, 1941–45, German Troops and the Barbarisation of War-fare* (Oxford: Macmillan Press, 1985); and idem, *Hitler's Army: Soldiers, Nazis, and War in the Third Reich* (New York: Oxford University Press, 1992).

27. Hörler and Müller, *Die Weltenuhr*, 101–103.

28. Franz Haun and Robert Ritter, eds., *Die Welt ist da damit wir alle leben. Ein Buch Von Krieg und Frieden* (Vienna: Hölder-Pichler-Tempsky, 1964), 38–44.

29. Ernst Joseph Görlich, Kurt Kren, and Josef Maderner, *Zeitgeschichte. Lehrbuch der Geschichte und Sozialkunde für den 5. Jahrgang der Handelsakademien* (Vienna: Österreichischer Gewerbeverlag, 1973), 68.

30. Moeller, *War Stories*, 148–149.

31. Franz Berger et al., eds., *Zeiten, Völker und Kulturen. Ein Lehr- und Arbeitsbuch für den Geschichtsunterricht an Haupt- und Untermittelschulen. 4. Band. Das Zeitalter der Weltpolitik und der Technik* (Vienna: Hölder-Pichler-Tempsky, 1957), 178. A 1965 text on Stalingrad emphasizes the German high command's carelessness in allowing the German army to get caught in a position where they knew it could not be supplied. See Theodor Plievier's story "Stalingrad," in *Wir Schweigen Nicht*, ed. Gross and Lein, 60–62.

32. *Bundesrealgymnasium, Henriettenplatz, Wien XV, Jahresbericht, 1964–1965* (Vienna, 1965), 10–11.

33. L. G. Stöger, ed., *Geschichte in Tafelbildern und Zusammenfassungen* (Wels: Verlagsbuchhandlung Leitner & Co., 1963), 303.

34. Lehrerarbeitsgemeinschaft beim Landesschulrat Salzburg, eds., *Unser Lesebuch. 4. Klasse Hauptschule. Du und die Gemeinschaft* (Salzburg: Otto Müller Verlag, 1960), 21–24.

35. "Like a winter storm, a rolling echo./The earthen wall of Bethlehem's stall, shot to pieces./Mary lies slain before the gate,/her bloody hair frozen on the stone.... Before Stalingrad the highway is covered with snow drifts./It leads to the death chamber of snow." Binder et al., *Aus dem Reich der Dichtung 4. Literatur für dich*, 52.

36. See Gertrud Kerschbaumer, "Wählerpotential 'Wehrmachtsoldat.' Die Nachkriegsparteien und die ehemaligen Wehrmachtsangehörigen," in *Eiszeit der Erinnerung*, ed. Brunnbauer, 89.

37. See Uhl, "Erinnern und Vergessen," 146–171.

38. Helene Berghofer et al., eds., *Unser schönes Buch. Lesebuch für die 4. Schulstufe. Ausgabe für Burgenland* (Eisenstadt: E. Rötzer Verlag, 1973), 34–35.

39. *Bundesgymnasium und -Realschule Bruck a. d. Mur, Festbericht Anlässlich des 50 Jährigen Bestandes der Anstalt (1907–1957)* (Bruck an der Mur, 1958), 44–46.

40. *Festschrift des B.R.G. Leoben 1962. Aus Anlass der 100 Jahrfeier und zur Eröffnung des neuen Schulgebäudes* (Leoben, 1962), 42–45.

41. Bukey, *Hitler's Austria*, 152.

42. Gerhard Botz, "The Dynamics of Persecution in Austria, 1938–45," in *Austrians and Jews in the Twentieth Century: From Franz Joseph to Waldheim*, ed. Robert S. Wistrich (New York: St. Martin's Press, 1992): 199–219.

43. Miller, *One, by One, by One*, 67.

44. Hanisch, *Der Lange Schatten des Staates*, 353, 370–385. For works on Mauthausen, see Gordon J. Horwitz, *In the Shadow of Death: Living Outside the Gates of Mauthausen* (New York: The Free Press, 1990); and Evelyn Le Chêne, *Mauthausen: The History of a Death Camp* (London: Methuen, 1971). Austria's prewar Jewish population was approximately 200,000. Around 120,000 Austrian Jews fled the country after the Anschluss. See Miller, *One, by One, by One*, 67.

45. Ebner and Partick, *Lehrbuch der Geschichte und Sozialkunde*, 119.

46. Zens, *Schaut Ringsumher*, 22.

47. Görlich et al., *Zeitgeschichte*, 72.

48. Christian Streit, *Keine Kameraden. Die Wehrmacht und die sowjetischen Kriegsgefangenen, 1941–1945* (Stuttgart: Deutsche Verlags-Anstalt, 1978).

49. Franz Berger et al., *Zeiten, Völker, und Kulturen. Ein Lehr- und Arbeitsbuch für den Unterricht in Geschichte und Sozialkunde. 3. Band für die 4. Klasser der Hauptschulen und der allgemeinbildenden höheren Schulen* (Vienna: Hölder-Pichler-Tempsky, 1967), 70. Also see the 1977 and 1987 editions of the same work.

50. Arbeitsgruppe Sprache als soziales Handeln, *Unter der Oberfläche. Band 4 für die 4. Klasse. Texte. Lese- und Arbeitsbuch für die Hauptschulen und die Unterstufe der allgemeinbildenden höheren Schulen* (Vienna: Österreichischer Bundesverlag, 1977), 32–35.

51. Gross and Lein, *Wir Schweigen Nicht*, 105–111.

52. Lang and Ritter, *Unser Österreich, 1945–1955*, 25.

53. Gerhard Atschko, Peter Dusek, and Helmut Rauch, *Sozial- und Wirtschaftskunde (inkl. Zeitgeschichte) für den Polytechnischen Lehrgang* (Vienna: Bohmann-Verlag, 1982), 23–24.

54. Herbert Hasenmayer, Johann Payr, and Kurt Tschegg, *Epochen der Weltgeschichte 3. Vom Ersten Weltkrieg bis zur Gegenwart. Ein approbiertes Arbeits- und Lehrbuch für Geschichte und Sozialkunde (Wirtschaftsgeschichte)* (Vienna: Verlag Ferdinand Hirt, 1983), 51–54.

55. The sentences include: "A citizen can only be someone who is a member of the [German] race (*Volksgenosse*). *Volksgenosse* can only be someone of German blood, regardless of religion. No Jew can be a *Volksgenosse*." On the following page, a sentence reads: "Every German citizen must have a genealogy pass to prove that he has no Jewish ancestry." These sentences are among the few specific mentions of Nazi anti-Semitism. See Herbert Hasenmayer et al., *Aus Vergangenheit und Gegenwart. Ein approbiertes Arbeits- und Lehrbuch für Geschichte und Sozialkunde* (Vienna: Verlag Ferdinand Hirt, 1985), 85–86.

56. Ibid., 97, 99.

57. Ibid., 99.

58. In a 1966 reader for polytechnic schools, Robert Jungk's story, "Die erste Atombombe," gives a straightforward account of the first atom bomb test in New Mexico. The same book also includes a story, "Die Wiege der Welt von Morgen," by Peter von Zahn, about the atomic research facility at Oak Ridge, Tennessee. This informative passage presents a positive view of the peaceful uses of nuclear technology in the fields of medicine and energy. This book for polytechnic students is an exception to the rule. See Arbeitsgemeinschaft, eds., *Das Leben Liegt vor Uns. Ein Arbeits- und Lesebuch für den Polytechnischen Lehrgang* (Vienna: Österreichischer Bundesverlag für Unterricht, Wissenschaft, und Kunst, 1966), 191–193, 199–202.

59. See Eleanor Coerr, *Sadako and the Thousand Paper Cranes* (New York: Putnam, 1977).

60. There are statues of Sadako at the Hiroshima Peace Park in Japan and in Seattle, Washington.

61. Adolf Harwalik et al., eds., *Schaffensfreude Lebensfreude. Ausgewähltes lebens- und berufskundliches Lesegut für den Polytechnischen Lehrgang* (Eisenstadt: E. Rötzer Verlag, 1966), 222–226.

62. Emanuel Bialonczyk and Otwald Kropatsch, *Begegnungen. Ein Lesebuch für die Oberstufe der allgemeinbildenden höheren Schulen einschließlich der Musisch-pädagogischen Realgymnasien*, 2nd ed. (Vienna: Österreichischer Bundesverlag für Unterricht, Wissenschaft und Kunst, 1974), 91–95. A 1982 polytechnic reader included the Sadako story, plus Marie Luise Kaschnitz's poem "Hiroshima." See Harawalik et al., *Schaffensfreude, Lebensfreude*, 189–196. Note that these stories were not in the 1966 edition of this work, which had presented a more positive image of the nuclear age. A 1985 reader includes a letter from Japanese schoolgirls to Major Claude Eatherly in a veterans hospital in Waco, Texas. Eatherly flew on the mission to drop the bomb and later suffered from psychiatric trouble. See Karl A. Dostal, *Umgang mit Texten 1. Lesestücke für die erste Klasse der Hauptschule* (Vienna: Verlag Leitner, 1985), 151–152.

63. Telford Taylor, *Nuremberg and Vietnam: An American Tragedy* (New York: Quadrangle Books, 1970). Also see Tom Engelhardt, *The End of Victory Culture: Cold War America and the Disillusioning of a Generation* (New York: Basic Books, 1995), 225–227.

64. See James W. Loewen, "The Vietnam War in High School American History," and David Hunt, "War Crimes and the Vietnamese People: American Representations and Silences," both in *Censoring History*, ed. Hein and Selden, 150–172 and 173–200, respectively.

65. Richard Pells, *Not Like Us: How Europeans Have Loved, Hated, and Transformed American Culture Since World War II* (New York: Basic Books, 1997), 284–285.

66. In his path-breaking book *The Pacific War, 1931–1945*, first published in 1968, the Japanese historian Saburo Ienaga not only exposes Japanese crimes in World War II, but also

castigates the Japanese government for its Cold War alliance with the United States—which, in Ienaga's words, is "the new aggressor in Asia"—and asserts that "Japan shares responsibility, as a partner in crime with the United States, in the illegal war against the Vietnamese people." See Saburo Ienaga, *The Pacific War, 1931–1945* (New York: Pantheon Books, 1978), 240, 244. The focus of Ienaga's work was not the United States, but the examples cited here demonstrate that in the context of 1968, the Vietnam War had an extremely negative impact on the international image of the United States.

67. The mixing of Auschwitz and Hiroshima is not unique to Austria. In Hiroshima, for example, there is a "Hiroshima-Auschwitz Committee." See Ian Buruma, *The Wages of Guilt: Memories of War in Germany and Japan* (New York: Meridian, 1994), 92.

68. Scheipl et al., *Geschichte und Sozialkunde*, 99.

69. *Bundesgymnasium für Mädchen in Graz, Jahresbericht über das Schuljahr 1964/65* (Graz, 1965), 20–22.

70. *Bundesgymnasium und Bundesrealgymnasium Lienz, Jahresbericht 1977/78* (Lienz, 1978), 34.

71. *Freinberger Stimmen*, 44. Jahrgang. 1. Heft. December 1973, v.

72. *Bundesgymnasium und Bundesrealgymnasium Leoben, LXXXVIII/124 Jahresbericht* (Leoben, 1986), 157.

73. "Mauthausen/Large and gray, it lies on a hill/Dominating/Swarms of school children spill into the square. Unknowing confused language puts new life into the cold/walls,/which have seen so many horrors.... One gets in his car, and drives, never to return./One drives to the next *Gasthaus* [restaurant/bar], to wash down the horror." *Jahresbericht des Bundesgymnasiums III Salzburg. Musisches Gymnasium. Neusprachliches Gymnasium* (Salzburg, 1985), 106.

74. *Bundesgymnansium und Budesrealgymnasium Bad Ischl, 13. Jahresbericht 1984/85* (Bad Ischl, 1985), 33–36.

75. See Heinz Strotzka, "Tonbandprotokolle im Unterricht am Beispiel des Berichts eines Ehemaligen Konzentrationslagerhäftlings," *Zeitgeschichte* 9, no. 8 (1982): 284–295; Gisela Buchinger and Elke Stöckl, "Konzentrationslager und Widerstand. Zwei Unterrichtseinheiten am Beispiel des Konzentrationslagers Mauthausen," *Zeitgeschichte* 10, no. 6 (1983): 240–248; Hermann Langbein, "Überlebende aus den Konzentrationslagern des Nationalsozialismus Sprechen mit Schülern," *Zeitgeschichte* 12, no. 2 (1984): 52–57; and Johann Mayr, "Praxisorientierte Vorbereitung einer Exkursion zur Gedenkstätte Mauthausen Ausserhalb der Lehrplankontinuität in einer Unterrichtsstunde," *Zeitgeschichte* 12, nos. 11–12 (1985): 439–450.

76. *HTL Braunau, Jahresbericht 1978/79* (Braunau, 1979), 25.

77. Quoted in Keyserlingk, *Austria in World War II*, 152.

78. Berger et al., *Zeiten, Völker und Kulturen*, 189.

79. Ebner et al., *Unsere Republik im Wandel der Zeit*, 44.

80. Knarr et al., *Der Mensch im Wandel der Zeiten*, 120.

81. Ibid., 121.

82. Bartov, "Defining Enemies, Making Victims," 794.

83. Schausberger, "Die Entstehung des Mythos," 40–41.

84. *Dreissig Jahre Dokumentationsarchiv des Österreichischen Widerstandes (1963–1993)* (Vienna, 1993), 3–5.

85. Uhl, "Transformationen des österreichischen Gedächtnisses," 56.

86. *Dreissig Jahre Dokumentationsarchiv des Österreichischen Widerstandes (1963–1993)*, 14. The work on the Fatherland Front referred to is Ludwig Reichhold, *Kampf um Österreich. Die Vaterländische Front und ihr Widerstand gegen den Anschluß, 1933–1938*, 2nd ed. (Vienna: Österreichischer Bundesverlag, 1985).

87. *Dreissig Jahre Dokumentationsarchiv des Österreichischen Widerstandes (1963–1993)*, 25.

88. Buruma, "Blood Libel," 82–86.

89. *Dreissig Jahre Dokumentationsarchiv des Österreichischen Widerstandes (1963–1993)*, 13.

90. See the chapter "Resistance Without the People?" in Ian Kershaw, *The Nazi Dictatorship: Problems and Perspectives of Interpretation*, 3rd ed. (London: Edward Arnold, 1993), 150–179.

91. Ian Kershaw remarks that "the story of dissent, opposition, and resistance in the Third Reich is indistinguishable from the story of consent, approval, and collaboration." Ibid., 179.

92. Detlev J. K. Peukert, *Inside Nazi Germany: Conformity, Opposition, and Racism in Everyday Life.* trans. Richard Deveson (New Haven: Yale University Press, 1987). Also see Christian Gerbel, Alexander Mejstrik, and Reinhard Sieder, "Die 'Schlurfs.' Verweigerung und Opposition von Wiener Arbeiterjugendlichen im 'Dritten Reich,'" in *NS-Herrschaft in Österreich*, ed. Tálos et al., 243–268.

93. The current director of the DÖW, Wolfgang Neugebauer, argues against this point, writing that resistance research cannot be accused of inappropriately contributing to state legitimacy, because resistance research "in no way owes its existence to state or official favor," and points out that the DÖW was independently founded in 1963. See Wolfgang Neugebauer, "Widerstand und Opposition," in *NS-Herrschaft in Österreich*, ed. Tálos et al. This argument is somewhat misleading, since Neugebauer was writing in 1988, and most criticism of DÖW work is leveled at works sponsored since the 1970s (and is not directed toward the founding of the DÖW).

94. *Dreissig Jahre Dokumentationsarchiv des Österreichischen Widerstandes (1963–1993)*, 13.

95. The first volume concentrates on workers, and ranges in subject from Austrian participation in the Spanish Civil War (on the Republican side), to the Anschluss, through the end of the war. See DÖW, ed., *Erzählte Geschichte. Berichte von Widerstandskämpfern und Verfolgten. Band I: Arbeiterbewegung* (Vienna: Österreichischer Bundesverlag, 1984). The second volume in the series chronicles the activities of Catholics, conservatives, and legitimists. See DÖW, ed., *Erzählte Geschichte. Berichte von Widerstandskämpfern und Verfolgten. Band II: Katholiken, Konservative, Legitimisten* (Vienna: Österreichischer Bundesverlag, 1992). The third volume is a collection of interviews with Jews. See DÖW, ed., *Erzählte Geschichte. Berichte von Widerstandskämpfern und Verfolgten. Band III: Jüdische Schicksale* (Vienna: Österreichischer Bundesverlag, 1993). The fourth volume in the series concentrates on the activities of Carinthian Slovenes. See DÖW, ed., *Erzählte Geschichte. Berichte von Widerstandskämpfern und Verfolgten. Band IV: Spurensuche. Erzählte Geschichte der Kärntner Slowenen* (Vienna: Österreichischer Bundesverlag, 1990).

96. See Brigitte Bailer, *Wiedergutmachung Kein Thema. Österreich und die Opfer des Nationalsozialismus* (Vienna: Löcker, 1993); Knight, *"Ich bin dafür, die Sache in die Länge zu ziehen"*; Robert Knight, "'Neutrality' Not Sympathy: Jews in Post-War Austria," in *Austrians and Jews in the Twentieth Century*, ed. Wistrich, 220–233; Richard Mitten, "Die 'Judenfrage' im Nachkriegsösterreich. Probleme der Forschung," *Zeitgeschichte* 19, nos. 11–12 (1992): 356–367; and idem, "'Die Sühne ... möglichst zu gestalten.' Die sozialdemokratische 'Bearbeitung' des Nationalsozialismus und des Antisemitismus in Österreich," in *Schwieriges Erbe. Der Umgang mit Nationalsozialismus und Antisemitismus in Österreich, der DDR und der Bundesrepublik Deutschland*, ed. Werner Bergmann, Rainer Erb, and Albert Lichtblau (Frankfurt: Campus Verlag, 1995), 102–119.

97. See Anton Pelinka and Sabine Mayr, eds., *Die Entdeckung der Verantwortung. Die Zweite Republik und die vertriebenen Juden* (Vienna: Wilhelm Braumüller, 1998).

98. The best survey in English of the Austrian resistance is Radomir Luza, *The Resistance in Austria, 1938–1945* (Minneapolis: University of Minnesota Press, 1984).

99. See the chapter "Der Österreichische Widerstand" by Erika Weinzierl, in *Österreich. Die Zweite Republik. Band 1*, ed. Erika Weinzierl and Kurt Skalnik (Graz: Verlag Styria, 1972), 109.

100. See Gottfried-Karl Kindermann, *Hitler's Defeat in Austria, 1933–1934: Europe's First Containment of Nazi Expansionism*, trans. Sonia Brough and David Taylor (London: C. Hurst & Company, 1988), title page, v, x.

101. See Neugebauer, "Widerstand und Opposition," in *NS-Herrschaft in Österreich*, ed. Tálos et al., 550. Neugebauer makes almost identical comments in Wolfgang Neugebauer, "Widerstand und Opposition," in *Österreicher und der Zweite Weltkrieg*, ed. Neugebauer and Morawek, 90.

102. The writer Jane Kramer claims that the Nazi Party figure was proportionately higher than in Germany. See Jane Kramer, *Europeans* (New York: Penguin Books, 1988), 404.

103. Siegwald Ganglmair (of DÖW), *Resistance and Persecution in Austria, 1938–1945* (Vienna: Federal Press Service, 1988).

104. Göhring and Hasenmayer, *Zeitgeschichte. Ein approbiertes Lehr- und Arbeitsbuch für Geschichte und Sozialkunde*, 103.

105. Harwalik et al., *Schaffensfreude Lebensfreude*, 205.

106. Werner Tscherne, Erich Scheithauer, and Manfred Gartler, *Weg durch die Zeiten 4. Arbeits- und Lehrbuch für Geschichte und Sozialkunde. Für die 8. Klasse der Oberstufe* (Graz: Leopold Stocker Verlag, 1980), 81–83.

107. Scheipl et al., *Geschichte und Sozialkunde*, 101–102.

108. Gross and Lein, *Wir Schweigen Nicht*, 153–154.

109. Carl Dolmetsch, *"Our Famous Guest": Mark Twain in Vienna* (Athens: University of Georgia Press), 27.

110. Ebner and Majdan, *Geschichte 4 für die Oberstufe*, 197.

111. Felix Riccabona et al., *Geschichte, Sozialkunde, Politische Bildung. 8 Schulstufe. 4. Klasse Hauptschule*, 2nd ed. (Linz: Veritas-Verlag, 1985), 73.

112. Ibid., 74.

113. Ernst Hanisch, "Gab es einen spezifisch Österreichischen Widerstand?" *Zeitgeschichte* 12, nos. 9–10 (1985): 339–350.

114. See the review article by Evan Burr Bukey, "Nazi Rule in Austria," *Austrian History Yearbook*, vol. 23 (1992): 230.

115. Arbeitsgemeinschaft, *Österreich Lesebuch. Band 4*, 120.

116. This question figures prominently in historian Matthew Paul Berg's examination of postwar veterans' organizations in Austria. See Matthew Paul Berg, "Challenging Political Culture in Postwar Austria: Veterans Associations, Identity, and the Problem of Contemporary History," *Central European History* 30, no. 4 (1997): 513–544. On the complexity of commemorating the German war dead, see Richard Mitten, "Bitburg, Waldheim, and the Politics of Remembering and Forgetting," in *From World War to Waldheim*, ed. Good and Wodak, 52–54.

PLATE 1 Flak tower near Mariahilferstrasse. "Smashed to Pieces in the Still of the Night." Vienna, spring 1996. Photo by the author.

PLATE 2 Memorial. "To Our Dead from Two World Wars." Bundesoberstufenrealgymnasium, Wiener Neustadt, spring 1988. Photo by the author.

PLATE 3 Monument at Morinzplatz commemorating victims of the Gestapo.
"Never Forget. Here stood the Gestapo building. For those loyal to Austria, it
was hell. For many of them, it was the vestibule to death. It sank in the ruins like
the Thousand Year Reich. Austria, however, rose again, and along with it, our
dead, the immortal victims." Vienna, spring 1996. Photo by the author.

PLATE 4 Memorial to "The Heroes of World War II." A similar memorial to World War I dead is on the opposite wall. Town church, Gablitz, Lower Austria, spring 1996. Photo by the author.

PLATE 5 View from the Old Jewish Section of Vienna Central Cemetery, looking toward the Christian section, Vienna, fall 1995. Photo by the author.

PLATE 6 Jewish gravestones in the Old Jewish Section of Vienna Central Cemetery, *Vienna*, fall 1995. Photo by the author.

PLATE 7 Monument against War and Fascism. The "Gate of Violence," Vienna, spring 1996. Photo by Claire Villalpando Utgaard.

PLATE 8 Monument against War and Fascism. The "Jew Scrubbing the Sidewalk," Vienna, spring 1996. Photo by Claire Villalpando Utgaard.

PLATE 9 Monument against War and Fascism. Man looking at two of Hrdlicka's pillars. Note the State Opera House in the background, Vienna, spring 1996. Photo by Claire Villalpando Utgaard.

Chapter Four

REMEMBERING AND FORGETTING THE ALLIED OCCUPATION, REBUILDING, AND THE STATE TREATY

The Second Rebirth of Austria and New Symbols of National Identity

━━━━━━━━━━━━━━━━━━━━━━━━━━━━━━

They [the Allies] declare that they wish to see re-established a free and independent Austria.

— Moscow Declaration, 1 November 1943[1]

Natirlich – es war eine harte Zeit...man hat ein befreites Volk hungern lassen.

— Der Herr Karl[2]

G'freit hab i mi scho...an den Tag, wo man 'n bekommen ham...den Staatsvertrag...Da san ma zum Belvedere zogn...san dag'standen... unübersehbar...lauter Österreicher...wie im Jahr achtadreißig...Und dann is er herausgetreten...der...der...Bundes-, der Poldl und hat die zwa andern Herrschaften bei der Hand genommen und mutig bekannt: "Österreich ist wieder frei!" Und wie i des g'hört hab, da hab i g'wußt: Auch das hab ich jetzt geschafft. Es ist uns gelungen – der Wiederaufbau.

— Der Herr Karl[3]

After years of painstaking negotiations, the Austrian State Treaty was signed on 15 May 1955. On 25 October 1955, the last Allied soldier left Austria, and the occupation was officially over. The next day, the Austrian government declared its permanent neutrality. Ten years later, in 1965, the twenty-sixth of October—already Austrian Flag Day—became the Austrian national holiday to honor that day when Austrian sovereignty was fully restored. Compared with East and West Germany, Austria found itself in an almost miraculous position. At the height of the

Cold War, Austria was united, unoccupied, and neutral, while the Federal Republic of Germany and the German Democratic Republic were armed camps filled with foreign soldiers. Given that Austria had been an integral part of Nazi Germany, the full restoration of Austrian sovereignty in 1955 was indeed remarkable. In the context of the Cold War, Austria was fortunate, but through the lens of the Austria-as-victim myth, the State Treaty did not amount to preferential treatment. Indeed, the opposite was true, as Austrian politicians viewed the Allies' evacuation as long overdue. Austrian political leaders continuously referred to the Allied occupation as the "second" occupation, which came on the heels of the German "occupation" (not annexation) of 1938–1945. As Foreign Minister (and former Chancellor) Leopold Figl put it, Austria had gone from "one foreign occupation to another foreign occupation."[4]

Of course, it was specious to link the Allied occupation of Austria with the Nazi regime, but in the context of the Austria-as-victim myth, this approach made perfect sense. Once one accepted the doctrine of Austrian victimization at the hands of Germany, the Allied presence in Austria became another theme of the victim myth. As Austria's fate became entwined with the Cold War, the Four Powers were portrayed as "betraying" their promise to restore Austria and as an obstacle to the rebuilding process. The occupation itself became part of the trial of rebuilding, or *Wiederaufbau*, and overcoming the Four Powers became an important symbol in the nation-building process. The Allies were the "they," which contrasted with the emerging Austrian "we."[5] Notably, this official memory of the Allied occupation included an official *forgetting* of denazification—a topic virtually absent in postwar Austrian textbooks. Besides its portrayal as the "second" occupation (which incorporated the Allied occupation into a larger ordeal of suffering dating to the First Republic), victimization at the hands of the Four Powers also intersected with new, key themes of postwar Austrian identity: rebuilding, the State Treaty (and being a pawn of the Cold War), neutrality, and eventually the national holiday, which celebrated overcoming the hardship of Allied occupation. Austria ultimately triumphed through the hard work of rebuilding to emerge as a neutral state that rose above the cynical politics of the Cold War.

The Roots of the "Unjust" Occupation: The Moscow Declaration and Allied Planning for Austria

The importance of the above themes is rooted in Austria's first encounter with the Allies—a moment which also signaled that the rebirth of Austria was a real possibility. On 1 November 1943, after a meeting of Allied foreign ministers in Moscow, the Moscow Declaration was issued. It stated:

> The Governments of the United Kingdom, the Soviet Union and the United States of America are agreed that Austria, the first free country to fall victim to Hitlerite aggression, shall be liberated from German domination.

They regard the annexation imposed upon Austria by Germany on March 15 [*sic*] 1938, as null and void. They consider themselves in no way bound by any changes effected in Austria since that date. They declare that they wish to see re-established a free and independent Austria, and thereby to open the way for the Austrian people themselves, as well as those neighboring states which will face similar problems, to find that political and economic security which is the only basis for lasting peace.

Austria is reminded, however, that she has a responsibility for participation in the war on the side of Hitlerite Germany, and that in the final settlement account will inevitably be taken of her contribution to her liberation.[6]

Taken at face value, the Moscow Declaration brought the Austrian corpse back to life. The Allies had stated clearly that Austria was "the first free country to fall victim to Hitlerite aggression" and that Austria "shall be liberated from German domination." After the war, Austrian political leaders understandably pointed to the Moscow Declaration as a source of legitimacy and as proof of Austria's victimization. But what was the intention and context of the Moscow Declaration in November 1943? At that time, the tide of the war had shifted against Nazi Germany. The battle for Stalingrad in the winter of 1942–1943, combined with serious reverses in North Africa and Italy, can rightly be called the turning point of the war, yet the war's final outcome was still uncertain in the fall of 1943. The Western Allies did not invade France until June 1944, and the German army was still well inside the Soviet Union. In the context of these circumstances, the Moscow Declaration was intended as a tactical device to promote resistance activity and weaken the Third Reich. In other words, the Moscow Declaration was part of the war effort and not meant as a meaningful political statement of Allied policy.

Historians who have carefully examined the process of drafting the Moscow Declaration have firmly established this point. Robert Graham Knight writes that the document "represented a political compromise, worked out by diplomats whose main concern was not Austria, but rather the defeat of Nazi Germany." Knight also cites the British diplomat Geoffrey Harrison, who had helped formulate the declaration. Early in 1945, Harrison stated that the declaration had "no particular legal validity in international law."[7] Gerald Stourzh, author of the definitive works on the Austrian State Treaty, also acknowledges that the Allied policy toward Austria should be seen in the larger context of an overall policy toward weakening Germany.[8] There is, however, no real consensus as to whether the restoration of Austria, promised by the Moscow Declaration, can be considered an "aim" or a "goal" of the Allies and by implication, therefore, among the reasons for defeating Nazi Germany. Stourzh argues that with the Moscow Declaration, the Four Powers had "finally established the re-establishment of an independent Austria as one of their war aims," despite the fact that the Allies continued to consider various options for Austria after November 1943.[9] Stourzh's argument is undermined by Robert Keyserlingk, whose *Austria in World II: An Anglo-American Dilemma* meticulously analyzes Allied wartime planning for Austria. His work calls into question the validity of referring to the restoration of Austria as a "war aim." Indeed, Keyserlingk points out that while some in the press took the Moscow Declaration at face value, many reporters perceived the tactical intention of the declaration. For example, the *New York Herald Tribune* called the declaration "their [the Allies'] best and brightest instrument for breaking down the crumbling structure of Hitler's empire of evil." The *New York Post* viewed the declaration as a "military weapon against Hitler," and the *Wall Street Journal* recognized that the Moscow Declaration was not a political statement, but rather "a statement of executive intent … it is not improbable that there will be some reservations on the one pertaining to Austria." American Secretary of State Cordell Hull left little doubt as to the intent of the Moscow Declaration. Upon his return from Moscow, Hull told reporters "off the record" that it, in Keyserlingk's words, "had been published solely for propaganda purposes and was certainly not official administration policy."[10]

In the end, the process of deciding to restore Austria was complicated, being both evolutionary and subject to sometimes rapid change, as was all of the planning for the postwar world. Once postwar planning began, it was clear that the post-1938 borders of Nazi Germany would not stand, so it only made sense that the Allies would take a retroactive principled stance on the Anschluss represented by the Moscow Declaration. Ultimately, it is most accurate to view the restoration of Austria as part of the dismemberment of Nazi Germany. Reviving Austria was the best and most logical way to weaken Germany and reverse the wrong of the Anschluss, but it is important to note that other options were being considered, such as detaching Bavaria from Germany and creating a Danubian confederation.[11] But because the Four Powers *did* restore Austria, there was never any reason to disavow the stated intent of the Moscow Declaration. Thus, in the postwar world, the Moscow Declaration took on a life of its own and became a kind of charter for the Second Republic. Austria's cadre of gifted and patriotic politicians did not miss the opportunity to seize upon the Moscow Declaration as a source of legitimacy. For their part, the Allied powers likewise encouraged and tolerated the myth of Austria as victim.

The Moscow Declaration and Allied Planning for Austria in Textbooks

As in the political sphere, school materials also addressed the significance of the Moscow Declaration. The first part of the document, which declared Austria a victim, was very valuable in legitimizing the Austria-as-victim stance, but the second part of the document, which reminded Austria "that she has a responsibility for participation in the war," was another matter. The declaration was too important to be ignored, but it was clearly a complex statement, which legitimized and simultaneously undermined the Austria-as-victim myth. Often, textbook authors simply ignored the second part of the document. For example, a 1957 history book mentions only the first part of the Moscow Declaration and includes a caption in the margin that reads: "The Moscow Declaration promises a free Austria."[12] As late as 1986, textbook authors made statements such as: "Since 1939, the re-establishment of the Republic of Austria was one of their [the Allies'] war aims."[13] In addition to overlooking the second part of the declaration, textbook authors often implied that Austria was betrayed by the Allies' failure to keep promises. In a 1968 history text, the authors ignore the second part of the declaration and then suggest that the Allies broke their word by delaying agreement to the State Treaty: "[With the Moscow Declaration, the Allies] ... declared the occupation of Austria by Germany to be null and void, and [they promised] a free and independent Austria.... No one thought, of all things, that it would take exactly twelve years to keep this promise."[14] Here, the authors both omit the second part of the Moscow Declaration and cast Austria as a victim of the Four Powers.

Perhaps because it was so obviously disingenuous to ignore the second part of the Moscow Declaration, history textbook authors began to address it in the 1970s. However, addressing the "responsibility" clause of the Moscow Declaration did not necessarily mean abandoning the victim theory, as authors resorted to qualifying statements or anti-Soviet arguments to explain away the "responsibility" passage of the document. A 1976 text explains the declaration in terms of the international law arguments used by Austrian politicians:

> This addendum stands in contradiction to the other contents of the Moscow Declaration, because it [the Moscow Declaration] assumes that Austria did not exist as an independent state during the National Socialist occupation, and therefore was unable to negotiate [on its own behalf]. Nevertheless, in the addendum it [Austria] is made responsible for participation in the war. Through this additional article, the Soviet Union wanted to secure her influence over our country after the war. However, in the State Treaty negotiations, the Austrian government succeeded in having the accusation of war guilt withdrawn.[15]

The authors refer here to Foreign Minister Figl's last-minute success in removing any mention of war responsibility in the State Treaty.[16] By placing the question of war responsibility only in the context of Soviet designs on Austria, the authors imply that questions of Austrian complicity in the war are to be understood only in the context o f the Russian desire to control Austria. A similar line of reasoning appears in a 1972 history text. Concerning the final part of the Moscow Declaration, students read: "This indefinite passage gave the Austrian resistance a further incitement, but also built the basis for later Soviet claims on Austria."[17] Again, it is clear that the responsibility clause of the Moscow Declaration was to be interpreted in terms of unjust Soviet designs on Austria. This passage is especially misleading, since most Russian claims to Austrian property originated out of the dispute over German property. At the August 1945 Potsdam

Conference, the Soviets agreed not to demand reparations from Austria, but reserved the right to claim German property. Since the Nazi state had taken control of many industries and had invested considerably in the Austrian economy, and since the Russians used a broad definition of German assets in their zone, in practice, the Soviet Union *did* exact reparations from Austria. Of course, the ultimate Soviet claim to reparations and political influence in Austria came through their military victory and the presence of the Red Army. Putting the responsibility clause only in the context of Soviet demands on Austria was disingenuous but understandable, in the context of the Austria-as-victim myth. Overall, it is not surprising that school texts embraced the legitimacy offered by the first part of the Moscow Declaration and took it at face value, while the "responsibility" clause was ignored or explained away.

Rebuilding in Spite of the Allies: The Marshall Plan and the *Wiederaufbau* in Textbooks

One of the most powerful and useful symbols of national renewal was the rebuilding *(Wiederaufbau)* of Austria that accompanied the Allied occupation. After 1955, rebuilding became an important symbol of national identity, as Austrians looked with justifiable pride on the physical and spiritual reconstruction of their Alpine republic. Peter Thaler argues that the Austrian version of the *Wirtschaftswunder* (economic miracle) became one of the most important factors in postwar national identity.[18] Indeed, the symbolism of rebuilding had a powerful resonance. Before-and-after pictures depicting the rubble of 1945 and the prosperous and rebuilt Austria of the mid 1950s clearly demonstrate Austria's rebirth. But while the *Wiederaufbau* was a powerful and legitimate symbol of national identity, it was also linked to the Austria-as-victim myth. Rebuilding was often seen as a process achieved *in spite of* the Allies, whose meddling hindered reconstruction. To some degree, this was true, for Allied demands on Austria (Soviet demands in particular) did hinder rebuilding efforts by draining Austria of resources. But when considered in a larger context, and by including the enormous amounts of European Recovery Program (ERP, better known as the Marshall Plan) investment and aid predating the Marshall Plan (e.g., food deliveries and other direct aid), outside help was essential to the rebuilding of Austria.[19] In the textbooks, however, rebuilding was presented as purely an Austrian achievement. Thus, coverage of the *Wiederaufbau* focused on the concrete aspects of overcoming the physical destruction of the war—destruction caused by the armies and air forces of the Four Powers. Furthermore, because the Allied occupation was seen as part of a series of injustices forced upon Austria, Allied "hindering" of the *Wiederaufbau* became one more chapter in Austria's long ordeal. But since in the end Austrians overcame these hardships, the narrative was ultimately a triumphant one. As Der Herr

Karl remarked: "Auch das hab ich jetzt geschafft. Es ist uns gelungen – der Wiederaufbau."[20]

Wiederaufbau symbolism was well understood by school officials. In the commentary to the 1970 polytechnic school lesson plan, the importance of the *Wiederaufbau* was placed in the context of remarks on World War II: "The hardships of the war and postwar time are important ... as background for the subsequent achievements of the rebuilding."[21] Thus, the destruction of the war and the devastation of the immediate postwar landscape were to serve as the basis for appreciation of the achievements of the *Wiederaufbau*. This "before-and-after" approach was already common in school texts in the mid 1950s, and several special publications from the Education Ministry emphasized the importance of rebuilding.[22] One of the most powerful symbols of the *Wiederaufbau* was the massive complex of dams and hydroelectric generating plants at Kaprun in the Austrian Alps. In a 1955 history text, students read about how Kaprun provided electricity for Austrian industry and for export, and that "Kaprun belongs to all of us. Free people created the marvelous project."[23] Numerous textbooks featured photos of the impressive complex at Kaprun.[24] There was even a feature film about Kaprun, *Das Lied von Kaprun* (The Song of Kaprun), which premiered in 1955.[25] But while Kaprun was a powerful and forward-looking symbol, the project was not purely a postwar phenomenon. Construction of the Kaprun project had begun after the Anschluss, and forced laborers from occupied Europe worked on the project during the war. Completed in 1955, the Kaprun project became a triumphant symbol of the *Wiederaufbau*. However, historian Georg Rigele estimates that between 1948 and 1955, around two-thirds of the project's cost came from Marshall Plan Counterpart Funds. As Rigele puts it, the "successful construction of Kaprun was not only an Austrian achievement, it was the most important project financed by the Marshall Plan."[26]

The initial work on the Kaprun project was one of many important investments made in the Austrian economy during the National Socialist years (though planning had begun before the Anschluss). Some scholars argue that these projects succeeded in diversifying the Austrian industrial economy by investing in Austria's western provinces. In 1937, 40 percent of Austrian industrial workers were in the west. Due, in part, to Nazi-era investments in the economy, the figure had risen to 51 percent by 1947. This westward shift in industrial production diversified the Austrian economy and was also important to the postwar rebuilding of Austria because most of the war damage had taken place in eastern Austria.[27] Furthermore, industries in the western provinces were not subject to Soviet claims regarding German property. But in the postwar period, the larger context of Kaprun's history was ignored. The narrative of rebuilding belonged to all Austrians, and Kaprun, as a key symbol of the *Wiederaufbau*, was portrayed almost solely as an Austrian achievement. Would an emphasis on the larger context of Kaprun have lessened its value as an Austrian accomplishment? While no precise motivation can be attributed to ignoring the Marshall Plan aid that was essential to completing Kaprun, it is clear that the omission served to strengthen Kaprun's status as a symbol of Austrian rebuilding, accomplished by Austrians working together.

The story of Kaprun raises the larger question: How important was the Marshall Plan to the rebuilding of Austria? On a per capita basis, Austria was number three (after Iceland and Norway) in Marshall Plan assistance with 131.7 dollars, which is more than seven times West Germany's amount of 18.6 dollars. Total American financial aid to Austria from 1945 to 1955 was 1.434 billion dollars.[28] Indeed, Marshall Plan funds are still at work in Austria to this day.[29] Early aid programs were essential for keeping Austrians fed in the meager years immediately after the war, while Marshall Plan assistance provided the investment capital needed to launch Austria's own version of the *Wirtschaftswunder*.[30] Given the importance of Marshall Plan aid, it is not surprising that the ERP was portrayed in a positive light in most Austrian postwar textbooks. For example, a 1967 text reads: "Through 1953 [Austria] received the enormous sum of a billion dollars. With the help of this huge contribution, agricultural production could be increased. Hydroelectric power plants were completed, the iron and steel industries modernized, and the damages to the transportation system were repaired."[31] A 1975 text states: "The Marshall Plan was the basis for Austria's economic upswing."[32] But while the Marshall Plan was discussed favorably, more often than not it was cited as merely one of many important factors of the successful rebuilding. In a 1973 textbook, the importance of the Marshall Plan is actually downplayed: "The supply problem remained unsolved for a long time; Austria was allotted help from the United Nations (UNRRA-Program) and afterwards to 1951 from the U.S. (Marshall Plan). While both of these aid programs contributed considerably to the alleviation of the misery, they could only replace a part of that which Austria lost in the war and through the dismantling [of factories] and oil shipments demanded by the Soviets in the postwar period."[33] In this case, the authors acknowledge the Marshall Plan, but they suggest that this aid cannot replace the losses of the war stemming from Allied bombing and Soviet reparations. In a 1985 textbook, the Marshall Plan is vaguely alluded to, but not mentioned by name: "With the industriousness and courage of the Austrian people and with foreign help, Austria stood anew. By 1953, one could speak of a *Wirtschaftswunder*, as in Germany."[34]

The above example of ignoring the Marshall Plan outright is an exception. The ERP was usually mentioned, though not discussed beyond a few sentences or a paragraph. But in no case did a textbook indicate that Austria received considerably more aid than most other ERP countries. Overall, Austrian textbooks acknowledged the importance of the Marshall Plan, but viewed it as only one of many factors in the triumphant narrative of the *Wiederaufbau*, which had become an important symbol for the Second Republic. Given the lack of coverage afforded to the Marshall Plan, it is no wonder then that, as Günter Bischof writes, the importance of the Marshall Plan "seems largely ignored by the political class and forgotten among the younger generation."[35] Why did the textbooks give so little coverage to the Marshall Plan and its importance? A possible explanation is the ambivalence many have always felt toward the ERP. From the beginning, European suspicion of the Marshall Plan ranged from fears of creeping American cultural influence to fears of becoming an outpost of an American "global empire." Tony Judt writes that in France, for example: "The campaign against the Marshall Plan (by no means limited to the PCF [the French Communist Party]) took as its central plank the thesis that the plan was the first stage of a peaceful occupation and takeover of France."[36] Historiography of the Marshall Plan has also at times been ideologically charged.[37] In Austria, as Günter Bischof points out, the entire subject of the ERP had been largely ignored by historians as late as 1997.[38] But aside from a general ambivalence toward the Marshall Plan, the most likely explanation for the ERP's minor presence in postwar Austrian textbooks is that the Marshall Plan was simply overshadowed by the great postwar Austrian narrative. Postwar Austria emerged from the ashes of the war led by the wisdom and leadership of its two great parties and the hard work of her people. The successful *Wiederaufbau* proved the virtue of cooperation and validated the coalition lesson. The Marshall Plan was part of that story, but it was of secondary importance, as presented in a 1962 text: "The Austrian population had learned from the past. It was not hate and radical political conflict that would change the situation, but rather appreciative cooperation of the parties, professional associations, and interest groups. With an unshakable belief in a better future, Austrians went about the rebuilding of the hard-hit economy. The U.S. supported their industriousness through generous help in the framework of the Marshall Plan."[39]

An earlier text from 1955 had conveyed the "working together" message to students by discussing the *Wiederaufbau* in schools: "[T]he professors and students had to clear the bomb debris from the libraries and laboratories; boy and girl students had to fit windows themselves and repair doors, tables, and benches.... And so it was everywhere. One person helpfully offered a hand to another. 'Come on, do your share! It's about our *Heimat*! It's about Austria's future!'"[40] This passage placed the coalition lesson at the grassroots level: when it came to rebuilding, everyone was needed, and everyone was called upon to do his or her share. The *Wiederaufbau* was a symbol of Austrian unity—a unity that was necessary to build the Second Republic physically and politically. This lesson had lasting impact, as demonstrated by a 1986 text stating that because of the terrors of Nazism and the war, "an especially strong Austrian consciousness developed. Fundamentally, one was unified [in the idea] that the rift, which had irreconcilably divided the parties during the time from 1918 to 1938, had to be overcome. [The] ... widespread devastation made it clear *that the future rebuilding of Austria would be possible only through the unity of all forces*" (emphasis added).[41] Again, a text linked the victim myth and the coalition lesson. Austria became an object of, rather than a participant in, aggression, and the pain and suffering of the war years forged a new sense of identity. Finally, the need to rebuild Austria cleared the way for putting aside differences from the First Republic.

The symbolism of rebuilding was further strengthened by emphasizing that the *Wiederaufbau* succeeded in spite of the presence of the Allies. The idea that the Allies had hindered the rebuilding was embraced immediately after the departure of the Four Powers in 1955. As soon as the last Allied soldier had left, the Education Ministry issued a new lesson plan. The foreword of the new *Lehrplan* discussed the need for a new syllabus in light of the failings of the 1946 provisional lesson plan, which was still in force:

> Never have lesson plans been drafted under circumstances as difficult as those in Austria after the last war.... [The] rebuilding of the school system demanded a rapid conclusion of work on the lesson plans. Thereby, the fervently appearing influences of the four occupying powers were to be heeded. One could not simply brush aside such claims, while on the other hand, [one] had to remain careful to meet these [detailed] wishes [while making sure] ... that the end result of the work could be justified [as our own].... The provisional lesson plans of 1946, as said, could not remain completely free from foreign influences.[42]

This idea of the "meddling Allies" was soon evident in history and reading texts. A 1962 text places the Allied presence squarely in the category of contributor to the general misery: "[T]he four-fold occupation weighed heavily on our republic. The Austrian government had to come up with the major part of the occupation costs.... The Soviet Union especially made demands that Austria could never accept."[43] A 1966 text reflects outrage at the occupation by the Four Powers. True, the war was over—"But what kind of a peace! A peace of the defeated with hunger, privation, and humiliations of every kind. The Four Powers held the land occupied, seized apartments and schools for their soldiers, set up borders between their occupation zones, across which there was no back and forth [allowed].... For ten long years the patience of Austrians was put to the test. It took that long, namely, until the Great Powers were ready actually to fulfill their promise to restore Austria's independence."[44] From these authors' point of view, it was a given that the Allied presence was unjust and signified yet another chapter of Austria's long ordeal. The idea of the "meddling Allies" was by no means unique to works of the 1960s. For example, a 1981 text emphasizes the hardships caused by the Allies: "For Austrians, the occupation period was an extremely difficult time. The occupation costs, which Austria had to pay, amounted to far more than 100 million schillings per year."[45]

The authors of a 1985 text point out that the occupation powers often took the most beautiful homes and the homes in the best condition for themselves, thereby putting Austrians out on the street.[46] The interference of the Allies in the rebuilding of Austria was also an occasional subject in yearbooks. In 1965, a student, Maria Szupanschitz, wrote an essay titled "Ein freies Österreich" (A Free Austria), in which she argues that the true recovery of Austria could begin only now that the Allied occupation was over: "Only now could agriculture, industry, business, and tourism properly develop."[47] Such an assertion neglected the impact of the Marshall Plan and other positive effects of the occupation, but given the contemporary portrayal of the occupation, it is understandable that a student would come to this conclusion. The Allied occupation had become fully incorporated into the Austria-as-victim myth, and the themes of the Allied occupation merged with the larger Austrian ordeal. Another example from a school principal in Graz reinforces this point. In 1970, M. Kössler opened a round table discussion in honor of the twenty-fifth anniversary of the founding of the Second Republic by linking the Allied occupation with the Nazi years: "[In 1945] Austria was now liberated from National Socialist rule, but was by no means free: four elephants climbed into the Austrian boat and threatened to sink it.... In this time, all of our countrymen knew that we had to stick together. It belongs in the golden book of Austrian history to properly honor the achievements of the politicians back then, but also the exemplary behavior of the Austrian people, whether farmer, worker, bureaucrat, or member of the middle class."[48]

Under the Thumb of the Great Powers: The Soviets and Americans in the Textbooks

Further strengthening the connection between the Austria-as-victim myth and the Allied occupation were specific portrayals of the occupation powers. Textbook authors often portrayed the Allies as brutal, capricious, and cynical. These depictions were not without foundation, but they were usually taken out of context, as Austria was routinely cast in the role of victim, and any notion of why the foreign armies were in Austria in the first place faded away. In some cases, the emphasis on negative aspects of Allied behavior was so strong or presented in such a way as to reduce implicitly the significance of Nazi crimes. Specific portrayals of the Four Powers were dominated by images of the Russians and the Americans.[49] The Soviets, with demands for reparations, political manipulations, and the initial brutal behavior of their troops, were not fondly remembered.[50] The Viennese appellation of the giant-sized Red Army soldier of the Soviet War Memorial as the "unknown rapist" attests to this. Indeed, as Matthew Paul Berg has written, rape was a crime routinely committed by soldiers of the Red Army, whose violent unpredictability was intensified by bouts of binge drinking, especially in the early years of the occupation.[51]

Austrian wariness of the Soviet Union was recognizable in textbooks and educational publications in the aftermath of the occupation. In a 1961 publication to honor Julius Raab, Austrian dialect demonstrates Austrian independence and defiance against the Russians. After the November 1945 elections, the new Austrian chancellor, Leopold Figl, proposed that Raab join his cabinet, but the Russian High Commissioner rejected Raab's appointment, citing his conservative roots dating to the First Republic.

The authors argue that the Russian refusal was a blessing in disguise, since Raab became such an effective leader in Parliament and went on to become chancellor. Recounting Raab's response to the Russian refusal, students read:

"I werd net Minister."
"Warum?"
"Die Russen san dagegen."
"Was tun wir jetzt?"
"Wir gehn ins Parlament."
"Was machen wir dort?"
"Das wirst schon sehn."[52]

In this passage the cool confidence of Raab, expressed in Lower Austrian dialect, represents Austrian perseverance in the face of the overwhelming force of the Soviet Union. A 1976 text quotes a 1955 speech made by Adolf Schärf, which made clear that the arrival of the Red Army was seen not as a liberation, but rather as a disaster for Austria: "In the eastern part of Austria, the Russians followed at the heels of the German troops. As soon as they came, there was plunder, arson, rape, and murder. Whoever led them to food, offered them a wine cellar, [or] whoever led them to women or girls was considered a friend. Whoever wanted to protect women, girls, or his property was easily labeled a fascist criminal. In almost every town of Lower Austria, there were, in addition to murders, also suicides, committed out of despair."[53] The Russians, who had indeed made rebuilding in their zone difficult, were not missed in the Lower Austrian town of Stockerau, either. In a 1973 yearbook article on the history of the town, the teacher Josef Mayer asserts that the rebuilding of Austria could begin only in 1955, after the Russians departed: "[Only] after the Russians had left Stockerau after those hot September days of the year 1955 could the building of the city proceed in peace and according to our own discretion."[54] The Red Army's behavior was notoriously bad, so it is hardly surprising that the Soviets would be remembered in a negative way. A rare positive statement about the Russians appears in a 1972 text, which accurately points out that Soviet troops had averted a famine by providing food to the local population in May 1945.[55]

Portrayals of Americans and the United States in general were more complicated. The attention given to the United States in Austrian school materials is no doubt linked to the larger cultural influence of the United States on postwar Austria and on postwar Europe in general.[56] In many cases, Austrian school texts and yearbooks portrayed Americans in a very positive light, often by pointing to the generosity of the Marshall Plan, albeit in a cursory manner (as discussed above). One place where the arrival of the Americans was genuinely seen as a liberation was the Catholic monastery and school at Kremsmünster. After the Anschluss, the Nazis secularized the school, and late in the war the Slovakian political puppet of the Nazis, Josef Tiso, was temporarily quartered there. When

American troops entered the area in the spring of 1945, the Nazi Security Service (SD) tried unsuccessfully to burn down the monastery. After the arrival of U.S. troops, Kremsmünster was turned back over to the Benedictines, and its school resumed instruction in the fall of 1945.[57] But from the beginning, there was also ambivalence about the American presence in Austria. While the Americans were clearly favored over the Russians, some critics feared the impact of American consumer culture on Austria. Resentment was also engendered by the relationships between American soldiers and Austrian women. Regardless of the true nature of such relationships, Ingrid Bauer writes that Austrian women were often accused of dragging Austria's reputation "into the dirt." In his sermon on New Year's Eve in 1946, the Bishop of Linz worried "that the number of those who would exchange their female honor and integrity as widows in return for a bottle of champagne, that the number of those who would sell their maidenly virtue for an American chocolate bar, is disgracefully high."[58]

During the years of the occupation, ambivalence felt toward the Americans was usually overshadowed by fear and dislike of the Russians.[59] As discussed above, textbook coverage of the Marshall Plan was generally positive, though cursory. By the late 1960s and early 1970s, the positive image of the United States—postwar American aid being one bright spot in an overall view of the United States—was turning negative as a result of the Vietnam War (as discussed in chapter 3). This change in viewpoint was especially evident in Austrian reading book stories that were not directly related to the occupation, but instead dealt with themes of discrimination and social injustice within American society. By far, the most popular theme relating to the United States concerned the Native Americans. A 1976 text includes several stories about Indians under the heading "Bei den nordamerikanischen Indianern" (With the North American Indians). Among the stories are "Nataju muß in die Schule der weißen Leute gehen" (Nataju Must Go to the School of the White People) and "Wir wollen nicht wie die Weißen leben" (We Do Not Want to Live Like the Whites).[60] A 1979 text presents three stories about Native Americans, including "Wie Indianer heute leben" (How Indians Live Today), which describes the poverty of Indians and includes a photograph of a shack in deplorable condition.[61] Second only to stories about Indians were stories about discrimination against African-Americans in the United States. In a 1977 reading book under the heading "Freiheit und Menschenwürde" (Freedom and Human Dignity), there is a story by Hans Georg Noack, titled "Birmingham, Alabama," about racial discrimination and violence in that Southern city.[62] In a 1979 text, another story by Noack appears, titled "Die Kämpfer" (The Fighters). This story is also about racial discrimination in the United States and includes an illustration of an American flag with the stripes representing bars in a jail, behind which stand two trapped blacks—caricatures with oversized lips.[63] Austrian textbook authors had discovered that there was no shortage of hypocrisy and injustice in American society to be exposed.

South Tyrol Betrayed: The Austrian Irredenta in the Textbooks

At the end of World War I, South Tyrol was awarded to Italy as part of the St. Germain peace settlement. Given the German-speaking majority of South Tyrol, this was a clear violation of President Wilson's promise of national self-determination and, in the words of Ernst Hanisch, "an ethnic injustice."[64] After World War II, the Austrian government, led by the young conservative Karl Gruber, again challenged the Italian claim to the South Tyrol, reasoning that since Italy had been an Axis power and Austria had not, a return of what the Italians call "Alto Adige" might be forthcoming. This assertion made sense, given the Austrian government's position that it had not been a belligerent in World War II. In any case, there was little chance that the Western powers, despite some sympathy on the part of the French and British, would support Austria's claim to South Tyrol. In the context of the emerging Cold War, the priority was to ensure Italy's place "in the Western camp," rather than adjust the Austrian border. In the end, the Austrian government did succeed in negotiating an agreement with Italy to protect the rights of German-speaking residents (the Gruber-De Gasperi agreement).[65] Yet tension, and even violence, has erupted periodically in the region since 1945.[66]

Emphasis on the South Tyrol issue in Austrian school materials stands as a reminder of Austria's vulnerability to international power politics.[67] A story in a 1960 reading book reminds Austrian children of South Tyrol's plight. In "Mein Vaterland" (My Fatherland), by Heinrich Kotz, child narrators from throughout Austria describe their provinces. When it comes to Tyrol, Michl, Klara, Toni, and Jörgl say: "Our Tyrol is torn. The most beautiful part belongs to Italy. But all Tyroleans hope that north and south Tyroleans will again come together."[68] A history text from 1968 explains the origins of the Tyrolean split in terms that extend the victim myth back to World War I:

> The murder of the heir to the throne in the summer of 1914 triggered World War I. For four long years, Austria-Hungary fought together with its allies against an immense number of enemies. The President of the United States of North America [*sic*], Wilson, had promised that after the war, every people could choose for itself in which state it wished to live.
>
> In the Peace Treaty of St. Germain, a suburb of Paris, South Tyrol was awarded to Italy against the will of its inhabitants. Why shouldn't the promised self-determination of peoples not have been applied here?[69]

It is a fair question, but the self-determination argument made more sense in 1919 than it did in 1946. A history text for polytechnic schools in 1982 takes a neutral approach. In this case, the authors simply state the government's reasoning behind its claim for South Tyrol, writing that after the war "Austrian officials demanded the return of South Tyrol. The hopes of Austria were fueled by the fact that this time, Italy was on the losing side.

But the Allies recognized the Brenner boundary. On the question of South Tyrolean autonomy, Austria was relegated to direct negotiations with Italy."[70] The authors of this text also cover issues of minority rights in Austria and include a photograph of Carinthian men tearing down bilingual road signs.[71]

Austrian Prisoners of War and Displaced Germans in the Textbooks

In addition to the South Tyrol question, the Allies were indirectly criticized regarding two matters that related to population transfers: returning prisoners of war (Heimkehrer), and German refugees from the east. In chapter 1, we already saw how returning prisoners of war were important to the birth of the victim myth. The symbolic importance of Heimkehrer continued in the post-occupation period, though the frequency of stories in reading books about returning POWs declined from the levels of the immediate postwar years.[72] Horror stories of Heimkehrer usually revolved around being a Soviet prisoner or the threat of becoming a Russian prisoner.

In a 1960 reading book, a story by Robert Wenzel, titled "Nacht der Entscheidung" (Night of Decision), tells about prisoners on a train traveling from Yugoslavia on Christmas Eve 1945. The captured troops are anxious about which way the train will turn, knowing that it will determine whether they are heading home or to Russia: "And then the train began to move faster, and turned—turned to the west! Weren't the stars suddenly shining more brightly? And hadn't the cold let up? Suddenly singing began ... and the songs eventually ran through the entire length of the train. The songs of this Christmas Eve rang far out into the quiet countryside."[73] While being a prisoner of the Russians was greatly feared, the Americans, too, could be capricious. An eyewitness account from a history text tells of an Austrian soldier who surrendered to American troops and was poorly treated:

> He expected humane treatment, but he had fooled himself. In the first camp where he was brought, the latrines overflowed. Machine gun fire just over their heads forced the prisoners to lie in the filth, which ran over the muddy ground of the camp.
>
> Meir did not know at the time that the head of the camp was a Jew, who had lost relatives in German death camps. Nor did he know that not far from the camp a freight train with tightly closed doors had been found. When the doors were forced open, human corpses fell out. In the overfilled cars, someone had starved or suffocated survivors of a concentration camp. Meir did not know any of that; now he wondered if had acted wisely when he, under life-threatening danger, tried to escape the Russians. He watched as one of his comrades lost his nerves, ran against the camp fence, and—hit by machine gun salvos—collapsed. Meir held out; he wanted to live.

Months later, he was at home. Despite this, he had no reason to celebrate. The bombs had slain his father, and he himself possessed barely more than what he wore on his body.[74]

This passage presents an example of a doubly victimized Austrian. Meir is clearly not a Nazi true believer, and the authors make it clear that he, like Sergeant Schultz in the television show *Hogan's Heroes*, "knows nothing." Meir simply wants to survive, but he almost does not because the camp where he is held prisoner is run by a revenge-seeking Jew. Furthermore, even though Meier is lucky enough to have survived, "he has no reason to celebrate," because his father has been unjustly killed in an Allied air raid. Stories like Meir's may well have been accurate. The bewildering events of military collapse and the devastation of homeland were formative experiences for many Austrians. On the other hand, Meir's opposite, a dyed-in-the-wool Nazi true believer, was rarely represented in a textbook.

One issue in which the Allies came across as particularly unfair, and even brutal, was their sanctioning of the expulsion of ethnic Germans from the east, a view shared by many historians.[75] For many textbook authors, the expulsion was no different from crimes committed by the Nazis. For example, under the heading "Crimes against Humanity," the authors of a 1968 text conflate Nazi and Allied actions: "The violent resettlement of different peoples on the orders of Hitler, or after the war, at the urging or toleration of the victorious powers, meant loss of home and property for around 40 million innocents, and, for several million, even death."[76] In a similar vein, a story in a 1973 text, titled "195,000 Kinder Gingen Verloren" (195,000 Children Went Missing), calls the plight of the refugees in the winter of 1944–1945 "the most terrible point in the war."[77] Another text, this one from 1984, manipulates the expulsion question to support the Austria-as-victim myth. The authors write that "of [twelve million Germans who fled or were resettled], more than two million died from cold and hunger. As with the resettlement and expulsion actions in Eastern Europe, but also in the South Tyrol, in southern Carinthia, and in Slovenia, [these actions] caused … material privation and immeasurable spiritual suffering."[78] Once again, a conflation of victims is put forth as all resettlements are placed into the same category. Overall, textbook portrayals of the resettlement/expulsion issue are not so much inaccurate as they are one-sided. Official memory again proved to be highly selective.

Ignoring Denazification in the Textbooks

One area of Austrian life in which the Allied presence had an impact on many was the denazification process; however, the topic is conspicuously absent from textbooks. This omission is revealing, though not surprising, given the potential of denazification to undermine the Austria-as-victim myth. Unlike in Germany (which did not have the advantage of a national government, as did Austria), the Austrian government had a large portion of responsibility for carrying out denazification from early on in the occupation. In general, the ability of the Austrian government to govern the country and even influence the Allies increased markedly in 1946, in large measure due to the June 1946 New Control Agreement.[79] Historian Dieter Stiefel, the leading scholar of Austrian denazification, divides denazification in Austria into five distinct phases: Phase One—April 1945 to June 1945, "military security phase" (characterized by arrests made by Allied military authorities); Phase Two—June 1945 to February 1946, "autonomous denazification by the Allies and the Austrian government" (characterized by varying policies on the part of the Austrian government and the Four Powers); Phase Three—February 1946 to February 1947, "Austrian denazification" (based on the denazification laws of 1945); Phase Four—February 1947 to May 1948, Austrian denazification continued (based on the 1947 denazification law); Phase Five—1948 to 1957: "amnesties."[80]

Of special importance in Stiefel's ordering is the shift from phase two to phase three, when the Allies began to pull back from denazification in Austria. This shift can also be noted upon examination of American Military Government reports. While the Four Powers retained oversight over the denazification process, by April 1946 the Austrian provincial governments were responsible for denazification with the role of the Military Government being "largely supervisory."[81] The trend continued when, in July 1946, the Austrian government enacted (and forwarded to the Allied Council for approval) the New Denazification Law, which specified levels of guilt and penalties for former Nazis.[82] The law was amended and approved by the Four Powers in December and formally went into effect in February 1947 (though actual implementation still required passage of "enabling ordinances").[83] Meanwhile, intensification of the Cold War changed priorities, and cooperation among the Allies was increasingly replaced by tension. By February 1948, the Four Powers, by American admission, "had abandoned responsibility for denazification."[84] Yet supervision and intervention in security matters, including matters related to denazification, and the court system remained a real possibility. For example, in 1947 the Americans convened a general court in the celebrated "Bad Ischl Milk Trial" in the American zone.[85] As recounted by Kurt Tweraser, in August 1947 a protest over a change from fresh milk to powdered milk in children's rations escalated into a near riot. Communist leaders protested to the mayor of Bad Ischl, and frustrated demonstrators vented their anger at a displaced persons camp (the "favored" status of DPs was a common source of resentment in postwar Austria), where some participants shouted anti-Semitic insults, such as "Down with the dirty Jews." Austrian authorities maintained order, but made no arrests because no Austrian law had been broken. The following day, six Communists were arrested on American orders and subsequently tried in an American general court in September on charges of inciting and/or participating in a riot. Despite the anti-Nazi records of the defendants, they were convicted and faced sentences "ranging from one to fifteen years." The United States High Commissioner, General Geoffrey Keyes, maintained that the verdicts were just, but reduced the sentences to approximately one year or less. This case indirectly indicates how much the denazification situation had changed by 1947, for, as Tweraser points out, the American motivation in the trial was not so much the protection of DPs (who themselves were subject to severe punishment by the Allies, though not the Austrian authorities, when they violated the law), but "the maintenance of law and order," to which the Communists were increasingly seen as a threat.[86]

This leads to the important question of why the Four Powers essentially abandoned denazification in Austria. A short answer to this complex issue has to consider the emerging politics of the Cold War, as well as the assumptions and political styles of the Four Powers. In the case of the Soviet Union, one would assume that denazification would have been an ideological imperative, given the violent anticommunism of Nazism. In practice, though, Soviet denazification policy in Austria was governed by pragmatism. Initially, the Russians were relatively lenient in Austria, but when the Austrian Communist Party was humiliated in the November 1945 parliamentary elections, the Soviets became more interested in denazification, often using the issue as a tool of obstruction or intimidation. French denazification policy was never firmly established, and was subject to change based on circumstances. According to Dieter Stiefel, the result was a combination of flexible and arbitrary actions by the French.[87] American denazification policy, by contrast, was initially somewhat idealistic, and was intended to be carried out with reformist zeal. However, the American system of using questionnaires (the infamous *Fragebogen*) to categorize and root out Nazis eventually collapsed under its own weight. When responsibility for denazification was turned over to the Austrian government early in 1946, only one-third of the eighty thousand questionnaires handed over to the Austrians had been processed.[88] The American system, based in positivist principles of New Deal-era social science, led to consternation for many Austrians who felt, with considerable justification, that the *Fragebogen* did not adequately take individual circumstances into account. For example, Albert Massiczek recounts the story of a woman who had joined the Nazi Party before the Anschluss—a criminal offense. After the Anschluss, she became disillusioned with Nazism and joined numerous Catholic groups. Without her knowledge, her mother continued to pay her Nazi Party dues. As a result, during the Allied occupation, she was required to register as an illegal Nazi, despite the fact that she had already "denazified" herself.[89] Robert Knight points out that because the British and the Americans had cooperated extensively on postwar planning, there were similarities in their policies, such as the use of *Fragebogen*. Overall, British policy differed from American policy in that it tended to be more lenient toward some former Nazis. By early 1946, the British had concluded that denazification should be largely abandoned.[90] While the Allies did continue to monitor (and sometimes protest) Austrian denazification, by way of summary it can be said that denazification in Austria rapidly lost its urgency as the Four Powers' focus shifted to the Cold War and pragmatic issues of rebuilding.

This change should be seen in the context of a larger shift in American policy toward Germany, which was moving away from punishment toward rehabilitation. In May 1946, General Lucius Clay, commander of US forces in Germany, suspended reparations in the American zone.[91] In September, American Secretary of State James Byrnes delivered a speech in Stuttgart, broadcast on German radio, announcing the economic unity of the British and American zones (the formation of "Bizonia"). In his speech, Byrnes committed the United States to stay in western Germany indefinitely: "I want no misunderstanding. We will not shirk our duty. We are not withdrawing. We are staying here. As long as there is an occupation army in Germany, American armed forces will be part of that occupation."[92] These events marked a fundamental change in American policy, culminating with the Marshall Plan. Collectively, these measures assured the Germans in the western zones that they would not be abandoned to the Russians. Given that Austria was generally treated much more favorably than Germany, it was unlikely that Austria would face stiffer denazification policies than Germany.

The Four Powers' abandonment of denazification made it easy for the Austrian government to retreat from a process that it had never pursued with great conviction. Indeed, even before the New Denazification Law had been implemented, President Renner promised leniency: "As President of the Republic, I say to you: The constitution gives me the right of pardon of even the capital criminal. And even the most debased citizen is for me an Austrian. I recognize no ostracism."[93] With the Allies giving up on denazification, even those Austrian politicians who had been committed to it were now forced by political circumstances to promote leniency. No party could afford to alienate the five hundred thousand disenfranchised Austrians who, sooner or later, would have their right to vote reinstated. Furthermore, Austria's two major parties had always insisted on differentiating between Nazi true believers and *Mitläufer* (those who jumped on the bandwagon), though the SPÖ was more wary of the fellow travelers than was the ÖVP.[94] Something close to an amnesty stampede began in the spring of 1948. In May, the Allied Council approved laws passed by the Austrian Parliament, granting amnesty to most former Nazis and revoking previously handed-down atonement penalties. By the summer of 1948, denazification was over for more than 92 percent of Austrian Nazis. As a punitive program, denazification now applied to only forty thousand former Nazis.[95] Of this remaining core, most either saw their punishments and sanctions lapse in the 1950s, or benefited from additional amnesties granted in 1955 and 1957.[96]

In retrospect, it is easy to criticize the Four Powers for abandoning denazification in Austria. For example, there is little doubt that the Soviet Union exploited the process for political gain, which ultimately undermined the moral authority of the Communists in Austria. Oliver Rathkolb points to several flaws in American denazification policy, including the arbitrary nature of the *Fragebogen*, a tendency to go easy on Nazis who had economic training that was needed for the recovery, and a Cold War-inspired shift in policy to ensure Austria's orientation with the West at the expense of more meaningful democratization.[97] Valid as these criticism are, an equal hindrance to the success of denazification was the lack of will on the part of the Austrian government and of all Austrian political parties. Dieter Stiefel points out that political cleansing was never a goal in and of itself, but was always seen in the context of other political aims, such as regaining sovereignty and achieving economic recovery.[98] In short, for most Austrian politicians the issue was how to avoid far-reaching denazification, instead of how best to carry it out. For democratically elected officials, achieving one's larger goals requires retaining political power, which means winning elections. In postwar Austria, winning elections meant aggressively seeking the votes of former Nazis and veterans. There was no better way to win them over than to let bygones be bygones and restore former Nazis to full citizenship as quickly as possible. Making matters easier for Austrian politicians, the Americans and the British had come to the same conclusion. Robert Knight points out that while British officials would not publicly admit their position, they privately agreed with President Karl Renner, who feared that overzealous denazification would create a permanent group of embittered political outcasts in Austria.[99] This sentiment was echoed by the American Military Government in December 1947:

> [W]ork has progressed to a point where Nazi ideology no longer constitutes the principal, or even a serious threat to democratic government or to its institutions. There remains some danger, however, that were denazification forced to an unreasonable extreme at the instigation of the Allies, there would develop a large unassimilable group which, barred from their normal participation in public and private enterprise, would be subversive in attitude.... It appears advisable that the Austrian Government should now be given full opportunity to implement and maintain, without Allied interference, the principles contained in the laws pertaining to denazification which it initiated.[100]

Further, the Americans and the British also shared the Austrian view that Nazism was intimately linked with Prussian (not Austrian) traditions.[101]

In the final analysis, criticism of Allied denazification policy should be qualified in at least three important ways. First, despite its numerous flaws (e.g., the *Fragebogen* system, lack of consistency in policy, etc.), the denazification process in Austria (as well as in Germany) could be considered a noble, though somewhat naïve, effort. Nothing of its sort had been tried before, and the nature of the Nazi regime called for some method of political cleansing. Second, there was a certain philosophical impossibility in denazification, as there is with all forms of re-education. Elimination of high Nazi officials was one thing, but the Nazi government and its policies had been enabled by millions of supporters. Did

Austrians and Germans give up on National Socialism because they recognized its inhumane and brutal nature? Or was it walking amidst ruins and scrounging for rations that made people change their minds about Nazism? This question cannot be answered, because after the war, there was no longer a future in Nazism. In the end, defeat (and the Allies' insistence on unconditional surrender) might be regarded as the most successful method of denazification. Third, as Robert Knight points out, though the British (and one could add the United States) can be criticized for not having a consistent denazification policy, denazification was ultimately an Austrian rather than a British (or American) problem.[102] As we have seen, it was a process that the Austrians had little desire to wade into, other than to end the business as soon as possible. This was largely achieved by the amnesty laws, which were completely justifiable in the context of the victim myth, according to which most of those subject to denazification were themselves victims. Most of them, after all, had been forced into a war that they did not want or had been led down a false path. But while this political justification for abandoning denazification was widely understood, it was not widely talked about—certainly not in postwar textbooks, which did not broach the subject.

Remembering the "Seventeen-Year Occupation": The Struggle for the State Treaty in the Textbooks

By far, the most important example cited as evidence of Austria's victimization at the hands of the Four Powers was the long struggle over the 1955 State Treaty. In the context of the Austria-as-victim myth, Austria did not receive preferential treatment compared to Germany—rather, the opposite was true. The official view was that the Four Powers had neither the right nor the reason to occupy Austria for an extended period, and that the State Treaty was long overdue. Furthermore, the treaty was achieved only through the tenacious work of Austrian politicians cooperating with one another. Thus, the State Treaty became the quintessential symbol of the coalition lesson. Given the prevailing view that the Allied occupation and the Nazi years were part of a single larger ordeal, the 1955 State Treaty became the benchmark for the new Austria. According to this view, Austria's continuity of suffering did not end in 1945, but only in 1955, when Austria was released from the Allied yoke. Finally, the State Treaty marked the official abandonment of Austrian responsibility for the war. On the eve of the signing of the treaty, the Four Powers agreed to Foreign Minister Figl's request to eliminate the war responsibility clause from the preamble of the State Treaty. Figl argued that the responsibility clause was counterproductive, since it would hinder Austria's new and future identity as a neutral state.[103]

The story of the Austrian State Treaty is a long and complex affair.[104] In the victim narrative of postwar Austrian history, there are two important themes that relate to the State Treaty: the tenacity of Austrian politicians of both parties in their negotiations, and the obstructionism of the Four Powers, especially the Soviet Union. There is nothing inherently mythological about these themes. Indeed, the talented cadre of Austrian politicians involved in the State Treaty negotiations became the leaders of the Second Republic as it marched into prosperity and remained neutral during the Cold War. They had proved that they could exercise what Günter Bischof calls "the leverage of the weak."[105] Second, there is no doubt that the State Treaty was obstructed by the Great Powers. The United States was concerned about security issues, including the danger of leaving a vacuum between Italy and West Germany. There were also secret American efforts to rearm western Austria. The Soviet Union was the most obstructionist of all. The Soviets, too, were concerned about security, and also exploited economic resources in eastern Austria to the fullest. Caught in the middle, Austria was indeed a pawn of sorts in the Cold War.[106] What makes the narrative of the State Treaty mythological is the lack of context. Successful negotiation of the State Treaty may have taken ten years, but in 1955 Austria was in a remarkable position. Austrians were enjoying an economic recovery akin to West Germany's, but partition had been avoided. Furthermore, while the German Democratic Republic and the Federal Republic of Germany had become independent states, parts of the two Germanys were filled with foreign troops, including Britain's "Army of the Rhine" (clearly indicating an indefinite presence in the Federal Republic),[107] and neither state, especially East Germany, was fully sovereign.[108] This larger context was generally absent from discussions about the State Treaty. Instead, the State Treaty marked a triumphant end to Austria's saga of unfair treatment. This idea had long been reflected in the rhetoric of Austrian politicians from the Socialist President Karl Renner, who spoke of "four elephants in a rowboat," to the Austrian People's Party Foreign Minister Karl Gruber, who in 1949 and 1950 complained of a "liberator's occupation" and opined that "liberation has long ago turned into an oppressive occupation."[109]

The victim view of the State Treaty is evidenced in the statements of Austrian politicians and in school materials. Sometimes the two overlap, as in the case of a 1962 text that quotes a speech by Foreign Minister Figl on the occasion of the signing of the State Treaty on 15 May 1955: "A seventeen-year, thorn-filled path of bondage has ended.... We have waited ten years for this day."[110] It is noteworthy that Figl linked the Nazi years in Austria with the Allied occupation by referring to them together as a "seventeen-year, thorn-filled path of bondage." Several history textbooks also reflect this sentiment. For example, the authors of a 1985 text wrote that the signing of the State Treaty in 1955 "brought our country the long-yearned-for freedom *after seventeen years of foreign rule*" (emphasis added).[111] It was also common to express frustration over Austria's position as a pawn of the Cold War when referring to the ordeal of negotiating the State Treaty. In 1972, students read: "In the year 1945, no one believed what a laborious and bitter path Austria would have to walk to [achieve] full freedom and independence. Based on the Moscow Declaration and the Potsdam resolutions, one was inclined to hope for a rapid withdrawal of the occupation troops. But the Austria question quickly became entwined in the realities of international politics."[112] Reading books also contributed to the idea that Austria's long wait for a treaty was an unjust ordeal. The story "Flug um die Freihiet" (Flight for Freedom), by Leopold Wally, in a 1956 text recounts the dramatic trip of the Austrian diplomats as they flew to Moscow for treaty negotiations. As they departed, men and women throughout Austria were hopeful and felt that "after ten years of occupation by foreign powers, Austria wants finally to be free, finally head of its own house." The mission succeeded, and on 15 May 1955, the State Treaty was signed: "Now we have our fatherland again, free and beautiful, its destiny lies in our own hands."[113] The overriding sentiment in treatments of the State Treaty is that there was no just reason for the Allied occupation of Austria. Armed with this point of view, the longer the occupation continued, the greater became the Austrian desire to be in charge of its own affairs—to be "Herr im eigenen Haus."

A 1960 text is especially significant as a demonstration of how textbook authors merged the State Treaty with other themes of the Austria-as-victim myth. The book includes a reproduction of a painting of the State Treaty ceremony at the Belvedere Palace in Vienna. The text accompanying the painting casts the Allied occupation as part of the larger ordeal suffered by Austria:

> But only with the signing of the Austrian State Treaty on Sunday, the fifteenth of May 1955, did bondage and occupation find an end.... Freedom was achieved, and a long painful path through bondage, war, privation, and occupation ended. This day of freedom did not emerge by itself; it is the fruit of a responsible and hard-working government and the result of a courageous cooperation of all the groups of our population.... This unanimity has its spiritual roots in the new and lively Austrian state consciousness. We had to lose Austria and win it back in the hard years of the war, privation, and bondage, in order to know and appreciate what Austria means for us all.[114]

The passage again demonstrates that the State Treaty was viewed as the culmination of a collective tribulation encompassing the Anschluss, the war, and Allied occupation. Because the State Treaty brought closure to this cumulative ordeal, it marked the genuine liberation of Austria. By implication, the collapse of Nazi rule brought about by the victory of the Allies was not Austria's true moment of liberation, but rather a shift from one occupation to another, or, in the words of Leopold Figl, "Von Fremdbetzung zu Fremdbesetzung."[115] The text also includes an Anton Wildgans poem (predating the war), "Das Österreichische Credo" (The Austrian Credo), which brackets the reproduction of the painting and its accompanying caption in the same book:

Von eben diesen Herzen will ich künden—
nicht nur als Lober der Vergangenheit:
Sie hatten ihren Irrtum, ihre Sünden;
wer hat sie nicht, welch Volk und welche Zeit?
...

Sie trauten ihren Obern leicht wie Kinder
und hielten Treu', selbst wo man sie verriet.
Je nun, die Treue ward darob nicht minder,
vielleicht gerad darum zu hohen Lied.
...

Sie ließen ihre Waffen gerne rosten,

brauchten als Zeichen: Kaiser und Altar.
Doch wo sie standen, hielten sie Posten,
selbst wenn der Posten ein verlorner war.
...

Unendlich ist, was dieses Volk gelitten,
Erniedrigung, Verfolgung, Hunger, Leid—
und trug es stark und trug's mit sanftem Bitten
in Stolz und Demut seiner Menschlichkeit.[116]

Wildgans portrays a loyal people whose suffering is never-ending, and whose only sin is, like everyone else, to have made mistakes. Even though this poem was written well before the Anschluss (Wildgans died in 1932), the themes of innocence and victimization took on even more significance after World War II and the Allied occupation. The textbook authors' bracketing of the State Treaty illustration with this poem makes it clear that they viewed Wildgans's poem in the post–World War II context.

The idea that the Allied occupation was one of many hardships in Austria's larger ordeal meant that the State Treaty took on a two-fold symbolic importance. First, as we have already seen, the long negotiations over the State Treaty joined Austria's litany of grievances. Second, the State Treaty took on great significance as a symbolic point of demarcation. While 1945 marked the rebirth of Austria, 1955 was the milepost for the "true" Austria, unencumbered by meddling outsiders and finally able to demonstrate its character as a nation.

New Symbols of Austrian National Identity:
The National Holiday and Neutrality in the Textbooks

It is hard to overstate the importance of the State Treaty for postwar Austrian identity. Historian Ernst Bruckmüller argues that the Anschluss, war, and resistance taken together dismantled Austrian identification with Germany, but that the development of true Austrian consciousness came only with the State Treaty and freedom from outside control. In the end, Bruckmüller writes, it was not so much the departure of the Wehrmacht from Austria as the decampment of the Red Army that made the Austrians begin to feel that they were a nation.[117] Post-occupation textbooks would seem to validate Bruckmüller's argument, for two great symbols of national identity emerged from the State Treaty to express this break in continuity: the national holiday and neutrality, both of which became staple themes in textbooks. With the Austrian Education Ministry taking the initiative, Austrian schools immediately began commemorating the twenty-sixth of October as a day to mark Austrian independence.[118] In 1965, the twenty-sixth of October was declared the Austrian national holiday and was strongly linked with Austria's declaration of permanent neutrality. Contributing to world peace was also declared a national goal.[119] The links among these symbols became a regular feature of school materials and an important part of Austria's official identity.

The importance of these new symbols of identity is reflected in the decrees and lesson plans for Austrian schools. For the 1960–1961 school year, the Education Ministry decreed that eighth class teachers must include postwar history. By Christmas they were to have covered the period through 1914, and by February, the year 1945 and the rebirth of Austria. Before the end of the school year, teachers were to have taught the period leading up to and including the 1955 State Treaty.[120] The 1967 lesson plan for the fourth class for AHS schools details more specific themes to incorporate than earlier lesson plans. The list of topics for postwar Austrian history clearly indicates an emphasis on coalition history and the importance of the State Treaty: "Austria between liberation and freedom. Associations, corporations, and parties in political life, the meaning of cooperation. The State Treaty. The declaration of permanent neutrality. Comprehensive national defense. Austria's role in all-European concerns, its participation in world organizations."[121] The 1984 AHS lesson plan for the fourth class also uses the phrase "Austria between liberation and freedom" to signify the occupation period.[122] For the seventh class lesson plan, the postwar themes relating to the occupation period to cover include: "The re-establishment of the Republic of Austria. The time of the occupation. The rebuilding. The State Treaty. Permanent neutrality."[123] As a whole, these additions to the lesson plans demonstrate the Education Ministry's emphasis on the importance of including Austria's postwar rehabilitation and its rebirth into the national narrative.

A 1966 reader for polytechnic students demonstrates how new national symbols such as rebuilding, neutrality, and the ordeal of the State Treaty were all linked together ten years after the Allied occupation ended. Among the passages included in the text are: "Österreich—ein neutraler Staat" (Austria—a Neutral State), "Landesverteidigung—eine Notwendigkeit und Verpflichtung für uns alle" (National Defense—a Necessity and Duty for Us All), "Soldaten!" (Soldiers! [an address to the Austrian army on the occasion of its first public parade on 26 September 1956, given by then President Theodor Körner]), "Österreich ist frei" (Austria Is Free [Leopold Figl's speech at the signing of the State Treaty]), and several poems and prose excerpts evoking Austria's triumphant rise from the ashes.[124] Among these was an untitled passage by Heimito von Doderer, which called Austria the "spiritually most deep country in Europe" and gave mighty praise to Austria's political leaders, likening their achievements to Austria's seventeenth-century heroic age, or *Heldenzeitalter*.[125] After 1965, the national holiday was also integrated into the seasonal topical readings in the readers for younger children: "All children in the class look forward to the 26th of October. On this day, our fatherland is honored and celebrated."[126] A story in a 1973 text for fourth-graders, "Zum Nationalfeiertag" (On the National Holiday), links the holiday with Austria's ordeal from 1918 to 1955. The story begins by describing a scene of a soccer match in Vienna. The narrator, speaking to a child, remarks on the prosperity represented by all of the material goods such as cars and refrigerators, adding that "[i]t was not always so good for the people of our country." After the collapse of the empire, "the country had suddenly become small" and "[m]any people could not find any work. There were bloody disturbances among the inhabitants," which led to the end of democracy. "Finally, Austria was incorporated into the National Socialist empire ... and [m]any people were imprisoned.... And then came the war.... Food became scarce.... Bombs fell on the cities, there were the dead, blood, and tears." The narrator then extends the story into the postwar period when democracy was restored:

> All Austrians knew it: together one would have to rebuild. Back then, foreign soldiers were in our country. They had brought peace to the country, yet they stayed for ten years and kept the country occupied.... After many negotiations, it finally came on the 15th of May 1955. In Vienna, history was made [and the State Treaty was signed].... That meant that Austria was now finally free.
>
> On the 25th of October 1955, the last foreign soldier left Austrian soil. And the first day of full independence, the 26th, is therefore celebrated yearly as the national holiday.[127]

This story clearly demonstrates the symbolic value of the national holiday. Not only is the twenty-sixth of October represented as the culmination of the State Treaty negotiations, it is seen as the end of an ordeal that began in 1918. It is also clear that Austria's status is one of a victim—bad things "happen" to Austria, and even the Allies, who admittedly "brought peace," are named only as "foreign soldiers" who occupy Austria for an unjustly long period.

A story in a 1984 text, "Unser Nationalfeiertag (Oma erzählt aus ihrem Leben)" (Our National Holiday [Grandma Tells about Her Life]), also emphasizes the national holiday as the symbolic demarcation of a free Austria:

> I went with my grandma to the attic to fetch the flag. She said to me: "Tomorrow is the national holiday, as you surely know. All of the houses will be covered with flags."

She opened a chest. On top lay the red-white-red flag, neatly rolled up. Underneath I saw something laying [there]. "What is that?" I asked curiously. "That is your grandfather's uniform from when he was still a soldier in 1945."

She stared for a while immersed in thought, sat on the chest, and began to speak:

"In May 1945 the most horrible of all wars, the Second World War, came to an end. But the people in the country suffered bitter privation. Cold, hunger, insecurity, a shortage of clothing—everywhere debris and rubble.... Your grandfather was still a prisoner of war. We did not even know where he was.... All of Austria was occupied by foreign soldiers, the Russians, the Americans, the English, and the French. In Carinthia it was the English. Many homes, this one also, were seized by the English. We were assigned a room in a barracks.... Soon thereafter your grandfather came home from his imprisonment. You can perhaps imagine how astounded he was, when he found not us, but foreign soldiers in our house.

Then followed the hard years of the rebuilding....

The foreign soldiers stayed in Austria for ten years. In May 1955 it had ended. The skillful statesmen of our government succeeded through long, difficult negotiations in concluding the State Treaty with the occupation powers....

So that we never forget, we observe our national holiday on the 26th of October. And that is why we need the flag now."

With these words, she put the flag in my hand.[128]

This story explains the significance of the national holiday in terms of marking the end of Austria's long ordeal. The Second Republic is seen as the legacy of Austria's suffering, and this tradition is literally passed on to Austria's youth when the grandmother places the flag in the young narrator's hand. Of course, the national holiday and 1955 *did* fundamentally change Austria, and it is a valid function of the holiday to symbolize this shift. But with 1955 clearly emphasized as *the* break in the continuity of Austrian suffering, the Allied occupation is quite deliberately included as part of the larger Austrian ordeal.

In a logical, but also paradoxical, move, the Austrian military was also associated with the national holiday. The federal army, or Bundesheer, was officially recognized and held up as the defender of Austrian neutrality. The Austrian Education Ministry directed schools to emphasize "spiritual national defense" (*geistige Landesverteidigung*) by making available to students information on the Austrian military, such as posters, army magazines, and films. Furthermore, students were to be given the opportunity to speak with officers and take field trips to military installations.[129] In one way, the decision to emphasize the military on the national holiday is obvious and logical, since the Bundesheer was responsible for maintaining Austrian independence and sovereignty. But at the same time, the choice of the Bundesheer as a symbol of Austrian independence is wrought with ironies. The Austrian army had very little to do with Austrian independence. The Austrian military had not resisted the German invasion in 1938, and after a purge of some officers, the army of the First

Republic had been incorporated into the Nazi armies. Indeed, those responsible for restoring the independence of Austria were not Austrian troops, but rather the foreign armies of the Allies.

Although the Bundesheer did have symbolic validity as the protector of Austrian independence and neutrality, Austrian neutrality initially had little resonance as a national symbol. Unlike Switzerland, Austria had no tradition of neutrality. Neutrality was a quid pro quo for the Soviet agreement to sign the State Treaty.[130] Nevertheless, neutrality became an important part of Austrian identity, and the idea gained credence over time as Austria became a model United Nations citizen. Moreover, neutrality further disassociated Austria from Germany and the Cold War, which strengthened the uniqueness of Austrian identity. By the mid 1980s, Austria had built an impressive record as a neutral country. Several UN organizations were headquartered in Vienna, many Austrian soldiers served in UN blue-helmet operations, and Austria became a major stopover point for refugees. For some Austrians, it was a cruel irony when former UN Secretary-General, Kurt Waldheim—once a proud symbol of Austria's newfound neutral and cosmopolitan world role—became the focal point for Austria's "unmastered past" in the 1980s.

But despite Austria's record as a neutral country, the Bundesheer and the Austrian national holiday remain a strange combination. A 1979 text links the national holiday more strongly with neutrality than with the end of the occupation. In the passage "Österreich—ein neutraler Staat" (Austria—a Neutral State), the authors point out that the last Allied troops left the country in September, though technically they could have remained until 25 October. Instead of focusing on the departure of Allied soldiers, the authors emphasize Austria's "permanent neutrality," which was ensured with the implementation of the neutrality law in a special session of Parliament on 26 October 1955.[131] The authors' emphasis is misleading because it suggests that the neutrality law came as a result of the end of the occupation. Even though the law was not enacted until 26 October, Austria's promise of neutrality was essential to Soviet agreement to the State Treaty negotiations. In other words, Austria did not become neutral because the Allies evacuated; Austria promised to be neutral so that the occupiers would leave.[132] This point is made more accurately in the passage "Am 26. Oktober ist der Österreichische Nationalfeiertag" (The Austrian National Holiday Is on October 26th) in a 1984 text for second-graders: "Do you know why we celebrate this day? After a long and hard war, Austria was occupied for ten years by foreign soldiers. Only when Austria promised to always be neutral, that is, not to become mixed up in a quarrel between other people, did it become a free country."[133] Overall, neutrality was a valuable symbol of Austrian independence, and because it was linked to the State Treaty, it contributed to the idea that the treaty marked Austria's moment of true liberation and the moment when its national character could be expressed.

Born out of the Cold War, Austrian neutrality after 1955 conveyed a morally superior status on Austria. This self-image was reinforced over time and was given credence by Austria's role as a mediator, weigh station for refugees, and host of important international conferences. Textbook authors soon embraced the moral high ground that neutrality ostensibly provides. A 1981 text demonstrates the symbolic importance of neutrality in a passage on the national holiday, "Zum Nationalfeiertag" (On the National Holiday): "On the 26th of October 1955, after many years of occupation, war, *and occupation again*, Austria was finally free. The Austrian government then enacted permanent neutrality; that means, Austria will always be the friend of all peoples and not take a side when other peoples have disagreements" (emphasis added).[134] Once again, it is significant that the same term—occupation (*Besetzung*)—is used for both the Nazi and the Allied occupations. Again, we see that the Anschluss, the war, and the Allied occupation became part of a single ordeal. The break in the continuity of suffering did not come in 1945, but in 1955. In addition, while the breach in this continuity of hardships comes with the State Treaty in May 1955, the break is finalized with Austria's declaration of permanent neutrality on 26 October 1955.

Looking Backward and Forward in 1965

To conclude this discussion of the Allies, the State Treaty, and new symbols of national identity, it is useful to return to the year 1965. It was during that year, twenty years after the war, ten years after the State Treaty, and twenty years before the Waldheim controversy, that the Austria-as-victim myth reached its zenith. The year 1965 marked the tenth anniversary of the State Treaty and the first celebration of the new national holiday, and the Education Ministry directed schools to commemorate these events. The school radio system (Österreichische Schulfunk) broadcast a thirty-minute program that included excerpts from speeches by former President Renner and former Chancellor Raab during the rebuilding period, as well as recordings of the original radio reports on the State Treaty.[135]

A commemorative publication on the State Treaty that was distributed to students employs the double-occupation theory: "The 15th of May 1955 was the greatest day of our *Heimat*. The day which a people of seven million had waited for ten years, yes, even seventeen years. The day on which the Austrian State Treaty was signed." The publication is accompanied by several photographs, including pictures of occupation troops leaving Austria with their suitcases in hand. The caption reads: "As it was agreed in the State Treaty, the soldiers of the occupying powers left our country: those from the east and those from the west."[136]

Two 1965 commemorative speeches by a school principal and a teacher clearly reflect how the victim myth was so important to building the new Austria. In the town of Gmunden, in Salzburg, Principal G. Rolletschek's speech at a school celebration of the ten-year anniversary of the signing of the State Treaty demonstrates how new symbols of national identity, such as rebuilding and the State Treaty, had been fully integrated with the Austria-as-victim myth by 1965. Rolletschek reminds the students that because of their youth, they cannot remember "the loss of Austria's independence, the war, the catastrophe, and the adjoining bitter years," which were characterized by "sorrow for the dead, for the destroyed homes, for the lost *Heimat*, sorrow and shame over the horrible crimes accountable to an unscrupulous regime, which we, after all, *were forced to obey*, and despair over the fate of our country, that *one pretended to liberate, and then divided up like a criminal*, and whose fate was altogether dark and uncertain" (emphasis added). The principal then explains that history demonstrates that a rebirth of civilization is by no means guaranteed, as evidenced by the fall of Egypt and Babylon, warning: "No, that we are an admired people of culture *[bewundertes Kulturvolk]*, not meaningful in size of population, but in creative powers, that does not give us claim to eternal life." Rolletschek then shifts to a positive tone, remarking that "as there is death …, *so there is also a resurrection*, an inner rebirth, often in the darkest hours…. And it happened. Thank God!" But as he then explains, standing in the way of Austria's rebirth were the Four Powers: "[W]e were not head of our own house *[wir waren nicht Herr im eigenen Haus]*." The principal then acknowledges the aid Austria received, but insists that the rebuilding is an achievement that belongs to the Austrians alone: "We do not want to be ungrateful in this hour of celebration and [we] remind ourselves that the occupation powers and international organizations like the UNRRA and the Red Cross kept us from the worst, from starvation, and that soon the generous assistance of the United States of America was implemented. *Yet everything decisive for the rebuilding of the state we had to achieve ourselves under difficult conditions*" (emphasis added). To conclude his speech, Rolletschek extols Austria's uniqueness vis-à-vis Germany and embraces the coalition lesson:

> And that a *small people*, which unlike *its great German neighbor*—to whose credit has a genial sense for planning and order *(Ordnung)*—has rather more of an understanding for affable nonchalance and comfortable routine, that this small people … achieved the unbelievable and solved problems—which even most of the victorious powers had failed to solve after the First World War … [is remarkable].
>
> In an inconspicuous and more modest form, we Austrians experienced something similar [to the rebirth of the Old Egyptian Empire] in the years before the State Treaty. When the people and government … avoided disintegration and chaos, when the parties, forgetting old feuds, worked together harmoniously in legislation and rebuilding…. But the most beautiful fruit from these years full of privation was a newly awakened simple love of *Heimat* without pathos and conceit, a new openness of the soul for the magic of the landscape and for the innate, unmistakable uniqueness of Austrian art and culture [emphasis added].[137]

This speech names nearly every major theme and subtheme of the victim myth and other themes of national identity, including victimization at the hands of Germany, Allied unfairness, Austria's status as a cultural powerhouse, the *Wiederaufbau*, Austrian uniqueness vis-à-vis Germany, and the coalition lesson. While the language of the school principal seems exaggerated in the post-Waldheim era, this speech was meant in earnest and reflects how the themes of the victim mythology had become an integral part of officially sanctioned national identity.

Another speech commemorating the first celebration of the new 26 October national holiday in 1965 demonstrates the same sentiment. In listening to their teacher Edeltrude Hubner, students again learned that Austrians were a culturally unique people who had been victimized by both the Germans and the Four Powers:

> The troops of the victorious powers, who in the fight against Hitler's Germany also had become the liberators of Austria, were—during the ten years of hope and disappointment—seen more and more as bothersome strangers. Who does not still think of the many seized factories and agricultural enterprises, of the chicanery of the checkpoints, of the four in the jeep, or of the identification cards?
>
> In a solemn declaration by the Allies still during the war, the re-establishment of a fully free and independent Austria had been decreed. Based on its experiences, what could Austria, already free and sovereign in 1945, have accomplished for world peace?… Now [after the State Treaty] our red-white-red flag no longer has to flutter modestly next to the flags of the great four; it can be the proud symbol of our national will…. It can wave above a state whose will to freedom and consciousness of cultural mission are documented by the reopening of the Vienna State Opera on 5 November 1955 with *Fidelio*.[138]

Once again, the Allied occupation is conflated with the Anschluss. It is also noteworthy that Ms. Hubner heralds the opera as a sign of Austria's rebirth, for as Sigrid Löffler points out, in Vienna, the State Opera and the Burgtheater are important sites of Austrian cultural identity and symbols of Austria's world cultural position.[139]

The previous speeches are emblematic of how the Austria-as-victim myth as a complex web of interlocking themes was entrenched in the rhetoric of school officials in 1965. Twenty years after the war, Austria had "found itself." [140] Ten years after the occupation, Austria was finally free from both the Germans and the meddling Allies. Officially, the Nazi past had been put to rest and was not an issue for Austria. But 1965 also witnessed a shocking event—Austria's first postwar political murder—an event which demonstrated that beneath the comfortable silence about the Nazi past, and amidst the *Gemütlichkeit* of rebuilt Vienna, there was some unfinished business.

Notes

1. Quoted from Keyserlingk, *Austria in World War II*, 152.
2. "Naturally—it was a hard time...one allowed a liberated people to go hungry." Merz and Qualtinger, *Der Herr Karl*, 26.
3. "I celebrated...on the day when we got it...the State Treaty...Then we went to Belvedere...[W]e stood there...a sea of us...lots of Austrians...like in the year thirty-eight... And then he walked out...the...the...Federal-, Poldl [Leopold Figl] and took the other gentlemen by the hand and courageously declared: 'Austria is free again!' And as I heard that, then I knew it: I made it through that, too. We succeeded with the rebuilding." See ibid., 29–30. Thanks to Günter Bischof for clarifying that "der Poldl" (roughly "lil' Leopold") refers to Leopold Figl.
4. See Leopold Figl's spring 1955 article "Von Fremdbesetzung zu Fremdbesetzung" in *Österreichische Monatshefte* 4 (April 1955): 5–6.
5. For works on Austria and the Four Powers, see James Jay Carafano, *Waltzing into the Cold War: The Struggle for Occupied Austria* (College Station: Texas A & M University Press, 2002); Manfried Rauchensteiner, *Der Sonderfall. Die Besatzungszeit in Österreich, 1945 bis 1955* (Graz: Verlag Styria, 1979); Anton Pelinka and Rolf Steininger, eds., *Österreich und die Sieger: 40 Jahre 2. Republik—30 Jahre Staatsvertrag* (Vienna: Wilhelm Braumüller, 1986); William B. Bader, *Austria Between East and West, 1945–1955* (Stanford: Stanford University Press, 1966); and Oliver Rathkolb, ed., *Gesellschaft und Politik am Beginn der Zweiten Republik. Vertrauliche Berichte der US-Militäradministration aus Österreich 1945 in englischer Originalfassung* (Vienna: Hermann Böhlaus Nachfolger, 1985).
6. Quoted from Keyserlingk, *Austria in World War II*, 152. Keyserlingk's work is the definitive account of the genesis and importance of the Moscow Declaration. Also see Günter Bischof, "Die Instrumentalisierung der Moskauer Erklärung nach dem 2. Weltkrieg," *Zeitgeschichte* 20, nos. 11–12 (1993): 345–366.
7. Robert G. Knight, "Besiegt oder befreit? Eine völkerrechtliche Frage historisch betrachtet," in *Die bevormundete Nation. Österreich und die Alliierten 1945–1949*, ed. Günter Bischof and Josef Leidenfrost (Innsbruck: Haymon Verlag, 1988), 76. Also see Fritz Fellner, "Die außenpolitische und völkerrechtliche Situation Österreichs 1938. Österreichs Wiederherstellung als Kriegsziel der Alliierten," in *Österreich. Die Zweite Republik. Band I*, ed. Weinzierl and Skalnik, 53–90.
8. Gerald Stourzh, *Geschichte des Staatsvertrages, 1945–1955. Österreichs Weg zur Neutralität* (Graz: Verlag Styria, 1980), 3.
9. Ibid., 5.
10. Keyserlingk, *Austria in World War II*, 153.
11. See Oliver Rathkolb, "Wie homogen war Österreich 1945? Innenpolitische Optionen," in *Inventur 45/55*, ed. Kos and Rigele, 157–180, *passim*.
12. Franz Berger et al., eds., *Zeiten, Völker und Kulturen. Ein Lehr- und Arbeitsbuch für den Geschichtsunterricht an Haupt- und Untermittelschulen. 4. Band. Das Zeitalter der Weltpolitik und der Technik* (Vienna: Hölder-Pichler-Tempsky, 1957), 191.
13. Walter Göhring and Herbert Hasenmayer, *Zeitgeschichte. Ein Lehr- und Arbeitsbuch für Geschichte und Sozialkunde*, 3rd rev. ed. (Vienna: Ed. Hölzel, 1986), 106.
14. Walter Knarr et al., *Der Mensch im Wandel der Zeiten, III. Teil. Lehrbuch für Geschichte und Sozialkunde. Vom Ausbruch des Ersten Weltkrieges bis zur Gegenwart* (Vienna: Österreichischer Gewerbeverlag, 1968), 158.
15. Novotny, *Österreichisches Lehrbuch für Geschichte und Sozialkunde*, 202.
16. See Stourzh, *Geschichte des Staatsvertrags*, 167; and Lonnie Johnson, "Die Österreichische Nation, Die Moskauer Deklaration und die Völkerrechtliche Argumentation. Bemerkungen zur Problematik der Interpretation der NS-Zeit in Österreich," in *Dokumentationsarchiv des österreichischen Widerstandes. Jahrbuch 1988*, ed. Siegwald Ganglmair (Vienna: Österreichischer Bundesverlag, 1989), 49–50.
17. Berger and Schausberger, *Zeiten, Völker und Kulturen*, 17. Except for pagination, the text of the 1977 second edition is identical.

18. Thaler, *The Ambivalence of Identity*, 32–35.

19. In assessing the degree to which the zonal boundaries hindered economic recovery, Fritz Weber argues that transport problems and fuel shortages were a much greater hindrance to the economy than were the boundaries. See Fritz Weber, "Wiederaufbau zwischen Ost und West," in *Österreich, 1945–1995. Gesellschaft, Politik, Kultur*, ed. Sieder et al., 68–79.

20. "I made it through that too. We succeeded with the rebuilding." Merz and Qualtinger, *Der Herr Karl*, 30.

21. Hans Spreitzer, ed., *Kommentar zum Lehrplan des Polytechnischen Lehrganges* (Vienna: Österreichischer Bundesverlag, 1970), 136.

22. See Johann Bernt and Helmut Zilk, *Wien. Stadt im Aufbau* (Vienna: Hölder-Pichler-Tempsky, 1965); Helmut Leiter, *Zwanzig Jahre Wien* (Vienna: Verlag für Jugend und Volk, 1965); Emmy Wohanka, *Zwanzig Jahre Wien, 1945–1965* (Vienna: Verlag für Jugend und Volk, 1965); and Karl Bruckner, *In Diesen Jahren. Wien 1945–1965* (Vienna: Verlag für Jugend und Volk, 1965).

23. Arbeitsgemeinschaft, *Unser Österreich, 1945–1955*, 46. Also see the story "Harte Arbeit in Kaprun," by Othmar Franz Lang, in Hans Bernt, Therese Schüssel, and Herta Zeman, *Arbeit—Freiheit—Menschenwürde. Von Biedermeier zur Gegenwart. Österreich—erlebt und erschaut* (Vienna: Hölder-Pichler-Tempsky, 1961), 159–164.

24. For an example, see Anton Ebner et al., *Unsere Republik im Wandel der Zeit*, plates between pages 48 and 49.

25. Hanisch, *Der Lange Schatten des Staates*, 438. "Das Lied von Kaprun" belongs to the genre of *Heimat* films. In the West German context, Elizabeth Boa and Rachel Palfreyman argue that the popular postwar *Heimat* films represent an escapist "flight from the past." See Boa and Palfreyman, *Heimat: A German Dream*, 10, 86–102, *passim*.

26. Georg Rigele, "The Marshall Plan and Austria's Hydroelectric Industry: Kaprun," in *The Marshall Plan in Austria*, ed. Bischof et al., 324, 328–329. Rigele argues that the hydroelectric industry in general was the most important beneficiary of Marshall Plan aid. See ibid., 335–338. Also see Margit Reiter, "The 'Myth' of Kaprun: Forced Labor at the Tauern Power Plant in Kaprun and How Postwar Austria Dealt With It," in *The Dollfuss/Schuschnigg Era in Austria*, ed. Bischof et al., 258–266.

27. Hanisch, *Der Lange Schatten des Staates*, 408; and Pelinka, *Austria: Out of the Shadow of the Past*, 186. Also see Gerald Stourzh, *Vom Reich zur Republik. Studien zum Österreichbewußtsein im 20. Jahrhundert* (Vienna: Edition Atelier, 1990), 67; and David Walker, "Industrial Location in Turbulent Times: Austria through Anschluss and Occupation," *Journal of Historical Geography* 12, no. 2 (1986): 182–195.

28. Figures cited from Bischof, *Austria in the First Cold War*, 102.

29. See Ferdinand Lacina, "The Marshall Plan—a Contribution to the Austrian Economy in Transition," and Kurt Löffler and Hans Fußenegger (trans. Mel Greenwald), "The Activities of the ERP Fund from 1962 to 1998," both in *The Marshall Plan in Austria*, ed. Bischof et al., 9–14 and 15–55, respectively.

30. Hanisch, *Der Lange Schatten des Staates*, 413. Also see Kurt Tweraser, "The Politics of Productivity and Corporatism: The Late Marshall Plan in Austria, 1950–54," in *Austria in the Nineteen Fifties*, ed. Bischof et al., 91–115.

31. Berger et al., *Zeiten, Völker, und Kulturen*, 196. Also see the 1977 and 1987 editions of the same book.

32. Ebner and Majdan, *Geschichte 4 für die Oberstufe*, 250.

33. Göbhart and Chvojka, *Geschichte und Sozialkunde*, 190.

34. Schödl and Forstner, *Sozialkunde, Wirtschaftskunde, Zeitgeschichte*, 117.

35. See Günter Bischof's introduction in *The Marshall Plan in Austria*, ed. Bischof et al., 1. Also see Bischof's analysis in Günter Bischof, "Der Marshall-Plan in Europa 1947–1952," *Aus Politik und Zeitgeschichte. Beilage zur Wochenzeitung Das Parlament*, B 22–23/97 (23 May 1997): 3–17.

36. Judt, *Past Imperfect*, 52.

37. For example, in a 1980 article in the Austrian journal *Zeitgeschichte*, Heinz Strotzka wrote about the Marshall Plan in the "Contemporary History and Teaching" section of

the journal. Strotzka came to the conclusion that the textbooks of the time (1970s to 1980) treated the Marshall Plan in an overly positive light, despite the fact that the ERP was, as discussed, typically only mentioned rather than discussed in any in-depth manner. Strotzka concluded his article with a lesson plan suggestion emphasizing the various American motivations, as well as suggestions for thought questions, including "The Marshall Plan—a Form of Dollar Imperialism?" See Heinz Strotzka, "Die Auswirkungen der Marshallplan-Hilfe auf Österreich als Didaktisches Problem," *Zeitgeschichte* 8, no. 2 (1980): 61–74.

38. See Günter Bischof, "Zum internationalen Stand de Marshallplan Forschung: Die Forschungsdesiderata für Österreich," in *Zeitgeschichte im Wandel. 3. Österreichische Zeitgeschichtetage 1997*, ed. Gertraud Diendorfer, Gerhard Jagschitz, and Oliver Rathkolb (Innsbruck: Studien Verlag, 1998), 61–72. For exceptions, see Tweraser, "The Politics of Productivity and Corporatism," 91–115; Wilfried Mähr, "Der Marshallplan in Österreich: Tanz nach einer ausländischen Pfeife?" in *Die Bevormundete Nation*, ed. Bischof and Leidenfrost, 245–272; and Wilfried Mähr, "Der Marshall-Plan in Österreich: Wirtschaftspolitischer Nachhilfeunterricht?" *Zeitgeschichte* 15, no. 3 (1987): 91–111.

39. Ebner and Partick, *Lehrbuch der Geschichte*, 157–158.

40. Lang and Ritter, *Unser Österreich, 1945–1955*, 38.

41. Göhring and Hasenmayer, *Zeitgeschichte*, 106.

42. *Verordnungsblatt für den Dienstbereich des Bundesministeriums für Unterricht*, Jahrgang 1955, Stück 10a, no. 87 [Erlaß: Neuverlautbarung der Provisorischen Lehrpläne für die Mittelschulen], 3.

43. Ebner and Partick, *Lehrbuch der Geschichte*, 151–152.

44. Zens, *Schaut Ringsumher*, 22–23.

45. Scheipl et al., *Geschichte und Sozialkunde*, 112.

46. Riccabona et al., *Geschichte, Sozialkunde, Politische Bildung*, 79.

47. Maria Szupanschitz, "Schüleraufsatz: Ein freies Österreich," *83./84. Jahresbericht der Hauptschule für Knaben und Mädchen in Eisenstadt, '63/64 '64/65* (Eisenstadt, n.p.: 1965), 19.

48. M. Kößler, "25 Jahre Zweite Republik Österreich. Ansprache über den Rundspruch anläßlich des Jubiläums der Zweiten Republik Österreich (25 Jahre) am 27. April. 1970 am 1. Bundesgymnasium Graz," *Bericht über das Schuljahr 1969/70*, erstattet von der Direktion (Graz: Selbstverlag des 1. Bundesgymnasiums Graz, 1970), 26.

49. In my research I did not find any specific portrayals of the French. In one instance, the behavior of the British was criticized. In a commemorative program to celebrate the 1957 fiftieth anniversary of a school in Bruck on the Mur, the British are taken to task for vandalizing the school during the occupation period. See Hans Valent, *"50 Jahre Brucker Mittelschule (1907–1957)," Bundesrealgymnasium und -Realschule Bruck a.d. Mur. Festbericht Anlässlich des 50 Jährigen Bestandes der Anstalt (1907–1957)* (Bruck an der Mur: Bundesrealgymnasium und -Realschule in Bruck an der Mur, 1957), 47.

50. See Raelynn J. Hillhouse, "A Reevaluation of Soviet Policy in Central Europe: The Soviet Union and the Occupation of Austria," *Eastern European Politics and Societies* 3, no. 1 (winter 1989): 83–104; and Reinhard Bollmus, "Ein kalkuliertes Risiko? Großbritannien, die USA und das 'Deutsche Eigentum' auf der Konferenz von Potsdam," in *Die Bevormundete Nation*, ed. Bischof and Leidenfrost, 107–126.

51. See Matthew Paul Berg, "'Caught Between Iwan and the Weihnachtsmann': Occupation, the Marshall Plan, and Austrian Identity," in *The Marshall Plan in Austria*, ed. Bischof et al., 156–164.

52. "I will not be minister."
"Why?"
"The Russians are against it."
"What are we going to do now?"
"We're going into the Parliament."
"What will we do there?"
"You'll see."

Heinrich Schramm-Schiessl, *Der Baumeister. Julius Raab—Kanzler der Freiheit* (Vienna: Österreichischer Bundesverlag, 1961); 24. The publication continued with a long account of the State Treaty negotiations. Also see Othmar Franz Lang, *Der Baumeister. Julius Raab—Kämpfer für Österreich* (Vienna: Österreichischer Bundesverlag, 1961); and Othmar Franz Lang, *Der Baumeister. Julius Raab—Freund der Jugend* (Vienna: Österreichischer Bundesverlag, 1961).

53. Novotny, *Österreichisches Lehrbuch für Geschichte und Sozialkunde*, 206.

54. Josef Mayer, "Eine Betrachtung der geschichtlichen Entwicklung der Stadt Stockerau," 103. *Jahresbericht des Bundes-Gymnasiums und des Bundes-Realgymnasiums in Stockerau* (Stockerau: Verlag des Studentenunterstützungsvereines Stockerau, 1973), 22.

55. Berger and Schausberger, *Zeiten, Völker und Kulturen*, 222.

56. See Reinhold Wagnleitner, *Coca-Colonization and the Cold War: The Cultural Mission of the United States in Austria after the Second World War*, trans. Diana M. Wolf (Chapel Hill: University of North Carolina Press, 1994).

57. Helmut Obermayr, Wolfgang Leberbauer, Studententeam, "40 Jahre seit dem Kriegsende. I. Erlebte Geschichte. Die Jahre 1938 bis 1955 im Gymnasium Kremsmünster," *Öffentliches Stiftsgymnasium Kremsmünster. 128. Jahresbericht 1985* (Kremsmünster, 1985), 20–23.

58. See Ingrid Bauer, "'Austria's Prestige Dragged into the Dirt'? The 'GI-Brides' and Postwar Austrian Society (1945–1955)," in *Women in Austria*, ed. Günter Bischof, Anton Pelinka, and Erika Thurner (New Brunswick: Transaction Publishers, 1998), 47.

59. See Berg, "'Caught Between Iwan and the Weihnachtsmann,'" 156–184.

60. Friederike Lanzelsdorfer and Ernst Pacolt, eds., *Unser Lesehaus 4. Bei uns und anderswo*, 9th ed. (Vienna: Jugend und Volk, 1976), 56–63.

61. Ludwig Boyer and Walter Fischer, *Westermann Leselehrgang. Lesebuch 4* (Vienna: Georg Westermann Verlag, 1979), 59–60.

62. Lucia Binder et al., eds., *Aus dem Reich der Dichtung 3. Sachlich—Kritisch—Informativ* (Vienna: Jugend und Volk, 1977), 57–63.

63. Richard Bamberger, ed., *Texte. Band 4. Lesebuch für die Hauptschulen und die Unterstufe der allgemeinbildender höheren Schulen* (Vienna: Österreichischer Bundesverlag für Unterricht, Wissenschaft und Kunst, 1979), 137–140.

64. Hanisch, *Der Lange Schatten des Staates*, 416.

65. See Günter Bischof, "The Making of a Cold Warrior: Karl Gruber and Austrian Foreign Policy, 1945–1953," *Austrian History Yearbook*, vol. 26 (1995): 110–112. Also see Karl Gruber's memoir *Between Liberation and Liberty*, trans. Lionel Kochan (New York: Praeger, 1955), 49–79.

66. For the definitive scholarly works on the South Tyrol question, see Rolf Steininger, *Südtirol zwischen Diplomatie und Terror, 1947–1969: Darstellungen in drei Bänden* (vol. 1, 1947–1959; vol. 2, 1960–1962; vol. 3, 1962–1969) (Bolzano: Verlagsanstalt Athesia, 1999).

67. The one-sided portrayal of the South Tyrol question is just one of the many faults Laurence Cole points to concerning Tyrolean historiography. See his blistering critique, "Fern von Europa? The Peculiarities of Tirolian Historiography," *Zeitgeschichte 23*, nos. 5–6 (1996): 181–204.

68. Heinrich Kotz et al., *Junge Saat. Lesebuch für Tiroler Volksschulen. Ausgabe B für Stadtschulen für die 3. Klasse* (Innsbruck: Tyrolia-Verlag, 1966), 207.

69. Franz Oberhammer, *Tirol in Gegenwart und Vergangenheit. Zeiten, Völker und Kulturen. Länderteil zum Einführungsband für die 1. Klasse der Hauptschulen* (Vienna: Österreichischer Bundesverlag, 1968). This text was reprinted unchanged in 1982.

70. Atschko et al., *Sozial- und Wirtschaftskunde (inlk. Zeitgeschichte) für den Polytechnischen Lehrgang*, 114.

71. For works on the Slovene minority in Carinthia, see Mirko Bogataj, *Die Kärntner Slowenen* (Klagenfurt: Hermagoras, 1989); and Arbeitsgemeinschaft Volksgruppenfragen Universität Klagenfurt, eds., *Kein einig Volk von Brüdern. Studien zum Mehrheiten-/Minderheitenproblem am Beispiel Kärntens* (Vienna: Verlag für Gesellschaftskritik, 1982).

72. For two poems on *Heimkehr*, see Ernst Wiechert "Heimkehrers Weihnacht," and Hans Kloepfer, "Heimkehr," both in *Lesebuch für Hauptschulen. 4. Teil*, ed. Adolf Harwalik and

Anton Afritsch (Graz: Stiasny Verlag, 1961), 167–168. For a text with two poems and a tragic short story about coming home, see Franz Theodor Czokor, "Heimkehr," Renate Seeliger, "Enttäuschte Hoffnung," and Erika Mitterer, "Oh, kehrst du heim ...," all in *Arbeit—Freiheit—Menschenwürde*, ed. Bernt et al., 154–158.

73. Lehrerarbeitsgemeinschaft beim Landesschulrat Salzburg, *Unser Lesebuch. 4. Klasse Hauptschule. Du und die Gemeinschaft*, 246.

74. Riccabona et al., *Geschichte, Sozialkunde, Politische Bildung*, 77.

75. See, for example, Alfred M. de Zayas, *Nemesis at Potsdam: The Expulsion of the Germans from the East*, 3rd rev. ed. (Lincoln: University of Nebraska Press, 1988). Also see John Keegan, *The Second World War* (New York: Penguin, 1989), 592–593.

76. Ebner et al., *Lehrbuch der Geschichte und Sozialkunde*, 156–157.

77. Hörler and Müller, *Die Weltenuhr*, 110. Also see *"Ostflüchtlinge"* (Eastern Refugees) about the hardships of refugees from East Prussia in Lehrerarbeitsgemeinschaft beim Landesschulrat Salzburg, *Unser Lesebuch 6.-8. Schulstufe. Heimat und Welt*, 437–439.

78. Franz Göbhart and Erwin Chvojka, *Zeitbilder. Geschichte und Sozialkunde 8. Vom Ersten Weltkrieg bis zur Gegenwart* (Vienna: Verlag Carl Ueberreuter, 1984), 119.

79. Kurt K. Tweraser, "Military Justice as an Instrument of American Occupation Policy in Austria 1945–1950: From Total Control to Limited Tutelage," *Austrian History Yearbook*, vol. 24 (1993): 161–162.

80. Dieter Stiefel, "Der Prozeß der Entnazifizierung in Österreich," in *Politische Säuberung in Europa. Die Abrechnung mit Faschismus und Kollaboration nach dem Zweiten Weltkrieg*, ed. Klaus-Dietmar Henke and Hans Woller (Munich: Deutscher Taschenbuch Verlag, 1991), 109–110. Also see Dieter Stiefel, *Entnazifizierung in Österreich* (Vienna: Europaverlag, 1981).

81. *Military Government Austria: Report of the United States Commissioner*, April 1946, 148.

82. Ibid., July 1946, 9–11.

83. Ibid., December 1946, 5, and *Military Government Austria: Report of the United States Commissioner*, February 1947, 15, 203.

84. Ibid., February 1948, 32.

85. See Tweraser, "Military Justice as an Instrument of American Occupation Policy," 161–170.

86. Ibid.

87. Stiefel, "Der Prozeß der Entnazifizierung in Österreich," 116–117.

88. Ibid., 113–115.

89. See Albert Massiczek, "'Zweimal illegal.' Bericht eines Zeitzeugen," in *Verdrängte Schuld, verfehlte Sühne. Entnazifizierung in Österreich, 1945–1955*, ed. Sebastian Meissl, Klaus-Dieter Mulley, and Oliver Rathkolb (Bad Vöslau: Verlag für Geschichte und Politik, 1986), 311.

90. Robert Knight, "Britische Entnazifizerungspolitik, 1945–1949," *Zeitgeschichte* 11, nos. 9–10 (1984): 287–295.

91. John H. Backer, *Winds of History: The German Years of Lucius Du Bignon Clay* (New York: Van Nostrand Reinhold, 1983), 123.

92. Committee on Foreign Relations, *United States Senate, Documents on Germany, 1944–1970* (Washington, D.C.: Government Printing Office, 1971), 59–67.

93. *Military Government Austria: Report of the United States Commissioner*, December 1946, 7.

94. Stiefel, "Der Prozeß der Entnazifizierung in Österreich," 117–120.

95. *Military Government Austria: Report of the United States Commissioner*, May 1948, 20–21; and ibid., June 1948, 36. One result of the amnesties was a competition among the parties for Nazi votes that was not always "dignified." See Karl Stadler, *Austria* (New York: Praeger, 1971), 270–271.

96. Dieter Stiefel, "Nazifizierung plus Entnazifizierung = Null? Bemerkungen zur besonderen Problematik der Entnazifizierung in Österreich," in *Verdrängte Schuld, verfehlte Sühne*, ed. Meissl et al., 28.

97. Oliver Rathkolb, "U.S.-Entnazifizierung in Österreich. Zwischen Kontrollierter Revolution und Elitenrestauration (1945–1949)," *Zeitgeschichte* 11, nos. 9–10 (1984): 302–325, *passim*.

98. Stiefel, "Nazifizierung plus Entnazifizierung = Null?" 33.

99. Knight, "Britische Entnazifizerungspolitik," 295.

100. *Military Government Austria: Report of the United States Commissioner*, December 1947, 14–15.

101. Knight, "Britische Entnazifizerungspolitik, 1945–1949," 288.

102. Ibid., 298.

103. Johnson, "Die Österreichische Nation, Die Moskauer Deklaration und die Völker-rechtliche Argumentation," 49–50.

104. Austrian politicians insisted on "State Treaty" over "Peace Treaty," since the Austrian state did not participate in the war. The definitive work on the Austrian State Treaty is Gerald Stourzh, *Um Einheit und Freiheit: Staatsvertrag, Neutralität und das Ende der Ost-West-Besetzung Österreichs 1945–1955*, 4th rev. and exp. ed. (Vienna: Böhlau, 1998) (revised from the earlier 1980 edition titled *Geschichte des Staatsvertrages, 1945–1955. Österreichs Weg zur Neutralität*). Also see Audrey Kurth Cronin, *Great Power Politics and the Struggle Over Austria, 1945–1955* (Ithaca: Cornell University Press, 1986).

105. Bischof, *Austria in the First Cold War*, 130–149, *passim*, and 153–155. Also see idem, "Spielball der Mächtigen? Österreichs außenpolitische Spielraum im beginnenden Kalten Krieg," in *Inventur 45/55*, ed. Kos and Rigele, 126–156.

106. Bischof, *Austria in the First Cold War*, 78–129, *passim*. On American security concerns, also see Oliver Rathkolb, "Von der Besatzung zur Neutralität: Österreich in den außenpolitischen Strategien des Nationalen Sicheheitsrates unter Truman und Eisenhower," in *Die bevormundete Nation*, ed. Bischof and Leidenfrost, 371–405. James Carafano demonstrates that the secret rearmament of Austria had the support of the ÖVP and the SPÖ, both of which feared a Communist coup. See Carafano, *Waltzing into the Cold War*, 179–188.

107. Wolfgang Weber, ed., *Die Streitkräfte der NATO auf dem Territorium der BRD* (Berlin: Militärverlag der Deutschen Demokratischen Republik, 1989), 171.

108. Of the numerous examples that demonstrate this, Berlin, where the Four Powers remained sovereign until the end of the Cold War, is the most outstanding.

109. See Günter Bischof, "Austria—a Colony in the U.S. Postwar 'Empire'?" in *Empire: American Studies*, ed. John G. Blair and Reinhold Wagnleitner (Tübingen: Gunter Narr Verlag, 1997), 123–124.

110. Ebner and Partick, *Lehrbuch der Geschichte*, 154.

111. Riccabona et al., *Geschichte, Sozialkunde, Politische Bildung*, 80.

112. Berger and Schausberger, *Zeiten, Völker und Kulturen*, 233.

113. Leherarbeitsgemeinschaft beim Landesschulrat Salzburg, *Unser Lesebuch. 6.-8. Schulstufe. Heimat und Welt*, 440–441. Also see "Das Jahr des Staatsvertrages" and "Aus dem Österreichischen Staatsvertrag" in Arbeitsgemeinschaft, *Österreich Lesebuch. Band 4.*, 121–126.

114. Lehrerarbeitsgemeinschaft beim Landesschulrat Salzburg, *Unser Lesebuch. 4. Klasse Hauptschule. Du und die Gemeinschaft*, unnumbered page between pages 240 and 241.

115. Figl, "Von Fremdbesetzung zu Fremdbesetzung," 5–6.

116. "From these hearts I want to bear witness—/not only as praiser of the past:/They had their mistakes, their sins;/who has not had them, which people and which time?/.../They trusted their superiors easily like children/and remained loyal, even where they were betrayed,/Yet the loyalty was not therefore less,/perhaps that is a reason for high praise./.../They gladly let their weapons rust,/as symbols they needed: emperor and altar./Yet wherever they stood, they kept their posts,/even if these posts were lost./.../It is never-ending what this people suffered,/Humiliation, persecution, hunger, pain—/and they carried it with strength and they carried it with quiet asking/in the pride and humility of their humanity." See Lehrerarbeitsgemeinschaft beim Landesschulrat Salzburg, *Unser Lesebuch. 4. Klasse Hauptschule. Du und die Gemeinschaft*, 240–241.

117. See Ernst Bruckmüller, *Nation Österreich. Sozialhistorische Aspekte ihrer Entwicklung* (Vienna: Hermann Böhlaus Nachfolger, 1984), 197–198. Also see Wodak et al., *The Discursive Construction of National Identity*, 53.

118. Christiana Potocnik, "Der Österreichische Nationalfeiertag—Nur Mehr Ein Tag der Fitnessmärsche?" *Zeitgeschichte* 17, no. 1 (1989): 19–32.

119. *Verordnungsblatt für den Dienstbereich des Bundesministeriums für Unterricht*, Jahrgang 1965, 12. Stück, no. 94, 245.

120. Ibid., Jahrgang 1960, 10. Stück, no. 113, 206.

121. *III. Sondernummer zum Verordnungsblatt für den Dienstbereich des Bundesministeriums für Unterricht*, Jahrgang 1967, Stück no. 10a, 107.

122. *Lehrpläne der allgemeinbildenden höheren Schulen. I. Band.* (Vienna: Österreichischer Bundesverlag, 1984), 83.

123. Ibid., 87–88.

124. Harwalik et al., *Schaffensfreude, Lebensfreude*, 12–28.

125. Ibid., 16.

126. See "Österreichischer Nationalfeiertag," in *Komm, lies mit mir! Lesebuch für die 2. Schulstufe*, ed. Josef Berghöfer et al. (Eisenstadt: E. Rötzer Verlag, 1970), 47.

127. Berghofer et al., *Unser schönes Buch*, 30–31.

128. Gertrude Langer et al., *Österreichisches Lesebuch. Lesebuch für die 4. Klasse der Volksschule* (Wolfsberg: Verlag Ernst Ploetz, 1984), 242–243.

129. *Verordnungsblatt für den Dienstbereich des Bundesministeriums für Unterricht*, Jahrgang 1965, 11. Stück, no. 85, 232.

130. Cronin, *Great Power Politics and the Struggle Over Austria*, 147–150.

131. Boyer and Fischer, *Westermann Leselehrgang. Lesebuch 4*, 36–37. This text also includes an account of Leopold Figl's State Treaty speech of 15 May 1955. See ibid., 124–125.

132. See the "historiography roundtable" discussion about Gerald Stourzh's work *Um Einheit und Freiheit* in *Neutrality in Austria*, ed. Bischof et al., 236–292. Vojtech Mastny states bluntly: "Austrian neutrality originated in Moscow" (240).

133. Karl A. Dostal and Irene Nieszner, *Lesequelle 2. Texte für die zweite Schulstufe* (Vienna: Verlag Leitner, 1984), 128.

134. Friederike Lanzelsdorfer and Ernst Pacolt, *Bei uns und anderswo. Lesebuch für die 4. Schulstufe* (Vienna: Jugend und Volk, 1982), 44.

135. *Verordnungsblatt für den Dienstbereich des Bundesministeriums für Unterricht*, Jahrgang 1965, 4. Stück, no. 20, 77.

136. Bernt and Zilk, *Wien. Stadt im Aufbau*, 63, 68–69.

137. G. Rolletschek, "Festrede zur zehnjährigen Wiederkehr der Unterzeichnung des österreichischen Staatsvertrages," *Bundes-Gymnasium Gmunden. 51. Jahresbericht. Schuljahr 1964/65* (Gmunden: Selbstverlag des Bundes-Gymnasiums Gmunden, 1965), 1–5.

138. Edeltrude Hubner, "Festrede zum Nationalfeiertag am 25. Oktober 1965," *Bundeshandelsakademie, Bundeshandelsschule Krems an der Donau. Jahresbericht, Schuljahr 1965/66* (Krems: Verlag der Bundeshandelsakademie u.-Handelsschule Krems in Zusammenarbeit mit dem Eltern- u. Forderungsverein der Anstalt, 1966), 7–8. "Four in the jeep" refers to the Allied patrols in the jointly occupied first district of Vienna. These patrols were unique in that military police from all of the Four Powers participated.

139. See Sigrid Löffler, "Zum Beispiel Burg und Oper—zwei kulturimperialistische Großmythen," in *Inventur 45/55*, ed. Kos and Rigele, 388.

140. For a collection of essays and articles that catalogues many of the themes of the Austria-as-victim myth, see Ludwig Reichhold, ed., *Zwanzig Jahre Zweite Republik. Österreich Findet zu sich Selbst* (Vienna: Verlag Herder, 1965).

Part III

The End of the Austria-as-Victim Myth?
Official Memory Since 1986

FRAGMENTATION OF THE VICTIM MYTH SINCE 1986

From Kurt Waldheim to Jörg Haider

> We share moral responsibility because many Austrians welcomed the 'Anschluss,' supported the Nazi regime and helped it to function.
>
> — Chancellor Franz Vranitzky, 1993[1]

The 25 February 1988 cover of the German glossy magazine *Stern* featured a young woman dressed in traditional Austrian attire holding a sacher torte decorated with an Austrian flag and a red-and-white striped swastika. The headline of the cover read "Österreich '88. Zuwenig Schnee, zuviel Waldheim" (Austria '88. Too little snow, too much Waldheim).[2] Meanwhile, the more respected German newsweekly *Der Spiegel* published a series on Austria, beginning with a cover story on 25 January 1988 featuring a photo of Hitler at Vienna's Heldenplatz and a smiling Kurt Waldheim, with the caption, "Trauma Anschluß, Trauma Waldheim."[3] Fifty years after the Anschluss, the German press was vehemently criticizing Austria and undermining Austria's claim to be a victim of Nazi Germany. Symbols of Austrian uniqueness were turned on their head and linked with Nazism through the image of a woman in *Trachten* dress bearing a Nazified chocolate cake. This allegorical assault on Austrian identity was an outrage to many in the Alpine republic. How could the Germans, who had invaded Austria in 1938, now have the audacity to judge Austria?

The Waldheim Controversy

The answer was the 1986 Austrian presidential election, with its attendant international media attention and the subsequent investigation into the background of the Wehrmacht veteran and former UN Secretary-General Kurt Waldheim. As chronicled by Melanie Sully, Waldheim was chosen by the Austrian People's Party to be its presidential candidate for the 1986 election, though Waldheim was, in fact, not a member of the ÖVP. Initially, the choice of Waldheim, who had had a long and distinguished career in the Austrian Foreign Service and the United Nations, was not controversial. But early in 1986, the Austrian newsmagazine *Profil* published details of Waldheim's war record that made it clear that he had not been forthcoming about his wartime role in the Wehrmacht. Waldheim had always claimed that he was a law student in Vienna after being wounded on the Eastern Front. Now it was revealed that he had neglected to mention his tour of duty in the Balkans, an area noted for Nazi deportations of Jews and savage reprisals against civilians. While Waldheim was stationed in the Balkans, at least forty thousand Greek Jews were deported to Auschwitz. Waldheim was also in the area during "Operation Black," an effective and brutal campaign against the partisans of Montenegro. Many felt it was inconceivable that Waldheim would not have known about war crimes in the Balkans, and to some, his "forgetting" suggested that the former officer may have been directly involved in Nazi atrocities. When the *New York Times* and the World Jewish Congress began to focus on the story, the issue of Waldheim's past received international attention. There was even a Home Box Office special about Waldheim and his wartime record. These revelations created a split in Austrian society between those who distrusted and rejected Waldheim and those who defended him. On 8 June 1986, Waldheim was elected president of Austria, winning 54 percent of the vote on the second ballot.[4]

But Waldheim's election only intensified the controversy. In the spring of 1987, the U.S. Justice Department placed the Austrian president on the immigration watch list, which barred Waldheim from receiving a visa to enter the United States. This move was resented not only by Waldheim supporters, but also by many who were incensed at outside interference. Waldheim rallied his supporters as he made an appeal to the population, citing his role as peacemaker at the UN and his work to help free American hostages in Iran. Many Austrians perceived Waldheim as a victim of an international conspiracy. A backlash with an anti-Semitic undercurrent became an important part of the Waldheim controversy, both during and after his election. The *New York Times* and the World Jewish Congress in particular engendered indignation among Waldheim supporters.[5] The ÖVP, led by Foreign Minister Alois Mock, staunchly defended Waldheim, while the Socialists found themselves in the uncomfortable position of leading a coalition government with Waldheim as head of state. Under the leadership of Franz Vranitzky, the SPÖ wanted the president to at least make official statements of atonement to ease the controversy. Waldheim did make a televised speech in the spring of 1987 in which he condemned the crimes of the Nazis, but also argued that he had had nothing to do with them. The Freedom Party condemned the international criticism, while contending that Waldheim should have done more to clear his name. The Greens, elected to Parliament for the first time, criticized Waldheim severely, but also pointed to American hypocrisy, since the United States had enlisted the aid of former Nazis after World War II.

One of the government's major efforts to end the affair was to establish the International Commission of Historians to examine Waldheim's war record. Meanwhile, in the summer of 1987, a "white book" on Waldheim's wartime record, researched by Waldheim's son and the aging conservative Karl Gruber, was published.[6] This was the same Karl Gruber who had been foreign minister during the early years of the Second Republic. (As Günter Bischof points out, there is a great irony here. In 1946, Gruber had hired Waldheim, who served as his personal secretary. Among other duties, Waldheim was almost certainly "involved" in the compilation of the *Red-White-Red-Book*—the manifesto of the victim myth.)[7] In the fall of 1987, ÖVP General Secretary Michael Graff was forced to resign after remarking to the French magazine *L'Express* that Waldheim would be in the clear, unless the Commission of Historians could prove that he had "personally strangled six Jews." Graff's crude prediction—which cost him his career—proved to be only partly accurate.[8] When the commission released its report in February 1988, they found that Waldheim was not a war criminal. However, the Commission of Historians also criticized Waldheim, pointing out that he must certainly have known about atrocities in his area of responsibility while serving in the Balkans. Furthermore, the authors noted that Waldheim had neither made any effort to modify orders nor offered any form of protest to protect innocent people: "The Commission has not noted a single instance in which Waldheim protested or took steps—to prevent, or at least to impede its execution—against an order to commit a wrong that he must doubtless have recognized as such. On the contrary: he repeatedly assisted in connection with unlawful actions and thereby facilitated their execution." In the commission's concluding remarks, Waldheim's lapses of memory are viewed as less than credible:

> The Commission views its task as one relating to Waldheim's statements and descriptions regarding his military record. In its report, it does not follow the numerous critical positions that have been made public, but limits itself to the materials examined.
>
> Waldheim's own description of his military past does not tally at many points with the findings of the Commission. He attempted to let his military past slip into oblivion and, when that no longer proved possible, to play it down and make it appear innocuous. His lapses of memory are, in the view of the Commission, so basic, that it was not able to obtain any elucidating indications from Waldheim for its work.[9]

The main result of the Commission of Historians report was that all sides retrenched further. Foreign Minister Mock and other defenders of Waldheim were angered by the report and felt that the commission had exceeded its mandate when it implied that Waldheim had some moral culpability in war crimes.[10] Karl Gruber publicly implied that the work was biased because many commission members were Jews and Socialists.

Meanwhile, Waldheim took the simple and creative position that the commission had exonerated him. Overall, the controversy had severely dam-
aged Austria's image abroad. Goose-stepping Nazis began to replace the
idyllic images from *The Sound of Music* as the favored stereotype for Austria. Some now began to fear that the very postwar consensus upon which
Austria was built was in danger. While Waldheim refused to resign, Vranitzky considered it as an option, complaining with justification that the
controversy took away from his ability to implement economic reforms.
Finally, in conjunction with the 1988 fiftieth anniversary of the Anschluss,
Waldheim made a televised speech in which he spoke of Austria's dual
role in World War II: "There were Austrians who were victims and others
who were accomplices.... [L]et us not create the impression that we had
nothing to do with this. Obviously, there can be no collective guilt, but as
head of state of the Republic of Austria, I want to apologize for the crimes
of National Socialism committed by Austrians." But Waldheim's remarks
had come too late. He spent the remaining term of office (until 1992) as a
largely ineffective president and rarely traveled on state visits. [11]

It should be noted that the Waldheim affair took place in the context of
the German *Historikerstreit*. The *Historikerstreit* refers collectively to a
series of related controversies in mid-1980s West Germany. In particular,
the controversy was sparked by Andreas Hillgruber's *Zwerlei Untergang*
(1986), which suggested a similarity between the fate of the Jews and that
of the Germans fleeing the Red Army. Also contributing to the debate
were the suggestions of historian Ernst Nolte that the time had come to
place the Nazi period into the "normal" flow of history. As scholars on
both sides of the Atlantic weighed in on the issues, related political controversies received more attention.[12] In particular, U.S. President Ronald
Reagan's placing a wreath at the military cemetery in Bitburg (where both
Wehrmacht and Waffen SS soldiers are buried) sparked heated debate.[13]
This meant that when the controversy arose about Waldheim's wartime
record, it was in a context of heightened historical awareness. In short, the
conditions were there for a kind of historical "perfect storm"—conditions
that continued on through 1988 as the fiftieth anniversary of the Anschluss
was called into memory.

The year 1988 was designated by the Austrian government as a year of
reflection ("Gedenkjahr 1938/1988"), and throughout the year there were
over six hundred lectures, films, and public discussions about the Anschluss
and National Socialism in Austria.[14] These public events were the result of
sponsorship from above, as well as the result of grassroots organizing.[15]
That year also saw the publication and performance of Thomas Bernhard's ultra controversial *Heldenplatz*, a work commissioned to commemorate the one-hundred-year anniversary of the Burgtheater. Bernhard's
bitterly critical play centered around the surviving family members of a
Viennese Jewish professor, Josef Schuster, who had fled to England after
the Anschluss. The professor then returned to Vienna, where he ultimately
committed suicide in 1988, in large part because so little had changed

since 1938.[16] Taken together, the years 1986–1988 were a time when extraordinary attention was paid to Austria's involvement in the Third Reich. The myths and silences surrounding Austrian history in the Nazi period were openly examined, and many began to doubt the validity of old mythologies. Though still very recent, there is already a consensus among scholars that 1986–1988 marked a true watershed in Austrians' view of their past. Austria's old myth of victimization had lost credibility. But how far-reaching was this re-examination of the past? What was the background to the shift away from the "ice age of memory"?[17] An examination of textbooks, public controversies about monuments, and changes in Austrian politics since 1986 suggests that the shift in Austrian official memory is best viewed as a fragmentation of consensus, rather than a pendulum swing away from the old victim myth. In place of consensus, Austrian official memory became characterized instead by a mixture of sometimes competing narratives, some of which represent significant breaks with the old consensus, while others demonstrate continuity with old mythologies. This fragmentation was reflected in Austrian political culture and could be seen in how various groups in Austrian society employed what Ruth Wodak refers to as different "languages" for different versions of the past.[18]

Der Herr Karl: Literature, Scandals, and Early Critics of Austria's Past

While the importance of the Waldheim affair is hard to overstate, its significance lies more in its sustaining influence and magnitude (reflected in the domestic and international attention it brought), rather than in its powers of revelation. Austrians did not wake up one morning in 1986 and suddenly discover that there were former Nazis and Wehrmacht veterans among themselves. Prior to this affair, there had in fact been several scandals that had periodically shaken the otherwise comfortable silence about the war. For example, in the early 1960s, business professor Taras Borodajkewycz, a former Nazi and an open anti-Semite, not only managed to maintain his academic position in Vienna, but also enjoyed the support of an enthusiastic student following. Borodajkewycz represented the worst of the hidebound conservatism that dominated Austrian universities in the postwar period. Borodajkewycz and his teaching did not go unchallenged, though. In March 1965, tensions turned violent when right-wing supporters of the business professor clashed with a group organized by the Anti-fascist Student Committee. In the fighting that ensued, 24-year-old chemistry student Günther Kümel beat 60-year-old Ernst Kirchweger to death (he died of his wounds two days after the street battle). Kirchweger, who had a record as a Communist resistance fighter, became the first postwar casualty of political violence in Austria. Despite his criminal record, Kümel was sentenced to a mere ten months in prison. Shortly thereafter, Borodajkewycz retired with his pension intact.[19] This affair is instructive in that it shows that former Nazis were able to have comfortable lives in postwar Austria, but only up to a point. Borodajkewycz's goading nature eventually sparked active protest.

The Nazi past was again evoked in the 1970s, when the Socialist (and Jewish) Chancellor Bruno Kreisky became embroiled in a bitter litigious battle with the famous Nazi hunter Simon Wiesenthal. Long an advocate of collaborating with the FPÖ for political reasons (in the 1960s, Kreisky had cooperated with Franz Olah's funneling of trade union money to the FPÖ), and in the Austrian spirit of letting go of the past, Kreisky had planned to form a coalition with the FPÖ after the 1975 elections. It was understood that FPÖ leader Friedrich Peter, a veteran of the First SS Infantry Brigade, would serve as vice chancellor. Because the election resulted in an absolute majority for the SPÖ, the coalition proved unnecessary. However, a few days before the election, Simon Wiesenthal had informed Austrian President Rudolf Kirchschläger that Peter had been in an extermination squad. After the election, Wiesenthal publicized his findings. Peter denied involvement in atrocities, while Kreisky defended Peter and implied that Wiesenthal had been a Nazi agent. Wiesenthal, in turn, sued for libel. After behind-the-scenes negotiating, Kreisky retracted his statements and Wiesenthal withdrew his lawsuit. (The Wiesenthal suit was revived in 1986 when Kreisky repeated his allegations. In the end, Kreisky had to pay AS 270,000 in damages.)[20] Another scandal erupted in 1985 surrounding the "Reder handshake." In this case, yet another SS veteran, convicted war criminal Walter Reder, was released from an Italian prison and then greeted formally by the Austrian defense minister upon his return.[21]

Besides these political scandals, which occasionally reminded Austrians of the Nazi past, there were numerous literary works that also dealt with themes related to Nazism and the horrors of war (though dealing with the horrors of war was not the same thing as exploring its origins). Individual authors and literary groups such as the Gruppe '47 (which, though mainly German, influenced Austrian writers) were not constrained by the consensus view that supported the victim myth and the coalition lesson. Ingeborg Bachmann, for example, influenced by Gruppe '47, often evoked the war and its aftermath in her works up until her death in 1973. Wendelin Schmidt-Dengler credits Bachmann as being the first to explore critically Austria's coming to terms with the war, referring to her short story "Unter Mördern und Irren" (Among Murderers and Lunatics) as "a total reckoning with the Austrian restoration."[22] Romanian-born Paul Celan also stands out for his poetry related to the war, in particular, his famous 1945 poem "Todesfuge" (Death Fugue), with its haunting refrain "Der Tod ist ein Meister aus Deutschland" (Death Is a Master from Germany)—a poem that has been routinely included in Austrian textbooks.[23] Helmut Qualtinger and Carl Merz's *Der Herr Karl* (cited throughout this work) stands out as a brilliant satire of the quintessential Viennese opportunist.[24] The play was first performed in 1961. While the degree to which these works penetrated Austrian consciousness is not at all clear, collectively they do again demonstrate that the Nazi period had not been forgotten by all. The Carinthian writer Egyd Gstättner recollects that in the 1970s her *Gymnasium* class worked extensively with the themes "Fascism, National Socialism, and the Second World War," which included reading and discussing works by Bertolt Brecht, Wolfgang Borchert, Paul Celan, and Max Frisch.[25] Indeed, the 1970s saw an increase in the number of publications that explored both the war and the generational conflicts of the postwar period. Peter Henisch's novel *Der Kleine Figur meines Vaters*, published in 1975, examines the relationship between a father (a wartime photographer) and his son.[26] The book was also made into a movie for television and broadcast in 1979.

May 1979 also saw the broadcast of the American-produced television miniseries *Holocaust* in Austria. It has been estimated that between 38 and 52 percent of all Austrians saw the series, with 61 percent seeing at least one episode. After the broadcast, some polls suggested that the number of Austrians who doubted the extent of Nazi crimes declined (for example, in response to the statement "In the Nazi period millions of Jews were killed," 81 percent agreed after the broadcast, as opposed to 72 percent before the broadcast).[27] This was seven years before the Waldheim scandal.

A very small number of historians had examined the Nazi era in Austria, notably Erika Weinzierl in her book *Zu wenig Gerechte. Österreich und Judenverfolgung, 1938–1945*, published in 1968. Also, many Austrian teachers had explored ways of teaching about the Nazi era well before the Waldheim controversy, though major changes in the textbooks did not occur until after the years 1986–1988.[28]

In summary, then, it can be said that well before the Waldheim controversy, there were numerous examples of critical reflection and several political furors that explicitly or implicitly called the Austria-as-victim myth into question. However, despite these challenges to the victim myth, the great narrative of victimization and postwar cooperation remained intact, especially at the official level. In contrast to earlier scandals, what distinguishes the Waldheim affair is that in retrospect it can be seen as the time when the two related narratives most important to the identity of the Second Republic—the victim myth and the coalition lesson—began to unravel. The Waldheim affair then, marked the beginning of the end for the postwar consensus.

Confronting the Past: The Historians and Vranitzky

Observers of American politics often refer to the president's power to persuade and the importance of using the office as a "bully pulpit" to influence issues of national concern. Indeed, the voices of leaders do have an important impact on how issues are framed. Faced with the difficulty of running the government during the Waldheim controversy, Chancellor

Franz Vranitzky of the SPÖ was instrumental in reframing the discussion about Austria's Nazi past, yet remained true to the coalition lesson. While President Waldheim defended and sometimes "forgot" about his wartime past, Chancellor Vranitzky spoke openly about the role Austrians played in the war and the Holocaust. Upon receiving an honorary doctorate at Hebrew University in Jerusalem in June 1993, Vranitzky said:

> There were those who were courageous enough to offer active resistance against the madness or tried to help the victims, risking their lives by doing so; but many more joined the Nazi machinery, and some rose through its ranks to be among the most brutal, hideous perpetrators.
>
> We have to live up to this side of our history, our share of the responsibility for the suffering, which not Austria—for the state no longer existed—but which some of her citizens inflicted upon other people, inflicted upon humanity.
>
> We have always felt, and still feel, that the connotation of "collective guilt" does not apply to Austria. But we do acknowledge collective responsibility, the responsibility of each and every one of us to remember and to seek justice.
>
> We share moral responsibility because many Austrians welcomed the 'Anschluss,' supported the Nazi regime, and helped it to function.[29]

These public statements by Austria's chancellor are very important and certainly a far cry from the official view of the Austrian government in the 1950s, when mention of responsibility for the war was excised from the State Treaty. While Vranitzky maintains the traditional position of the innocence of the Austrian state, the tone of his remarks is one of atonement, and he prominently mentions Austrian perpetrators of Nazi crimes.

Historians and other scholars, too, played an important role in the 1986–1988 shift, as many focused more attention on the era of National Socialism and World War II. Some of the attention to the past was contrived, as the Austrian government scrambled to improve Austria's image, but there was much genuine concern with Austria's Nazi past.[30] In the introduction to a collection of essays, the Austrian political scientist Anton Pelinka and the historian Erika Weinzierl scorn the public relations campaign, writing: "For us it is not about a better advertising campaign for this country, for us it is about the country, about Austria itself."[31] Since the Waldheim affair, Austrian and other academics (e.g., Robert Keyselingk of Canada, Evan Bukey of the United States, and Robert G. Knight of the United Kingdom) have vigorously examined Austria's Nazi past, producing numerous works on the Nazi years, anti-Semitism, Austrian *Vergangenheitsbewältigung*, and Austrian monuments. Sometimes Austrian scholars have been severe in their criticism of their own country, embracing the language of "guilt" over the long-favored "responsibility."[32] Austrian writers, who long played an important role in questioning and undermining the victim myth, also continued to express criticism, which at times has been extreme in its severity. Consider an excerpt from a 1993 interview by Eva Brenner with the provocative feminist writer and playwright Elfriede Jelinek:

Brenner: The Salzburg Festival and winter sports seem to be the only international assets Austria has left.... By the way, Alpine sports appear in almost all of your works, and mostly they are ridiculed. Why is that so?

Jelinek: I was born in the mountains. Mountains imply a certain narrowness. All of Austria, in fact, lies in the shadow of these gigantic mountains. For me, winter sports are total terrorism. You cannot escape it. Championship skiers are our national heroes.

Brenner: Are you referring to Alpine tourism as a perfect means to cover up history in Austria?

Jelinek: Yes. Everything that has been done in this country since 1945 was the result of an intricate cover-up. We managed to do this better than any other country—for example, better than Germany, where the dead are haunting the living, where deeds of repentance are common. Especially in the cultural arena, Austrians have perfected this technique of covering up history.[33]

Such voices have created a simplistic and somewhat gratuitous counter-caricature of Austria as the land of unrepentant Nazis. This is perhaps what Ernst Hanisch refers to in his article about "self-hate" as a part of Austrian identity.[34] But many others on the literary front have continued the tradition of thoughtful criticism and exploration of Austria's past. The novels of Elisabeth Reichart *(February Shadows)*, Anton Fuchs *(Deserter)*, Gerald Szyszkowitz *(Puntigam, or The Art of Forgetting)*, Lili Koerber *(Night over Vienna)*, among others, attest to the literary interest in Austria's wartime past.[35] Robert Menasse stands out as a cultural critic who has made a point of lambasting Austrian mythologies and the Red-Black (SPÖ-ÖVP) coalition.[36]

The post-1986 emphasis on Austria's Nazi past eventually led to changes in commemoration as well. For years, the old Jewish section of the Central Cemetery stood in stark contrast to the neighboring Christian section.[37] One crossed from a well-maintained paved road to a rundown dirt path lined with overgrown trees and weeds. The old Jewish graves were in complete disrepair. Vines and roots had slowly pulled some of the grave stones apart (see plates 5 and 6). In the aftermath of the war, there were few survivors to care for the graves. The old Jewish section of the Central Cemetery had long been a haunting site of forgetting. But in 1997, restoration of the cemetery began.[38]

Confronting the Past in Austrian Schools and Textbooks

Those interested in education in Austria have been particularly involved in the new emphasis on examining the Nazi era in Austria, and the Austrian Education Ministry has taken the lead in publishing numerous important works.[39] Indeed, Austrian schools were profoundly affected by the events of 1986–1988. During the 1987–1988 school year, the Education Ministry sponsored a special publication dealing specifically with the Anschluss and the dangers of National Socialism.[40] Many Austrian schools also undertook special projects to commemorate the year 1988.[41] During and after 1986–1988, education-related publications often featured articles on National Socialism, fascism, the Holocaust, and other related themes.[42]

This new emphasis was also reflected in Austrian schoolbooks published after the late 1980s. When reading about the Anschluss, for example, students no longer were taught that there was no support for the annexation within Austria:

> The entrance of the German troops into Austria on 12 March 1938 meant the end of the independent and autonomous state, a state that above all was no longer a democracy, but rather an authoritarian regime, which was distanced from, indeed hostile to, a great part of the population….
>
> The 'Anschluss' enthusiasm of great masses of people is not to be denied, yet it [this feeling] was not held by all Austrians.[43]

This passage not only mentions prominently support for the Anschluss, but also clearly states the oft-forgotten point that the Austria taken over by the Nazis had already ceased to be a democracy. Another text from 1992 prominently mentions support for the Anschluss and also includes a special section on anti-Semitism in Austria.[44] The authors of a different text published in 1992 challenge students to think about how they would react in a similar situation: "In 1938 the Austrians did not defend their state. How would we act today?" In another question, students are asked to think about the validity of the Austria-as-victim idea: "Historians today discuss to what degree Austria is to be portrayed as a victim and in a related question, how much Austria itself became guilty of the fateful developments."[45] Inclusion of historiographical questions about the Austria-as-victim myth in the texts is clear evidence that the victim myth had been severely undermined.

After 1986–1988, textbook authors were also much more forthright about World War II and the Holocaust. A history text from 1992 can only be described as remarkable in comparison to earlier texts. The authors quote a speech by Chancellor Franz Vranitzky in which, in reference to Austria's past, Vranitzky asserts that Austrians must not forget that "there were not a few Austrians who brought great pain to others in the name of this [the Nazi] regime." In an unusually unequivocal statement, the authors assert: "As a whole, Austrians were—whether National Socialist party member, opportunistic follower, Christian opposition, or middle-class or leftist resistance fighter—neither better nor worse than the Germans in the Reich."[46] A 1990 reading book includes several passages critical of Austria's role in World War II, among which is an excerpt from a speech by Erwin Ringel wherein he clearly states that Austrians played a role in the fate of countless innocent victims.[47] In a section titled "The Inhumanity of War: Example, Russian Campaign," the authors of a 1991 history text accurately point to the racist nature of the war against Russia. The book also links the Holocaust with the war in the East and mentions the murder of Jews and civilians by the SS.[48] In an attempt to make the Holocaust more relevant to students, many textbook authors also included questions for discussion and sought to relate contemporary issues to the Holocaust. In one case, after two-page coverage of the Holocaust, students are instructed to ask the older generation about the fate of Jewish citizens and are posed the question: "How do you react to fellow students who are considered outsiders?"[49] A 1992 text includes a special section on Jewish history dating to the late eighteenth century. Among the themes discussed is "Die Juden—keine Gottesmörder" (The Jews—No Murderers of God). Later in the text, the authors include extensive coverage of the Holocaust and address the problem of postwar "revisionists."[50] A 1988 text emphasizes that Jews were the primary targets of Nazi ideology and covers the anti-Jewish measures implemented in Austria after the Anschluss. The authors also include a section under the heading "What Happened in the Concentration Camps?" Unlike in many earlier books, Jews are accurately presented as the primary victims of the Holocaust.[51] Another text even mentions the victim myth itself and points out that relying on the myth to help forge Austria's postwar identity resulted in ignoring Austria's involvement in the Third Reich.[52]

The examples above are strong evidence that the myth of Austria as a victim, and only a victim, collapsed in the aftermath of 1986–1988. No longer did history textbook authors justify the war against Russia, and coverage of anti-Semitism increased considerably compared to pre-Waldheim textbooks. By 1993, "racial ideology and anti-Semitism" were part of the official lesson plan for the fourth class, which meant they were required subjects in both textbooks and the classroom,[53] whereas in 1984, the official lesson plan had required the more vague formulation "crimes against humanity."[54] Collectively, these examples represent a remarkable shift away from the old Austria-as-victim myth.

Continuities: Persistent Myths in the Textbooks

After the Waldheim affair, the notion that Austria was solely a victim of Nazi aggression had been discredited, but upon close examination, it is clear that some themes related to the victim myth remained entrenched in Austrian school materials and throughout Austrian society. There is also some evidence that certain themes that contributed to the victim mythology received more emphasis in textbooks, especially reading books. Language usage and the passive voice, for example, continued subtly to distance perpetrators from their actions.[55] For example, in the same 1993 text that mentions victim mythology, students also read the following about the pogrom that accompanied the Anschluss: "The Jewish fellow citizens, who were declared fair game, publicly humiliated, beaten, and robbed, suffered the most. The entire world was dismayed at how many

Austrians allowed themselves to be swept up in the anti-Semitic vio-lence."[56] Compared to works from the 1950s, this passage could be seen as anti-mythological, since it actually covers the Anschluss pogrom, but the passive construction gives the impression of somewhat anonymous per-petrators. A reading book from 1990 likewise employs the passive voice, which again imparts an impression of anonymous perpetrators and pres-ents nearly everyone as part of the collective of victims:

> On the twelfth and thirteenth of March 1938 German soldiers under their 'Führer' Adolf Hitler marched into Austria. The 'Anschluss' with the German Reich was implemented. Many people cheered about it. One now called our country the *Ostmark*. Many people were arrested immediately. The Jews were especially affected [by the invasion].
>
> One year later, the Austrian men had to go to war for Greater Germany. Whoever refused was jailed and shot. Many soldiers lost their lives in the war. Women and children died in the hail of bombs. More and more people suffered from the war. Courageous women and men formed resistance groups through-out the entire country.[57]

Although this story was meant for younger children, for whom the themes of World War II were surely daunting, this short passage still manages to encompass several aspects of Austrian victim mythology. The community of suffering theme is especially evident: Jews were persecuted, but every-one else suffered as well, including soldiers and those killed in the "hail of bombs." Resistance mythology also makes an appearance as children read that men and women throughout Austria resisted the Nazis.

Post-1986 texts continued to qualify Austrian support for Nazism, but, more significantly, also continued to emphasize the links between the Anschluss and the coalition lesson. Consider the following example from a 1993 text:

> With his march into Austria, Hitler found many enthusiastic supporters. In addition, the number of fellow-travelers grew rapidly. But there were also avowed opponents of National Socialist rule *in all sectors of society* ... [empha-sis added]. The Gestapo came to Austria along with the German army and arrested the opponents of National Socialism. On 1 April the first transport of prominent Austrians departed for the concentration camp Dachau. Among the 150 prisoners were the later Federal Chancellor Figl and the Social Democratic *Stadtrat* Dannenberg. [There they learned the coalition lesson of cooperation.]

Then, in a departure from pre-Waldheim texts, the authors emphasize the Jewish question, noting that "especially severe suffering was brought upon" the Jews, who "were at the mercy of every kind of arbitrary action and could be humiliated and beaten. Many Austrians *allowed themselves to be swept off into anti-Semitic violent actions*" (emphasis added). The authors then cover the Nazi economic exploitation of Austria and the April 1938 plebiscite, which was approved by "more than 99 percent, as is normal in dictatorships.... Historians are of the opinion that in the plebiscite desired by Schuschnigg of 13 March 1938, the majority of Austrians—some 60 percent—would have voted for an autonomous Austria." The text then addresses the fundamental question: "Why in 1938 did so many Austrians cheer Hitler?" The answer is that hopes "for an improvement of the economic conditions drove many into the arms of Hitler, whose real intentions they did not see." Further, "many voted yes because they were afraid. Then there was [the fact] that Anschluss with Germany had already been sought in 1918, and many Austrians doubted the ability of the republic to survive."[58] Compared to earlier texts, these authors are remarkably forthright about the Anschluss, yet this passage remains true to the coalition lesson. Many supported the Anschluss, but many—from "all sectors"—resisted. The Jews were subjected to especially harsh persecution, but prominent Austrian politicians, too, were sent to Dachau. The plebiscite was passed by a wide margin, but Schuschnigg's plebiscite would have also succeeded, if given the chance. Finally, there were many reasons to support the Anschluss, but heartfelt support for Nazism was not among them. The major lesson of the war is again the familiar coalition lesson.

World War II likewise remained divorced from its ideological roots in many post-1986 Austrian schoolbooks. Many reading books especially continued to impart platitudes and often portrayed Austrians as the primary victims of the war. Stories about air raids on Austrian cities also remained common. A 1991 text features the story "Kriegszerstörungen in Wiener Neustadt" (War Destruction in Wiener Neustadt) about the damage caused by American air raids and the heroic rebuilding of the city after the war.[59] In "Als die Väter weg waren" (When the Fathers Were Away), by Christine Nöstlinger, students read: "Hilde's father was missing in Russia. My grandmother said that he is as good as dead. The father of Bauer Otto was a prisoner of war in Siberia. My grandmother said that to be a prisoner of the Russians is much worse than to be dead."[60] Of course, grandmother's view of being a POW of the Soviets is largely accurate, but she neglects to mention that for Russians, it was usually worse to be a prisoner of the Germans and Austrians.

Above all, the "war is bad" theme remained a common feature in post-Waldheim Austrian reading books. A text from 1991 includes an antiwar story featuring a young boy, Florian, who wants to play war with his uncle, who had been severely wounded in World War II. Florian's enthusiasm for war is dashed when his uncle teaches him a lesson by throwing him in the mud, screaming at him, and then playing dead to the point where the young Florian is terrified. Florian decides he no longer wants to play war, and the uncle explains his reasoning behind the harsh lesson: "It wasn't easy for me. But I did it because … I want to make it clear to you how war really is." A distraught Florian then tells his uncle he was afraid because "[y]ou looked like an animal," to which the uncle responds seriously: "In war people become animals."[61] There is nothing inherently mythological about this story, but in the context of a lesson about pacifism,

World War II easily loses its ideological significance. It becomes a war like all other wars, and all wars are "bad."

Another example in which World War II and Nazism were taught out of ideological context was through screenings of the film *Die Welle*, or *The Wave*. *The Wave* is an American-produced television program originally broadcast as an ABC Afterschool Special. The program features a teacher who instructs his class about the dangers of fascism by forming a special club for them. The students become avid members and embrace the discipline and camaraderie they feel from their membership. At the end of the film, the teacher shows the class films of cheering Nazi crowds, and the students are horrified to discover what they have become. *The Wave* teaches a basic lesson about blindly following a leader, and in the context of a lesson plan that emphasizes blind obedience as one of many factors that gave rise to Nazism, the film is a powerful pedagogical tool. It could also be argued, though, that the dubbed German version of *The Wave* takes on a subtly different meaning. While Nazi propaganda and mass group activities were certainly important to the support of Nazism, National Socialism did not emerge from an ideological or political vacuum in either Austria or Germany.[62] Placing fascism in the context of an American junior high school could be misleading to Austrian students, as it makes it easier to divorce Nazism from its specific German and Austrian context.

By far, the most common theme that continued to subtly support the Austria-as-victim myth was the indirect (and sometimes direct) relativization of the Holocaust by juxtaposing it with the American atomic bombings of Japan. In this case, there has been an increase in the tendency to conflate the Holocaust and Hiroshima since 1986. Stories and poems about Hiroshima—especially the ubiquitous *Sadako will leben*—have become more common than ever before.[63] But even more problematic is an increased tendency to link the Holocaust and Hiroshima directly. This trend is visible both in the spatial layout of the texts, as well as in some analytical passages. For example, a 1990 reading book includes excerpts from a play about the trial of a guard at a concentration camp. The very next story on the following page is "Hiroshima—eine Warnung für uns alle" (Hiroshima—a Warning for All of Us), which features a photo of Hiroshima in the aftermath of the atomic bombing. This story begins a seven-page section on Hiroshima, which includes poems, an interview with the pilot Colonel Tibbets, and an excerpt from Karl Bruckner's *Sadako will leben*.[64] A 1991 history text includes a photo of Hiroshima after it was bombed. The paragraph immediately following starts coverage of the Holocaust and is introduced by a boldface caption, parallel to the photo of Hiroshima, that reads "Persecution and Attempted Destruction of the Jews."[65] A 1992 text puts a different twist on the same theme. Immediately following the story "Heimkehr aus dem KZ" (Homecoming from the Concentration Camp), excerpted from Rudolf Kalmar's *Zeit ohne Gnade* (Time without Mercy), is an account of the bombing of Dresden.[66] A 1992 reading book embraces moral relativism to an extreme degree. In *Lesezeichen 4*, the authors include an excerpt from the

Auschwitz commandant Rudolf Höss's statement at the Nuremberg war crimes trials. In an obvious comparison and juxtaposition, the facing page features an excerpt from President Harry Truman's memoirs about his decision to drop the atomic bomb.[67]

A 1995 text stands out for its explicit relativization of the Holocaust. The book contains extensive excerpts from Käthe Recheis's work *Lena, unser Dorf und der Krieg* (Lena, our Village and the War) (immediately followed by Tamiki Hara's "Hiroshima, August 1945"), including the following passage:[68]

> I only found out the whole truth about Hitler's regime of horror after 1945. Back then, I believed that there was no other people on earth, who had placed such guilt on itself as we Austrians and Germans. But the study of history and the [events of the] following decades have taught me that inhumanity was (and is) to be found elsewhere. So many genocides, often only a few years in the past, are forgotten…. Today, too, people are persecuted and oppressed throughout the world, be it because of their religion, because they are opponents of a political regime, or [because they are] members of an ethnic minority. Because of economic interests the life and existence of the last native peoples is threatened. The genocide goes on![69]

While trying to bring the attention of students to other problems in the world, the author conflates both religious persecution and the threat to native peoples posed by economic interests with the genocide of World War II. Further, by using vague comparisons, the author fails in her attempt to make a profoundly serious point—namely, that there are concrete examples of genocide that should be discussed (e.g., in Cambodia and Rwanda)—and actually contributes to the "forgetting" she is ostensibly criticizing. The student Oliver Michael Tatzmann, reporting on his trip to Mauthausen, expresses a similar world-view, whereby the Holocaust was horrible, but something to be seen in the greater context of world discrimination and oppression of peoples:

> I believe that through our visit to the concentration camp Mauthausen (not a death camp—still, over 170,000 persons died there!), we were made aware how horrible man can be. In light of the current situation—there are only five (!) states worldwide where there is no torture—and [because of] this horrible past, so terribly brought before our eyes, the maxim of the "young generation," and those who will come, must be: *"Never again war, no more violence—instead, tolerance, understanding, love for the neighbor"* [emphasis in original].[70]

This passage shows that the student views Mauthausen with horror and has no doubts about what happened at the camp. On the other hand, he clearly places Mauthausen in a global context and points to continued problems in the world, claiming that there are only five countries in the world where people are not tortured. In short, Mauthausen is divorced from its Austrian and Nazi context. It is seen as a symbol of an oppressive regime, of which there are many in the world. The important thing is "Never again war, no more violence—instead tolerance, understanding, love for the neighbor!" Some of this view is attributable to the age and inexperience of the student (between seventeen and nineteen years old), but in large part the lesson taken by the student reflects the pacifist truisms so frequently found in Austrian textbooks.

Of course, many passionately believe that a pacifist renunciation of war is a valid way of rejecting the violent Nazi past. It can be added that when it comes to genocide, there are numerous legitimate comparisons and analogies that can be made to the Shoah, though there are also good scholarly arguments for its uniqueness.[71] The point should not be automatically to dismiss historical comparisons, but rather to call into question those comparisons lacking sufficient context. In general, what might be called "defensive comparisons" (as seen in the above example) often stem from a pacifist view of war that ultimately rejects the consequences of violent regimes, as opposed to exploring the root causes of that destruction. This suggests that these defensive comparisons have less to do with broadening historical understanding than they do with maintaining one's self-image in the present. Thus, when the Japanese memorialize Auschwitz in Hiroshima, they are in fact reflecting on the incineration of their own people.[72] In a similar vein, it can be argued that when discussion of a concentration camp in Austria immediately evokes atrocities elsewhere, the function (if not the purpose) of such a comparison is to diminish the significance of a site such as Mauthausen.

The resistance, too, remained mythologized in Austrian textbooks. In particular, the coalition lesson of "resistance for everybody" persisted in post-Waldheim textbooks. Students continued to read about this outdated idea in a 1993 text, which claims that "resistance groups from all political camps strove for the fall of the Hitler dictatorship," and that wartime suffering "and bombing raids of Allies caused many people to engage in passive resistance."[73] This is a clear example of how passive noncompliance with the demands of the regime was portrayed as resistance: the concept of *Resistenz* was used to bolster *Widerstand*. Astonishingly, as recent as 2002, in an English-language textbook to introduce college students to contemporary Austrian history, Erika Weinzierl reaffirms Karl Stadler's aforementioned all-encompassing definition of resistance.[74]

Austrian textbooks' emphasis on resistance should be understood in the context that it is an important mission of the Austrian schools to instill democratic values, and teaching about the resistance is an important vehicle for imparting these lessons. These purposes are explicitly mentioned in the 1996 lesson plan, which links the resistance with state legitimacy and also casts the resistance a counterpoint to the Holocaust. For the fourth class, the theme of resistance is listed as "[t]he Austrian resistance against the National Socialist regime; the Moscow Declaration." For the seventh class, resistance is listed immediately following the Holocaust: "Persecution and mass exterminations; freedom and resistance movements."[75]

In the end, when it comes to the resistance, the issue of balance remains. Indeed, one textbook directly addresses the issue of overemphasizing the resistance. In the 1993 text *Zeitbilder*, the authors explain that it is dangerous and inaccurate to view National Socialism as having any positive side. They then examine the resistance in a section titled "Widerstand—der Beitrag zur Freiheit" (Resistance—the Contribution to Freedom), which includes excerpts by the University of Vienna historian Gerhard Jagschitz, who argues for at least five categories of resistance. The authors then quote Jagschitz's summation of those who lost their lives in the resistance and argue specifically that the resistance has not been exaggerated for political reasons.[76] These pages not only demonstrate the importance of the resistance to postwar Austrian legitimacy, but also represent an open defense of the official memory of the resistance. Given the continued relevance of the resistance to Austrian identity, it is not surprising that the authors conclude this section with a summation of war casualties; 247,000 Austrian soldiers and 65,459 Austrian Jews appear in the same list.[77]

Themes related to the Allies and the Austria-as-victim myth were the least affected by the post-Waldheim shift. There was no discernible change from the view that the Four Powers were an occupying force that treated Austria unfairly. Negative portrayals of the Allies, both direct and indirect, continued, especially through the themes of the American atomic and conventional bombings and Soviet reparations from Austria.[78] The importance of the national holiday continued to be explained in terms of liberation from the "meddling" Allies. In the passage "26. Oktober—Nationalfeiertag" in a 1991 reading book, students read that "foreign soldiers marched in and used furniture and household items. All Austrians received a photo identification card. Only he who had this with him could go from one occupation zone to the other." Furthermore, people were afraid that they would be "taken away" and shot: "Usually, they were war criminals ... but also among them were innocent victims of the postwar troubles." The occupiers remained in the country "for ten long years."[79] In this passage, the "double occupation" idea appears again, as the threat of being carted off, or even shot, marks a continuity between Nazi rule and the Allied occupation. This not-so-subtle association suggests that Austrians were the victims of the arbitrariness of both the Nazis and the Four Powers. This idea is also expressed in a 1991 text that rehashes the familiar theme of Allied soldiers "unjustly" seizing living quarters and denying Austrians' rule over their own country: "The Austrians were not head of their own house. The quartering and provisioning of the occupation troops caused great problems. The shortage of housing was oppressive as the occupiers laid claim to entire homes, yes, even hotels, for their officers."[80]

The end of the occupation brought by the State Treaty continued to be portrayed as the demarcation for a free Austria, and neutrality continued to serve as the characteristic that distinguished Austria from the occupiers. For example, in a 1991 reading book, students read: "The Second World War lasted six years. Many people were killed in this war, and much was destroyed. Austria was occupied for ten long years by foreign soldiers. Austria wanted to be free. That is why it was decided to be neutral forever. That means Austria will defend its freedom. Austria does not want to join any military alliances. We do not allow foreign soldiers bases in Austria. We children also want to live in peace. Weapons are not toys. We do not want to start any fights."[81] Similar to earlier texts, the authors of a 1992 text describe the year 1955 as a year of fulfilled visions: "After ten years of occupation [*Besatzung*] by the Allies, and after seven years of occupation [*Okkupation*] by Hitler's Germany, Austria had recovered its full sovereignty with [the State Treaty]."[82] The use of two synonyms for "occupation" does not diminish the view presented in this passage that Austria's ordeal was that of a "double occupation." Of course, the State Treaty *did* mark the full return of Austrian sovereignty, as well as the beginning of Austria's neutral status. In this context, the State Treaty was an extremely important point of demarcation—both politically and symbolically—in postwar Austria. However, except for the common denominator of denying Austria complete sovereignty, the Allied occupation and the Nazi annexation shared nothing meaningful in common. But an official memory which maintained that Austria survived a two-stage, but ultimately single, period of occupation supported the legitimacy of the Second Republic and embraced a kind of teleology in reverse. Austria had not been reborn after all, because Austria had never disappeared. Austria had been occupied from 1938 to 1955.

Explaining Continuity: The Coalition Lesson and Other Factors

To explain why many themes of the Austria-as-victim myth continue to be relevant, it is useful to turn to a final example from a 1992 history text. In the passage "Österreichbewußtsein" (Austrian Consciousness) students read:

At the end of World War II, Austria found itself in a precarious position. The east had suffered heavily from the fighting, and the air raids had left behind great damage in many locations. Over 400,000 Austrians were killed in the war or were missing. Economic production had sunk to one-third of prewar production; there was a shortage of food, heating material, and goods of all kinds.

Although the situation was worse than that after World War I, only a few showed doubt as to the ability of Austria to survive. A fundamental change had taken place in the consciousness of the people. During National Socialist rule, people had again learned to appreciate independence. People no longer wanted to be integrated into a larger group; the Anschluss idea was dead. [Lessons from] the dictatorship of 1934 had also shown the value of democratic freedom. Politicians of different persuasions, who had been together in the concentration camps, had recognized the value of cooperation and entered into partnership for a democratic Austria. Once, people put [Austria] at risk for ideological goals; now, after the [recent] experiences, people returned to [their belief in

Austria]. This Austrian consciousness allowed the population, despite all of their hardships, to look to the future with assurance.[83]

Several by now familiar themes are evident in this excerpt: the conflation of victims, the coalition lesson, and the new Austrian consciousness that emerged from the unity of suffering. In short, this passage clearly demonstrates that many themes and subthemes of victim mythology continued to play a key role in the formation of national identity after 1986. Indeed, fostering Austrian consciousness remained a stated goal of the 1996 official lesson plans.[84] The link between themes of victim mythology and a unique Austrian consciousness that had been forged in the late 1940s continued into the mid 1990s. The example above exemplifies this tradition, with the coalition lesson as the key point of the narrative. Here, the positive function of the coalition lesson (linked to the victim myth) should be reiterated, for it can be argued that the coalition lesson of cooperation and consensus has served Austria well. The idea that Austrians learned to appreciate their independence only after the Nazi takeover also has validity, though the timing of this shift in attitude had more to do with the war turning sour than with the events of 1938. But while these themes may have served Austria in a positive way, there are other aspects of this official narrative that simply ring hollow more than fifty years after the war. To say that four hundred thousand Austrians were killed in the war, without distinguishing between victims of racist discrimination and those killed fighting in the Nazi armies, homogenizes victims and perpetrators into a single category—a kind of retroactive community of victims. Likewise, the continued use of the concentration camp primarily as a symbol of political unity can be seen as problematic.

A second reason for the ongoing life of the Austria-as-victim myth is simply that many Austrians are still tied to the comfort it brings. For example, a 1995 letter to the "Staberl" column in the *Neue Kronen Zeitung* from Eduard Strimitzer of Vienna-Stammersdorf demonstrates that some Austrians continue to have a personal investment in the victim myth:

> Not a day goes by when the suffering of the Jews during the Hitler years is not called into memory on television, on the radio, or in the newspapers. After fifty years, one knows this by heart to the point of disgust.... I myself as an eleven-year-old child had to experience the inferno of the American bombing raids. From that, my health has suffered my whole life long. It has been the same for hundreds of thousands of others as it was with me, without them all having been fanatical Nazis and murderers of Jews. I therefore find it to be a shabby mockery and an insult that it is always assumed that only the Jews had to suffer greatly under Hitler.[85]

Strimitzer makes it clear that he, too, feels like a victim. As far as he is concerned, there is no fundamental difference between what happened to him and what happened to many Jews. It is also possible that many people who benefited financially from the seizure of Jewish property or by other means do not want the comfort of the victim myth taken away. While the Waldheim controversy marked a significant shift in attitudes, for many Austrians, like Strimitzer, it resulted in the retrenchment of strongly held beliefs. The controversy of the mid 1980s may have started people talking, but this did not necessarily mean abandoning the victim mythology.

Complicating matters further was that international criticism of Waldheim was often seen as unfair and was bitterly resented. When *Time* magazine published an article on the Waldheim election in the summer of 1986, its description of the Lower Austrian town Wiener Neustadt prompted an angry response from students at a Tyrolean high school, who felt that Austrians were being stereotyped. They voiced their protest in a letter to *Time* (which the magazine chose not to publish):

> Hi, you guys with Stetsons, cowboy boots, and lassos! Best regards from some "leathery faced," backwards, anti-Semitic lads and lasses in *"lederhosen"* and *"dirndls."* We are putting these on especially for you, when you come across the Atlantic to ogle us, to hear us yodeling, and to leave a couple of bucks in our country. But, as young Austrians, we are really not very happy with the way you use these stale stereotypes to convey a negative image of an entire people.
>
>   Sincerely,
>   Class 6I
>   Bundesgymnasium St. Johann/Tirol[86]

This letter to the editor reflects frustration that because of Waldheim, all Austrians were being criticized. Indeed, to some degree Waldheim's troubles added yet another chapter to Austria's litany of unfair treatment, as the once-honored Secretary-General of the United Nations was "picked on" by the World Jewish Congress and put on the United States immigration "watch list" (as discussed above). As recently as 1996, Waldheim himself referred to a "worldwide network" that had influenced his presidential candidacy.[87]

A final reason for the continuation—and, in some cases, elaboration—of the victim myth is the trend to embrace ethical relativism. Ethical relativism is not an explicit aspect of victim mythology, but it indirectly supports the idea of victimization by legitimizing a pacifist and ultimately platitude-based understanding of history, whereby events are considered out of context. Related to this is ethical relativism—most evident in the "Auschwitzification" of Hiroshima—which undermines the ideological nature of World War II. It is important to point out that the increase in materials relativizing the war and the Holocaust is not unique to Austria, but part of a larger intellectual trend in scholarship. Admittedly, relativism is a philosophically difficult problem, for as the great intellectual historian Jacques Barzun points out: "[T]he opposite of the Relative is the Absolute, and the Absolute means one principle only, a single standard of thought and behavior. One must therefore ask the anti-relativist: 'Whose Absolute are we to adopt and impose?'"[88]

With Barzun's warning in mind, one might yet criticize the approach of Eric Markusen and David Kopf in their 1995 book, *The Holocaust and Strategic Bombing: Genocide and Total War in the Twentieth Century.*[89] Among the more problematic statements of the authors is the following:

> A family cowering in its basement in a German or Japanese city under massive incendiary attack was no more able to escape or defend itself than its counterpart confined in a Polish ghetto. By the same token, just as most of the victims of the Holocaust were killed indiscriminately because they were members of a group deemed undesirable or threatening to the Nazis rather than for what they had done or not done as individuals, so were many of the victims of strategic bombing. Large numbers of these victims were disabled or elderly; many were women and children—all killed anonymously and indiscriminately simply because they happened to live in areas targeted for annihilation.[90]

A moralist might legitimately argue that this is a case of relativism. Historically, though, the passage is subject to criticism at other levels, for Markusen and Kopf's view of the war is one without cause, effect, and context. In their view, the war was underway and all sides slaughtered indiscriminately. There is no indication that strategic bombing, as morally questionable as it may have been in many cases, should be seen in the context of a response to a total war begun by Germany. Second, the authors strip the war of ideological context when they fail to distinguish between Jews, who were ideological targets of Nazism, and casualties of strategic bombing, who were targeted more for *where* they were than *who* they were. Finally, in a related criticism, Markusen and Kopf do not differentiate between the aims of killing. Whatever conclusions one draws from the strategic bombing campaign, the ultimate goal of strategic bombing was to aid in winning (and therefore ending) the war.[91] If Germany had surrendered, strategic bombing would have stopped. The reverse is not true. Only through Allied victory did the slaughter of Jews, Gypsies, and others, not to mention the slow starvation and mistreatment of slave laborers, come to an end. This does not excuse the well-documented failure of the Allied countries to accept Jewish refugees before the war, or, as some argue (more controversially), the failure to use air power to stop or slow the killing in the death camps. Indeed, it cannot be said that the Allies fought a war to save the Jews. Nevertheless, the differences between the Allied and Axis causes were extreme. In this context, it is worth asking whether the comparisons made by Markusen and Kopf obscure more than they clarify. This kind of scholarship should be taken seriously, for as we have seen in the Austrian case, similar relativist ideas have made their way into school materials. The evidence indicates that authors and editors of Austrian history textbooks and reading books have chosen both to emphasize Hiroshima more than Auschwitz or Mauthausen and to equate concentration camps with Hiroshima. It is ultimately a question of judgment as to whether or not relativist comparisons in textbooks serve to elucidate or obfuscate historical problems.

Continuities and Fragmentation in the Mainstream: The Durability of the Coalition Lesson

Scholars, to their dismay, are awed by the power of television to influence popular views of history. A widely watched documentary can reach more viewers in one showing than a lifetime of publications will find readers. In the late 1980s and 1990s, Hugo Portisch's ORF (Austrian television) documentaries on the First and Second Republics ("Österreich I" and "Österreich II") reached millions of viewers. The series was unprecedented in its ambition. "Österreich II" consists of thirty-one 90-minute episodes, and there have been several book companions to the series.[92] A systematic analysis of the series and its impact would improve our understanding of Austrian popular memory. Some have severely criticized the series for its "all-knowing narrator" and for promoting the victim theory of Austrian history. In general, it can be said that the series, which has its strengths (e.g., its high production values, extensive use of film and photographic archives, and broad scope), is a work of consensus history, which indeed can be seen as its purpose.[93] Portisch might be seen as a kind of Austrian Shelby Foote (the Southern writer and historian featured in Ken Burns's *Civil War* television series, who showed sympathy and admiration for Southerners but also Abraham Lincoln and Ulysses S. Grant) for steering the safe course that honors all sides. This is what the coalition lesson was all about.

One of the more revealing episodes of continuity can be seen in the controversy over the "Monument against War and Fascism." As recounted by Ruth Wodak, on 30 September 1983, the Vienna City Council unanimously approved funding for a monument to be built by the prominent Austrian sculptor Alfred Hrdlicka, who had been a Communist up until the 1956 Soviet invasion of Hungary. In the wake of the Waldheim scandal, controversy erupted over where the monument should be placed. The Social Democrats insisted that the Albertinaplatz in the First District behind the State Opera House, Austria's cultural flagship, had already been agreed to. The ÖVP, however, wanted a different site and a change of artist. This most likely was partly motivated by Hrdlicka's anti-Waldheim activism, which had included unveiling a giant mobile horse in front of Saint Stephen's Cathedral. Hrdlicka's horse was in reference to Chancellor Fred Sinowatz's wry remark in 1986 that it was only Waldheim's horse, rather than Waldheim, who had been a member of the SA equestrian club.[94] ÖVP City Council member Robert Kauer argued that the rights of those Austrians killed in an air raid, and still buried beneath the Albertinaplatz, needed protection. The conservatives proposed that the Morinzplatz on the bank of the Danube canal, which was the former site of Vienna Gestapo headquarters, would be a more appropriate site for the monument. The sculptor Hrdlicka replied that he had not envisioned "a monument on wheels" to be moved from site to site. Meanwhile, the Freedom Party and the powerful tabloid the *Kronen Zeitung* demanded a referendum.

As the debate became national, the major politicians weighed in on the side of their parties. Jörg Haider of the Freedom Party singled out Hrdlicka for criticism and accused him of supporting fascist ideas, as well as being a Stalinist. But while the national debate was intensifying, the final decision was a local one. When Social Democrat Mayor Helmut Zilk (who had favored the project from its inception) returned from vacation, he announced his decision in favor of Hrdlicka's monument at the Albertinaplatz on 26 July 1988.[95] Work began on 3 August, and on 24 November, the monument, "seven-eighths" completed, was unveiled in a ceremony boycotted by the ÖVP and the Freedom Party. The final piece of the monument was put into place on 21 June 1991.[96]

The controversy over the "Monument against War and Fascism" is a microcosm of the debate over Austria's past. During the dispute over the site of the monument and the choice of the artist, those against the original plan (the ÖVP and the Freedom Party) were portrayed as wanting to forget or not face up to the past.[97] Some scholars see the debate about the monument as echoing the larger debates about Austria's past brought on by the Waldheim affair. Matti Bunzl, for example, contends that the conservatives argued against the monument because it presented "a lasting symbol of resistance to Austria's founding myth," and that "Hrdlicka's monument could be perceived as a threat to the country's historiographical status quo."[98] However, it can be argued that the conservative rejection of the monument had more to do with the choice of Hrdlicka as the artist than the message of the monument; indeed, upon completion, the monument reflected continuity with the great coalition lesson. While many on the Left framed the debate in terms of the "enlightened" versus the "unenlightened," it was a false dichotomy, especially given that there were numerous reasons to criticize the monument. To better understand the controversy, it is useful to turn to the monument and the vision behind it as described by the artist. The monument is composed of four sculpted pillars with a bronze figure in the middle (see plates 7, 8, 9):

[The viewer of the monument] will go through the gate of violence. That is two granite blocks, each one meter and fifty [centimeters] high. On each of these two blocks there is a large block of asymmetric marble. Four meters twenty and three meters forty. The blocks are ninety centimeters apart. When you enter, it has something like a fearful [feeling] of collapsing. When you walk through this gate, you encounter the street-scrubbing Jew who is poured out of bronze. He is no higher than eighty centimeters. From this uncanny descent and from this huge difference [in scale], you can judge [how small] the individual is against violence. Then you come to a stone, the limestone, one meter and 20 [centimeters] high. And therein, a figure disappears into the stone in order to show that the people who went into the basement, who were the victims at that place, entered Hades, entered hell. As we know, there were knocking noises from the basement and building for days on end. The people in the basement were buried alive and suffocated and starved down there. Orpheus meeting Hades is also a greeting to the State Opera and to the Albertina. That is why I wanted to build a monument right at this location. And afterwards comes once again a final concluding stone. It is [made] of polished granite, with the Declaration of Independence from 27 April 1945 chiseled in with rough edges. For Austria declared itself independent when the Greater German Reich had not yet capitulated. I find that a very decisive point, because it is not only a negative and terrifying monument, but there is also a view toward the Second Republic there.[99]

As Ruth Wodak argues, then, Hrdlicka's monument actually continues what had long been a theme of the postwar narrative: the conflation of victims. Indeed, the site itself links the bombing casualties with the victims of the Holocaust through the figure of the bronze Jew scrubbing the sidewalk. Furthermore, the legitimacy of the Second Republic is directly connected with the victims of the war—again, a list that is all-encompassing.[100] Given the context of the postwar victim myth, Hrdlicka's monument is neither surprising nor shocking. What was new and unusual about the monument was that viewers were now confronted with an unmistakable victim in the form of the street-scrubbing Jew (who, incidentally, had to have a crown of thorns added to his head to prevent exhausted passers-by by from sitting on him). The inclusion of the Jew marked a significant departure from earlier monuments, but the principle of conflation was not new. For example, in 1953 the city government in Knittelfeld, Styria, countered the Communist-oriented KZ-Verband's (Concentration Camp Union) "Monument for the Victims of Fascism" by dedicating a monument to "all of the victims from the time 1938 to 1945," by which they meant resisters, bombing casualties, and Wehrmacht soldiers; Jews were not explicitly mentioned. The monument was dedicated to the "victims of the war."[101] Hrdlicka's street-washing Jew was something new, but it was not a radical departure from the past; rather, it represented an update on the postwar consensus. The Jews were now included as victims, but in Hrdlicka's monument, the Jew is one of many victims. In the end, Hrdlicka's "Monument against War and Fascism" represents continuity in a long history of conflation that legitimizes the victim mythology underpinning the Second Republic. Finally, the fact that the interpretive flaws of the monument were not part of the debate in the first place indicates that "coming to terms with the past" in Austria was a complex matter that went beyond the "enlightened" versus "the unenlightened," or the political Left versus the political Right. For example, Vienna's small Jewish community was not consulted about the "street-washing Jew," to which many took offense. In the end, the Jewish *Kultusgemeinde* supported the monument, but as Matti Bunzl points out, they were left with little choice, given that the alternative was to oppose the monument altogether.[102] Ultimately, the victims and their descendants remained largely outside the frame of debate. When some Jews complained that Hrdlicka's "scrubbing Jew" figure was humiliating, the artist remarked: "Humiliation was a symbol of resistance among Christians. Learn something from the Christians."[103]

While they may not have learned the lesson from the Christians, Vienna's Jewish community did become more proactive in planning a monument that would memorialize the victims of the Holocaust outside the constraints of the coalition lesson. Some monuments specifically commemorating Jewish victims—such as the Dounaustadt Forest, which was planted by school children to commemorate Austria's 65,000 murdered Jews—were already being erected in the city's outer districts.[104] In terms of symbolically important space, more significant is the Holocaust monument erected on Judenplatz (in the First District) in 1999. As Heidemarie Uhl writes, this marked a true change in the culture of commemoration. No longer was the discussion about whether to commemorate, nor was the monument conceived as part of the coalition lesson; instead, it was an artistic discussion about how to memorialize Austrian Holocaust victims. In the end, a design by Rachel Whiteread was chosen.[105] Of course, the Whiteread monument did not replace the Hrdlicka monument, so collectively, commemoration of the war and the Holocaust in Vienna's First District represents a fragmentation of the consensus, rather than its elimination.

The controversy over the exhibition "Vernichtungskrieg. Verbrechen der Wehrmacht, 1941 bis 1944"(War of Annihilation: Crimes of the Wehrmacht, 1941 to 1944), sponsored by the Hamburger Institut für Sozialforschung (Hamburg Institute for Social Research), represents a similar fragmentation of Austrian memory. The exhibition was provocative and explicitly didactic in intent. The introduction to the 23-page illustrated brochure accompanying the exhibit reads:

> In 1945, when Nazi Germany had just been defeated, the former generals began to fabricate a legend—the legend of the "clean Wehrmacht." The troops, supposedly, had kept their distance from Hitler and the Nazi regime, and fulfilled their soldierly duty with decency and honor. In all cases, they had only later been informed of the atrocities of Himmler's Einsatzgruppen.
>
> This assertion, which exonerated millions of former German and Austrian soldiers, defines public opinion to this day. Now in 1995, fifty years later, it is time finally to depart from this lie and accept the reality of a great crime: from 1941 to 1944, the Wehrmacht did not wage a "normal" war in the Balkans or in the Soviet Union, but rather a war of annihilation against Jews, prisoners of war, and the civilian population, which killed millions of victims.[106]

In terms of scholarship, the exhibition did not break new ground, for the direct involvement of the Wehrmacht in war crimes (especially those committed on the Eastern Front) had long been established. Nevertheless, the provocative title and obvious purpose of the exhibition to highlight publicly the crimes of the regular army created national and local political controversies throughout Germany and Austria, where, beginning in 1995, it was shown in Vienna, Innsbruck, Klagenfurt, Linz, Graz, and Salzburg. The political parties reacted along lines that represented a fragmentation of the postwar consensus. The Greens and the Liberals gave unqualified support to the exhibition, while the Freedom Party condemned it. The two great coalition parties generally split their position, with the ÖVP against the exhibition and the SPÖ generally in favor of it—though somewhat reluctantly.[107] (In Styria, for example, the SPÖ showed concern over the timing of the exhibition, fearing that the controversy would benefit the FPÖ in elections.)[108] Throughout Austria, school groups and citizens from all walks of life, including many Wehrmacht veterans, visited the exhibition. There was no consensus on the exhibition, as reactions varied from rejection (often expressed in angry letters to newspapers) to thoughtful reflection and catharsis.[109] In the end, as Walter Manoschek points out, reaction to the exhibit proved that ten years after the Waldheim debate, controversies over Austrian participation in the war had hardly been resolved.[110]

Confronters of the Coalition: Jörg Haider and the Victim Myth

In October 1999, the Freedom Party of Austria (FPÖ) placed second in the general election.[111] After nine rounds of failed negotiations between the Social Democrats (SPÖ) and the conservative Austrian People's Party (ÖVP), in February 2000, Wolfgang Schüssel of the ÖVP turned to the FPÖ and its rightist leader Jörg Haider to form a coalition government. The inclusion of Haider's party in the government sparked major controversy within Austria and in Europe. The new government set a series of unprecedented actions into motion. First, it can be argued that the inclusion of the FPÖ in the coalition marked the first time in postwar Europe that a party so far to the Right had gained a large share of political power.[112] Second, Austria's President Thomas Kleistl accepted the coalition only after Haider and Schüssel signed a joint declaration committing themselves to democracy, human rights, and racial tolerance, as well as acceptance of Austria's "responsibility" for crimes committed during the Nazi years.[113] None of this impressed the European Union, which led to another precedent—bilateral sanctions against Austria on the part of EU member states. These sanctions were problematic, for they were essentially ideological in nature as the EU made an example of Austria. Because the sanctions were not in response to any policy enacted by the democratically elected Austrian government, the EU, in the end, was redefining its authority.[114] Complicating matters further was that Haider resigned as head of the FPÖ on 18 February 2000. Many of Haider's opponents dismissed the resignation as a ploy, and indeed, FPÖ Vice Chancellor, Susanne Riess-Passer declared: "The Freedom Party is still Jörg Haider's party!"[115] By the fall of 2000, the EU's sanctions against Austria had come to be seen as untenable by most member states and were dropped.[116]

No figure since Waldheim has generated such negative publicity abroad for Austria nor polarized Austrian society as has Jörg Haider. The rise of Haider has been explained in terms ranging from rightist-populist-opportunist politician to yuppie-neo-fascist.[117] Haider's career has been characterized by inflammatory rhetoric and controversial and unsavory comments (often followed by apologies) on themes including immigrants, the European Union, the Austrian nation, the Nazi past, and the role Austrians played in the Nazi regime. Haider's comments about Nazism in particular (including, at times, praise for the Nazi labor policy and for the veterans of the Waffen SS) have made him a symbol of Austrians' "unenlightened" view of their past. But for all of his faults, Haider has not been a propagator of Austria's victim mythology; rather, he has been forthright, though unapologetic, about Austria in the Nazi years. Consider this 1988 exchange between Haider and Hubertus Czernin and Ernst Schmiederer of *Profil* magazine:

> *Profil:* There is a quote from you from the previous year: "Just because we lost a war, one does not need to believe that we must eternally dance to the tune of the victors." Doesn't that have something to do with your inability to accept the Austrian nation as such?
> *Haider:* I am noble enough, likewise, not to attest to you an inability to interpret history correctly. But Austria was among the losers. And therefore had to share in many of the losses.
> *Profil:* Austria was among the losers? Who actually lost the war?
> *Haider:* The National Socialist Regime and the areas and states ruled by it.
> *Profil:* That is us?
> *Haider:* We were also a part of that. That is why one built up the following combination: Austria was invaded in 1938, and we only came back to ourselves in 1945, and in principle we had no part in it.
> *Profil:* The Austrian state cannot have lost this war, because it did not exist.
> *Haider:* It was the Austrians who were with the German Wehrmacht.[118]

This exchange helps explain Haider's appeal. His statement that Austria was part of Nazi Germany rings much more true than *Profil*'s legally accurate but ultimately unsatisfying position that the Austrian state did not exist (the position long held by the Austrian government). Thus, as Ruth Beckermann points out, Haider undermined the consensus on which the Second Republic was built. But as many of Haider's statements demonstrate, part of his reason for undercutting the myth of the Second Republic is his belief that National Socialism was in some ways admirable.[119] The mythology propagated by Haider is that of the "noble Wehrmacht" doing its duty. As we have seen, this idea has been used at times to support the victim myth, but Haider's comments challenge the legitimacy of the Second Republic because he is not apologetic about the Nazi past. When Haider praised veterans of the Waffen SS in October 1995, he again was undermining the Austria-as-victim myth. Rather than excusing the veterans by arguing that they were led down a false path, Haider simply praised their sense of duty.[120]

While Haider's attitude should be deplored, his statements on the birth of the Second Republic are in large part accurate (this does *not* include his assertion, which he has since retracted, that the concept of the Austrian nation was an "ideological abortion"). The position Haider took in his *Profil* interview raises the ire of many because it undermines the consensus on which the Second Republic was built. This is in part because the Freedom Party has historically had the least investment in the nation-building mythologies of postwar Austria and therefore has no reverence for them. Initially made up mostly of former Nazis, the FPÖ never had a stake in the great coalition lesson.

This analysis is not meant to validate Haider's positions, and it can be argued that Haider has contributed to an atmosphere that has encouraged violence against immigrants in Austria.[121] Furthermore, it should be reiterated that Haider supports his own brand of mythology, which in many ways is a throwback to the earlier, crude ideas that justified the war against the Soviet Union and ignored the crimes of the Nazis. But Austria's postwar mythology of victimization and its related themes were not the products of right-wing revisionism and a rightist "failure to confront the past"; rather, these myths were created by the mainstream parties. It is more accurate to say that different aspects of victim mythology are defended to varying degrees by several different political groups in Austrian society, which often have diametrically opposed agendas. Thus, the anti-right-wing Archive of the Austrian Resistance is one of the leading perpetuators of resistance mythology, while a chief foe of the archive, Jörg Haider defends other and often older aspects of victim mythology, such as the idea of the upstanding army and even the upstanding Waffen SS.[122] The left-wing parties, too, are by no means untainted by the failure "to confront the past." When human bones were discovered at a controversial dam construction site in 1996, some members of the Green Party (die Grünen) openly hoped the remains would prove to belong to Jewish victims of a nearby concentration camp, thereby forcing a halt to construction.[123] Of the many lessons to be learned from the Holocaust, environmental protection is perhaps low on the list. For years, Austria's two largest parties, the conservative ÖVP and the SPÖ, put up only limited resistance to Haider for reasons of political expediency and out of fear of opening old wounds, some of which date to the First Republic. In the coalition view, reliving old battles could have had devastating consequences for Austrian stability.

Despite genuinely deep political differences, the success of the postwar coalition has been an acknowledged part of Austria's postwar success story. Cooperation meant prosperity, a share of political power, and the creation of a unique sense of Austrian identity. It is thus not surprising that the coalition lesson and the mythologies that supported it were jealously defended. But fifty years after the end of the war, the coalition lesson began to run out of steam. Perhaps the leading parties' failure to stop the increasing popularity of Haider stemmed in part from their continued adherence to various strands of national mythology. As many themes of mythology increasingly rang hollow, they lost their ability to work effectively as pillars upon which the Second Republic could stand. When the Austrian People's Party formed a coalition with the Freedom Party in

2000, they crossed two lines at the same time. First, they joined forces with a party that many regard as beyond the pale and not fit to serve in a democracy. The second line crossed by the ÖVP was to prioritize political power over the traditional coalition (a line, which to some degree, had been crossed earlier by the SPÖ when it had governed with the pre-Haider FPÖ). This amounted to jettisoning the niceties of the postwar coalition lesson and may come to be seen as a key moment in the history of the Second Republic. To call the ÖVP's move "dangerous," however, implies that the Austrian political system and social peace remain as fragile as they were fifty years ago. Most seasoned observers of Austrian politics reject this notion.[124] Since 1945, many new themes of identity, such as the reconstruction, fifty years of parliamentary democracy, active participation in the United Nations, and neutrality, have combined with the old themes of culture, *Heimat*, *Landschaft*, and Catholicism to forge an Austrian identity that is both unquestioned and democratically oriented. More than anything, the ÖVP's move may be a sign that Austrian politics are becoming more "normal."[125]

Austria as a Given: The Students Speak

A major reason for the "normality" of contemporary Austria is that the great postwar question of whether Austria can survive as a nation (or even *if* Austria is a nation) has been definitively answered. Austria has the resource of a population that now sees the Austrian nation as a given.[126] According to polling data, in 1994, 72 percent of Austrians believed that the Austrians "are a nation," while 14 percent agreed that the Austrians "are slowly beginning to see themselves as a nation."[127] Flaws inherit to polling notwithstanding, this represents a remarkable change from the mid 1950s. The results of a 1956 survey indicate that 49 percent agreed that the "Austrians are a people of their own," while 46 percent answered that the "Austrians are part of the German people."[128] The struggle to build an Austrian identity and a sense of nationhood, in which the schools have played an important role, has clearly been successful. By the 1990s then, the postwar victim myth, no longer being necessary, became an awkward and disingenuous way of defining Austria. Further, as Anton Pelinka argues, the Austria of the 1990s had become something new, to be compared with the smaller and medium-sized EU states, rather than being seen as the land of the Habsburgs or being compared to the First Republic.[129]

There is much anecdotal evidence to suggest that Austria's young people in particular are ready and even eager to confront Austria's past, without the need for the same old lessons of identity based on the idea of a victimized Austria. In their yearbook contributions, many Austrian students openly state that they want honest answers about their history. In one case, a student expresses worry about the dangers of fascism and writes of the need to learn from the past, and of the danger of racism in contemporary Austria.[130] The Holocaust and the role Austrians played in it are a particular source of interest. Field trips to the Mauthausen camp remain an important event in the education of many of Austria's students, and some students report making more than one visit to the camp.[131] In describing their discussions after watching the film *Schindler's List*, many students write that they were deeply moved. One student reports that he did not have much success when discussing the film with his relatives: "I talked about it with all of my relatives. Some of them were shaken, others were fed up with the constant reports about the Jews and the Nazis—they believe that one should finally put it to rest."[132]

Yearbook reports from student history projects also indicate a desire for more information and a keen interest in the role of Austrians in World War II. In one project, a student learned that the nearby brewery in Zipf had been converted to a rocket-fuel plant and employed slave labor.[133] At another school, students and teachers conducted an oral-history project about the underground aircraft factory at Hinterbrühl, south of Vienna.[134] During the 1991–1992 school year, students in Klagenfurt organized a detailed exhibition with posters for their German class. The organizers saw their project as *geistigen Widerstand* (spiritual resistance) against the dangers of neo-Nazis speaking about the alleged "Auschwitz lie" and against those who distributed the extremist newspaper *Gäck* near their school. One student remarked: "They should explain more about the Third Reich to us students. Perhaps then, there would not be any more young people who are obsessed with National Socialism, beat up foreigners, burn down homes for asylum seekers, and carry out other 'antics.'" The students noted that there was also some negative reaction, such as that of an anonymous student who wrote "forgery" on a poster about Anne Frank.[135]

These examples demonstrate that there is genuine student interest in openly examining and confronting Austria's Nazi past. Even more significant is evidence that some students are rejecting themes of mythology presented to them in their school materials. Students at a Vienna school took an unusual and bold step in their yearbook report from the 1994–1995 school year. In an article titled "50 Jahre Danach" (Fifty Years After), the students lambaste their own textbook, *Gestalteten Welt*, for its woeful lack of coverage of the Holocaust and severely criticize the authors' implication that everyone, including the Nazis, were victims.[136] At another school, a student wrote an essay on the significance of the national holiday in which he expressed the desire to abandon old clichés. In his essay, Mario Rausch states his appreciation for the achievements of the generation that rebuilt Austria, but expresses disgust with the usual speeches that accompany the national holiday. He states a desire to look to the future and defends the right of the younger generation to criticize Austrian society:

> But it is no longer a destructive criticism, no pessimistic denial of nationality, not a criticism without suggestions for solutions. It is a constructive criticism ... we place great importance upon the values Austria offers us, we value the

independence of the state, and the advantages of a great society, like our state Austria is.... We are ready. Ready in the future to work for the well-being of this entity that is called the nation of Austria. Ready to live in a state that, while no island of the blessed, also is no ideological abortion. [Ready to live for a country] that has a thousand-year-old independent culture, around which we can orient ourselves. A culture that should have more meaning for us than we often give due today. A culture that clearly separates us from other peoples and nations, but also [a culture] that links us to the other European cultures.[137]

This passage is significant because it represents the point of view of a student who does not need convincing about Austria's identity. For him, Austria is a given, and the continued exhortations from politicians to believe in Austria have become tiresome and hollow clichés.

In 1998 the Austrian Education Ministry announced a renewed effort to revise history textbooks and to provide better and more comprehensive coverage of the Nazi era in Austria. It remains to be seen how extensive these changes will be, nor is it clear if any significant changes will also be made to reading books, which, as seen throughout this work, often cover important historical themes. What can be said is that revisions in Austrian school materials reflect an ongoing dialogue in Austrian society on the role its citizens played in the Nazi era. This dialogue in itself is evidence of important changes in the landscape of Austrian official memory.

Notes

1. Quoted from the appendix of Botz and Sprengnagel, *Kontroversen um Österreichs Zeitgeschichte*, 577–580.
2. *Stern*, no. 9, 25 February 1988, cover.
3. *Der Spiegel*, no. 4, 25 January 1988, cover.
4. Melanie Sully, *A Contemporary History of Austria* (London: Routledge, 1990), 81–88; and Miller, *One, by One, by One*, 75.
5. Richard Mitten, "Die Kampagne mit 'der Kampagne': Waldheim, der Jüdische Weltkongress und 'Das Ausland,'" *Zeitgeschichte* 17, no. 4 (1990): 175–195. Also see Richard Mitten, "New Faces of Anti-Semitic Prejudice in Austria: Reflections on the 'Waldheim Affair,'" in *Austrians and Jews in the Twentieth Century*, ed. Wistrich, 252–273.
6. Sully, *A Contemporary History of Austria*, 89–98. For the "white book," see *Kurt Waldheim's Wartime Years: A Documentation* (Vienna: Carl Gerold's Sohn, 1987).
7. Bischof, *Austria in the First Cold War*, 65.
8. Sully, *A Contemporary History of Austria*, 98–105.
9. *International Commission of Historians, The Waldheim Report Submitted February 8, 1988 to Federal Chancellor Dr. Franz Vranitzky, authorized English translation of the unpublished German report* (Copenhagen: Museum Tusculanum Press, 1993), 211, 214–215.
10. According to the commission members, the Austrian government reneged on its agreement to publish the report. See ibid., 7–26.
11. Sully, *A Contemporary History of Austria*, 105–115. On the Waldheim affair, see also Richard Mitten, *The Politics of Antisemitic Prejudice: The Waldheim Phenomenon in Austria* (San Francisco: Westview Press, 1992); Hanspeter Born, *Für die Richtigkeit. Kurt Waldheim* (Ulm:

Schneekluth, 1987); and Robert Edwin Herzstein, *Waldheim: The Missing Years* (New York: Arbor House/William Morrow, 1988).

12. On the *Historikerstreit*, see Peter Baldwin, ed., *Reworking the Past: Hitler, the Holocaust, and the Historians' Debate* (Boston: Beacon Press, 1990); and Maier, *The Unmasterable Past*.

13. Mitten, "Bitburg, Waldheim, and the Politics of Remembering and Forgetting," 51–84.

14. Some 607 lectures, films, exhibits, and other events in 1988 dealt with the National Socialist past in Austria. See Katinka Tatjana Nowotny, "Erinnerung an den National-sozialismus. Eine Analyse zum Österreichischen Bedenkjahr 1938/88" (Diplomarbeit, University of Vienna, 1990), appendix.

15. Uhl, *Zwischen Versöhnung und Verstörung*, 20.

16. Thomas Bernhard, *Heldenplatz* (Frankfurt am Main: Suhrkamp, 1988). On the controversy, see Wodak et al., *Die Sprachen der Vergangenheiten*, 114–119.

17. This phrase is, of course, borrowed from Ulf Brunnbauer, editor of *Eiszeit der Erinnerung*.

18. See Wodak et al., *Die Sprachen der Vergangenheiten*, 9–17.

19. See Gerard Kasemir, "Spätes Ende für 'wissenschaftlich' vorgetragenen Rassismus. Die Borodajkewycz-Affäre 1965," in *Politische Affären und Skandale in Österreich*, ed. Michael Gehler and Hubert Sickinger (Thaur: Kulturverlag, 1996), 486–501.

20. Kreisky and Wiesenthal had originally come into conflict in 1971, when Wiesenthal revealed the Nazi backgrounds of four Kreisky cabinet appointees. See Herbert Pierre Secher, "Kreisky and the Jews," in *The Kreisky Era in Austria*, ed. Günter Bischof and Anton Pelinka (New Brunswick: Transaction Publishers, 1994), 16–22. Also see Ingrid Böhler, "'Wenn die Juden ein Volk sind, so ist es ein mieses Volk.' Die Kreisky-Peter-Wiesenthal-Affäre 1975," in *Politische Affären und Skandale in Österreich*, ed. Gehler and Sickinger, 502–531.

21. See Heidi Trettler, "Der umstrittene Handschlag. Die Affäre Frischenlager—Reder," in *Politische Affären und Skandale in Österreich*, ed. Gehler and Sickinger, 592–613.

22. Wendelin Schmidt-Dengler, "Das neue Land. Die Konzeption einer neuen österreichischen Identität in der Literatur," in *Inventur 45/55*, ed. Kos and Rigele, 429–436. The story can be found in Ingeborg Bachmann, *Das Dreissigste Jahr. Erzählungen* (Munich: R. Piper & Co. Verlag, 1961), 105–141.

23. On Ingeborg Bachmann and Paul Celan, see Beth Bjorklund, "Ingeborg Bachmann," and Michael Winkler, "Paul Celan," both in *Major Figures of Modern Austrian Literature*, ed. Donald G. Daviau (Riverside, Cal.: Ariadne Press, 1988), 49–82 and 139–159, respectively.

24. See Fiona Steinert and Heinz Steinert, "Reflexive Menschenverachtung: die Wiener-ische Variante von Herrschaftskritik. Der Herr Karl—ein echter Wiener geht nicht unter," in *Österreich 1945–1995*, ed. Sieder et al., 236–249.

25. See Egd Gstättner, "Eiszeit, Schweigen, Erinnern," in *Eiszeit der Erinnerung*, ed. Brunn-bauer, 162–170.

26. See the English translation, Peter Henisch, *Negatives of My Father*, trans. Anne Close Ulmer (Riverside, Cal.: Ariadne Press, 1990).

27. See Heinz P. Wassermann, *"Zuviel Vergangenheit tut nicht gut!" Nationalsozialismus im Spiegel der Tagespresse der Zweiten Republik* (Innsbruck: Studien Verlag, 2000), 307–309.

28. Several examples from the "Zeitgeschichte im Unterricht" section of the journal *Zeit-geschichte* demonstrate this point. Among the many is Hermann Langbein, "Über-lebende aus den Konzentrationslagern des Nationalsozialismus Sprechen mit Schülern," *Zeitgeschichte* 12, no. 2 (1984): 52–57.

29. Botz and Sprengnagel, *Kontroversen um Österreichs Zeitgeschichte*, 577–580. Vranitzky made similar remarks before the Austrian Parliament in 1991. See ibid., 574–576. Chancellor Viktor Klima echoed Vranitzky's statements in a 1997 address before Jewish émi-grés upon a visit to Vienna. See "Viktor Klima, Federal Chancellor of Austria: Remarks before former Austrian citizens who had to flee their native country to escape Nazi ter-ror," *Austrian Information* 50, nos. 7–8 (1997): 2–3.

30. See Sully, *A Contemporary History of Austria*, 88.

31. Pelinka and Weinzierl, *Das grosse Tabu*, 7.

32. For example, Bernhard Schausberger writes: "No one can and will demand that an indi-vidual during the National Socialist dictatorship should have openly challenged the

regime and thereby have spoken out his own death sentence. But what one can and must demand is that these individuals recognize the facts of a certain guilt *[Mitschuld]* and not to constantly flee into excuses." See Schausberger, "Die Entstehung des Mythos," 17–18.

33. See "'Where Are the Big Topics, Where Is the Big Form?' Elfriede Jelinek in Discussion with Eva Brenner about Her Play, *Totenauberg* (1991), Theater and Politics," in *Elfriede Jelinek: Framed by Language*, ed. Jorun B. Johns and Katherine Arens (Riverside, Cal.: Ariadne Press, 1994), 29–30.

34. See Ernst Hanisch, "'Selbsthaß' als Teil der österreichischen Identität," *Zeitgeschichte* 23, nos. 5–6 (1996): 136–145.

35. These selections are all available in English. See the "Literature and Literary Criticism" section of the bibliography.

36. See Robert Menasse, *Die sozialpartnerschaftliche Ästhetik. Essays zum österreichischen Geist* (Vienna: Sonderzahl, 1990); idem, *Das Land ohne Eigenschaften. Essay zur österreichischen Identität* (Vienna: Sonderzahl, 1992); and idem, *Dummheit ist machbar. Begleitende Essays zum Stillstand der Republik* (Vienna: Sonderzahl, 1999).

37. There is also a newer Jewish section that has been well maintained.

38. "Measures Against Anti-Semitism in Austria: An Overview," *Austrian Information* 50, no. 6 (1997): 3.

39. The best example is the book *Österreicher und der Zweite Weltkrieg*, jointly edited by Wolfgang Neugebauer of the DÖW and Elisabeth Morawek of the Austrian Education Ministry.

40. See Peter Malina and Gustav Spann, *1938, 1988. Vom Umgang mit unserer Vergangenheit* (Vienna: Bundesministerium für Unterricht, Kunst und Sport, 1988).

41. For a summation of these projects, see Veronika Ratzenböck, Elisabeth Morawek, and Sirikit M. Amann, eds., *Die zwei Wahrheiten. Eine Dokumentation von Projekten an Schulen zur Zeitgeschichte im Jahr 1988* (Vienna: Löcker Verlag, 1989).

42. Among others, see Albert G. Absenger, ed., *Schriftenreihe zur Lehrerbildung im Berufsbildenden Schulwesen, Heft 97. Zeitgeschichte—Politische Bildung VIII. Österreichbewußtsein, Vergangenheitsbewältigung, Neutralitätspolitik* (Vienna: Pädagogisches Institut des Bundes in Wien, 1986).

43. Albert G. Absenger et al., *Aus Geschichte lernen. 7. Klasse. Von der industriellen Revolution bis zum Zweiten Weltkrieg* (Vienna: ÖVB Pädagogischer Verlag, 1993), 148.

44. Alois Scheucher et al., *Zeitbilder. Geschichte und Sozialkunde 7. Vom Beginn des Industriezeitalters bis zum Zweiten Weltkrieg* (Vienna: Österreichischer Bundesverlag, 1992), 117. Note that this book is a completely reworked edition of the earlier book of the same title by Lein and Weissensteiner. This explains why this book is considered a first edition.

45. The same book also included coverage of the pogrom that accompanied the Anschluss. See Leopold Rettinger and Friedrich Weissensteiner, *Zeitbilder. Geschichte und Sozialkunde 4*, 3rd ed. (Vienna: Österreichischer Bundesverlag, 1992), 31.

46. Michael Floiger, Ulrike Ebenhoch, and Manfred Tuschel, *Stationen 4. Spuren der Vergangenheit—Bausteine der Zukunft. Lehr- und Arbeitsbuch für die 8. Klasse an allgemeinbildenden höheren Schulen* (Vienna: Ed. Hölzel, 1992), 71–72.

47. Christine Schönach et al., eds., *Strickleiter 4. Band 4 für die 4. Klasse. Lesebuch für die Hauptschulen und die Unterstufe der allgemeinbildenden höheren Schulen* (Vienna: Österreichischer Bundesverlag, 1990), 146.

48. Floiger et al., *Stationen 3. Spuren der Vergangenheit—Bausteine der Zukunft. Lehr- und Arbeitsbuch für die 7. Klasse an allgemeinbildenden höheren Schulen*, 175–176.

49. Rettinger and Weissensteiner, *Zeitbilder. Geschichte und Sozialkunde* (Vienna: 1992), 44–45.

50. Scheucher et al., *Zeitbilder. Geschichte und Sozialkunde*, 157–160.

51. Norbert Schausberger, Erich Oberländer, and Heinz Strotzka, *Wie? Woher? Warum? 3. Geschichte und Sozialkunde 4. Klasse* (Vienna: Österreichischer Bundesverlag, 1988), 52–53.

52. Absenger et al., *Aus Geschichte lernen*, 162.

53. Gerhard Münster, ed., *Schul-Lehrpläne. Lehrplan für die Allgemeinbildende Höhere Schule-AHS. Gymnasium, Realgymnasium, Wirtschaftskundliches Realgymnasium. 1. bis 4. Klasse (Unterstufe) in der Fassung der Lehrplanreform 1993 bis 1996 (weitgehend ident mit der*

Hauptschule) 5. bis 8. Klasse (Oberstufe). Kodex des Österreichischen Rechts, ed. Werner Doralt (Vienna: Verlag Orac, 1996), 91.

54. *Lehrpläne der allgemeinbildenden höheren Schulen.* 1. Band (Vienna: Österreichischer Bundesverlag, 1984), 82.

55. See Peter Malina, "Auschwitz: Betroffenheit Statt Einsicht. Schulbuchtexte als Indikator öffentlichen Geschichtsbewußtseins," *Materialien zur Geschichts-Didaktik* 1 (1995): 36–48.

56. Absenger et al., *Aus Geschichte lernen*, 148.

57. Arbeitsgemeinschaft, eds., *Österreich Lesebuch 4 für die 4. Klasse der Volksschulen. Tirol* (Vienna: Bundesverlag—Ueberreuter, 1991), 104.

58. Oskar Achs et al., *Zeiten, Völker, Kulturen 3. Lehr- und Arbeitsbuch für Geschichte und Sozialkunde. 4. Klasse der Hauptschulen und der allgemeinbildenden höheren Schulen* (Vienna: ÖBV Pädagogischer Verlag, 1993), 74–77, 81.

59. Leopold Eibl, *Bücherwurm 4. Länderteil Niederösterreich* (Linz: Veritas Verlag, 1991), 73. Also see the story "In Graz fallen Bomben" (Bombs Are Falling in Graz) in Alois Almer and Ernst A. Ekker, *Leseheft Steiermark* (Vienna: Österreichischer Bundesverlag, 1991), 10–11.

60. Gabriele Bauer et al., *Bücherwurm 4. Basisteil* (Linz: Veritas Verlag, 1991), 35–36.

61. Agnes Larcher et al., eds., *Strickleiter 3. Band 3 für die 3. Klasse. Lesebuch für die Hauptschulen und die Unterstufe der allgemeinbildenden höheren Schulen* (Vienna: Österreichischer Bundesverlag, 1991), 148–151.

62. See *Bundesrealgymnasium Steyr. 105. Jahresbericht, Schuljahr 1987/88* (Steyr: 1988), 74. I too watched *Die Welle* in an Austrian history class as a student at the Lower Austrian Teacher's College in the spring of 1988. *The Wave* is the property of Columbia Tristar Television, a Sony Pictures Entertainment Company, Culver City, California. The program was produced by Tandem Productions in association with Embassy Television.

63. A 1991 reading book includes a ten-page excerpt from *Sadako will leben*. See Robert Killinger, ed., *Lesebuch 2. für die 2. Klasse der Hauptschulen und der allgemeinbildenden höheren Schulen* (Vienna: Österreichischer Bundesverlag, 1991), 52–62. Another reading book from 1995 includes a six-page excerpt from *Sadako will leben*. See Jakob Ebner et al., *Auslese Buch 3. Ein Lesebuch für die 7. Schulstufe* (Vienna: ÖBV Pädagogischer Verlag, 1995), 73–78.

64. Wolfgang Pramper et al., *Lesestunde. Lesebuch für die 8. Schulstufe. Teil A* (Linz: Veritas, 1990), 105–114.

65. Werner Tscherne and Manfred Gartler, *Wege durch die Zeiten 3* (Graz: Leopold Stocker Verlag, 1991), 136.

66. Erich Benedikt et al., eds., *Erlebnis Literatur 8. Lesebuch für die 8. Klasse der AHS* (Vienna: Österreichischer Bundesverlag, 1992), 113–119.

67. Josef Donnenberg et al., eds., *Lesezeichen 4* (Vienna: Österreichischer Bundesverlag, 1992), 80–81.

68. Jakob Ebner et al., *Auslese Buch 4. Eine Lesebuch für die 8. Schulstufe* (Vienna: ÖBV Pädagogischer Verlag, 1995), 150–167.

69. Ibid., 151.

70. *Jahresbericht Bundesgymnasium Klagenfurt. Völkermarkter Ring 27. Schuljahr 1988/89* (Klagenfurt, 1989), 33.

71. On the question of the uniqueness of the Holocaust, see the thoughtful comments by Inga Clendinnen, *Reading the Holocaust* (Cambridge: Cambridge University Press, 1999), 10–16.

72. See Buruma, *The Wages of Guilt*, 92–111, *passim*. As in Europe, in Japan the onset of the Cold War resulted in American complicity in rapid retreat from punishing war criminals to economic rehabilitation and rearmament. On the complexity of Japanese *Vergangenheitsbewältigung*, see John Dower's Pulitzer Prize-winning work, *Embracing Defeat: Japan in the Wake of World War II* (New York: Norton, 1999), 485–521, *passim*.

73. Achs et al., *Zeiten, Völker, Kulturen*, 107.

74. Erika Weinzierl, "Resistance, Persecution, Forced Labor," in *Austria in the Twentieth Century*, ed. Rolf Steininger, Günter Bischof, and Michael Gehler (New Brunswick: Transaction Publishers, 2002), 137.

75. Münster, *Schul-Lehrpläne*, 91, 304.
76. Anton Wald et al., *Zeitbilder. Geschichte und Sozialkunde 8. Vom Ende des Zweiten Weltkrieges bis heute. Mit "Aktuellem Journal"* (Vienna: ÖBV Pädagogischer Verlag, 1993), 6–9.
77. Ibid., 9.
78. One yearbook includes two popular European caricatures of American life: poverty in the United States, and American "Puritanism." In his essay "Österreich—eine Skandalrepublik?" (Austria—a Republic of Scandals?), the student Thomas Gaigg asserts: "There are no slums in our country like in so many other Western industrialized nations, and in Austria, 30 percent do not live below the poverty line as in the USA." In the same yearbook there is an article by a teacher, Karl Steinkogler, titled "Von der protestantischen Diktatur zum pluralistischen Basar—Amerika zwischen Hexenprozessen und Drogenkulturen" (From Protestant Dictatorship to Pluralistic Bazaar—America between Witch Trials and Drug Cultures). See *Bundesgymnasium und Bundesrealgymnasium Bad Ischl. 15. Jahresbericht 1986/87* (Bad Ischl, 1987), 111–113, 143–145.
79. Gabriele Bauer, *Bücherwurm 3. Lesebuch* (Linz: Veritas, 1991), 26.
80. Hannelore Tscherne and Sylvia Krampl, *Spuren der Zeit 4.* (Vienna: Verlag E. Dorner, 1991), 75.
81. Gabriele Bauer, *Bücherwurm 2. Lesebuch* (Linz: Veritas, 1991), 37.
82. Erlefried Schröckenfuchs and Georg Lobner, *Spuren der Zeit 8* (Vienna: E. Dorner, 1992), 102.
83. Werner Tscherne and Manfred Gartler, *Wege durch die Zeiten 4* (Graz: Leopold Stocker Verlag, 1992), 82.
84. Münster, *Schul-Lehrpläne*, 8.
85. See "Staberl," *Neue Kronen Zeitung*, 31 October 1995, 12. The letter was written after the Austrian Parliament passed a law to give compensation to Jewish war victims.
86. *Jahresbericht 1986/87. Bundesgymnasium St. Johann in Tirol* (St. Johann, 1987), 37–38.
87. See the interview, G. Hoffmann-Ostenhof, "'Jeder hat Angst,'" *Profil*, no. 25, 17 June 1996. 35. Also see Harold H. Tittmann III, *The Waldheim Affair: Democracy Subverted* (New York: Olin Frederick, 2000).
88. Jacques Barzun, *From Dawn to Decadence: 500 Years of Western Cultural Life, 1500 to the Present* (New York: Perennial, 2000), 761–762.
89. On the problem of relativism and World War II, see Friedlander, *Probing the Limits of Representation*; and Deborah Lipstadt, *Denying the Holocaust: The Growing Assault on Truth and Memory* (New York: The Free Press, 1993).
90. Eric Markusen and David Kopf, *The Holocaust and Strategic Bombing: Genocide and Total War in the Twentieth Century* (San Francisco: Westview Press, 1995), 247.
91. Questions about the morality and ultimate effectiveness of strategic bombing were raised during the war and have been ever since. See Keegan, *The Second World War*, 432–433.
92. See, for example Hugo Portisch, *Österreich II. Jahre des Aufbruchs. Jahre des Umbruchs* (Vienna: Kremayr & Scheriau, 1996).
93. See Susanne Eybl and Elke Renner, "Überlegungen zu einem Ideologiekritischen Einsatz von 'Österreich II' im Unterricht," *Zeitgeschichte* 17, no. 1 (1989): 33–43, *passim*. Portisch responded to these criticisms, arguing that Eybl and Renner had analyzed his films out of context. See Hugo Portisch, "Ideologiekritische Überlegungen: Eine Replik," *Zeitgeschichte* 14, no. 4 (1990): 196–201. Thanks to Günter Bischof for pointing how Portisch's documentaries match the theme of coalition history.
94. Wodak et al., *Die Sprachen der Vergangenheiten*, 107–108; and Matti Bunzl, "On the Politics and Semantics of Austrian Memory: Vienna's Monument against War and Fascism," *History and Memory* 7, no. 2 (fall/winter 1996): 16–17.
95. Zilk later became the target of a terrorist letter bomb, which he survived with a severe hand injury. After serving as mayor, Zilk worked as the "Ombudsman" columnist for the *Kronen Zeitung*.
96. Wodak et al., *Die Sprachen der Vergangenheiten*, 108–112.
97. Ibid., 113.
98. See Bunzl, "On the Politics and Semantics of Austrian Memory," 16 and 20.

99. Wodak et al., *Die Sprachen der Vergangenheiten*, 106–107.
100. Ibid., 112–113.
101. See Heidemarie Uhl, "Erinnerung als Versöhnung. Zur Denkmalkultur und Geschichts-politik der Zweiten Republik," *Zeitgeschichte* 23, nos. 5–6 (1996): 151.
102. See Bunzl, "On the Politics and Semantics of Austrian Memory," 28–31.
103. Beckermann, *Unzugehörig. Österreicher und Juden nach 1945*, 11.
104. See Dokumentationsarchiv des österreichischen Widerstand, ed., *Gedenken und Mahnen in Wien 1934–1945* (Vienna: DÖW, 1998), 453–454.
105. Heidemarie Uhl, "Transformation des Österreichischen Gedächtnisses. Geschichtspoli-tik und Denkmalkultur in der Zweiten Republik," in *Eiszeit der Erinnerung*, ed. Brunn-bauer, 60–61.
106. See Hamburger Institut für Sozialforschung, *Vernichtungskrieg. Verbrechen der Wehrmacht 1941 bis 1944* (Hamburg: Institut für Sozialforschung, 1995), 2–3.
107. Walter Manoschek, "Austrian Reaction to the Exhibition 'War of Extermination: Crimes of the Wehrmacht 1941 to 1944,'" in *The Vranitzky Era in Austria*, ed. Günter Bischof, Anton Pelinka, and Ferdinand Karlhofer (New Brunswick: Transaction Publishers, 1999), 193–197.
108. Ulf Brunnbauer, "'Ich will Ausstellungen, die Freude bereiten.' Die Wehrmachtausstel-lung in Graz—zwischen Gedächtnis und Geschichte," in *Eiszeit der Erinnerung*, ed. Brunnbauer, 19–20.
109. See Helga Embacher, "'Mein Vater war kein Mörder,'" and the comments of the Wehr-macht veteran Friedrich R. Besl, "Erinnern. Gedanken über Kriegsgeschehen und die Ausstellung 'Vernichtungskrieg. Verbrechen der Wehrmacht 1941–1944,'" both in *Eiszeit der Erinnerung*, ed. Brunnbauer, 31–37 and 135–148, respectively.
110. Manoschek, "Austrian Reaction to the Exhibition," 199–200.
111. "Fascism Resurgent?" *The Economist*, 9 October 1999, 57–59.
112. "Broken Taboo?" *The Economist*, 20 January 2000, 59
113. "Younger, Fresher, and Harder Right," *The Economist*, 19 February 2000, 52.
114. See "A Conundrum for Austria—and for Europe," *The Economist*, 5 February 2000, 45–46; and "The Union Expects Europe's Voters to Fit Its Political Space," *The Economist*, 11 March 2000, 53–54.
115. See "Poker Game," *The Economist*, 4 March 2000, 50–51; and "Is Haider in or Out?" *The Economist*, 6 May 2000, 54.
116. "Who Is Serving Whom?" *The Economist*, 2 September 2000, 43–44.
117. See, for example, the comments of Jacob Heilbrunn, who argues that a line of continuity can be drawn between Haider and Karl Lueger, Vienna's fin-de-siècle mayor and a polit-ical anti-Semite, who stood up for the "little man." See Jacob Heilbrunn, "A Disdain for the Past: Jörg Haider's Austria," *World Policy Journal* 17, no. 1 (spring 2000): 71–78.
118. Quoted from Beckermann, *Unzugehörig. Österreicher und Juden nach 1945* (Vienna: 1989), 35. The interview appeared in *Profil* no. 35, 29 November 1988.
119. Ibid.
120. Thomas Vasek, "Haiders Anständige Menschen," *Profil*, no. 52, 23 December 1995, 24–26.
121. For examples of terrorist actions in Austria, see Andy Kaltenbrunner, Oliver Tanzer, and Paul Yvon, "Hilflos im Terrornetz," *Profil*, no. 7, 13 February 1995, 24–28.
122. Vasek, "Haiders Anständige Menschen," 24–26. For an example of the DÖW's battle against Haider, see the meticulously documented *Handbuch des Österreichischen Rechts-extremismus*. A lawsuit forced the DÖW to remove Haider's picture from the cover. See Dokumentationsarchiv des Österreichischen Widerstandes, ed., *Handbuch des Österrei-chischen Rechtsextremismus. Aktualisierte und Erweiterte Neuausgabe* (Vienna: Deuticke, 1994). For another anti-Haider work, see Hans-Henning Scharsach, *Haider's Kampf*, 8th ed. (Vienna: Verlag Orac, 1992). For Haider's political philosophy in his own words, see Jörg Haider, *Die Freiheit die ich meine. Das Ende des Proporzstaates. Plädoyer für die Dritte Republik* (Frankfurt am Main: Ullstein Verlag, 1993).
123. Eva Mensasse, "Achtung, Geschichte!" *Profil*, no. 12, 18 March 1996, 72–73.
124. See Tony Judt, "Tale from the Vienna Woods," *New York Review of Books*, 23 March 2000, 8–9; Robert S. Wistrich, "Haider and His Critics," *Commentary*, April 2000, 30–35;

and Lonnie Johnson, "On the Inside Looking Out: Austria's New ÖVP-FPÖ Government, Jörg Haider, and Europe," Habsburg Occasional Papers 2 (February 2000) [http://www2.h-net.msu.edu/~habsweb/occasionalpapers/haider.html]; and the contributions in Ruth Wodak and Anton Pelinka, eds., *The Haider Phenomenon in Austria* (New Brunswick: Transaction Publishers, 2002).

125. For a thorough analysis of the changing nature of Austrian politics and society, see Pelinka, *Austria: Out of the Shadow of the Past*.

126. See Hanns Haas, "Zur Österreichischen Nation—Eine Spätlese," *Zeitgeschichte* 18, nos. 9–10 (1991): 304–313; and Stourzh, *Vom Reich zur Republik*, 99–102.

127. See the data in Thaler, *The Ambivalence of Identity*, 168. These figures compared with responses of 66 percent and 16 percent respectively in 1970, and 47 percent and 23 percent in 1964. Also see Peter Gerlich, "National Consciousness and National Identity: A Contribution to the Political Culture of the Austrian Party System," in *The Austrian Party System*, ed. Anton Pelinka and Fritz Plasser (Boulder: Westview Press, 1989), 223–258; and Stourzh, *Vom Reich zur Republik*, 99–113. Also see the linguistic study by Wodak et al., *The Discursive Construction of National Identity*. Among the authors' conclusions are that "[a]lthough the term 'Austrian nation' hardly ever occurs explicitly in our data, there can be no doubt that the Austrians who made up our sample perceived its existence in their speeches" (190).

128. Thaler, *The Ambivalence of Identity*, 167.

129. See Pelinka, *Austria: Out of the Shadow of the Past*, 232.

130. *Erster Jahresbericht. Handelsakademie und Handelsschule Steyr, 1987/88* (Steyr, 1988), 40–41.

131. *Bundes-Oberstufenrealgymnasium Wolfsberg. Jahresbericht über das Schuljahr 1993/94* (Wolfsberg, 1994), 46–49.

132. *Siebter Jahresbericht. Handelsakademie und Handelsschule Steyr, 1993/94* (Steyr, 1994), 44–45.

133. *Öffentliches Stiftsgymnasium Kremsmünster. 138. Jahresbericht, 1995* (Kremsmünster, 1995), 141–143.

134. *Festschrift und Jahresbericht im 125. Bestandsjahr des BG & BRG Baden, Biondekgasse* (Baden, 1988), 71–74.

135. *Bundesgymnasium und Bundesrealgymnasium 9020 Klagenfurt, Mössingerstrasse 25. Bericht über das Schuljahr 1991/1992* (Klagenfurt, 1992), 24–25.

136. *Höhere Technische Bundeslehranstalt Wien 10. Jahresbericht 1994/95* (Vienna, 1995), 94–106.

137. *Jahresbericht Bundesgymnasium Klagenfurt. Völkermarkter Ring 27. Schuljahr 1988/89* (Klagenfurt, 1989), 32–33.

BIBLIOGRAPHY

Austrian Textbooks, *Ständestaat* (Austro-fascist) Period, 1934–1938

Burger, Wolfgang, and Hans Groll. *Handbuch der vormilitärischen Erziehung*. Vienna: Deutscher Verlag für Jugend und Volk, 1936.

Der Österreicher hat ein Vaterland. Vienna: Österreichischer Bundesverlag, 1935.

Ender, Otto. *Das neue Österreich. Staatsbürgerkunde mit Bildern*. Innsbruck: Tyrolia Verlag, 1935.

Fedra, Franz, ed. *Methodik der vormilitärischen Ausbildung im Turnunterricht*. Vienna: Deutscher Verlag für Jugend und Volk, 1936.

Hoch Österreich. Vienna: Österreichischer Bundesverlag, 1935.

Ich bin ein Österreicher! Vienna: Österreichischer Bundesverlag, 1935.

Lesebuchausschüssen für Salzburg und Kärnten. *Unser Lesebuch für die vierte Stufe der alpenländischen Volksschulen. Ausgabe für Kärnten*. 6th rev. ed. Vienna: Österreichischer Bundesverlag für Unterricht, Wissenschaft und Kunst, 1937.

Mein Vaterland, mein Österreich. Vienna: Österreichischer Bundesverlag, 1935.

Salzburger Lesebuchausschuss. *Unser Lesebuch für die dritte Stufe der alpenländischen Volksschulen. Ausgabe für niederösterreichische Landschulen*. 3rd rev. ed. Vienna: Österreichischer Bundesverlag für Unterricht, Wissenschaft und Kunst, 1937.

Tzöbl, Josef A. *Vaterländische Erziehung*. Preface by Kurt von Schuschnigg. Vienna: Österreichische Volkschriften, 1933. [Published during the First Republic, but also used in the *Ständestaat* period]

National Socialist Period Textbooks, 1938–1945

Bock, Bernhard, Ernst Falke, Friedrich Hackenberg, Erich Kirsch, and Ludwig Pohnert. *Deutsches Lesebuch für Jungen. Dritter Teil*. 3rd ed. Vienna: Ostmärkischer Landesverlag, 1942.

Graf, Jakob. *Familienkunde und Rassenbiologie für Schüler*. Munich: J.F. Lehmanns Verlag, 1934.

Hackenberg, Friedrich, Erich Kirsch, Ludwig Pohnert, and Albert Streuber. *Deutsches Lesebuch für Jungen. Zweiter Teil*. Frankfurt am Main: Verlag Moritz Diesterweg, 1942.

Krieck, Ernst. *Weltanschauliche Entscheidung*. Vienna: Österreichischer Landesverlag vormals Österreichischer Bundesverlag, 1939.

Austrian History Textbooks and Commemorative Publications, Second Republic, 1945–1996

Absenger, Albert G., Walter Knarr, Herbert Pfeifer, and Irmfried Speiser. *Der Mensch im Wandel der Zeiten. 3. Teil. Lehr- und Arbeitsbuch der Geschichte und Sozialkunde*. Vienna: Österreichischer Gewerbeverlag, 1992.

———. *Aus Geschichte lernen. 7. Klasse. Von der industriellen Revolution bis zum Zweiten Weltkrieg*. Vienna: ÖBV Pädagogischer Verlag, 1993.

Achs, Oskar, Manfred Scheuch, and Eva Tesar. *Aus Geschichte lernen. 8. Klasse. Vom Ende des Zweiten Weltkrieges bis zur Gegenwart.* Vienna: ÖBV Pädagogischer Verlag, 1994.

Achs, Oskar, Werner Adelmaier, Edith Loebenstein, and Hermann Schnell. *Zeiten, Völker, Kulturen 3. Lehr- und Arbeitsbuch für Geschichte und Sozialkunde. 4. Klasse der Hauptschulen und der allgemeinbildenden höheren Schulen.* Vienna: ÖBV Pädagogischer Verlag, 1993.

Aicher, Ferdinand, and Richard Pacher. *Kärnten in Gegenwart und Vergangenheit. Zeiten, Völker und Kulturen. Länderteil zum Einführungsband für die 1. Klasse der Hauptschulen.* Vienna: Österreichischer Bundesverlag für Unterricht, Wissenschaft und Kunst, 1972.

Aigner, Manfred, and Irmgard Bachl. *Geschichte, Sozialkunde, Politische Bildung. 8. Schulstufe.* Linz: Veritas-Verlag, 1988.

Arbeitsgemeinschaft, eds. *Unser Österreich, 1945–1955. Zum 10. Jahrestag der Wiederherstellung der Unabhängigkeit der Republik Österreich der Schuljugend gewidmet von der Österreichischen Bundesregierung.* Vienna: Österreichischer Bundesverlag, 1955.

Aspernig, Walter, Albert Atzl, Klaus Volker, and Gerhard Winkler. *Gestaltete Welt 3. Von der Neuzeit zur Gegenwart. Ein Lehr- und Arbeitsbuch für Geschichte und Sozialkunde.* Vienna: Ed. Hölzel, 1988.

Atschko, Gerhard, Peter Dusek, and Helmut Rauch. *Sozial- und Wirtschaftskunde (inkl. Zeitgeschichte) für den Polytechnischen Lehrgang.* Vienna: Bohmann-Verlag, 1982.

Berger, Franz, Edith Loebenstein, Hermann Schnell, and Klemens Zens. *Zeiten, Völker und Kulturen. Ein Lehr- und Arbeitsbuch für den Geschichtsunterricht an Haupt- und Untermittelschulen. 4. Band. Das Zeitalter der Weltpolitik und der Technik.* Vienna: Hölder-Pichler-Tempsky, 1957.

———. *Zeiten, Völker und Kulturen. Ein Lehr- und Arbeitsbuch für den Unterricht in Geschichte und Sozialkunde. 3. Band für die 4. Klasse der Hauptschulen und der allgemeinbildenden höheren Schulen. Das Zeitalter der Weltpolitik und der Technik. Einführung in die Sozialkunde und in die Staatsbürgerkunde.* Vienna: Hölder-Pichler-Tempsky, 1967.

———. *Bilder aus Wiens Vergangenheit. Zeiten, Völker und Kulturen. Länderteil Wien.* 3rd ed. Vienna: Österreichischer Bundesverlag für Unterricht, Wissenschaft und Kunst, 1974.

———. *Zeiten, Völker und Kulturen. 3. Band für die 4. Klasse der Hauptschulen und der allgemeinbildenden höheren Schulen. Arbeitsbuch.* Vienna: Österreichischer Bundesverlag für Unterricht, Wissenschaft und Kunst, 1977.

———. *Zeiten, Völker und Kulturen. Ein Lehr- und Arbeitsbuch für den Unterricht in Geschichte und Sozialkunde. 3. Band für die 4. Klasse der Hauptschulen und der allgemeinbildenden höheren Schulen. Das Zeitalter der Weltpolitik und der Technik.* 1st ed. (Neubearbeitung). Vienna: Hölder-Pichler-Tempsky, 1977.

———. *Zeiten, Völker und Kulturen. Ein Lehr- und Arbeitsbuch für den Unterricht in Geschichte und Sozialkunde. 3. Band für die 4. Klasse der Hauptschulen und der allgemeinbildenden höheren Schulen. Das Zeitalter der Weltpolitik und der Technik.* 2nd ed. (Neubearbeitung). Vienna: Hölder-Pichler-Tempsky, 1982.

Berger, Franz, and Norbert Schausberger. *Zeiten, Völker und Kulturen. Lehrbuch der Geschichte und Sozialkunde für die Oberstufe der allgemeinbildenden höheren Schulen. Band für die 8. Klasse. Geschichte des 20. Jahrhunderts.* 2nd ed. Vienna: Österreichischer Bundesverlag für Unterricht, Wissenschaft und Kunst, 1977.

Berger, Franz, Anton Kolbabek, and Hermann Schnell. *50 Jahre Republik Österreich.* Vienna: Österreichischer Bundesverlag, 1968.

———. *Unsere Republik ist 50 Jahre alt.* Vienna: Österreichischer Bundesverlag, 1968.

Bernt, Johann, and Helmut Zilk. *Wien. Stadt im Aufbau.* Vienna: Hölder-Pichler-Tempsky, 1965.

Bohunovsky, Irmgard, Helmut Rumpler, and Gerd Schindler. *Weltgeschichte im 20. Jahrhundert.* Vienna: Verlag für Geschichte und Politik, 1979.

Breitfuss, Wilhelm, and Herbert Glaser. *Sozialkunde und Wirtschaftskunde (mit Einschluß der Zeitgeschichte) für den Polytechnischen Lehrgang.* 2nd rev. ed. Salzburg: Otto Müller Verlag, 1973.

Bruckner, Karl. *In Diesen Jahren. Wien 1945–1965.* Vienna: Verlag für Jugend und Volk, 1965.

Ebner, Anton. *Arbeitsheft zu Ebner-Partick "Lehrbuch der Geschichte und Sozialkunde," Band IV für die 4. Klasse der Hauptschulen.* 2nd ed. Salzburg: Salzburger Jugend-Verlag, 1983.

Ebner, Anton, and Harald Majdan. *Geschichte 4 für die Oberstufe der allgemeinbildenden höheren Schulen.* Vienna: Österreichischer Bundesverlag für Unterricht, Wissenschaft und Kunst, 1975.

———. *Geschichte 4 für die Oberstufe der allgemeinbildenden höheren Schulen.* 2nd ed. Vienna: Österreichischer Bundesverlag für Unterricht, Wissenschaft und Kunst, 1978.

Ebner, Anton, and Matthias Partick. *Lehrbuch der Geschichte für die 4. Klasse der Hauptschulen und Mittelschulen.* Salzburg: Salzburger Jugend-Verlag, 1962.

———. *Lehrbuch der Geschichte und Sozialkunde. Band IV für die 4. Klasse der Hauptschulen.* Salzburg: Salzburger Jugend-Verlag, 1967.

Ebner, Anton, Anton Kolbabek, Matthias Laireiter, and Hermann Schnell. *Unsere Republik im Wandel der Zeit.* Vienna: Österreichischer Bundesverlag, 1962.

Ebner, Anton, Matthias Partick, and Georg Stadler. *Lehrbuch der Geschichte und Sozialkunde. Vom Wiener Kongreß bis zur Gegenwart. Band III für die 4. Klasse der allgemeinbildenden höheren Schulen.* Salzburg: Otto Müller Verlag, 1968.

Endres, Robert. *Österreichische Staatsbürgerkunde.* 6th rev. ed. Vienna: Verlag für Jugend und Volk, 1950.

Fadrus, Viktor. *Gedenkblatt für Herrn Bundespräsident Dr. Adolf Schärf.* Vienna: Verlag für Jugend und Volk, 1965.

Floiger, Michael, Ulrike Ebenhoch, and Manfred Tuschel. *Stationen 4. Spuren der Vergangenheit—Bausteine der Zukunft. Lehr- und Arbeitsbuch für die 8. Klasse der allgemeinbildenden höheren Schulen.* Vienna: Ed. Hölzel, 1992.

Floiger, Michael, Ulrike Ebenhoch, Kurt Tschegg, and Manfred Tuschel. *Stationen 3. Spuren der Vergangenheit—Bausteine der Zukunft.* Vienna: Ed. Hölzel, 1991.

Förstner, Renate, and Anna Schödl. *SWZ. Sozialkunde, Wirtschaftskunde, Zeitgeschichte.* Vienna: Jugend und Volk, 1993.

Fortbildungsschulrat für Niederösterreich. *Aus Österreichs Vaterlandskunde.* Vienna: Verlag Carl Ueberreuter, 1946.

Gey, Roderich. *Durch die Vergangenheit zur Gegenwart. ein Lehr- und Arbeitsbuch. Geschichte und Sozialkunde für die 8. Klasse der allgemeinbildenden höheren Schulen.* Vienna: Österreichischer Agrarverlag, 1974.

———. *Durch die Vergangenheit zur Gegenwart. ein Lehr- und Arbeitsbuch. Geschichte und Sozialkunde für die 8. Klasse der allgemeinbildenden höheren Schulen.* 2nd rev. ed. Vienna: Österreichischer Agrarverlag, 1987.

Göbhart, Franz, and Erwin Chvojka. *Geschichte und Sozialkunde. Vom Ersten Weltkrieg bis zur Gegenwart. Lern- und Arbeitsbuch.* Vienna: Verlag Carl Ueberreuter, 1973.

———. *Zeitbilder. Geschichte und Sozialkunde 8. Vom Ersten Weltkrieg bis zur Gegenwart.* Vienna: Verlag Carl Ueberreuter, 1984.

Göhring, Walter, and Herbert Hasenmayer. *Zeitgeschichte. Ein approbiertes Lehr- und Arbeitsbuch für Geschichte und Sozialkunde.* Vienna: Verlag Ferdinand Hirt, 1972.

———. *Zeitgeschichte. Ein approbiertes Lehr- und Arbeitsbuch für Geschichte und Sozialkunde.* 3rd rev. ed. Vienna: Verlag Ferdinand Hirt, 1986.

Görlich, Ernst Joseph, Kurt Kren, and Josef Maderner. *Zeitgeschichte. Lehrbuch der Geschichte und Sozialkunde für den 5. Jahrgang der Handelsakademien.* Vienna: Österreichischer Gewerbeverlag, 1973.

Hammerschmid, Helmut, and Wolfgang Pramper. *Meilensteine der Geschichte. Geschichtsbuch für die 4. Klasse HS und AHS.* Linz: Veritas, 1993.

Hasenmayer, Herbert, Johann Payr, and Kurt Tschegg. *Epochen der Weltgeschichte 3. Vom Ersten Weltkrieg bis zur Gegenwart. Ein approbiertes Arbeits- und Lehrbuch für Geschichte und Sozialkunde (Wirtschaftsgeschichte)*. Vienna: Verlag Ferdinand Hirt, 1983.

Hasenmayer, Herbert, Erich Scheithauer, and Werner Tscherne. *Aus Vergangenheit und Gegenwart. Ein approbiertes Arbeits- und Lehrbuch für Geschichte und Sozialkunde.* Vienna: Verlag Ferdinand Hirt, 1985.

Heilsberg, Franz, and Friedrich Korger, eds. *Lehrbuch der Geschichte für die Oberstufe der Mittelschulen. 4. Band. Allgemeine Geschichte der Neuzeit von der Mitte des 19. Jahrhunderts bis zur Gegenwart.* Vienna: Verlag Hölder-Pichler-Tempsky, 1953.

———. *Lehrbuch der Geschichte für die Oberstufe der Mittelschulen. 4. Band. Allgemeine Geschichte der Neuzeit von der Mitte des 19. Jahrhunderts bis zur Gegenwart.* 3rd ed. Revised by Ferdinand Hübner. Vienna: Verlag Hölder-Pichler-Tempsky, 1961.

———. *Lehrbuch der Geschichte für die Oberstufe der Mittelschulen. 4. Band. Allgemeine Geschichte der Neuzeit von der Mitte des 19. Jahrhunderts bis zur Gegenwart.* 4th rev. ed. Revised by Ferdinand Hübner. Vienna: Verlag Hölder-Pichler-Tempsky, 1965.

———. *Lehrbuch der Geschichte für die Oberstufe der Mittelschulen. 4. Band. Allgemeine Geschichte der Neuzeit von der Mitte des 19. Jahrhunderts bis zur Gegenwart.* 5th rev. ed. Revised by Ferdinand Hübner. Vienna: Verlag Hölder-Pichler-Tempsky, 1969.

Hörler, Hans. *Vielgerühmtes Österreich.* Vienna: Österreichischer Bundesverlag, 1966.

Jähnl, Walter, and Franz Stidl. *Das österreichische Gewerbebuch. Band I, Teil 7. Staatsbürgerkunde.* 3rd rev. ed. Vienna: Österreichischer Gewerbeverlag, 1954.

Janetschek, Kurt. *Österreich—wie es war und wurde.* 2nd ed. Mödling: Missionsdruckerei, 1968.

Klein, A., and Heinz Weber. *Einst und Jetzt. Bilder aus der Geschichte. 1. Teil.* Graz: Stiasny Verlag, 1961.

Knarr, Walter, Gustav Otruba, and Hans Mairinger. *Der Mensch im Wandel der Zeiten. III. Teil. Lehrbuch für Geschichte und Sozialkunde. Vom Ausbruch des Ersten Weltkrieges bis zur Gegenwart.* Vienna: Österreichischer Gewerbeverlag, 1968.

Krawarik, Hans, Erlefried Schröckenfuchs, and Brigitte Weiser. *Spuren der Zeit 7.* Vienna: Verlag E. Dorner, 1991.

Kreuzer, Franz. *Ein Leben für Österreich.* Vienna: Verlag für Jugend und Volk, 1969.

Kurfürst, Richard. *Franz Jonas unser Bundespräsident.* Vienna: Verlag für Jugend und Volk, 1969.

Lang, Othmar Franz. *Der Baumeister. Julius Raab—Freund der Jugend.* Vienna: Österreichischer Bundesverlag für Unterricht, Wissenschaft, und Kunst, 1961.

———. *Der Baumeister. Julius Raab—Kämpfer für Österreich.* Vienna: Österreichischer Bundesverlag für Unterricht, Wissenschaft, und Kunst, 1961.

———. *Das war Bundespräsident Dr. Adolf Schärf.* Vienna: Österreichischer Bundesverlag, 1965.

Lang, Othmar Franz, and R. Ritter, *Unser Österreich, 1945–1955. Zum 10. Jahrestag der Wiederherstellung der Unabhängigkeit der Republik Österreich der Schuljugend gewidmet von der Österreichischen Bundesregierung.* Vienna: Österreichischer Bundesverlag, 1955.

Leitner, Helmut. *Zwanzig Jahre Wien.* Vienna: Verlag für Jugend und Volk, 1965.

Leitner, Leo, Theodor Tomandl, and Manfried Welan. *Der Mensch in Gesellschaft und Staat. Lehrbuch der Sozialkunde.* Vienna: Österreichischer Bundesverlag für Unterricht, Wissenschaft und Kunst, 1970.

Malina, Peter, and Gustav Spann. *1938, 1988. Vom Umgang mit unserer Vergangenheit.* Vienna: Bundesministerium für Unterricht, Kunst und Sport, 1988.

Novotny, Alexander, ed. *Österreichisches Lehrbuch für Geschichte und Sozialkunde. Menschen und Völker im Wandel der Zeiten. Ausgabe für die 4. Klasse. Vom Wiener Kongreß bis zur Gegenwart.* 3rd rev. ed. Eisenstadt: E. Rötzer Verlag, 1976.

Oberhammer, Franz. *Tirol in Gegenwart und Vergangenheit. Zeiten, Völker und Kulturen. Länderteil zum Einführungsband für die 1. Klasse der Hauptschulen.* Vienna: Österreichischer Bundesverlag für Unterricht, Wissenschaft und Kunst, 1968.

Oberländer, Erich, and Heinz Strotzka. *Wie? Woher? Warum? 3. Geschichte und Sozialkunde 4. Klasse. Lehrerhandbuch.* Vienna: Österreichischer Bundesverlag, 1991.

Rettinger, Leopold. *Geschichte und Sozialkunde. Vom Wiener Kongreß bis zur Gegenwart. Für die 4. Klasse.* Vienna: Carl Ueberreuter, 1982 [reprint].

Rettinger, Leopold, and Leopold Hohenecker, *Zeitbilder. Geschichte und Sozialkunde 4. Vom Wienerkongreß bis zur Gegenwart.* Vienna: Verlag Carl Ueberreuter, 1982.

Rettinger, Leopold, and Friedrich Weissensteiner. *Zeitbilder. Geschichte und Sozialkunde 4.* 3rd ed. Vienna: Österreichischer Bundesverlag, 1992.

Riccabona, Felix, Karl-Heinz Kopeitka, Klaus Markovits, Norbert Riccabona, and Hermine Schuster. *Geschichte, Sozialkunde, Politische Bildung. 8. Schulstufe. 4. Klasse Hauptschule.* 2nd ed. Linz: Veritas Verlag, 1985.

Schausberger, Norbert, Erich Oberländer, and Heinz Strotzka. *Wie? Woher? Warum? 3. Geschichte und Sozialkunde 4. Klasse.* Vienna: Österreichischer Bundesverlag, 1988.

Scheipl, Josef, et al. *Geschichte und Sozialkunde 4. Arbeitsbuch für die 4. Klasse der Hauptschulen.* Vienna: Ferdinand Hirt, 1981.

Scheipl, Josef, Eric Scheithauer, Werner Tscherne, and Wehl. *Lehrerbegleitheft zu Geschichte und Sozialkunde 4.* Vienna: Ferdinand Hirt, 1981.

Scheucher, Alois, Anton Wald, Hermann Lein, and Eduard Staudinger. *Zeitbilder. Geschichte und Sozialkunde 7. Vom Beginn des Industriezeitalters bis zum Zweiten Weltkrieg.* Vienna: Österreichischer Bundesverlag, 1992.

Schimper, Arnold, Harald Hitz, Herbert Hasenmayer, Senta Göhring, and Manfred Tuschel. *Geschichte miterlebt. Ein Lehr- und Arbeitsbuch für Geschichte und Sozialkunde.* Vienna: Ed. Hölzel, 1989.

Schmidberger, Gustav. *Österreich. Eine Kleine Vaterlandskunde.* Arbeitsblätter für Erdkunde, ed. Adalbert Schwarz, Heft 15. Graz: Verlag Stiasny, 1955.

Schödl, Anna, and Renate Forstner. *SWZ. Sozialkunde, Wirtschaftskunde, Zeitgeschichte.* Vienna: Jugend und Volk, 1974.

———. *SWZ. Sozialkunde, Wirtschaftskunde, Zeitgeschichte.* Vienna: Jugend und Volk, 1985.

Schramm-Scheissl, Heinrich. *Der Baumeister. Julius Raab—Kanzler der Freiheit.* Vienna: Österreichischer Bundesverlag für Unterricht, Wissenschaft, und Kunst, 1961.

Schröckenfuchs, Erlefried, and Georg Lobner. *Spuren der Zeit 8.* Vienna: Verlag E. Dorner, 1992.

Stockinger, Josef, and Ferdinand Prillinger. *Salzburg in Gegenwart und Vergangenheit. Zeiten, Völker und Kulturen. Länderteil zum Einführungsband für die 1. Klasse der Hauptschulen.* Vienna: Österreichischer Bundesverlag für Unterricht, Wissenschaft und Kunst, 1973.

Stöger, L. G., ed. *Geschichte in Tafelbildern und Zusammenfassungen.* Wels: Verlagsbuchhandlung Leitner & Co., 1963.

Tesarek, Anton. *Bundespräsident Dr. Adolf Schärf. Zum Gedenken.* Vienna: Österreichischer Bundesverlag, 1965.

Tscherne, Hannelore, and Sylvia Krampl. *Spuren der Zeit 4.* Vienna: Verlag E. Dorner, 1991.

Tscherne, Werner. *Steiermark in Gegenwart und Vergangenheit. Zeiten, Völker und Kulturen. Länderteil zum Einführungsband für die 1. Klasse der Hauptschulen.* Vienna: Österreichischer Bundesverlag, 1974.

Tscherne, Werner, and Manfred Gartler. *Wege durch die Zeiten 3.* Graz: Leopold Stocker Verlag, 1991 [reprint, 1994].

———. *Wege durch die Zeiten 4.* Graz: Leopold Stocker Verlag, 1992 [reprint 1994].

Tscherne, Werner, Josef Scheipl, Erich Scheithauer, and Robert Machacek. *Geschichte und Sozialkunde. 4. Klasse.* 3rd ed. Vienna: Österreichischer Bundesverlag, 1992.

Tscherne, Werner, Erich Scheithauer, and Manfred Gartler. *Weg durch die Zeiten 4. Arbeits- und Lehrbuch für die Geschichte und Sozialkunde. Für die 8. Klasse der Oberstufe.* Graz: Leopold Stocker Verlag, 1980.

Wachter, Rosa, and Ludwig Welti. *Vorarlberg in Gegenwart und Vergangenheit. Zeiten, Völker und Kulturen. Länderteil zum Einführungsband für die 1. Klasse der Hauptschulen.* Vienna: Hölder-Pichler-Tempsky, 1967.

Wagner, Reinhard. *Sozial-und Wirtschaftskunde. Mit Zeitgeschichte.* Vienna: Verlag Carl Ueberreuter, 1981.

———. *Sozial- und Wirtschaftskunde mit Zeitgeschichte.* Vienna: Jugend und Volk, 1991.

Wald, Anton, Eduard Staudinger, Alois Scheucher, and Josef Scheipl. *Zeitbilder. Geschichte und Sozialkunde 8. Vom Ende es Zweiten Weltkrieges bis heute. Mit "Aktuellem Journal."* Vienna: ÖBV Pädagogischer Verlag, 1993.

Wohanka, Emmy. *Zwanzig Jahre Wien, 1945–1965.* Vienna: Verlag für Jugend und Volk, 1965.

Zens, Klemens. *Schaut Ringsumher. Zum Österreichischen Nationalfeiertag.* Vienna: Österreichischer Bundesverlag, 1966.

Zimmermann, Edmund. *Zum Österreichischen Nationalfeiertag.* Vienna: Verlag für Jugend und Volk, 1966.

Zimmermann, Edmund, and Irmgard Strauß, eds. *Burgenland in Gegenwart und Vergangenheit. Zeiten, Völker und Kulturen. Länderteil zum Einführungsband für die 1. Klasse der Hauptschulen.* Vienna: Österreichischer Bundesverlag, 1969.

Austrian Reading Books, Second Republic, 1945–1996

Almer, Alois, and Ernst A. Ekker. *Leseheft Steiermark.* Vienna: Österreichischer Bundesverlag, 1991.

Arbeitsgemeinschaft, eds. *Die Sonnenuhr. Ein Lesebuch für Schule und Haus. 5.–8. Schulstufe.* 2nd ed. Vienna: Hölder-Pichler-Tempsky, 1961.

———. *Das Leben Liegt vor Uns. Ein Arbeits- und Lesebuch für den Polytechnischen Lehrgang.* Vienna: Österreichischer Bundesverlag für Unterricht, Wissenschaft und Kunst, 1966.

———. *Das Neue Lesebuch für die 4. Schulstufe. Ausgabe für Kärnten.* 3rd rev. ed. Graz: Leykam, Pädagogischer Verlag, 1968.

———. *Das Neue Lesebuch für die 4. Schulstufe. Ausgabe für Vorarlberg.* Graz: Leykam, Pädagogischer Verlag, 1969.

———. *Die Sonnenuhr. Ein Lesebuch für Schule und Haus.* 2nd ed. Vienna: Hölder-Pichler-Tempsky, 1969.

———. *Aus dem Reich der Dichtung. Ein Lesewerk für 10- bis 14-jährige in vier Teilen. Neue Ausgabe, Teil 1.* Vienna: Jugend und Volk, 1974.

———. *Österreich Lesebuch. Band 4.* Vienna: Verlag Carl Ueberreuter, 1983.

———. *Das Neue Lesebuch für die 4. Schulstufe. Ausgabe für Burgenland.* 3rd ed. Vienna: Österreichischer Bundesverlag, 1986.

———. *Österreich Lesebuch Band 3.* Vienna: Verlag Carl Ueberreuter, 1987.

———. *Österreich Lesebuch 4 für die 4. Klasse der Volksschule. Tirol.* Vienna: Bundesverlag-Ueberreuter, 1990.

———. *Horizonte. Lesebuch für den Polytechnischen Lehrgang.* Vienna: Österreichischer Bundesverlag, 1992.

Arbeitsgruppe Sprache als soziales Handeln, eds. *Unter der Oberfläche. Band 4. für die 4. Klasse. Texte. Lese- und Arbeitsbuch für die Hauptschulen und die Unterstufe der allgemeinbildenden höheren Schulen.* Vienna: Österreichischer Bundesverlag, 1977.

———. *Unter der Oberfläche. Band 3. für die 3. Klasse. Texte. Lese- und Arbeitsbuch für die Hauptschulen und die Unterstufe der allgemeinbildenden höheren Schulen.* Vienna: Österreichischer Bundesverlag, 1984.

Auf der Wanderschaft. Kreuz und quer durch Niederösterreich und das Burgenland. Anhang zum österreichischen Lesebuch "Mein Heimatland" für die vierte Schulstufe. 6th ed. Vienna: Vienna: Hölder-Pichler-Tempsky, 1962.

Aus da Hoamat. Anhang zum Lesebuch "Mein Heimatland" für die vierte Schulstufe der oberösterreichischen Volksschulen. 3rd rev. ed. Vienna: Hölder-Pichler-Tempsky, 1953.

Autoren Arbeitsgemeinschaft. *Deutsch Lesen für den Polytechnischen Lehrgang.* Vienna: Bohmann-Verlag, 1982.

Bamberger, Richard, and Inge Auböck. *Lesebuch für die 2. Schulstufe.* Vienna: Österreichischer Bundesverlag, 1992.

Bamberger, Richard, Inge Auböck, and Lehrerarbeitsgemeinschaft. *Texte 4. Band 3. Lesebuch für die Hauptschulen und die Unterstufe der allgemeinbildenden höheren Schulen.* Vienna: Österreichischer Bundesverlag, 1987.

Bamberger, Richard, and Lehrerarbeitsgemeinschaft. *Texte. Band 4. Lesebuch für die Hauptschulen und die Unterstufe der allgemeinbildender höheren Schulen.* Vienna: Österreichischer Bundesverlag für Unterricht, Wissenschaft, und Kunst, 1979.

Bamberger, Richard, and J. Stöger, eds. *Lesebogen für Schule und Heim. Aus der Heimat.* Vienna: Verlag Leinmüller, 1949.

Bauer, Gabriele, Ursula Bugram, Silvia Lukarsch, and Maria Rögner. *Bücherwurm 2. Lesebuch.* Linz: Veritas-Verlag, 1991.

———. *Bücherwurm 3. Lesebuch.* Linz: Veritas-Verlag, 1991.

———. *Bücherwurm 4. Lesebuch.* Linz: Veritas-Verlag, 1991.

Bei uns Daheim. Lesestoffe für die zweite Schulstufe der österreichischen Volksschulen. 24th ed. Vienna: Hölder-Pichler-Tempsky, 1964.

Benedikt, Erich, and Arbeitsgemeinschaft, eds. *Erlebnis Literatur 5. Lesebuch für die 5. Klasse der AHS.* Vienna: Ueberreuter-Bundesverlag, 1990.

———. *Erlebnis Literatur 8. Lesebuch für die 8. Klasse der AHS.* Vienna: Österreichischer Bundesverlag, 1992.

Berghofer, Helene, Ida Brandstätter, Franz Glavantis, Herbert Niklas, Franz Schwarz, and Gertrude Sapper. *Unser schönes Buch. Lesebuch für die 4. Schulstufe. Ausgabe für Burgenland.* Eisenstadt: E. Rötzer Verlag, 1973.

———. *Unser schönes Buch. Lesebuch für die 4. Schulstufe. Ausgabe für Oberösterreich.* Eisenstadt: E. Rötzer Verlag, 1973.

———. *Unser schönes Buch. Lesebuch für die 4. Schulstufe. Ausgabe für Steiermark.* Eisenstadt: E. Rötzer Verlag, 1973.

Berghöfer, Josef, Ida Brandstätter, Leopold Gartner, Franz Glavantis, Herbert Niklas, and Franz Schwarz. *Komm, lies mit mir! Lesebuch für die 2. Schulstufe.* Eisenstadt: E. Rötzer Verlag, 1970.

Berghöfer, Josef, Maximilian Führing, Leopold Gartner, Hans Hörler, and Ernst Löger, eds. *Das Neue Lesebuch für die 4. Schulstufe. Ausgabe für Niederösterreich.* Graz: Leykam, Pädagogischer Verlag, 1964.

Bernt, Hans, Therese Schüssel, and Herta Zeman, eds. *Arbeit—Freiheit—Menschenwürde. Vom Biedermeier zur Gegenwart. Österreich—erlebt und erschaut.* Vienna: Hölder-Pichler-Tempsky, 1961.

Bialonczyk, Emanuel, and Otwald Kropatsch. *Begegnungen. Ein Lesebuch für die Oberstufe der allgemeinbildenden höheren Schulen einschließlich der Musisch-pädagogischen Realgymnasien. 1. Band.* Vienna: Österreichischer Bundesverlag für Unterricht, Wissenschaft und Kunst, 1974.

———. *Begegnungen. Ein Lesebuch. 2. Band.* Vienna: Österreichischer Bundesverlag für Unterricht, Wissenschaft und Kunst, 1978.

Binder, Lucia, Norbert Griesmayer, Wolfram Hiebl, Franz Lux, Jutta Modler, and Peter Schneck. *Hallo Leser! Teil 1. Für die 5. Schulstufe.* Vienna: Jugend und Volk, 1985 [reprint 1993].

Binder, Lucia, Viktor Fadrus, Therese Heckerling, Johann Lenz, Peter Schneck, and Karl Sretenovic, eds. *Aus dem Reich der Dichtung 3. Sachlich—Kritisch—Informativ.* Vienna: Jugend und Volk, 1977.

———. *Aus dem Reich der Dichtung 2.Literatur für dich.* Vienna: Jugend und Volk, 1978.

———. *Aus dem Reich der Dichtung 4. Literatur für dich.* Vienna: Jugend und Volk, 1978.

Bitsche, Josef, Albert Eberle, and Rudolf Hansen. *Heimat und Vaterland. Lesebuch für die Mittelstufe der Vorarlberger Volksschulen (4. und 5. Schulstufe).* Dornbirn: Verlag der Vorarlberger Verlagsanstalt, 1953.

———. *Von heut' und ehedem. Lesebuch für die Oberstufe der Vorarlberger Volksschulen. 6. bis 8. Schulstufe.* Bregenz: J. R. Teutsch, 1953.

Bitsche, Josef, and Rudolf Hansen. *Meine Welt. Lesebuch für die Unterstufe der Vorarlberger Volksschulen (2. und 3. Schulstufe).* Bregenz: Verlag Eugen Ruß, 1955.

Boyer, Ludwig, and Walter Fischer. *Westermann Leselehrgang. Lesebuch 2.* Vienna: Westermann, 1976.

———. *Westermann Leselehrgang. Lesebuch 4.* Vienna: Westermann, 1979.

Boyer, Ludwig, and Cornelius Mayr. *Miteinander Lesen 4.* Vienna: Jugend und Volk, 1989.

Brunner, Wolfgang, Susi Chamrad, Wolfram Hiebl, Monika Kainrath, and Manfred Porsch. *Lebendige Sprache 4.* Vienna: Bohmann Verlag, 1988.

Chamrad, Susi, Edgar Grubich, Wolfram Hiebl, Monika Kainrath, Margit Oswald, and Manfred Porsch. *Lebendige Sprache 3.* 2nd ed. Vienna: Bohmann Verlag, 1988.

Demel, Friedrich, and Wilfrieda Lindner. *Lesebuch für Handelsakademien. I. Band.* Vienna: Hölder-Pichler-Tempsky, 1948.

Die Welt ist Da, Damit Wir Alle Leben. Ein Buch von Krieg und Frieden. Vienna: Hölder-Pichler-Tempsky, 1964.

Donnenberg, Josef, Alfred Bauer, Emanuel Bialonczyk, Eva Salomon, and Wolfgang Wiener. *Lesezeichen 1. Lesebuch für die 5. Klasse der allgemeinbildenden höheren Schulen.* Vienna: Österreichischer Bundesverlag, 1983.

Donnenberg, Josef, Alfred Bauer, Emanuel Bialonczyk, Adelgunde Haselberger, and Eva Salomon. *Lesezeichen 2. Lesebuch.* Vienna: Österreichischer Bundesverlag, 1992.

———. *Lesezeichen 4. Lesebuch.* Vienna: Österreichischer Bundesverlag, 1992.

Dostal, Karl A., ed. *Umgang mit Texten 2. Lesestücke für die zweite Klasse der Hauptschule und der AHS.* Vienna: Verlag Leitner, 1983.

———. *Umgang mit Texten 3. Lesestücke für die dritte Klasse der Hauptschule und der AHS.* Vienna: Verlag Leitner, 1983.

———. *Umgang mit Texten 1. Lesestücke für die erste Klasse der Hauptschule.* Vienna: Verlag Leitner, 1985.

———. *Lesestücke für das Schuljahr.* Vienna: Bundesverlag-Ueberreuter, 1990.

Dostal, Karl A., and Irene Nieszner. *Lesequelle 2. Texte für die zweite Schulstufe.* Vienna: Verlag Leitner, 1984.

Dungl, Waltraud, and Franz Franta. *Kunterbuntes Lesekarussell. 3. Schulstufe.* Eisenstadt: E. Weber Verlag, 1995.

Ebner, Jakob, Siegfried Ferschmann, Dietmar Kaindlstorfer, and Siegfried Wlasaty. *Lesen und Verstehen 1. Ein Lesebuch für die 5. Schulstufe. Neubearbeitung.* Vienna: Österreichischer Bundesverlag, 1989.

———. *Lesen und Verstehen 2. Ein Lesebuch für die 6. Schulstufe. Neubearbeitung.* Vienna: Österreichischer Bundesverlag, 1990.

Ebner, Jakob, Siegfried Ferschmann, Dietmar Kaindlstorfer, Barbara Moser, and Irmelin Stockmair. *Auslesebuch 2. Ein Lesebuch für die 6. Schulstufe.* Vienna: ÖBV Pädagogischer Verlag, 1994.

———. *Auslesebuch 3. Ein Lesebuch für die 7. Schulstufe.* Vienna: ÖBV Pädagogischer Verlag, 1995.

————. *Auslesebuch 4. Ein Lesebuch für die 8. Schulstufe.* Vienna: ÖBV Pädagogischer Verlag, 1995.

Eibl, Leopold. *Bücherwurm 4. Länderteil Niederösterreich.* Linz: Veritas-Verlag, 1991.

Frohes Kinderland. Lesestoffe für die dritte Schulstufe der österreichischen Volksschulen. Vienna: Hölder-Pichler-Tempsky, 1964.

Griesmayer, Norbert, Franz Lux, Jutta Modler, Helga Pinterits, and Peter Schneck. *Hallo Leser! Teil 3. Für die 7. Schulstufe.* Vienna: Jugend und Volk, 1987.

————. *Hallo Leser! Teil 4. Für die 8. Schulstufe.* Vienna: Jugend und Volk, 1988.

Griesmayer, Norbert, Helmuth Lang, Christine Wildner, and Paul Peter Wildner, eds. *Impulse 2. Lese- und Arbeitsbuch.* Vienna: Österreichischer Bundesverlag, 1990.

————. *Impulse 4. Lese- und Arbeitsbuch.* Vienna: Österreichischer Bundesverlag, 1992.

Griesmayer, Norbert, Walter Klaus, Helmuth Lang, Christine Wildner, and Paul Peter Wildner, eds. *Impulse 1. Lese- und Arbeitsbuch.* Vienna: Österreichischer Bundesverlag, 1989.

Gross, Wilhelm, Hermann Lein, and Hermann Schnell, eds. *Um der Menschlichkeit Willen. Wir Schweigen Nicht. Dokumentarische und literarische Aussagen zur Zeitgeschichte.* Vienna: Österreichischer Bundesverlag, 1965.

Harmer, Anna, and Arbeitsgemeinschaft. *Lesebuch für die Lehranstalten für Frauenberufe. 1. Teil.* St. Pölten: Preßverein St. Pölten, 1949.

Harwalik, Adolf, and Anton Afritsch. *Lesebuch für Hauptschulen. 1. Teil.* Graz: Stiasny Verlag, 1961.

————. *Lesebuch für Hauptschulen. 4. Teil.* Graz: Stiasny Verlag, 1961.

Harwalik, Adolf, Adolf März, Walther Pluhar, and Erich Schratzer. *Schaffensfreude, Lebensfreude. Ausgewähltes lebens- uns berufskundliches Lesegut für den Polytechnischen Lehrgang.* Eisenstadt: E. Rötzer Verlag, 1966.

————. [Revised by Christine Ziegler and Hermann Weber]. *Schaffensfreude, Lebensfreude. Ausgewähltes lebens- uns berufskundliches Lesegut für Schüler(innen) des Polytechnischen Lehrganges.* Eisenstadt: E. Rötzer Verlag, 1982.

Heimat und weite Welt. Lesestoffe für die 7. und 8. Schulstufe der österreichischen Volksschulen. 3rd rev. ed. Vienna: Österreichischer Bundesverlag, 1954.

Hörler, Hans, and Hans Müller, eds. *Die Weltenuhr. Ein Lesebuch für Schule und Haus.* Vienna: Österreichischer Bundesverlag für Unterricht, Wissenschaft und Kunst, 1973.

Kefer, Rudolf, Franz Karl Eidenberger, and Rudolf Kluger, eds. *Welt im Wort 4. Ein Lesebuch. Ausgabe für Hauptschulen. 4. Band für die 4. Klasse.* Vienna: Österreichischer Bundesverlag, 1976.

Killinger, Robert, ed. *Lesebuch 2 für die 2. Klasse der Hauptschulen und der allgemeinbildenden höheren Schulen.* Vienna: Österreichischer Bundesverlag, 1991.

————. *Lesebuch 3 für die 3. Klasse der Hauptschulen und der allgemeinbildenden höheren Schulen.* Vienna: Österreichischer Bundesverlag, 1992.

Knotzinger, Franz, and Josef Nemetz. *Heimat Österreich.* Vienna: Vienna: Hölder-Pichler-Tempsky, 1963.

————. *Österreich. Land und Leute.* Vienna: Hölder-Pichler-Tempsky, 1964.

Korger, Friedrich, and Josef Lehrl, eds. *Lesebuch für Mittelschulen. I. Band.* Vienna: Österreichischer Bundesverlag, 1947.

————. *Lesebuch für Mittelschulen. II. Band.* Vienna: Österreichischer Bundesverlag, 1951.

————. *Lesebuch für Mittelschulen. IV. Band.* Vienna: Österreichischer Bundesverlag, 1952.

————. *Lesebuch für Mittelschulen. III. Band.* Vienna: Österreichischer Bundesverlag, 1954.

Kostroun, Susi, and Arbeitsgemeinschaft. *Österreich Lesebuch 4 für die 4. Klasse der Volksschulen. Wien.* Vienna: Bundesverlag-Ueberreuter, 1991.

Kotz, Heinrich. *Frohe Fahrt. Lesebuch für Hauptschulen. Ausgabe für die 4. Klasse an Tiroler Hauptschulen.* Innsbruck: Tyrolia-Verlag, 1972.

Kotz, Heinrich, and Sylvia Del-Pero. *Der Weggenoss. Vierter Band eines Tiroler Lesewerkes.* Innsbruck: Tyrolia Verlag, 1954.

Kotz, Heinrich, and Martin Singer. *Goldene Welt. Lesebuch für Stadtsvolksschulen. Ausgabe für die 3. Klasse an Tiroler Stadtvolksschulen.* Innsbruck: Tyrolia-Verlag, 1968.

——. *Goldene Welt. Lesebuch für Stadtsvolksschulen. Ausgabe für die 2. Klasse an Tiroler Stadtvolksschulen.* Innsbruck: Tyrolia-Verlag, 1969.

Kotz, Heinrich, Emil Ladstätter, and Walter Mahringer. *Frohe Fahrt. Lesebuch für Hauptschulen. Ausgabe für die 2. Klasse an Tiroler Hauptschulen.* Innsbruck: Tyrolia-Verlag, 1969.

——. *Frohe Fahrt. Lesebuch für Hauptschulen. Ausgabe für die 3. Klasse an Tiroler Hauptschulen.* Innsbruck: Tyrolia-Verlag, 1970.

Kotz, Heinrich, and Lehrerarbeitsgemeinschaft. *Tirolerland. Anhang zum Lesebuch "Mein Heimatland" für die vierte Schulstufe der Tiroler Volksschulen.* Vienna: Hölder-Pichler-Tempsky, 1949.

——. *Junge Saat. Lesebuch für Tiroler Volksschulen. Band I (2. und 3. Schulstufe).* Innsbruck: Tyrolia Verlag, 1952.

——. *Junge Saat. Lesebuch für Tiroler Volksschulen. Band II (4. und 5. Schulstufe).* Innsbruck: Tyrolia Verlag, 1952.

——. *Junge Saat. Lesebuch für Tiroler Volksschulen. Band III (6. bis 8. Schulstufe).* Innsbruck: Tyrolia Verlag, 1953.

——. *Junge Saat. Lesebuch für Tiroler Volksschulen. Ausgabe B für Stadtschulen für die 2. Klasse.* Innsbruck: Tyrolia Verlag, 1960.

——. *Junge Saat. Lesebuch für Tiroler Volksschulen. Ausgabe B für Stadtschulen für die 3. Klasse.* Innsbruck: Tyrolia Verlag, 1960.

Kracher, Silvana. *Das Dorner Lesebuch 4. Wien, für die 4. Klasse der Volksschulen.* Vienna: E. Dorner, 1994.

Lampée-Baumgartner, Traute, and Josef Paulis. *Bücherwurm. Länderteil Wien.* Linz: Veritas-Verlag, 1994.

Langer, Gertraude, and Arbeitsgemeinschaft. *Österreichisches Lesebuch. Lesebuch für die 4. Klasse der Volksschule.* Wolfsberg: Verlag Ernst Ploetz, 1984.

Lanzelsdorfer, Friederike, and Ernst Pacolt, eds. *Unser Lesehaus 2.* Vienna: Jugend und Volk, 1975.

——. *Unser Lesehaus 4. Bei uns und anderswo.* Vienna: Jugend und Volk, 1979.

——. *Bei uns und anderswo.* Vienna: Jugend und Volk, 1982.

Larcher, Agnes, Dietmar Larcher, Ines Morocutti, Fred Reumüller, and Ferdinand Stefan (Arbeitsgruppe Sprache als soziales Handeln), eds. *Strickleiter 3. Band 3 für die Hauptschulen und die Unterstufe der allgemeinbildenden höheren Schulen.* Vienna: Österreichischer Bundesverlag, 1991.

——. *Strickleiter 2. Band 2 für die Hauptschulen und die Unterstufe der allgemeinbildenden höheren Schulen.* Vienna: Österreichischer Bundesverlag, 1992.

Leherarbeitsgemeinschaft beim Landesschulrat Salzburg. *Unser Lesebuch. 4. Schulstufe. Heimat Salzburg.* Salzburg: Otto Müller Verlag, 1954.

——. *Unser Lesebuch. 5. Schulstufe. Vaterland Österreich.* Salzburg: Otto Müller Verlag, 1955.

——. *Unser Lesebuch. 6.-8. Schulstufe. Heimat und Welt.* Salzburg: Otto Müller Verlag, 1956.

——. *Unser Lesebuch. 3. Schulstufe. Daheim in Dorf und Stadt.* Salzburg: Otto Müller Verlag, 1957.

——. *Unser Lesebuch. 4. Klasse Hauptschule. Du und die Gemeinschaft.* Salzburg: Otto Müller Verlag, 1960.

Mechler-Schönach, Christine. *Strickleiter 5. Band 5. Lesebuch für den Polytechnischen Lehrgang.* Vienna: Jugend und Volk, 1991.

Mein Heimatland. Lesestoffe für die vierte Schulstufe der österreichischen Volksschulen. Vienna: Hölder-Pichler-Tempsky, 1947.

Meissel, Wilhelm. *Leseheft Burgenland.* Vienna: Österreichischer Bundesverlag, 1992.

Österreich Lesebuch 3 für die 3. Klasse der Volksschulen. Vienna: Verlag Karl Ueberreuter, 1985.

Pramper, Wolfgang, Helmut Hammerschmid, and Gertrud Neumann. *Lesestunde. Lesebuch für die 6. Schulstufe. Teil A.* Linz: Veritas-Verlag, 1989.

Pramper, Wolfgang, Wilma Emerich, Helmut Hammerschmid, and Erich Neuwirth. *Lesestunde. Lesebuch für die 8. Schulstufe. Teil A.* Linz: Veritas-Verlag, 1989.

Pramper, Wolfgang, Helmut Hammerschmid, Gertrud Neumann, and Erich Neuwirth. *Lesestunde. Lesebuch für die 5. Schulstufe. Teil A.* Linz: Veritas-Verlag, 1990.

Ruzicka, Ruth. *Das Dorner Lesebuch 3 für die 3. Klasse der Volksschulen.* Vienna: E. Dorner, 1994.

Sanz, Wilhelm. *Aus dem Reich der Dichtung. Vom Naturalismus bis zur Gegenwart.* Vienna: Österreichischer Bundesverlag, 1971.

Schönach, Christine, Almud Greiter, Hansjörg Gutweniger, Evi Laimer, Hans-Jürgen Mechler, and Bernhard Rathmayer (Arbeitsgruppe "Sprache als soziales Handeln"), eds. *Strickleiter 4. Band 4 für die 4. Klasse. Lesebuch für die Hauptschulen und die Unterstufe der allgemeinbildenden höheren Schulen.* Vienna: Österreichischer Bundesverlag, 1990.

Sklenitzka, Franz S. *Lesefuchs 2.* Vienna: Jugend und Volk, 1995.

Sperandio, Hans. *Leseheft Vorarlberg.* Vienna: Österreichischer Bundesverlag, 1992.

Steirische Heimat. Anhang zum Lesebuch "Mein Heimatland" für die vierte Schulstufe der steirischen Volksschulen. 2nd ed. Vienna: Hölder-Pichler-Tempsky, 1951.

Tramer-Soeser, Helene. *Die Valtbauernkinder. Anhang zum Lesebuch "Mein Heimatland" für die vierte Schulstufe der Salzburger Volksschulen.* Vienna: Hölder-Pichler-Tempsky, 1947.

Türk, Heinz. *Bücherwurm 4. Länderteil Kärnten.* Linz: Veritas-Verlag, 1993.

Viertes Lesebuch. Ausgabe für das Bundesland Kärnten. Vienna: Hölder-Pichler-Tempsky, 1954.

Viertes Lesebuch. Ausgabe für das Bundesland Steiermark. 3rd rev. ed. Vienna: Hölder-Pichler-Tempsky, 1954.

Austrian School Yearbooks and Commemorative Programs *(Festschriften)*, National Socialist Period, 1938–1945

88. Jahresbericht des Obergymnasiums der Benediktiner zu Kremsmünster. Schuljahr 1938. Kremsmünster, 1938.

Jahresbericht 1937–38 der Handelsakademie und der kaufm. Wirtschaftsschule in Klagenfurt. Klagenfurt, 1938.

Jahresbericht des Oberlyzeums und Realgymnasiums für Mädchen der Gesellschaft für erweiterte Frauenbildung in Baden b. Wien, Frauengasse 3. Baden, 1938.

Jahresbericht des Staatsgymnasiums in Krems a. d. D. am Schuljahres 1937/8. Krems, 1938.

Staats-Realgymnasium in Laa a.d. Thaya (1911/12–1937/38). XI Jahresbericht über die Schuljahre 1936/37 und 1937/38. Laa a.d. Thaya, 1938.

Unser Heim. Blätter der Staatserziehungsanstalt Traiskirchen. Heimjahr 1937/38. 13. Jahr. 6. Folge. Traiskirchen, 1938.

Austrian School Yearbooks and Commemorative Programs *(Festschriften)*, Austrian Second Republic, 1945–1996

(Listed by Province)

Burgenland

40. Jahre Mittelschule in Fürstenfeld, 1909/19–1949/50. 20. Jahresbericht des Bundesgymnasiums in Fürstenfeld (zugleich Festschrift). Fürstenfeld, 1950.

75. Jahre Hauptschule für Knaben und Mädchen in Eisenstadt. Eisenstadt, 1956.

83., 84. Jahresbericht der Hauptschule für Knaben und Mädchen in Eisenstadt '63/64, '64/65. Eisenstadt, 1965.

Bundes-Realgymnasium in Eisenstadt. Jahresbericht über das Schuljahr 1949/50. Eisenstadt, 1949.

Bundes-Realgymnasium in Eisenstadt. Jahresbericht über das Schuljahr 1950/51. Eisenstadt, 1951.

Hauptschule für Knaben und Mädchen in Eisenstadt. 73. Jahresbericht, Schuljahr 1953/54. Eisenstadt, 1954.

XXXV. Jahresbericht des Bundesgymnasiums und Bundesrealgymnasiums Fürstenfeld über das Schuljahr 1964/65. Fürstenfeld, 1965.

Carinthia

1945–1946 Jahresbericht der Handelsakademie und der kaufm. Wirtschaftsschule in Klagenfurt. Klagenfurt, 1946.

Bundesgymnasium und Bundesrealgymnasium, 9020 Klagenfurt, Mössingerstrasse 25. Bericht über das Schuljahr 1991/92. Klagenfurt, 1992.

Bundesgymnasium und Bundesrealgymnasium, 9020 Klagenfurt, Mössingerstrasse 25. Bericht über das Schuljahr 1994/95. Klagenfurt, 1995.

Bundes-Oberstufenrealgymnasium Wolfsberg. Jahresbericht über das Schuljahr 1986/87. Wolfsberg, 1987.

Bundes-Oberstufenrealgymnasium Wolfsberg. Jahresbericht über das Schuljahr 1989/90. Wolfsberg, 1990.

Bundes-Oberstufenrealgymnasium Wolfsberg. Jahresbericht über das Schuljahr 1990/91. Wolfsberg, 1991.

Bundes-Oberstufenrealgymnasium Wolfsberg. Jahresbericht über das Schuljahr 1992/93. Wolfsberg, 1993.

Bundes-Oberstufenrealgymnasium Wolfsberg. Jahresbericht über das Schuljahr 1993/94. Wolfsberg, 1994.

Jahresbericht. 1. Bundesgymnasium Klagenfurt. Schuljahr 1969/70. Klagenfurt, 1970.

Jahresbericht Bundesgymnasium Klagenfurt, Völkermarkter Ring 27. Schuljahr 1987/88. Klagenfurt, 1988.

Jahresbericht Bundesgymnasium Klagenfurt, Völkermarkter Ring 27. Schuljahr 1988/89. Klagenfurt, 1989.

Lower Austria

103. Jahresbericht des Bundes-gymnasiums und des Bundes-Realgymnasiums in Stockerau. Stockerau, 1973.

Achtundvierzigster Jahresbericht vom Bundesgymnasium Amstetten herausgegeben am Schlusse des Schuljahres 1985/86. Amstetten, 1986.

Bundesgymnasium und -Realgymnasium in Hollabrunn. 83. Jahresbericht 1960/61. Hollabrunn, 1961.

Bundesgymnasium und -Realgymnasium in Hollabrunn. 84. Jahresbericht 1961/62. Hollabrunn, 1962.

Bundesgymnasium und Bundesrealgymnasium Wieselburg. Jahresbericht 1994/95. Wieselburg, 1995.

Bundeshandelsakademie, Bundeshandelsschule Krems an der Donau. Jahresbericht Schuljahr 1965/66. Krems, 1966.

Bundesrealgymnasium in Laa a.d. Thaya. XV. Jahresbericht. Städt. Wirtschaftsschule in Laa a.d. Thaya. V. Jahresbericht. Schuljahr 1945–46. Laa an der Thaya, 1946.

Bundesrealgymnasium Mödling, Franz Keimgasse 3. Jahresbericht 1955/56. 59. Schuljahr. Mödling, 1956.

Festschrift und 50. Jahresbericht, herausgegeben vom Bundesgymnasium Amstetten am Schlusse des Schuljahres 1987/88. Amstetten, 1988.

Festschrift und Jahresbericht im 125. Bestandsjahr des BG & GRG Baden, Biondekgasse, 1987/88. Baden, 1988.

Fünfundfünfzigster Jahresbericht vom Bundesgymnasium Amstetten herausgegeben am Schlusse des Schuljahres 1992/93. Amstetten, 1993.

GRC, WIKU 23. 6. Jahresbericht, 1992/93. Krems, 1993.

Höhere Technische Landes- Lehr- und Versuchanstalt in Waidhofen a.d. Ybbs. Bericht über das Schuljahr 1965/1966. Waidhofen a.d. Ybbs, 1966.

Jahresbericht des Bundesgymnasiums Krems am Schlusse des Schuljahres 1987/88. Krems, 1988.

Jahresbericht des Bundesgymnasiums Krems am Schlusse des Schuljahres 1988/89. Krems, 1989.

Siebenundfünfzigster Jahresbericht vom Bundesgymnasium Amstetten herausgegeben am Schlusse des Schuljahres 1994/95. Amstetten, 1995.

Städtische Handelsschule Baden mit Öffentlichkeitsrecht für Knaben und Mädchen. Jahresbericht, Schuljahr 1954/55. Baden, 1955.

Salzburg

Bundes-Gymnasium Gmunden. 51. Jahresbericht, Schuljahr 1964/64. Gmunden, 1965.

Jahresbericht des Akademischen Gymnasiums Salzburg. Schuljahr 1982/83. Salzburg, 1983.

Jahresbericht des Akademischen Gymnasiums Salzburg. Schuljahr 1984/85. Salzburg, 1985.

Jahresbericht des Akademischen Gymnasiums Salzburg. Schuljahr 1987/88. Salzburg, 1988.

Jahresbericht des Akademischen Gymnasiums Salzburg. Schuljahr 1988/89. Salzburg, 1989.

Jahresbericht des Bundesgymnasiums III Salzburg. Musisches Gymnasium Neusprachliches Gymnasium, Franz-Josef-Kai 41, für das Schuljahr 1981/82. Salzburg, 1982.

Jahresbericht des Bundesgymnasiums III Salzburg. Musisches Gymnasium Neusprachliches Gymnasium, Franz-Josef-Kai 41, für das Schuljahr 1984/85. Salzburg, 1985.

Jahresbericht des Bundesgymnasiums III Salzburg. Musisches Gymnasium Neusprachliches Gymnasium, Franz-Josef-Kai 41, für das Schuljahr 1985/86. Salzburg, 1986.

Jahresbericht des Bundesgymnasiums III Salzburg. Musisches Gymnasium Neusprachliches Gymnasium, Franz-Josef-Kai 41, für das Schuljahr 1986/87. Salzburg, 1987.

Jahresbericht des Bundesgymnasiums III Salzburg. Musisches Gymnasium Neusprachliches Gymnasium, Franz-Josef-Kai 41, für das Schuljahr 1993/94. Salzburg, 1994.

Jahresbericht des Bundesgymnasiums III Salzburg. Musisches Gymnasium Neusprachliches Gymnasium, Franz-Josef-Kai 41, für das Schuljahr 1994/95. Salzburg, 1995.

Jahresbericht des Bundesgymnasiums III Salzburg. Musisches Gymnasium Neusprachliches Gymnasium, Haunspergstrasse 77, für das Schuljahr 1988/89. Salzburg, 1989.

Styria

20. Jahresbericht des Bundes-Oberstufenrealgymnasiums mit Gewerbe-BORG, 1988/89. Bad Radkersberg, 1989.

25. Jahresbericht des Bundes-Oberstufenrealgymnasiums mit Gewerbe-BORG, 1993/94. Bad Radkersburg, 1994.

Bundesgymnasium für Mädchen in Graz. Jahresbericht über das Schuljahr 1963/64. Graz, 1964.

Bundesgymnasium für Mädchen in Graz. Jahresbericht über das Schuljahr 1964/65. Graz, 1965.

Bundesgymnasium Graz, Carnerigasse 30–32. Bericht über das Schuljahr 1969/70. Graz, 1970.

Bundesgymnasium und Bundesrealgymnasium Leibnitz. Jahresbericht 1985/86. Leibnitz, 1986.

Bundesrealgymnasium und -Realschule Bruck a.d. Mur. Festbericht Anlässlich des 50 Jährigen Bestandes der Anstalt (1907–1957). Bruck an der Mur, 1958.

Festschrift des B.R.G. Leoben, 1962. aus Anlass der 100 Jahrfeier und zur Eröffnung des neuen Schulgebäudes. Leoben, 1962.

Jahresbericht Bundesgymnasium und Bundesrealgymnasium Leibnitz. Expositur Radkersburg Musisch-pädagogisches Realgymnasium, 1968/69. Leibnitz, 1969.

Jahresbericht des Akademischen Gymnasiums in Graz, 1987/88. Graz, 1988.

Jahresbericht des Stiftsgymnasiums Admont. Schuljahr 1985/86. Stiftsgymnasium der Benediktiner in Admont. Admont, 1986.

LII. (LXXXVIII.) Jahresbericht des Bundesrealgymnasiums in Leoben, 1949/50. Leoben, 1950.

LXXXVIII/124 Jahresbericht des Bundesgymnasiums und Bundesrealgymnasiums Leoben, 1985/86. Leoben, 1986.

LXXXX/126 Jahresbericht des Bundesgymnasiums und Bundesrealgymnasiums Leoben, 1987/88. Leoben, 1988.

LXXXXII/128 Jahresbericht des Bundesgymnasiums und Bundesrealgymnasiums in Leoben, 1989/90. Leoben, 1990.

Tyrol

Bundesgymnasium Innsbruck. Jahresbericht 1963/64. Innsbruck, 1964.

Bundesgymnasium und 1. Bundesrealgymnasium in Innsbruck. Jahresbericht 1956/57. Innsbruck, 1957.

Bundesgymnasium und Bundesrealgymnasium Innsbruck—Sillgasse. 78. Jahresbericht über das Schuljahr 1987/88. Innsbruck, 1988.

Bundesgymnasium und Bundesrealgymnasium Innsbruck—Sillgasse. 79. Jahresbericht über das Schuljahr 1988/89. Innsbruck, 1989.

Bundesgymnasium und Bundesrealgymnasium Innsbruck—Sillgasse. 84. Jahresbericht über das Schuljahr 1993/94. Innsbruck, 1994.

Bundesgymnasium und Bundesrealgymnasium Innsbruck—Sillgasse. 85. Jahresbericht über das Schuljahr 1994/95. Innsbruck, 1995.

Bundesgymnasium und Bundesrealgymnasium Lienz. Jahresbericht 1976/77. Lienz, 1977.

Bundesgymnasium und Bundesrealgymnasium Lienz. Jahresbericht 1977/78. Lienz, 1978.

Bundesgymnasium und Bundesrealgymnasium Lienz. Jahresbericht 1979/80. Lienz, 1980.

Bundesgymnasium und Bundesrealgymnasium Lienz. Jahresbericht 1982/83. Lienz, 1983.

Bundesgymnasium und Bundesrealgymnasium Lienz. Jahresbericht 1984/85. Lienz, 1985.

Bundesgymnasium und Bundesrealgymnasium Lienz. Jahresbericht 1987/88. Lienz, 1988.

Bundesrealgymnasium Lienz. Jahresbericht 1961/62. Lienz, 1962.

Festschrift zum 400 jährigen Jubiläum des Gymnasiums Innsbruck. Innsbruck, 1962.

Jahresbericht 1986/87 Bundesgymnasium St. Johann in Tirol. St. Johann, 1987.

Jahresbericht 1991/92 Bundesgymnasium und Bundes-Oberstufenrealgymnasium St. Johann in Tirol. St. Johann, 1992.

Jahresbericht des Bundesrealgymnasium Reutte, 1990/91. Reutte, 1991.

Jahresbericht des Bundesrealgymnasium Reutte, 1992/93. Reutte, 1993.

Upper Austria

7. Jahresbericht, Bundesrealgymnasium Schärding. Schuljahr 1954/55, 1955/1956. Schärding, 1956.

16. Jahresbericht 1975/76 des Bundesgymnasiums und Bundesrealgymnasiums, Braunau am Inn. Braunau am Inn, 1976.

16. Jahresbericht der Hauptschule Lenzing. Schuljahr 1964/65. Lenzing, 1965.

89. Jahresbericht des Obergymnasiums der Benediktiner zu Kremsmünster, Schuljahr 1946. Kremsmünster, 1946.

104. Jahresbericht, Schuljahr 1961. Öffentl. Gymnasium der Benediktiner zu Kremsmünster. Kremsmünster, 1961.

Achter Jahresbericht. Handelsakademie und Handelsschule Steyr, 1994/95. Steyr, 1995.

Bundesgymnasium für Mädchen und Wirtschaftskundliches Bundesrealgymnasium für Mädchen, Linz. 79. Jahresbericht 1967/68. Linz, 1968.

Bundesgymnasium und Bundesrealgymnasium Bad Ischl. 9. Jahresbericht 1980/81. Bad Ischl, 1981.

Bundesgymnasium und Bundesrealgymnasium Bad Ischl. 10. Jahresbericht 1981/82. Bad Ischl, 1982.

Bundesgymnasium und Bundesrealgymnasium Bad Ischl. 13. Jahresbericht 1984/85. Bad Ischl, 1985.

Bundesgymnasium und Bundesrealgymnasium Bad Ischl. 15. Jahresbericht 1986/87. Bad Ischl, 1987.

Bundesgymnasium und Bundesrealgymnasium Bad Ischl. 16. Jahresbericht 1987/88. Bad Ischl, 1988.

Bundeshandelsakademie, Bundeshandelsschule Braunau am Inn. Jahresbericht 1992/93. Braunau am Inn, 1993.

Bundeshandelsakademie, Bundeshandelsschule Braunau am Inn. Jahresbericht 1994/95. Braunau am Inn, 1995.

Bundesrealgymnasium Steyr. 79. Jahresbericht, Schuljahr 1961/1962. Steyr, 1962.

Bundesrealgymnasium Steyr. 105. Jahresbericht, Schuljahr 1987/88. Steyr, 1988.

Bundesrealgymnasium Steyr. 112. Jahresbericht, Schuljahr 1994/95. Steyr, 1995.

Erster Jahresbericht. Handelsakademie und Handelsschule Steyr, 1987/88. Steyr, 1988.

Freinberger Stimmen. 44. Jahrgang. 1. Heft. Dezember 1973. Linz, 1973.

Fünfter Jahresbericht. Handelsakademie und Handelsschule Steyr, 1991/92 Steyr, 1992.

HTL Braunau, Jahresbericht 1978/79. Braunau, 1979.

Jahres-Bericht der Städtischen Handelsschule in Braunau am Inn, Schuljahr 1955/56. Braunau am Inn, 1956.

Öffentliches Stiftsgymnasium Kremsmünster. 128. Jahresbericht, 1985. Kremsmünster, 1985.

Öffentliches Stiftsgymnasium Kremsmünster. 138. Jahresbericht, 1995. Kremsmünster, 1995.

Siebter Jahresbericht. Handelsakademie und Handelsschule Steyr, 1993/94. Steyr, 1994.

Zweites Bundesgymnasium Linz, 1969–1970. Linz, 1970.

Vienna

1889–1989. Festschrift. Höhere Technische Bundeslehranstalt, Wien 10. Jahresbericht 1988/89. Vienna, 1989.

AKG Präsentation des Akademischen Gymnasiums Wien, 1979/80. Vienna, 1980.

Brigittenauer Bundesrealgymnasium, 1962/63. Vienna, 1963.

Bundesgymnasium Wien VIII (Piaristengymnasium). Jahresbericht 1966/67. Vienna, 1967.

Bundesrealgymnasium und Bundesoberstufenrealgymnasium, Wien 22. Achter Jahresbericht mit Beiträgen von Schülern, Lehrern, Eltern und Absolventen. Schuljahr 1987/88. Vienna, 1988.

Bundesstaatliche Arbeitermittelschule Wien, Bericht über das Schuljahr 1962/63. Vienna, 1963.

Ein Bericht des Akademischen Gymnasiums Wien I., 1986/87. Vienna, 1987.

Ein Bericht des Akademischen Gymnasiums Wien I., 1987/88. Vienna, 1988.

Ein Bericht des Akademischen Gymnasiums Wien I., 1988/89. Vienna, 1989.

GRGWIKU 23. 2. Jahresbericht, 1988/89. Vienna, 1989.

Höhere Gewerbliche Bundeslehranstalt für Tourismus und Höhere Bundeslehranstalt für Wirtschaftliche Berufe. 1130 Wien. Jahresbericht 1994/95. Vienna, 1995.

Höhere Technische Bundeslehranstalt, Wien 10. Jahresbericht 1991/92. Vienna, 1991.

Höhere Technische Bundeslehranstalt, Wien 10. Jahresbericht 1994/95. Vienna, 1995.

Jahresbericht 1959/60. Bundesrealgymnasium für Mädchen, Wien XVIII. Vienna, 1960.

Jahresbericht 1964/1965. Bundesrealgymnasium, Henriettenplatz, Wien XV. Vienna, 1965.

Jahresbericht 1965/66. Bundesgymnasium und -Realgymnasium Simmering, Wien XI. Vienna, 1966.

Jahresbericht des Bundesgymnasiums und des Bundesrealgymnasiums, Wien XV, Schuljahr 1964/64. Vienna, 1965.

Jahresbericht des Bundesrealgymnasiums Wien XVI. über das Schuljahr 1949/50. Vienna, 1950.

Sechsundachtzigster Jahresbericht des Brigittenauer Bundesrealgymnasiums, 1960/61. Vienna, 1961.

Währinger Gymnasium. Jahresbericht 1958–1959. Vienna, 1959.

Währinger Gymnasium. Jahresbericht 1960/61. Vienna, 1961.

Wiedner Gymnasium. Jahresbericht 1994. Vienna, 1994.

Vorarlberg

Bundesgymnasium Bregenz. Jahresbericht, Schuljahr 1971/1972. Bregenz, 1972.

Bundesgymnasium Bregenz. Jahresbericht, Schuljahr 1972/1973. Bregenz, 1973.

Bundesgymnasium Bregenz. Jahresbericht, Schuljahr 1973–74. Bregenz, 1974.

Bundesgymnasium Bregenz. Jahresbericht, Schuljahr 1984/85. Bregenz, 1985.

Bundesgymnasium und Bundesrealgymnasium Bludenz. Jahresbericht, Schuljahr 1968/69. Bludenz, 1969.

Mehrerauer Grüße zugleich Jahresbericht des Gymnasiums Mehrerau, 1991/92. Neue Folge/Heft 68. Mehrerau, 1992.

Lesson Plans, Austrian Second Republic, 1945–1996

(In some cases, lesson plans are also printed in the *Verordnungsblatt für den Dienstbereich des Bundesministeriums für Unterricht.*)

Lang, Ludwig, ed. *Kommentar zum Österreichischen Hauptschullehrplan.* Vienna: Österreichischer Bundesverlag, 1966.

Lehrplan der Hauptschule. 5th ed. Vienna: Österreichischer Bundesverlag, 1974.

Lehrplan der Hauptschule. Vienna: Österreichischer Bundesverlag, 1979.

Lehrplan des Polytechnischen Lehrganges. Vienna: Österreichischer Bundesverlag für Unterricht, Wissenschaft und Kunst, 1976.

Lehrplan des Polytechnischen Lehrganges. Vienna: Österreichischer Bundesverlag, 1967.

Lehrplan des Polytechnischen Lehrganges. Vienna: Österreichischer Bundesverlag, 1981.

Lehrpläne der allgemeinbildenden höheren Schulen. 2. Band. Vienna: Österreichischer Bundesverlag, 1979.

Lehrpläne der allgemeinbildenden höheren Schulen. I. Band. Vienna: Österreichischer Bundesverlag, 1984.

Lehrpläne für die Hauptschulen. With a foreword by Viktor Fadrus. Vienna: Verlag für Jugend und Volk, 1947.

Lehrplan-Service. *Deutsch AHS Kommentarheft 1.* Vienna: Österreichischer Bundesverlag, 1985.

———. *Geschichte und Sozialkunde (HS und AHS) Kommentarheft 1.* Vienna: Österreichischer Bundesverlag, 1985.

———. *Deutsch AHS Kommentarheft 2.* Vienna: Österreichischer Bundesverlag, 1988.

———. *Geschichte und Sozialkunde (HS und AHS) Kommentarheft 2.* Vienna: Österreichischer Bundesverlag, 1988.

———. *Lehrplan des Polytechnischen Lehrganges. Vollständige, mit Anmerkungen und Ergänzungen versehene Ausgabe.* Vienna: Österreichischer Bundesverlag, 1989.

———. *Deutsch AHS-Oberstufe Kommentar.* Vienna: Österreichischer Bundesverlag, 1990.

———. *Geschichte und Sozialkunde. Kommentar Oberstufe.* Vienna: Österreichischer Bundesverlag, 1990.

———. *Kommentar zum Lehrplan der Volksschule.* Vienna: ÖBV Pädagogischer Verlag, 1995.

Münster, Gerhard, ed. *Schul-Lehrpläne. Lehrplan für die Allgemeinbildende Höhere Schule-AHS, Gymnasium, Realgymnasium, Wirtschaftskundliches Realgymnasium. 1. bis 4. Klasse (Unterstufe) in der Fassung der Lehrplanreform 1993 bis 1996 (weitgehend ident mit der Hauptschule). 5. bis 8. Klasse (Oberstufe).* Kodex des Österreichischen Rechts, Werner Doralt, ed. Vienna: ORAC, 1996.

Provisorische Lehrpläne für die Hauptschulen. Amtliche Ausgabe. Vienna: Österreichischer Bundesverlag, 1947.

Provisorische Lehrpläne für die Hauptschulen. 2nd rev. ed. Official ed. Vienna: Österreichischer Bundesverlag, 1948.

Provisorische Lehrpläne für die Mittelschulen. Vienna: Österreichischer Bundesverlag, 1946.

Spreitzer, Hans. *Kommentar zum Lehrplan des Polytechnischen Lehrganges.* Vienna: Österreichischer Bundesverlag, 1970.

Austrian and German Government Documents and Publications, Anschluss and Nazi Periods, 1938–1945

Verordnungsblatt für den Dienstbereich des Ministeriums für innere und kulturelle Angelegenheiten. Abteilung IV: Erziehung, Kultus und Volksbildung.

Verordnungsblatt für den Dienstbereich des Österreichischen Unterrichtsministeriums, bzw. des Ministeriums für innere und kulturelle Angelegenheiten, Abt. IV: Erziehung, Kultus, und Volksbildung.

Austrian Government Documents and Publications, Second Republic, 1945–1996

Austrian Information. [Newsletter]

Austrian State Printing House. *Justice for Austria! Red-White-Red-Book. Descriptions, Documents and Proofs to the Antecedents and History of the Occupation of Austria (from Official Sources) First Part.* Vienna: Austrian State Printing House, 1947.

Bundesministerium für Finanzen und Bundesministerium für Unterricht und Kunst. *10 Jahre Schulbuchaktion.* Graz: Leykam Universitätsbuchdruckerei, 1982.

Bundesministerium für Justiz. *Volksgerichtsbarkeit und Verfolgung von Nationalsozialistischen Gewaltverbrechen in Österreich. Eine Dokumentation.* 2nd ed. Vienna: Bundesministerium für Justiz, 1987.

Bundesministerium für Unterricht, ed. *Freiheit für Österreich. Dokumente.* Vienna: Österreichischer Bundesverlag, 1955.

———. *Österreich frei. Dokumente II.* Vienna: Österreichischer Bundesverlag, 1956.

Federal Press Service. *Austria Documentation: Resistance and Persecution in Austria, 1938–1945.* Vienna: Federal Press Service, 1988.

———. *Austria Documentation: The Austrian Educational System.* Vienna: Federal Press Service, 1990.

———. *Austria: Facts and Figures.* Vienna: Federal Press Service, 1993.

Marboe, Ernst. *The Book of Austria.* Trans. G. E. R. Gedye. Vienna: Österreichische Staatsdruckerei, 1948.

———. *The Book of Austria.* Rev. ed. Trans. Gordon Shepherd, Richard Rickett, and Emmy Molles. Vienna: Österreichische Staatsdruckerei, 1969.

Österreichische Staatsdruckerei. *Gerechtigkeit für Österreich! Rot-Weiss-Rot-Buch. Darstellungen, Dokumente und Nachweise zur Vorgeschichte und Geschichte der Okkupation Österreichs (Nach Amtlichen Quellen). Erster Teil.* Vienna: Österreichische Staatsdruckerei, 1946.

———. *The Case of South Tyrol.* Vienna: Österreichische Staatsdruckerei, 1960.

Österreichischer Akademischer Austauschdienst. *Kooperationen. Austria's Cooperation with the United States.* [Published periodically, n.d.]

Verordnungsblatt für den Dienstbereich des Bundesministeriums für Unterricht. [Issued monthly]

Weinberg, Gerhard L. *Der Gewaltsame Anschluss 1938. Die deutsche Außenpolitik und Österreich*. Vienna: Bundespressedienst, 1988.

U.S. Documents

Committee on Foreign Relations, United States Senate. *Documents on Germany, 1944–1970*. Washington, D.C.: Government Printing Office, 1971.

Military Government Austria: Report of the United States Commissioner, 1945–1950.

Periodicals and Newspapers

Der Spiegel [Germany]
Der Standard [Austria]
Die Zeit [Germany]
Falter [Austria]
Neue Kronen Zeitung [Austria]
Politische Bildung und Zeitschrift für Erwachsenenbildung [Austria]
Profil [Austria]
Stern [Germany]
The Economist [Great Britain]

Literature and Literary Criticism

Bachmann, Ingeborg. *Das Dreissigste Jahr*. [Short stories] Munich: R. Piper & Co, 1961.

Bernhard, Thomas. *Heldenplatz*. Frankfurt am Main: Suhrkamp, 1988.

Boa, Elizabeth, and Rachel Palfreyman. *Heimat, a German Dream: Regional Loyalties and National Identity in German Culture, 1890–1990*. Oxford Studies in Modern European Culture, ed. Elizabeth Fallaize, Robin Fiddian, and Katrin Kohl. New York: Oxford University Press, 2000.

Daviau, Donald G., ed. *Major Figures of Modern Austrian Literature*. Studies in Austrian Literature, Culture, and Thought. Riverside, Cal.: Ariadne Press, 1988.

Dolmetsch, Carl. *"Our Famous Guest": Mark Twain in Vienna*. Athens: University of Georgia Press, 1992.

Fuchs, Anton. *Deserter*. Trans. Todd C. Hanlin. Riverside, Cal.: Ariadne Press, 1991.

Henisch, Peter. *Negatives of My Father*. Trans. Anne Close Ulmer. Riverside, Cal.: Ariadne Press, 1990.

———. *Stone's Paranoia*. Trans. Craig Decker. Riverside, Cal.: Ariadne Press, 2000.

Johns, Jorun B., and Katherine Arens, eds. *Elfriede Jelinek: Framed by Language*. Studies in Austrian Literature, Culture, and Thought. Riverside, Cal.: Ariadne Press, 1994.

Koerber, Lili. *Night over Vienna*. Trans. Viktoria Hertling and Kay M. Stone. Riverside, Cal.: Ariadne Press, 1990.

Menasse, Robert. *Die sozialpartnerschaftliche Ästhetik. Essays zum österreichischen Geist*. Vienna: Sonderzahl, 1990.

———. *Das Land ohne Eigenschaften. Essay zur österreichischen Identität*. Vienna: Sonderzahl, 1992.

———. *Dummheit ist machbar. Begleitende Essays zum Stilstand der Republik*. Vienna: Sonderzahl, 1999.

Merz, Carl, and Helmut Qualtinger. *Der Herr Karl*. Theater program, no. 5. Vienna: Burgtheater, 1 October 1986.

Reichart, Elisabeth. *February Shadows*. Trans. Donna L. Hoffmeister. London: The Women's Press, 1988.

Roth, Joseph. *Radetzkymarsch.* Munich: Deutscher Taschenbuch Verlag, 1986.

Szyszkowitz, Gerald. *Puntigam, or the Art of Forgetting.* Trans. Adrian del Caro. Riverside, Cal.: Ariadne Press, 1990.

Vansant, Jacqueline. "Challenging Austria's Victim Status: National Socialism and Austrian Personal Narratives." *The German Quarterly* 67, no. 1 (winter 1994): 38–57.

Wickham, Christopher. *Constructing Heimat in Postwar Germany: Longing and Belonging.* Studies in German Thought and History, vol. 18. Lewiston, N.Y.: The Edwin Mellen Press, 1999.

Historical Works: Books and Articles

Absenger, Albert G., ed. *Zeitgeschichte-Politische Bildung VIII. Österreichbewußtsein, Vergangenheitsbewältigung, Neutralitätspolitik.* Schriftenreihe zur Lehrerbildung im Berufsbildenden Schulwesen, Heft 97. Vienna: Pädagogisches Institut des Bundes in Wien, 1986.

Alcock, Anthony Evelyn. *The History of the South Tirol Question.* London: Michael Joseph, 1970.

Alexander, Helmut, Stefan Lechner, and Adolf Leidlmair. *Heimatlos. Die Umsiedlung der Südtiroler.* Vienna: Deuticke, 1993.

Alter, Peter. *Nationalism.* Trans. Stuart McKinnon-Evans. London: Edward Arnold, 1989.

Anderson, Benedict. *Imagined Communities: Reflections on the Origin and Spread of Nationalism.* Rev. ed. London: Verso, 1991.

Arbeitsgemeinschaft Volksgruppenfrage Universität Klagenfurt, eds. *Kein einig Volk von Brüdern. Studien zum Mehrheiten/Minderheitenproblem am Beispiel Kärntens.* Österreichische Texte zur Gesellschaftskritik, Band 9. Vienna: Verlag für Gesellschaftskritik, 1982.

Backer, John H. *Winds of History: The German Years of Lucius Du Bignon Clay.* New York: Van Nostrand Reinhold, 1983.

Bader, William B. *Austria Between East and West, 1945–1955.* Palo Alto: Stanford University Press, 1966.

Bailer, Brigitte. *Wiedergutmachung kein Thema. Österreich und die Opfer des Nationalsozialismus.* Vienna: Löcker Verlag, 1993.

Baldwin, Peter, ed. *Reworking the Past: Hitler, the Holocaust, and the Historians' Debate.* Boston: Beacon Press, 1990.

Balfour, Michael, and John Mair. *Four-Power Control in Germany and Austria, 1945–1946.* Survey of International Affairs, 1939–1946, ed. Arnold Toynbee. London: Oxford University Press, 1956.

Barker, Elisabeth. *Austria: 1918 to 1972.* London: Macmillan, 1973.

Bartov, Omer. *The Eastern Front, 1941–45: German Troops and the Barbarisation of Warfare.* London: Macmillan, 1985.

———. *Hitler's Army: Soldiers, Nazis, and War in the Third Reich.* New York: Oxford University Press, 1992.

———. "Defining Enemies, Making Victims: Germans, Jews, and the Holocaust." *American Historical Review* 103, no. 3 (June 1998): 771–816.

Barzun, Jacques. *From Dawn to Decadence, 1500 to the Present: 500 Years of Western Cultural Life.* New York: Perennial, 2000.

Baumgartner, Marianne. "'Jo, des waren halt schlechte Zeiten…'. Das Kriegsende und die unmittelbare Nachkriegszeit in den lebensgeschichtlichen Erzählungen von Frauen aus dem Mostviertel.* Europäische Hochschulschriften. Reihe III. Geschichte und ihre Hilfswissenschaften. Bd. 610. Frankfurt am Main: Peter Lang, 1994.

Becker, Hans. *Österreichs Freiheitskampf.* Vienna: Verlag der Freien Union der ÖVP, 1946.

Beckermann, Ruth. *Unzugehörig. Juden und Österreicher nach 1945.* Vienna: Löcker Verlag, 1989.

Berg, Matthew Paul. "Challenging Political Culture in Postwar Austria: Veterans Associations, Identity, and the Problem of Contemporary History." *Central European History* 30, no. 4 (1997): 513–544.

———. "Between Kulturkampf and Vergangenheitsbewältigung: The SPÖ, the Roman Catholic Church, and the Problem of Reconciliation. *Zeitgeschichte* 24, nos. 5–6 (1997): 147–169.

Berghan, Volker R., and Hanna Schissler, eds. *Perceptions of History: International Textbook Research on Britain, Germany and the United States.* Oxford: Berg, 1987.

Bergmann, Werner, Rainer Erb, and Albert Lichtblau, eds. *Schwieriges Erbe. Der Umgang mit Nationalsozialismus und Anti-Semitismus in Österreich, der DDR und der Bundesrepublik Deutschland.* Schriftenreihe des Zentrums für Anti-Semitismusforschung, Berlin, Band 3. Frankfurt: Campus Verlag, 1995.

Bhabha, Homi K., ed. *Nation and Narration.* New York: Routledge, 1990.

Bischof, Günter. "Die Instrumentalisierung Der Moskauer Erklärung Nach Dem 2. Weltkrieg." *Zeitgeschichte* 20, nos. 11–12 (1993): 345–366.

———. "The Making of a Cold Warrior: Karl Gruber and Austrian Foreign Policy, 1945–1953." *Austrian History Yearbook*, vol. 26 (1995): 99–127.

———. "Der Marshall-Plan in Europa 1947–1952." *Aus Politik und Zeitgeschichte. Beilage zur Wochenzeitung Das Parlament* 22–23 (23 May 1997): 3–17.

———. *Austria in the First Cold War, 1945–55: The Leverage of the Weak.* Cold War History. General editor: Saki Dockrill. New York: St. Martin's Press, 1999.

Bischof, Günter, and Josef Leidenfrost, eds. *Die bevormundete Nation. Österreich und die Alliierten 1945–1949.* Innsbrucker Forschungen zur Zeitgeschichte, ed. Rolf Steininger, Band 4. Innsbruck: Haymon Verlag, 1988.

Bischof, Günter, and Anton Pelinka, eds. *Austria in the New Europe.* Contemporary Austrian Studies, vol. 1. New Brunswick: Transaction Publishers, 1993.

———. *The Kreisky Era in Austria.* Contemporary Austrian Studies, vol. 2. New Brunswick: Transaction Publishers, 1994.

———. *Austrian Historical Memory and National Identity.* Contemporary Austrian Studies, vol. 5. New Brunswick: Transaction Publishers, 1997.

Bischof, Günter, Anton Pelinka, and Michael Gehler, eds. *Austria in the European Union.* Contemporary Austrian Studies, vol. 10. New Brunswick: Transaction Publishes, 2002.

Bischof, Günter, Anton Pelinka, and Ferdinand Karlhofer, eds. *The Vranitzky Era in Austria.* Contemporary Austrian Studies, vol. 7. New Brunswick: Transaction Publishers, 1999.

Bischof, Günter, Anton Pelinka, and Alexander Lassner, eds. *The Dollfuss/Schuschnigg Era in Austria: A Reassessment.* Contemporary Austrian Studies, vol. 11. New Brunswick: Transaction Publishers, 2003.

Bischof, Günter, Anton Pelinka, and Rolf Steininger, eds. *Austria in the Nineteen Fifties.* Contemporary Austrian Studies, vol. 3. New Brunswick: Transaction Publishers, 1995.

Bischof, Günter, Anton Pelinka, and Dieter Stiefel, eds. *The Marshall Plan in Austria.* Contemporary Austrian Studies, vol. 8. New Brunswick: Transaction Publishers, 2000.

Bischof, Günter, Anton Pelinka, and Erika Thurner, eds. *Women in Austria.* Contemporary Austrian Studies, vol. 6. New Brunswick: Transaction Publishers, 1998.

Bischof, Günter, Anton Pelinka, and Ruth Wodak, eds. *Neutrality in Austria.* Contemporary Austrian Studies, vol. 9. New Brunswick: Transaction Publishers, 2001.

Bissinger, H. G. *Friday Night Lights: A Town, a Team, and a Dream.* New York: HarperPerennial, 1991.

Blair, John G., and Reinhold Wagnleitner, eds. *Empire: American Studies.* Swiss Papers in English Language and Literature. General editor: Andreas Fischer, vol. 10. Tübingen: Gunter Narr Verlag, 1997.

Bluhm, William T. *Building an Austrian Nation: The Political Integration of a Western State.* London and New Haven: Yale University Press, 1973.

Bogataj, Mirko. *Die Kärntner Slowenen.* Klagenfurt: Hermagoras Verlag, 1989.

Born, Hanspeter. *Für die Richtigkeit. Kurt Waldheim.* Ulm: Schneekluth, 1987.

Botz, Gerhard. *Die Eingliederung Österreichs in das Deutsche Reich. Planung und Vewirklichung des politisch-administrativen Anschlusses (1938–1940).* 2nd rev. ed. Schriftenreihe des Ludwig Boltzmann Instituts, ed. Karl R. Stadler. Vienna: Europa Verlag, 1976.

———. *Der 13. März und die Anschluss-Bewegung. Selbstaufgabe, Okkupation und Selbstfindung Österreichs, 1918–1945.* Zeitdokumente, Dr. Karl Renner Institute, 14. Vienna: Dr. Karl Renner Institute, 1978.

———. *Wien vom 'Anschluß' zum Krieg.* Vienna: Jugend und Volk Verlag, 1978.

Botz, Gerhard, and Gerald Sprengnagel, eds. *Kontroversen um Österreich Zeitgeschichte.* Verdrängte Vergangenheit, *Österreich-Identität, Waldheim und die Historiker.* Ludwig-Boltzmann-Institut für Historische Sozialwissenschaft: Studien zur Historischen Sozialwissenschaft, ed. Gerhard Botz, Albert Müller, and Gerald Sprengnagel, Band 13. Frankfurt: Campus Verlag, 1994.

Boyer, John W. "Some Reflections on the Problem of Austria, Germany, and Mitteleuropa." *Central European History* 21, nos. 3–4 (September–December 1989): 301–315.

Brook-Shepherd, Gordon. *The Anschluss.* Philadelphia: J.B. Lippincott, 1963.

———. *The Austrians: A Thousand-Year Odyssey.* New York: Carroll & Graf Publishers, 1997.

Browning, Christopher. *Ordinary Men: Reserve Police Battalion 101 and the Final Solution in Poland.* New York: HarperPerennial, 1992.

Bruckmüller, Ernst. *Nation Österreich. Sozialhistorische Aspekte ihrer Entwicklung.* Studien zu Politik und Verwaltung, ed. Christian Brünner, Wolfgang Mantl, and Manfried Welan, Band 4. Vienna: Hermann Böhlaus Nachfolger, 1984.

Brunnbauer, Ulf, ed. *Eiszeit der Erinnerung. Vom Vergessen der eigenen Schuld.* Vienna: Promedia, 1999.

Bucur, Maria, and Nancy M. Wingfield, eds. *Staging the Past: The Politics of Commemoration in Habsburg Central Europe, 1848 to the Present.* Central European Studies, ed. Charles W. Ingrao. West Lafayette: Purdue University Press, 2001.

Buchinger, Gisela, and Elke Stöckl. "Konzentrationslager und Widerstand. Zwei Unterrichtseinheiten am Beispiel des Konzentrationslagers Mauthausen." *Zeitgeschichte* 10, no. 6 (1983): 240–248.

Bukey, Evan Burr. *Hitler's Hometown: Linz, Austria 1908–1945.* Bloomington: Indiana University Press, 1986.

———. "Nazi Rule in Austria." [Review article] *Austrian History Yearbook,* vol. 23 (1992): 202–233.

———. *Hitler's Austria: Popular Sentiment in the Nazi Era, 1938–1945.* Chapel Hill: University of North Carolina Press, 2000.

Bullock, Alan. *Hitler: A Study in Tyranny.* Rev. ed. New York: HarperTorchbooks, 1964.

Bullock, Malcolm. *Austria 1918–1938: A Study in Failure.* London: MacMillan, 1939.

Bunzl, John, and Bernd Marin. *Antisemitismus in Österreich. Sozialhistorische und soziologische Studien.* Vergleichende Gesellschaftsgeschichte und politische Ideengeschichte der Neuzeit, Band 3. Innsbruck: Inn-Verlag, 1983.

Bunzl, Matti. "On the Politics and Semantics of Austrian Memory: Vienna's Monument against War and Fascism." *History and Memory: Studies in Representation of the Past* 7, no. 2 (winter 1996): 7–40.

Burger, Johann, and Elisabeth Morawek, eds. *1945–1995. Entwicklungslinien der Zweiten Republik.* Vienna: Jugend und Volk, 1995.

Buruma, Ian. *The Wages of Guilt: Memories of War in Germany and Japan.* New York: Meridian, 1994.

———. "Blood Libel: Hitler and History in the Dock." *The New Yorker,* 16 April 2001, 82–86.

Butterworth, Neil. *Haydn: His Life and Times.* Tunbridge Wells: Midas Books, 1977.

Carafano, James Jay. *Waltzing into the Cold War: The Struggle for Occupied Austria.* Texas A & M University Military History Series 81, ed. Joseph G. Dawson III. College Station: Texas A & M University Press, 2002.

Clendinnen, Inga. *Reading the Holocaust.* Cambridge: Cambridge University Press, 1999.

Coerr, Eleanor. *Sadako and the Thousand Paper Cranes.* New York: Putnam, 1977.

Cohen, Bernard, and Luc Rosenzweig. *Waldheim.* Trans. Josephine Bacon. London: Robson Books, 1986.

Cole, Laurence. "Fern von Europa? The Peculiarities of Tirolian Historiography." *Zeitgeschichte* 23, nos. 5–6 (1996): 181–204.

Cronin, Audrey Kurth. *Great Power Politics and the Struggle Over Austria, 1945–1955.* Cornell Studies in Security Affairs. Ithaca: Cornell University Press, 1986.

———. "East-West Negotiations over Austria in 1949: Turning-Point in the Cold War." *Journal of Contemporary History* 24, no. 1 (January 1989): 125–145.

Cubitt, Geoffrey, ed. *Imagining Nations.* York Studies in Cultural History. New York: Manchester University Press, 1998.

Dachs, Herbert, et al., eds. *Handbuch des Politischen Systems Österreichs. Die Zweite Republik.* 2nd rev. ed. Vienna: Manzsche Verlags- und Universitätsbuchhandlung, 1992.

Danimann, Franz, and Hugo Pepper, eds. *Österreich im April '45.* Vienna: Europaverlag, 1985.

Deák, István, Jan T. Gross, and Tony Judt, eds. *The Politics of Retribution in Europe: World War II and Its Aftermath.* Princeton: Princeton University Press, 2000.

de Zayas, Alfred M. *Nemesis at Potsdam: The Expulsion of the Germans from the East.* 3rd rev. ed. Lincoln: University of Nebraska Press, 1988.

Diendorfer, Gertraud, Gerhard Jagschitz, and Oliver Rathkolb, eds. *Zeitgeschichte im Wandel.* Innsbruck: Studien Verlag, 1988.

Dokumentationsarchiv des österreichischen Widerstandes, ed. *Erzählte Geschichte. Berichte von Widerstandskämpfern und Verfolgten.* Band I: *Arbeiterbewegung.* Vienna: Österreichischer Bundesverlag, 1984.

———. *Erzählte Geschichte. Berichte von Widerstandskämpfern und Verfolgten.* Band 4: *Spurensuche. Erzählte Geschichte der Kärntner Slowenen.* Vienna: Österreichischer Bundesverlag, 1990.

———. *Erzählte Geschichte. Berichte von Widerstandskämpfern und Verfolgten.* Band 2: *Katholiken, Konservative, Legitimisten.* Vienna: Österreichischer Bundesverlag, 1992.

———. *Dreissig Jahre Dokumentationsarchiv des Österreichischen Widerstandes (1963–1993).* Vienna: Special Printing from DÖW Jahrbuch 1993, 1993.

———. *Erzählte Geschichte. Berichte von Widerstandskämpfern und Verfolgten.* Band 3: *Jüdische Schicksale. Berichte von Verfolgten.* 2nd ed. Vienna: Österreichischer Bundesverlag, 1993.

———. *Handbuch des Österreichischen Rechtsextremismus. Aktualisierte und Erweiterte Neuausgabe.* Vienna: Deuticke, 1994.

———. *Gedenken und Mahnen in Wien, 1934–1945. Gedenkstätten zu Widerstand und Verfolgung, Exil, Befreiung. Eine Dokumentation.* Vienna: Deuticke 1998.

Doumanis, Nicholas. *Italy.* Inventing the Nation. General editor: Keith Robbins. London: Arnold, 2001.

Dower, John W. *War Without Mercy: Race and Power in the Pacific War.* New York: Pantheon, 1996.

———. *Embracing Defeat: Japan in the Wake of World War II.* New York: Norton, 1999.

Dressel, Johannes. "Politische Bildung am Beispiel Faschismus—einige Ansätze." *Zeitgeschichte* 7, no. 4 (1980): 128–133.

Eichstädt, Ulrich. *Von Dollfuss zu Hitler. Geschichte des Anschlusses Österreichs, 1933–1938.* Veröffentlichungen des Instituts für Europäische Geschichte Mainz, ed. Joseph Lortz and Martin Göhring. Wiesbaden: Franz Steiner Verlag, 1955.

Engelbrecht, Helmut. *Geschichte des österreichischen Bildungswesens. Erziehung und Unterricht auf dem Boden Österreichs. Band 5. Von 1918 bis zur Gegenwart.* Vienna: Österreichischer Bundesverlag, 1988.

————. *Erziehung und Unterricht im Bild. Zur Geschichte des österreichischen Bildungswesens.* Vienna: ÖBV Pädagogischer Verlag, 1995.

Engelhardt, Tom. *The End of Victory Culture: Cold War America and the Disillusioning of a Generation.* New York: Basic Books, 1995.

Erdmann, Karl Dietrich. *Die Spur Österreichs in der deutschen Geschichte. Drei Staaten, zwei Nationen, ein Volk?* Zürich: Manesse-Verlag, 1989.

Ermacora, Felix. *Südtirol und das Vaterland Österreich.* Vienna: Amalthea Verlag, 1984.

————. *Südtirol. Die Verhinderte Selbstbestimmung.* Vienna: Amalthea Verlag, 1991.

Esden-Tempska, Carla. "Civic Education in Authoritarian Austria, 1934–38." *History of Education Quarterly* 30, no. 2 (summer 1990): 187–211.

Evans, Richard. *In Defense of History.* New York: Norton, 1999.

Ewing, Blair G. *Peace Through Negotiation: The Austrian Experience.* Washington, D.C.: Public Affairs Press, 1966.

Eybl, Susanne, and Elke Renner. "Überlegungen zu einem Ideologiekritischen Einsatz von 'Österreich II' im Unterricht." *Zeitgeschichte* 17, no. 1 (1989): 33–43.

Fellner, Fritz. "The Problem of the Austrian Nation after 1945." *The Journal of Modern History* 60 (June 1988): 264–289.

Fest, Joachim C. *Hitler.* Trans. Richard and Clara Winston. New York: Penguin Books, 1974.

Figl, Leopold. "Von Fremdbesetzung zu Fremdbesetzung." *Österreichische Monatshefte* 4 (April 1955): 5–6.

Fischer, Ernst. *Das Ende Einer Illusion. Erinnerungen 1945–1955.* Vienna: Verlag Fritz Molden, 1973.

Freund, Florian. *Vertreibung und Ermordung. Zum Schicksal der österreichischen Juden 1938–1945: das Projekt "Namentliche Erfassung der österreichischen Holocaustopfer."* Vienna: Dokumentationsarchiv des österreichischen Widerstandes, 1993.

Freund, Florian, and Gustav Spann. "Zur Aueinandersetzung mit der Apologie des Nationalsozialismus im Schulunterricht am Beispiel der Vernichtung der Juden." *Zeitgeschichte* 8, no. 2 (1981): 192–212.

Friedlander, Saul, ed. *Probing the Limits of Representation: Nazism and the "Final Solution."* Cambridge: Harvard University Press, 1992.

Fuchs, Eduard. *Schule und Zeitgeschichte oder wie Kommen Jugendliche zu Politischen Klischeevorstellungen.* Veröffentlichungen zur Zeitgeschichte, ed. Erika Weinzierl, Ernst Hanisch, and Karl Stuhlpfarrer, Band 5. Salzburg: Geyer Edition, 1986.

Fussell, Paul. *The Great War and Modern Memory.* New York: Oxford University Press, 1975.

————. *Wartime: Understanding and Behavior in the Second World War.* New York: Oxford University Press, 1989.

Gallup, Stephen. *A History of the Salzburg Festival.* London: Weidenfeld and Nicolson, 1987.

Gedye, G. E. R. *Betrayal in Central Europe—Austria and Czechoslovakia: The Fallen Bastions.* New York: Harper and Brothers, 1939.

Gehler, Michael, and Hubert Sickinger, eds. *Politische Affären und Skandale in Österreich. Von Mayerling bis Waldheim.* 2nd rev. ed. Thaur: Kulturverlag, 1996.

Geiringer, Karl. *Haydn: A Creative Life in Music.* New York: W.W. Norton, 1946.

Göhring, Walter. *1000 Daten SPÖ. Zur Entwicklung der Sozialistischen Partei Österreichs, 1945–1985.* Eisenstadt: Edition Roetzer, 1985.

Good, David F., and Ruth Wodak, eds. *From World War to Waldheim: Culture and Politics in Austria and the United States.* Austrian History, Culture, and Society. General editor: Richard L. Rudolph. New York: Berghahn Books, 1999.

Grandner, Margarete, Gernot Heiss, and Oliver Rathkolb. "Österreich und seine deutsche Identität. Bemerkungen zu Harry Ritter's Aufsatz 'Austria and the Struggle for German Identity.'" *German Studies Review* 16, no. 3 (October 1993): 515–520.

Grell, Heinz, ed. *Der Österreich Anschluss 1938. Zeitgeschichte im Bild.* Leoni am Starnberger See: Druffel-Verlag, n.d.

Gruber, Karl. *Between Liberation and Liberty.* Trans. Lionel Kochen. New York: Praeger, 1955.

Gutkas, Karl. *Die Zweite Republik. Österreich 1945–1985.* Munich: R. Oldenbourg Verlag, 1985.

Haas, Hanns. "Zur Österreichischen Nation—eine Spätlese." *Zeitgeschichte* 18, nos. 9–10 (1991): 304–313.

Hagspiel, Hermann. *Die Ostmark. Österreich im Großdeutschen Reich 1938 bis 1945.* Vienna: Wilhelm Braumüller, 1995.

Haider, Jörg. *Die Freiheit, die ich meine. Das Ende des Proporzstaates. Plädoyer für die Dritte Republik.* Frankfurt am Main: Ullstein Verlag, 1993.

Halbwachs, Maurice. *On Collective Memory.* Ed. and trans. Lewis A. Coser. The Heritage of Sociology, ed. Donald N. Levine. Chicago: University of Chicago Press, 1992.

Hamann, Brigitte. *Hitler's Vienna: A Dictator's Apprenticeship.* New York: Oxford University Press, 1999.

Hamburger Institut für Sozialforschung. *Vernichtungskrieg. Verbrechen der Wehrmacht 1941 bis 1944.* Hamburg: Hamburger Institut für Sozialforschung, 1995.

Hanisch, Ernst. "Gab es einen Spezifisch Österreichischen Widerstand?" *Zeitgeschichte* 12, nos. 9–10 (1985): 339–350.

———. *Der Lange Schatten des Staates. Österreichische Gesellschaftsgeschicthe im 20. Jahrhundert.* Österreichische Geschichte, ed. Herwig Wolfram. Vienna: Ueberreuter, 1994.

———. "'Selbsthaß' als Teil der österreichischen Identität." *Zeitgeschichte* 23, nos. 5–6 (1996): 136–145.

Harms, Kathy, Lutz Reuter, and Volker Dürr, eds. *Coping with the Past: Germany and Austria after 1945.* Monatshefte Occasional Volumes, ed. Reinhold Grimm. Madison: University of Wisconsin Press, 1990.

Hause, Steven C. "The Evolution of Social History." *French Historical Studies* 19, no. 4 (1996): 1191–1214.

Heilbrunn, Jacob. "A Disdain for the Past: Jörg Haider's Austria." *World Policy Journal* (spring 2000): 71–78.

Hein, Laura, and Mark Selden, eds. *Censoring History: Citizenship and Memory in Japan, Germany, and the United States.* Asia and the Pacific. Series editor: Mark Selden. New York: M.E. Sharpe, 2000.

Heineman, Elizabeth. "The Hour of the Woman: Memories of Germany's 'Crisis Years' and West German National Identity." *American Historical Review* 101, no. 2 (April 1996): 354–395.

Heinemann, Manfred, ed. *Umerziehung und Wiederaufbau. Die Bildungspolitik der Besatzungsmächte in Deutschland und Österreich.* Stuttgart: Klett-Cotta, 1981.

Heiss, Gernot. "Pan-Germans, Better Germans, Austrians: Austrian Historians on National Identity from the First to the Second Republic." *German Studies Review* 16, no. 3 (October 1993): 411–433.

Henke, Klaus-Dietmar, and Hans Woller, eds. *Politische Säuberung in Europa. Die Abrechnung mit Faschismus und Kollaboration nach dem Zweiten Weltkrieg.* Munich: Deutscher Taschenbuch Verlag, 1991.

Herf, Jeffrey. *Divided Memory: The Nazi Past in the Two Germanys.* Cambridge: Harvard University Press, 1997.

Herzstein, Robert Edwin. *Waldheim: The Missing Years.* New York: Arbor House/William Morrow, 1988.

Hilberg, Raul. *Perpetrators, Victims, Bystanders: The Jewish Catastrophe, 1933–1945.* New York: HarperCollins, 1992.

Hildebrand, Klaus. *The Foreign Policy of the Third Reich.* Trans. Anthony Fothergill. Berkeley: University of California Press, 1973.

Hiller, Alfred. "US-Amerikanische Schulpolitik in Österreich 1945–1950." *Österreich in Geschichte und Literatur* 24, no. 2 (1980): 65–79.

Hillhouse, Raelynn J. "A Reevaluation of Soviet Policy in Central Europe: The Soviet Union and the Occupation of Austria." *Eastern European Politics and Societies* 3, no. 1 (winter 1989): 83–104.

Hindels, Josef. *1938. Aus der Vergangenheit lernen. Österreichs Weg vom Austrofaschismus zur Nazi-Barbarei.* Vienna: Zukunft Verlag, 1988.

Hiscocks, Richard. *The Rebirth of Austria.* London: Oxford University Press, 1953.

Hobsbawm, Eric, and Terence Ranger, eds. *The Invention of Tradition.* London: Cambridge University Press, 1983.

Hofmann, Paul. *The Viennese: Splendor, Twilight, and Exile.* New York: Anchor Books, 1988.

Hölzl, Norbert. *Propaganda-Schlachten. Die österreichischen Wahlkämpfe, 1945–1971.* Munich: R. Oldenbourg Verlag, 1974.

Horwitz, Gordon J. *In the Shadow of Death: Living Outside the Gates of Mauthausen.* New York: The Free Press, 1990.

Hutton, Patrick H. *History as an Art of Memory.* Hanover, N.H.: University of Vermont, 1993.

Ienaga, Saburo. *The Pacific War, 1931–1945.* New York: Pantheon Books, 1978.

Iggers, Georg G. *Historiography in the Twentieth Century: From Scientific Objectivity to the Postmodern Challenge.* Hanover, N.H.: Wesleyan University Press, 1997.

Janik, Allan. Review of *Austrian Historical Memory and National Identity*, ed. Günter Bischof and Anton Pelinka. *Central European History* 30, no. 4 (1997): 625–628.

Jászi, Oscar. *The Dissolution of the Habsburg Monarchy.* Chicago: University of Chicago Press, 1929 [reprint, Chicago: University of Chicago Press, Phoenix Books, 1961].

Johnson, Lonnie R. "Die Österreichische Nation, Die Moskauer Deklaration und die Völkerrechtliche Argumentation. Bemerkungen zur Problematik der Interpretation der NS-Zeit in Österreich." *Dokumentationsarchiv des österreichischen Widerstandes Jahrbuch 1988*, ed. Siegwald Ganglmair. Vienna: Österreichischer Bundesverlag, 1988.

———. ."On the Inside Looking Out: Austria's New ÖVP-FPÖ Government, Jorg Haider, and Europe." *Habsburg Occassional Papers* 2 (February 2000) [http://www2.h-net.msu.edu/~habsweb/occasionalpapers/haider.html].

———. *Central Europe: Enemies, Neighbors, Friends.* 2nd ed. New York: Oxford University Press, 2002.

Judt, Tony. *Past Imperfect: French Intellectuals, 1944–1956.* Berkeley: University of California Press, 1992.

———. "The Past Is Another Country: Myth and Memory in Postwar Europe." *Daedalus* 121, no. 4 (fall 1992): 83–118.

———. "Tale from the Vienna Woods." *The New York Review of Books*, 23 March 2000, 8–9.

Kater, Michael H. *The Twisted Muse: Musicians and Their Music in the Third Reich.* New York: Oxford University Press, 1997.

Keegan, John. *The Second World War.* New York: Penguin, 1989.

Kershaw, Ian. *The Nazi Dictatorship: Problems and Perspectives of Interpretation.* 3rd ed. London: Edward Arnold, 1993.

———. *Hitler, 1889–1936: Hubris.* New York: W.W. Norton, 1998.

———. *Hitler, 1936–1945: Nemesis.* New York: W.W. Norton, 2000.

Keyserlingk, Robert K. *Austria in World War II: An Anglo-American Dilemma.* Montreal: McGill-Queen's University Press, 1988.

Kindermann, Gottfried-Karl. *Hitler's Defeat in Austria, 1933–1934: Europe's First Containment of Nazi Expansionism.* Trans. Sonia Brough and David Taylor. London: C. Hurst Company, 1988.

Klamper, Elizabeth. "Ein einig Volk von Brüdern. Vergessen und Erinnern im Zeichen des Burgfriedens." *Zeitgeschichte* 24, nos. 5–6 (1997): 170–185.

Knight, Robert, ed. *"Ich bin dafür, die Sache in die Länge zu ziehen." Wortprotokolle der österreichischen Bundesregierung von 1945–52 über die Entschädigung der Juden.* Frankfurt am Main: Athenäum, 1988.

———. "Britische Entnazifizierungspolitik, 1945–1949." *Zeitgeschichte* 11, nos. 9–10 (1984): 287–301.

Konrad, Helmut, ed. *Sozialdemokratie und "Anschluß." Historische Wurzeln. Anschluß 1918 und 1938. Nachwirkungen.* Schriftenreihe des Ludwig Boltzmann Instituts für Geschichte der Arbeiterbewegung, 9. Vienna: Europaverlag, 1978.

Kos, Wolfgang, and Georg Rigele, eds. *Inventur 45/55. Österreich im ersten Jahrzehnt der Zweiten Republik.* Vienna: Sonderzahl, 1996.

Kramer, Jane. *Europeans.* New York: Penguin Books, 1988.

———. "Letter from Germany: The Politics of Memory." *The New Yorker*, 14 August 1995, 48–65.

———. "Manna from Hell: Nazi Gold, Holocaust Accounts, and What the Swiss Must Finally Confront." *The New Yorker: Special Europe Issue*, 28 April and 5 May 1997, 74–89.

Kritzman, Lawrence D., ed. *Realms of Memory: Rethinking the French Past. Volume I: Conflicts and Divisions. Under the Direction of Pierre Nora.* Trans. Arthur Goldhammer. New York: Columbia University Press, 1996.

Kurt Waldheim's Wartime Years: A Documentation. Vienna: Carl Gerold's Sohn Verlagsbuchhandlung, 1987.

Kurz, Hans Rudolf, James L. Collins, Hagen Fleischer, Gerald Fleming, Manfred Messerschmidt, Jean Vanwelkenhuyzen, and Jehuda L. Wallach. *The Waldheim Report. Submitted February 8, 1988 to Federal Chancellor Dr. Franz Vranitzky by the International Commission of Historians Designated to Establish the Military Service of Lieutenant/1st Lieutenant Kurt Waldheim.* Authorized English translation of the unpublished German report. Copenhagen: Museum Tusculanum Press—University of Copenhagen, 1993.

Langbein, Hermann. "Überlebende aus den Konzentrationslagern des Nationalsozialismus Sprechen mit Schülern." *Zeitgeschichte* 12, no. 2 (1984): 52–57.

Large, David Clay, ed. *Contending with Hitler: Varieties of German Resistance in the Third Reich.* Publications of the German Historical Institute. Cambridge: Cambridge University Press, 1991.

Lauber, Wolfgang. *Wien—ein Stadtführer durch den Widerstand.* Vienna: Böhlau Verlag, 1988.

Le Chêne, Evelyn. *Mauthausen: The History of a Death Camp.* London: Methuen & Co., 1971.

Lehne, Inge, and Lonnie Johnson. *Vienna: The Past in the Present.* Studies in Austrian Literature, Culture, and Thought. Vienna: Österreichischer Bundesverlag and Riverside, Cal.: Ariadne Press, 1985.

Lennhoff, Eugene. *The Last Five Hours of Austria.* New York: Frederick A. Stokes, 1938.

Levi, Erik. *Music in the Third Reich.* London: Macmillan, 1994.

Lipstadt, Deborah. *Denying the Holocaust: The Growing Assault on Truth and Memory.* New York: The Free Press, 1993.

Loewenberg, Peter. "Karl Renner and the Politics of Accommodation: Moderation versus Revenge." *Austrian History Yearbook*, vol. 22 (1991): 35–56.

Low, Alfred D. *The Anschluss Movement 1918–1919 and the Paris Peace Conference.* Memoirs of the American Philosophical Society, vol. 103. Philadelphia: American Philosophical Society, 1974.

———. *The Anschluss Movement 1931–1938, and the Great Powers.* East European Monographs, no. 185. New York: Columbia University Press, 1985.

Lowenthal, David. *The Past is a Foreign Country*. London: Cambridge University Press, 1985.

Luza, Radomir V. *Austro-German Relations in the Anschluss Era*. Princeton: Princeton University Press, 1975.

———. *The Resistance in Austria, 1938–1945*. Minneapolis: University of Minnesota Press, 1984.

Lyon, Dirk, Joseph Marko, Eduard Staudinger, and Franz Christian Weber, eds. *Österreich 'bewußt'sein—bewußt Österreicher sein? Materialien zur Entwicklung des Österreichbewußtseins seit 1945*. Vienna: Österreichischer Bundesverlag, 1985.

Maass, Walter B. *Country Without a Name: Austria under Nazi Rule, 1938–1945*. New York: Frederick Ungar Publishing Co., 1979.

Mähr, Wilfried. "Der Marshall-Plan in Österreich: Wirtschaftspolitischer Nachhilfeunterricht?" *Zeitgeschichte* 15, no. 3 (1987): 91–111.

Maier, Charles S. *The Unmasterable Past: History, Holocaust, and German National Identity*. Cambridge: Harvard University Press, 1988.

Malina, Peter. "Die Diagnose Gilt Noch…Zur Aufarbeitung und 'Bewältigung' von Vergangenheit." *Zeitgeschichte* 15 (1988): 180–195.

———. "Auschwitz. Betroffenheit Statt Einsicht. Schulbuchtexte als Indikator öffentlichen Geschichtsbewußtseins." *Materialien zur Geschichts-Didaktik* 1 (1995): 36–48.

Mantl, Wolfgang, ed. *Politik in Österreich. Die Zweite Republik: Bestand und Wandel*. Studien zur Politik und Verwaltung, ed. Christian Brünner, Wolfgang Mantl, and Manfried Welan, Band 10. Vienna: Böhlaus Verlag, 1992.

Markusen, Eric, and David Kopf. *The Holocaust and Strategic Bombing: Genocide and Total War in the Twentieth Century*. Boulder: Westview Press, 1995.

Mastny, Vojtech. "Kremlin Politics and the Austrian Settlement." *Problems of Communism* 31, no. 4 (1982): 37–51.

Mayr, Johann. "Praxisorientierte Vorbereitung einer Exkursion zur Gedenkstätte Mauthausen Ausserhalb der Lehrplankontinuität in einer Unterrichtsstunde." *Zeitgeschichte* 12, nos. 11–12 (1985): 439–450.

McGovern, William Montgomery. *From Luther to Hitler: The History of Fascist-Nazi Political Philosophy*. New York: Houghton Mifflin, 1941.

Meissl, Sebastian, Klaus-Dieter Mulley, and Oliver Rathkolb, eds. *Verdrängte Schuld, verfehlte Sühne. Entnazifizierung in Österreich, 1945–1955*. Symposion des Instituts für Wissenschaft und Kunst Wien, März 1985. Vienna: Verlag für Geschichte und Politik, 1986.

Miller, Judith. *One, by One, by One: The Landmark Exploration of the Holocaust and the Uses of Memory*. New York: Touchstone Books, 1990.

Mitten, Richard. "Die Kampagne mit 'der Kampagne': Waldheim, der Jüdische Weltkongress und 'Das Ausland.'" *Zeitgeschichte* 17, no. 4 (1990): 175–195.

———. "Die 'Judenfrage' im Nachkriegsösterreich. Probleme der Forschung." *Zeitgeschichte* 19, nos. 11–12 (1992): 356–367.

———. *The Politics of Antisemitic Prejudice: The Waldheim Phenomenon in Austria*. Boulder: Westview Press, 1992.

Mittermaier, Karl. *Südtirol. Geschichte, Politik, und Gesellschaft*. Vienna: Österreichischer Bundesverlag, 1986.

Moeller, Robert G. *War Stories: The Search for a Usable Past in the Federal Republic of Germany*. Berkeley: University of California Press, 2001.

Neck, Rudolf, and Adam Wandruszka, eds. *Anschluß 1938. Protokoll des Symposions in Wien am 14. und 15. März 1978*. Vienna: Verlag für Geschichte und Politik, 1981.

Neugebauer, Wolfgang (Dokumentationsarchiv des österreichischen Widerstands), and Elisabeth Morawek (Bundesministerium für Unterricht, Kunst und Sport, Abteilung für politische Bildung), eds. *Österreicher und der Zweite Weltkrieg*. Vienna: Österreichischer Bundesverlag, 1989.

Niven, Bill. *Facing the Nazi Past: United Germany and the Legacy of the Third Reich.* London: Routledge, 2002.

Nora, Pierre. "Between Memory and History: *Les Lieux de Mémoire.*" *Representations* 26 (spring 1989): 7–25.

Palumbo, Michael. *The Waldheim Files: Myth and Reality.* London: Faber and Faber, 1988.

Parkinson, Frank, ed. *Conquering the Past: Austrian Nazism Yesterday and Today.* Detroit: Wayne State University Press, 1989.

Pauley, Bruce F. *Hitler and the Forgotten Nazis: A History of Austrian National Socialism.* Chapel Hill: University of North Carolina Press, 1981.

———. *From Prejudice to Persecution: A History of Austrian Anti-Semitism.* Chapel Hill: University of North Carolina Press, 1992.

Pelinka, Anton. *Windstille. Klagen über Österreich.* Vienna: Medusa Verlag, 1985.

———. *Zur Österreichischen Identität. Zwischen deutscher Vereinigung und Mitteleuropa.* Vienna: Ueberreuter, 1990.

———. "Karl Renner—a Man for All Seasons." *Austrian History Yearbook,* vol. 23 (1992): 111–119.

———. "Dismantling Taboos: Antisemitism in the Austrian Political Culture of the 1980s." *Patterns of Prejudice* 27, no. 2 (1993): 39–48.

———. *Austria: Out of the Shadow of the Past.* Nations of the Modern World: Europe, ed. Rand Smith and Robin Remington. Boulder: Westview Press, 1998.

Pelinka, Anton, and Fritz Plasser. *The Austrian Party System.* Boulder: Westview Press, 1989.

Pelinka, Anton, and Sabine Mayr, eds. *Die Entdeckung der Verantwortung. Die Zweite Republik und die vertriebenen Juden.* Vienna: Wilhelm Braumüller, 1998.

Pelinka, Anton, and Rolf Steininger, eds. *Österreich und die Sieger: 40 Jahre 2. Republik—30 Jahre Staatsvertrag.* Vienna: Wilhelm Braumüller, 1986.

Pelinka, Anton, and Erika Weinzierl, eds. *Das große Tabu. Österreichs Umgang mit seiner Vergangenheit.* Vienna: Edition S., 1987.

Pells, Richard. *Not Like Us: How Europeans Have Loved, Hated, and Transformed American Culture Since World War II.* New York: Basic Books, 1997.

Peterlini, Oskar. *Autonomy and the Protection of Ethnic Minorities in Trentino-South Tyrol: An Overview of the History, Law and Politics.* Ethnos, no. 48, trans. Marie Fraser. Vienna: Braumüller, 1997.

Peukert, Detlev J. K. *Inside Nazi Germany: Conformity, Opposition, and Racism in Everyday Life.* Trans. Richard Deveson. New Haven: Yale University Press, 1987.

Pick, Hella. *Guilty Victim: Austria from the Holocaust to Haider.* New York: I.B. Tauris, 2000.

Pohl, Walter. "Ostarrîchi Revisited: The 1946 Anniversary, the Millennium, and the Medieval Roots of Austrian Identity." *Austrian History Yearbook,* vol. 27 (1996): 21–39.

Portisch, Hugo. "Ideologiekritische Überlegungen: Eine Replik." *Zeitgeschichte* 17, no. 4 (1990): 196–201.

———. *Österreich II. Jahre des Aufbruchs, Jahre des Umbruchs.* Vienna: Kremayr & Scheriau, 1996.

Potocnik, Christiana. "Der Österreichische Nationalfeiertag—nur mehr ein Tag der Fitness-märsche?" *Zeitgeschichte* 17, no. 1 (1989): 19–32.

Psichari, Henriette, ed. *Oeuvres complètes de Ernest Renan.* Tome 1. Édition Définitive établie par. Paris: Calmann-Lévy, 1947.

Pulzer, P. G. J. *The Rise of Political Anti-Semitism in Germany and Austria.* New Dimensions in History. Essays in Comparative History, ed. Norman F. Cantor. New York: John Wiley & Sons, 1964.

Rathkolb, Oliver. "U.S.-Entnazifizierung in Österreich. Zwischen Kontrollierter Revolution und Elitenrestauration (1945–1949)." *Zeitgeschichte* 11, nos. 9–10 (1984): 302–325.

————, ed. *Gesellschaft und Politik am Beginn der Zweiten Republik. Vertrauliche Berichte der US-Militäradministration aus Österreich 1945 in englischer Originalfassung.* Vienna: Hermann Böhlaus Nachfolger, 1985.

Ratzenböck, Veronika, Elisabeth Morawek, and Sirkit M. Amann. *Die zwei Wahrheiten. Eine Dokumentation von Projekten an Schulen zur Zeitgeschichte im Jahr 1988.* Vienna: Löcker Verlag, 1989.

Rauchensteiner, Manfried. *Der Sonderfall. Die Besatzungszeit in Österreich, 1945 bis 1955.* Ed. Heeresgeschichtlichen Museum/Militärwissenschaftliches Institut, Vienna. Graz: Verlag Styria, 1979.

————. *Die Zwei. Die große Koalition in Österreich. 1945–1966.* Vienna: Österreichische Bundesverlag, 1987.

Reichhold, Ludwig. *Kampf um Österreich. Die Vaterländische Front und ihr Widerstand gegen den Anschluß, 1933–1938.* 2nd ed. Vienna: Österreichischer Bundesverlag, 1985.

————, ed. *Zwanzig Jahre Zweite Republik. Österreich Findet zu sich Selbst.* Vienna: Verlag Herder, 1965.

Reiterer, Albert F., ed. *Nation und Nationalbewusstsein in Österreich. Ergebnisse einer empirischen Untersuchung.* Vienna: Verband der wissenschaftlichen Gesellschaften Österreichs, 1988.

Rewadikar, Nalini. *Conference Diplomacy Austrian Model: A Study of the Dynamics of Negotiations and Disengagement of Big Powers.* Meerut and Delhi: Meenakshi Prakashan, 1973.

Riedlsperger, Max E. *The Lingering Shadow of Nazism: The Austrian Independent Party Movement Since 1945.* East European Monographs, no. 42. Boulder: East European Quarterly, distributed by Columbia University Press, 1978.

Riesenfellner, Stefan, and Heidemarie Uhl, eds. *Todeszeichen. Zeitgeschichtliche Denkmalkultur in Graz und in der Steiermark vom Ende des 19. Jahrhunderts bis zur Gegenwart.* Kulturstudien Bibliothek der Kulturgeschichte, ed. Hubert Ch. Ehalt and Helmut Konrad, Sonderband 19. Vienna: Böhlau Verlag, 1994.

Ritter, Harry. "Austria and the Struggle for German Identity." *German Studies Review.* Special Issue: German Identity (winter 1992): 111–129.

————. "On Austria's German Identity: A Reply to Margarete Grandner, Gernot Heiss, and Oliver Rathkolb." *German Studies Review* 16, no. 3 (October 1993): 521–523.

Robertson, Ritchie, and Edward Timms, eds. *The Habsburg Legacy: National Identity in Historical Perspective.* Austrian Studies, vol. 5. Edinburgh: Edinburgh University Press, 1994.

Rosenbaum, Eli M., with William Hoffer. *Betrayal: The Untold Story of the Kurt Waldheim Investigation and Cover-Up.* New York: St. Martin's Press, 1993.

Roth, Michael S. *The Ironist's Cage: Memory, Trauma, and the Construction of History.* New York: Columbia University Press, 1995.

Rousso, Henry. *The Vichy Syndrome: History and Memory in France since 1944.* Trans. Arthur Goldhammer. Cambridge: Harvard University Press, 1991.

Saltman, Jack. *Kurt Waldheim: A Case to Answer?* London: Robson Books, in association with Channel Four Television Company, 1988.

Scharsach, Hans-Henning. *Haider's Kampf.* Vienna: Ein trend-profil-Buch im Verlag Orac, 1992.

Schermaier, Josef. *Geschichte und Gegenwart des allgemeinbildenden Schulwesens in Österreich.* Vienna: Verband der wissenschaftlichen Gesellschaften Österreichs, 1990.

Schlesinger, Thomas O. *Austrian Neutrality in Postwar Europe: The Domestic Roots of a Foreign Policy.* Vienna: Wilhelm Braumüller, 1972.

Schmidl, Erwin A. *Der "Anschluß" Österreichs. Der Deutsche Einmarsch im März 1938.* Bonn: Bernard & Graefe Verlag, 1994.

Schoiswohl, Johann. "Schule nach Auschwitz. Fünf Thesen zur Struktur der Österreichischen Pflichtschule in der unmittelbaren Nachkriegszeit." *Zeitgeschichte* 15, no. 6 (1988): 245–261.

Schorske, Carl E. *Fin-de-Siècle Vienna: Politics and Culture.* New York: Vintage Books, 1981.

Schuschnigg, Kurt von. *My Austria.* New York: Alfred A. Knopf, 1938.

———. *Austrian Requiem.* Trans. Franz von Hildebrand. New York: G.P. Putnam's Sons, 1946.

———. *The Brutal Takeover: The Austrian Ex-Chancellor's Account of the Anschluss of Austria by Hitler.* Trans. Richard Barry. New York: Athenaeum, 1971.

Scrinzi, Otto, ed. *Chronik Südtirol, 1959–1969. Von der Kolonie Alto Adige zur Autonomen Provinz Bozen.* Graz: Leopold Stocker Verlag, 1996.

Shumway, Nicolas. *The Invention of Argentina.* Berkeley: University of California Press, 1991.

Sieder, Reinhard, Heinz Steiner, and Emmerich Tálos, eds. *Österreich 1945–1995. Gesellschaft, Politik, Kultur.* Österreichische Texte zur Gesellschaftskritik, ed. Verein Kritische Sozialwissenschaft und Politische Bildung, Band 60. Vienna: Verlag für Gesellschaftskritik, 1995.

Stadler, Karl R. *Austria.* Nations of the Modern World. New York: Praeger, 1971.

Stearman, William Lloyd. *The Soviet Union and the Occupation of Austria (an Analysis of Soviet Policy in Austria, 1945–1955).* Bonn: Siegler & Co., 1961.

Steinbach, Peter, ed. *Widerstand. Ein Problem zwischen Theorie und Geschichte.* Cologne: Verlag Wissenschaft und Politik Berend von Nottbeck, 1987.

Steinberg, Michael P. *The Meaning of the Salzburg Festival: Austria as Theater and Ideology, 1890–1938.* Ithaca: Cornell University Press, 1990.

Steiner, Herbert. "The Role of the Resistance in Austria, with Special Reference to the Labor Movement." *Journal of Modern History* 64, suppl. (December 1992): S128–S133.

Steininger, Rolf. *Los von Rom? Die Südtirolfrage 1945/46 und das Gruber-De Gasperi-Abkommen.* Innsbrucker Forschungen zur Zeitgeschichte, Band 2. Innsbruck: Haymon-Verlag, 1987.

———. *Südtirol zwischen Diplomatie und Terror, 1947–1969: Darstellungen in drei Bänden* (vol. 1, 1947–1959; vol. 2, 1960–1962; vol. 3, 1962–1969). Veröffentlichungen des Südtiroler Landesarchivs. Bolzano: Verlagsanstalt Athesia, 1999.

Steininger, Rolf, Günter Bischof, and Michael Gehler, eds. *Austria in the Twentieth Century.* Studies in Austrian and Central European History and Culture, ed. Günter Bischof. New Brunswick: Transaction Publishers, 2002.

Stiefel, Dieter. *Entnazifizierung in Österreich.* Vienna: Europaverlag, 1981.

Stourzh, Gerald. *Geschichte des Staatsvertrages. Österreichs Weg zur Neutralität.* Graz: Verlag Styria, 1980.

———. *Vom Reich zur Republik. Studien zum Österreichbewußtsein im 20. Jahrhundert.* Vienna: Edition Atelier, 1990.

———. *Um Einheit und Freiheit. Staatsvertrag, Neutralität und das Ende der Ost-West Besetzung Österreichs 1945–1955.* 4th rev. and exp. ed. Vienna: Böhlau, 1998.

Streim, Alfred. *Die Behandlung sowjetischer Kriegsgefangenen im "Fall Barbarossa." Eine Dokumentation.* Motive—Texte—Materialien (MTM), Band 13. Heidelberg: C.F. Müller Juristischer Verlag, 1981.

Streit, Christian. *Keine Kameraden. Die Wehrmacht und die sowjetischen Kriegsgefangenen, 1941–1945.* Studien zur Zeitgeschichte, Band 13. Ed. Institut für Zeitgeschichte. Stuttgart: Deutsche Verlags-Anstalt, 1978.

Strotzka, Heinz. "Tonbandprotokolle im Unterricht am Beispiel des Berichts eines Ehemaligen Konzentrationslagerhäftlings." *Zeitgeschichte* 9, no. 8 (1982): 284–295.

Suppanz, Werner. *Österreichische Geschichtsbilder. Historische Legitimationen in Ständestaat und Zweiter Republik.* Vienna: Böhlau Verlag, 1998.

Sully, Melanie. *A Contemporary History of Austria.* London: Routledge, 1990.

Suval, Stanley. "The Search for a Fatherland." *Austrian History Yearbook,* vols. 4–5 (1968–1969): 275–299.

———. *The Anschluss Question in the Weimar Era: A Study of Nationalism in Germany and Austria, 1918–1932.* Baltimore: The Johns Hopkins University Press, 1974.

Tálos, Emmerich, and Wolfgang Neugebauer, eds. *"Austrofaschismus." Beiträge Über Politik, Ökonomie und Kultur, 1934–1938.* 2nd ed. Österreichische Texte zur Gesellschaftskritik, Band 18. Vienna: Verlag für Gesellschaftskritik, 1984.

Tálos, Emmerich, Ernst Hanisch, and Wolfgang Neugebauer, eds. *NS-Herrschaft in Österreich, 1938–1945.* Österreichische Texte zur Gesellschaftskritik, Band 36. Vienna: Verlag für Gesellschaftskritik, 1988.

Tálos, Emmerich, Herbert Dachs, Ernst Hanisch, and Anton Staudinger, eds. *Handbuch des Politischen Systems Österreichs. Erste Republik, 1918–1933.* Vienna: Manzsche Verlags- und Universitätsbuchhandlung, 1995.

Taylor, Telford. *Nuremberg and Vietnam: An American Tragedy.* New York: Quadrangle Books, 1970.

Terkel, Studs. *The Good War.* New York: Ballantine, 1984.

Thaler, Peter. *The Ambivalence of Identity: The Austrian Experience of Nation-Building in a Modern Society.* Central European Studies, ed. Charles W. Ingrao. West Lafayatte: Purdue University Press, 2001.

Thonhauser, Josef. Österreichbewusstsein und Vergangenheitsbewältigung im Spiegel der Lehrbücher." *Zeitgeschichte* 15, no. 1 (1987): 37–53.

Timms, Edward. "National Memory and the 'Austrian Idea': From Metternich to Waldheim." *The Modern Language Review* 86 (October 1991): 898–910.

Tittmann, Harold H., III. *The Waldheim Affair: Democracy Subverted.* New York: Olin Frederick, 2000.

Todrova, Maria. *Imagining the Balkans.* New York: Oxford University Press, 1997.

Toscano, Mario. *Alto Adige—South Tyrol: Italy's Frontier with the German World.* Ed. and trans. George A. Carbone. Baltimore: The Johns Hopkins University Press, 1976.

Tweraser, Kurt K. "Military Justice as an Instrument of American Occupation Policy in Austria 1945–1950: From Total Control to Limited Tutelage." *Austrian History Yearbook,* vol. 24 (1993): 153–178.

Uhl, Heidemarie. *Zwischen Versöhnung und Verstörung. Eine Kontroverse um Österreichs historische Identität fünfzig Jahre nach dem "Anschluß."* Böhlaus Zeitgeschichtliche Bibliothek, ed. Helmut Konrad, Band 17. Vienna: Böhlau Verlag, 1992.

———. "Erinnerung als Versöhnung. Zur Denkmalkultur und Geschichtspolitik der Zweiten Republik." *Zeitgeschichte* 23, nos. 5–6 (1996): 146–160.

van Amerongen, Martin. *Kreisky und seine unbewältigte Gegenwart.* Graz: Verlag Styria, 1977.

Wagner, Dieter, and Gerhard Tomkowitz. *"Ein Volk, Ein Reich, Ein Führer," Der Anschluß Österreichs, 1938.* Munich: n.p., 1968.

Wagnleitner, Reinhold. *Coca-Colonization and the Cold War: The Cultural Mission of the United States in Austria after the Second World War.* Trans. Diana M. Wolf. Chapel Hill: University of North Carolina Press, 1994.

Waldheim, Kurt. *Im Glaspalast der Weltpolitik.* Düsseldorf and Vienna: Econ, 1985.

———. *Worauf es mir ankommt. Gedanken, Appelle, Stellungnahmen des Bundespräsidenten, 1986–1992.* Ed. Hanns Sassmann. Graz: Styria Medien Service, 1992.

Walker, David. "Industrial Location in Turbulent Times: Austria through Anschluss and Occupation." *Journal of Historical Geography* 12, no. 2 (1986): 182–195.

Wassermann, Heinz P. *"Zuviel Vergangenheit tut nicht gut!" Nationalsozialismus im Spiegel der Tagespresse der Zweiten Republik.* Innsbruck: Studien Verlag, 2000.

Weber, Eugene. *Peasants into Frenchmen.* Stanford: Stanford University Press, 1976.

Weber, Wolfgang, ed. *Die Streitkräfte der NATO auf dem Territorium der BRD.* Berlin: Militärverlag der Deutschen Demokratischen Republik, 1989.

Weinzierl, Erika. *Zu wenig Gerechte. Österreicher und Judenverfolgung, 1938–1945.* 3rd ed. Graz: Verlag Styria, 1986.

———. "Kirche und Schule in Österreich 1945–1948." *Kirchliche Zeitgeschichte* 2, no. 1 (1989): 165–170.

Weinzierl, Erika, and Kurt Skalnik, eds. *Österreich. Die Zweite Republik.* 2 vols. Graz: Verlag Styria, 1972.

Whitnah, Donald R., and Edgar L. Erickson. *The American Occupation of Austria: Planning and Early Years.* Contributions in Military Studies, no. 46. Westport, Conn.: Greenwood Press, 1985.

Wistrich, Robert S., ed. *Austrians and Jews in the Twentieth Century: From Franz Joseph to Waldheim.* New York: St. Martin's Press, 1992.

———. "Haider and His Critics." *Commentary,* April 2000, 30–35.

Witek, Hans, and Hans Safrian. *Und keiner war dabei. Dokumente des alltäglichen Antisemitismus in Wien 1938.* Foreword by Erika Weinzierl. Vienna: Picus Verlag, 1988.

Wodak, Ruth, Florian Menz, Richard Mitten, and Frank Stern. *Die Sprachen der Vergangenheiten. Öffentliches Gedenken in österreichischen und deutschen Medien.* Frankfurt am Main: Suhrkamp, 1994.

Wodak, Ruth, Peter Nowak, Johanna Pelikan, Helmut Gruber, Rudolf de Cillia, and Richard Mitten. *"Wir sind alle unschuldige Täter!" Diskurshistorische Studien zum Nachkriegsantisemitismus.* Frankfurt am Main: Suhrkamp, 1990.

Wodak, Ruth, and Anton Pelinka, eds. *The Haider Phenomenon in Austria.* New Brunswick: Transaction Publishers, 2002.

Wodak, Ruth, Rudolf de Cillia, Martin Reisigl, and Karin Liebhart, eds. *The Discursive Construction of National Identity.* Trans. Angelika Hirsch and Richard Mitten. Critical Discourse Analysis Series, ed. Norman Fairclough. Edinburgh: Edinburgh University Press, 1999.

Wright, William E., ed. *Austria Since 1945.* Minneapolis: Center for Austrian Studies, University of Minnesota, 1982.

———. *Austria, 1938–1988. Anschluss and Fifty Years.* Studies in Austrian Literature, Culture, and Thought. Riverside, Cal.: Ariadne Press, 1994.

Wyman, David S., ed. *The World Reacts to the Holocaust.* Baltimore: The Johns Hopkins University Press, 1996.

Zammito, John H. "Are We Being Theoretical Yet? The New Historicism, the New Philosophy of History, and 'Practicing Historians.'" *The Journal of Modern History* 65 (December 1993): 783–814.

Zentner, Christian. *Heim ins Reich. Der Anschluß Österreichs 1938.* Munich: Südwest Verlag, 1988.

Ziegler, Meinrad, and Waltraud Kannonier-Finster. *Österreichisches Gedächtnis. Über Erinnern und Vergessen der NS-Vergangenheit.* With a contribution by Mario Erdheim. Böhlaus Zeitgeschichtliche Bibliothek, ed. Helmut Konrad, Band 25. Vienna: Böhlau Verlag, 1993.

Zöllner, Erich, ed. *Österreichs Erste und Zweite Republik. Kontinuität und Wandel ihrer Strukturen und Probleme.* Schriften des Institutes für Österreichkunde, no. 47. Vienna: Österreichischer Bundesverlag, 1985.

Dissertations and Master's Theses

Berg, Matthew Paul. "Political Culture and State Identity: The Reconstruction of Austrian Social Democracy, 1945–1958." Ph.D. diss., University of Chicago, 1993.

Fuchs, Sabine. "Geschichtsbewußtsein von Maturanten Allgemeinbildender Höher Schulen in Oberösterreich." Ph.D. diss., University of Salzburg, 1990.

Nowotny, Katinka Tatjana. "Erinnerung an den Nationalsozialismus. Eine Analyse zum Österreichischen Bedenkjahr 1938/88. Eine Inhaltsanalyse wichtiger Printmedien und eine Dokumentation von Veranstaltungen und politischen Kontroversen." Diplomarbeit, University of Vienna, 1990.

Schausberger, Bernhard. "'Die Entstehung des Mythos: Österreich als Opfer des Nationalsozialismus.' Eine Dokumentation." Diplomarbeit. Paris-Lodron-Universität, Salzburg, 1991.

Sitte, Christian. "Entwicklung des Unterrichtsgegenstandes Geographie, Erdkunde, Geographie und Wirtschaftskunde an den Allgemeinbildenden Schulen (APS u. AHS) in Österreich nach 1945." Ph.D. diss., University of Vienna, 1989.

INDEX

Advent, 48
African Americans, 133
air raids, 15, 93–95, 101, 108, 136, 173, 178, 182
Alm, 40, 43, 45, 65nn. 105, 106
Alto Adige, 79, 134
Americans, textbook portrayal of, 1, 94–95, 101–2, 104–6, 129–33, 135–36, 142–44, 153–54n. 37, 162–63, 174, 177, 179, 195n. 78
Anschluss, 27–29, 85–86n. 20, 87n. 20
  1988 anniversary, 161, 164–65, 169–70
  Austrian memory of, x, 13
  Austrian reaction to, 9, 72–74
  textbook portrayal of, 53–54, 74–85, 170–73
anti-Semitism, 8, 14, 20–21n. 72, 73, 86n. 11, 92, 103, 106, 117n. 55, 168, 170–71
appeasement, 74–76
Austrian People's Party. *See* ÖVP
Austrianism, 34
Austro-Fascism, 1–2, 26

Bachmann, Ingeborg, 166
Bad Ischl, 107, 137–38
Balkans, 90, 185
Balkans, and Kurt Waldheim, 162–63
Beethoven, Ludwig van, 38–39
Bernhard, Thomas, 164–65
Bonaparte, Napoleon, 36–37
Borchert, Wolfgang 94, 167
Borodajkewycz (Taras), scandal, 165–66
Bundesheer (Austrian federal army), 147–48
Byrnes, James, 139

Cardinal Innitzer, 72, 82, 84, 86n. 9
Catholicism
  Austrian identity and, 1, 65n. 114, 189

Catholic schools, 7, 132–33
  links with politics, 30, 34, 73, 138
  textbook portrayal of, 26, 35, 46–48, 52, 55, 58, 78, 95, 100–101
Celan, Paul, 166–67
Central Cemetery, Vienna, 169, plates 5–6
Clay, Lucius, 139
coalition history, 5, 8, 30–32, 61n. 32, 77–80, 101, 109–13, 145, 195n. 93
coalition lesson, the, 80–81, 83–84, 96, 102, 114, 129–30, 141, 150–51, 166–68, 172–73, 176, 178, 182–85, 188–89
coalition, postwar, 85, 162–63, 166–67, 169, 186, 188–89
Cold War, ix, 6, 12, 104–5, 117–118n. 66. 122, 134, 137–40, 142–43, 148–49, 194n. 72
Commission of Historians, 163–164
culture *(Kultur)*
  textbook portrayal of, 32–35, 37–40, 52
  uniqueness of Austrian, 15, 26, 30, 33–34, 58–59, 94, 102, 150–51, 191
curriculum
  Nazi, 27–28
  postwar, 6–7, 17nn. 27, 28, 32–35, 46–47, 52–53
  See also education policy

Dachau, 55, 78, 87n. 39, 102, 172–73
denazification, 31–33, 122, 136–141
Der Herr Karl, 8, 18n. 38, 71, 85n. 1, 90, 95, 115n. 1, 121, 152nn. 2, 3, 153n. 20, 165–66
Dokumentationsarchiv des österreichischen Widerstands (DÖW), 109–14, 119nn. 93, 95, 193n. 39, 196nn. 104, 122

Education Ministry, Austrian, ix, xii, 5, 27, 32, 38, 62nn. 39, 44, 45, 127, 130, 145, 147, 149, 169–70, 191

education policy
  Allied, 32–33, 5, 130
  Austrian (Second Republic), 7, 32–35,
    62nn. 39, 44, 45, 83, 169–70, 191
  Nazi, 27–28
  Ständestaat, 26–27
ERP. *See* Marshall Plan
Eugene, Prince of Savoy, 37, 63n. 68
European Union (EU), 186–87

farmers, textbook portrayal of, 36, 49–52,
  54, 78
Figl, Leopold, 122, 125, 131, 141–43, 145,
  152n. 4, 158n. 131, 172
Fischer, Ernst, 33–35, 47, 62n. 47
flag, Austrian national, 35–36, 61n. 23, 121,
  146–47, 151, 161
FPÖ, 31, 61n. 37, 166, 186–89
Fragebogen, 138, 140
France, 12–13, 54, 75, 108, 123, 129
Frederick the Great, 47
Freedom Party of Austria. *See* FPÖ

Germany, 40, 47, 52, 55, 99, 136–37, 144,
  148, 150
  Federal Republic of Germany (West
    Germany and united Germany), 2,
    12–13, 15, 20nn. 69, 70, 71, 105,
    121–22, 128, 139–42, 164, 169
  Imperial Germany, 1
  Nazi Germany, 1, 13, 15, 25–30, 33–36,
    38, 54, 58, 73, 75–77, 81–84, 92, 96, 98,
    100–102, 105–11, 119nn. 91, 92, 102,
    122–25, 151, 161, 166, 172–74, 178,
    181, 185–87
  German Democratic Republic (East
    Germany), 12–13, 121–22
Great Britain, 75, 110, 134, 138–142, 154n. 49
Green Party, Austrian, 162–63, 185, 188
Grillparzer, Franz, 33, 39
Gruber, Karl, 74, 134, 142, 163–64
Gruber-De Gasperi Agreement, 134
Grünwald, Béla, 4
Gruppe '47, 166–67

Habsburgs, 1, 27–28, 189
Haider, Jörg, x, 183, 186–89, 196nn. 116, 121
Hamburg Institute for Social Research, 185
Haydn, Joseph, 33, 36, 39, 64n. 82
Heimat (homeland), textbook portrayal of, 26–
  27, 30, 34–35, 39–49, 52, 54, 56–58, 92,
  99, 108, 114, 129, 149–50, 153n. 25, 189

Heimkehr, textbook portrayal of 56–58,
  135–36, 174
Heldenplatz (play), 164–65
Heldenplatz, 71–72, 161
Hiroshima, textbook portrayal of, 101–6,
  117nn. 60, 62, 118n. 67, 174–76,
  180–81
Historikerstreit, 164–65
historiography, 4, 47, 92, 129, 155n. 67
  of history and memory, 9–11
  of victim myth, 7–9
Hitler Youth, 27
Hitler, Adolf, 13, 20–21n. 72, 27–28, 39,
  53–54, 71–81, 91, 96–97, 101, 103, 106,
  108–9, 113–14, 124, 136, 151, 161,
  172–73, 175–76, 178–79, 185
Hofer, Andreas, 36–37, 63n. 65
Holocaust (television mini-series), 167
Holocaust, x, 8, 13, 19n. 55, 21n. 74, 110,
  168, 170, 180–81, 184–85, 188, 190,
  194n. 71
  textbook portrayal of 5, 80–81, 91, 99–
  107, 113, 170–71, 174–76, 190
Hrdlicka, Alfred, 182–85, plates 7–9
Hull, Cordell, 124
Hurdes, Felix, 34–35

Irving, David, 19n. 55, 110

Jelinek, Elfriede, 168–69
Jews, Austrian, 14–15, 30, 39, 48, 55, 78–81,
  87n. 39, 92, 99–107, 111, 113–14, 116n.
  44, 137, 162–64, 167, 171–74, 177, 179,
  181, 184–85, 190

Kaprun, 50, 127–28, 153nn. 23, 25, 26
Katyn massacre, 12, 100–101
Keyes, Geoffrey, 138
Kindermann, Gottfried-Karl, 111–12
Kirchschläger, Rudolf, 31, 166
Kleistl, Thomas, 186
Kreisky, Bruno, 19n. 45, 166, 192n. 20
Kremsmünster, 132–33

Landschaft (landscape), as textbook theme,
  26–27, 30, 35, 44–47, 49, 52, 189
lesson plan(s), official, 5, 7, 33–34, 53, 91–92,
  107, 127, 130, 145, 171, 174, 176, 179
L'Express, 163
Luftwaffe, 72, 90, 102

Maria Theresa, 39, 47
Marshall Plan, x, 25, 45, 126–133, 139, 153n. 26, 153–54n. 37
Mauthausen, 90, 100, 103, 106–7, 175–76, 181, 190
memorials, war, 31, 98–99, 113, 131, 176, 185, plates 2, 4
memory, historical
	Austrian official, ix–x, 2, 4–5, 9–11, 26, 74, 113, 122, 136, 165, 177–78, 191
	uniqueness of Austrian, 11–15
	See also historiography
Merz, Carl, 8, 18n. 38, 166
Mock, Alois, 112, 162–63
Monument against War and Fascism, 182–185, plates 7–9
Moscow Declaration, x, 8, 13, 29–30, 71, 85n. 2, 108, 112, 121–24
	textbook portrayal of, 124–126, 143, 176
Mozart, Wolfgang Amadeus, 33, 36, 39, 58
music, textbook portrayal of, 37–40
Mussolini, Benito, 79–80

national anthem, Austrian, 35–36, 63n. 63
national holiday, Austrian, textbook portrayal of, 106–7, 121–22, 144–51, 177, 190
national identity, Austrian, and victim myth. *See* victim myth
Native Americans, 133
Neue Kronen Zeitung, 179, 182, 195n. 95
neutrality, x, 13, 121
neutrality, textbook portrayal of, 144–45, 147–49, 177, 189
New York Times, 162

Occident, the *(Abendland),* 37, 40, 59
occupation, Allied, x, 2, 13–15, 32, 56, 79
	conflation with German annexation, 77, 121–22, 131, 141–43, 149–51, 177–78
Olah, Franz, 166
"Österreich II" (television series), 182, 195nn. 92, 93
Ottoman Turks, 37
ÖVP, 5, 34, 61n. 38, 99, 112, 139, 157n. 106, 162–63, 169, 182–89

Peter, Friedrich, 166
plebiscite, April 1938, textbook portrayal of, x, 27, 71–72, 74, 82–85, 86n 9, 172–73
polytechnic schools, 6, 83, 92, 103–4, 117nn. 58, 62, 127, 134, 145

Portisch, Hugo, 182, 195nn. 92, 93
postmodernism, 19nn. 52, 55
Potsdam Conference, 125–26, 143
Proclamation of 27 April 1945, 28–29, 38, 54
Profil, 162, 187–88
Proporz, 5
provisional government, Austrian, 25–26, 29, 33
Prussia, 1–2, 13, 39, 47, 3, 58, 65n. 115, 91, 97, 140

Qualtinger, Helmut, 8, 18n. 38, 166

Raab, Julius, 131–32, 149, 154–55n. 52
Reagan, Ronald, 164
rebuilding, ix–x, 25, 45, 48, 50, 58, 121–22, 126–32, 139, 145–46, 149–50, 152n. 3, 153n. 20, 173
Red Army, 38, 40, 97, 113–14, 126, 131–32, 144, 164
Reder, Walter, 166
Red-White-Red-Book, 29–30, 108, 113
Renan, Ernest, 3, 16n. 14
Renner, Karl, 5, 37, 82, 84, 88n. 53, 139–40, 142, 149
reparations, 13, 20, 32, 74, 126, 128, 131, 139, 177
resistance, x, 2, 12–14, 29–31, 53–54, 78–80, 86n. 17, 90–92, 97–98, 109–12, 119n. 91, 123, 144, 165, 168, 170, 183–84, 188
	resistance, textbook portrayal of, 92, 103, 108–9, 112–14, 125, 172, 176–77
Resistenz, 110, 176
Riess-Passer, Susanne, 186
Roth, Joseph, 3
Russians, textbook portrayal of, 58, 93, 96, 98, 108, 135, 170–71, 173. *See also* Soviet Union

Sadako will leben, 104–5, 174, 194n. 63
Schärf, Adolf, 77, 95, 132
Schulbuchaktion, 6, 17–18n. 29
Schuschnigg, Kurt von, 27, 71–72, 74–76, 81, 87n. 20, 155nn. 66, 67, 164, 173
Seyss-Inquart, Arthur, 71–72
Sinowatz, Fred, 182
Socialist Party of Austria. *See* SPÖ
Sound of Music, The (film), 52, 66n. 38
South Tyrol (Alto Adige), 79–80, 134–36
Soviet Union, 55, 96, 100–101, 122–23, 125–26, 130–32, 138–40, 142, 185, 188. *See also* Russians

SPÖ (Socialists), 5, 27, 30–32, 34, 47, 49, 52,
61nn. 37, 38, 73, 78, 80, 83–84, 86n.
14, 99, 101, 139, 162–63, 166, 168–69,
186, 188–89
St. Germain, Treaty of, 29, 134
Staatsbürgerkunde, 53–54
Stalingrad, battle of, 73–74, 123
   textbook portrayal of, 97–98, 108, 116nn.
   31, 35
State Treaty, Austrian, x, 13, 79, 121–23, 125,
141–51, 157n. 104, 168, 177–78
Stern, 161

Taylor, Telford, 105
textbooks, study of, 3–6, 16–17n. 18, 17n. 25
Tiso, Josef, 132
Twain, Mark, 113

United States, textbook portrayal of. *See*
   Americans, textbook portrayal of
Unterrichtssprache, 34–35

Vergangenheitsbewältigung, 15, 168, 194n. 72
victim myth, Austria as, ix–xi, 16n. 9, 149,
158n. 140
   Allied occupation, and, 122–33, 135–36,
   141
   Anschluss, and, 71, 74–75, 79, 85
   birth of, 14–15, 29–30, 52–53, 56
   challenges to, 165–71, 189–91
   coalition history, and, 5, 182–86
   historiography of. *See* historiography
   Holocaust, and, 100–107
   Jörg Haider, and, 186–89
   national identity, and, ix, 2–3, 11, 13,
   25–26, 39–40, 58–59, 149–51

persistence of, 171–86
resistance, and, 108–14
South Tyrol, and, 134–35
State Treaty, and, 141–44
uniqueness of, 13
Waldheim Controversy, and. *See* Wald-
   heim, Kurt
World War II, and, 90–99
Vienna State Opera, 1, 38, 94–95, 151,
182–84, plate 9
Vietnam War 94, 101–2, 104–5, 117–18n. 66,
133
Vranitzky, Franz ,161–62, 164, 167–68, 170,
192n. 29

Waldheim, Kurt, ix–x, 3, 8–9, 18n. 36,
148–49, 151, 161–65, 167–68, 171–73,
176–77, 18–, 182–83, 186
Wave, The (television program), 174, 194n. 62
Wehrmacht, 12, 14–15, 30, 72, 76, 90, 96–99,
112–13, 144, 161–62, 164–65, 184–87
Whiteread, Rachel, 185
Wiederaufbau. See rebuilding
Wiesenthal, Simon, 100, 166, 192n. 20
Wildgans, Anton, 40–41, 44, 143–44
Wirtschaftswunder, 126, 128
work, textbook portrayal of, 26, 35, 45–46,
48–53, 128
World Jewish Congress, 162, 180
World War I, 2, 35, 134, 178

Yugoslavia, 108, 135

Zilk, Helmut, 183, 195n. 95